SIZE
WISE

SIZE
WISE

JUDY SULLIVAN

AVON BOOKS ◆ NEW YORK

SIZE WISE is an original publication of Avon Books. This work has never before appeared in book form.

The photographs on pages 6, 80, 81 and 91 are used courtesy of Making it Big. The photograph on page 14 is used courtesy of Fit to Be Tried. The photographs on pages 61 and 75 are by Lisa M. Hoytt and are used courtesy of Sally's Place. The photo on page 71 is used courtesy of King Size. The illustration on page 269 is © PAWS; Garfield is a registered copyright and trademark property of PAWS, Inc. and is used courtesy of PAWS, Inc. and Jim Davis.

Additional permissions are listed on pages 368–369 which serve as an extension of this copyright page.

AVON BOOKS
A division of
The Hearst Corporation
1350 Avenue of the Americas
New York, New York 10019

Copyright © 1997 by Judy Sullivan
Published by arrangement with the author
Visit our website at http:AvonBooks.com
ISBN: 0-380-78711-3

Library of Congress Cataloging in Publication Data:

Sullivan, Judy.
   Size wise / by Judy Sullivan.
      p.   cm.
   Includes bibliographical references and index.
   1. Overweight persons.   2. Overweight persons—Information
resources.   I. Title.
RC628.S88   1997   96-36904
155.2'34—DC21   CIP

First Avon Books Trade Printing: April 1997

AVON TRADEMARK REG. U.S. PAT. OFF. AND IN OTHER COUNTRIES, MARCA REGISTRADA, HECHO EN U.S.A.

Printed in the U.S.A.

QPM   10   9   8   7   6   5   4   3   2   1

This book is dedicated to my children, Elizabeth and Michael, for putting up with my long hours at the computer, erratic work schedule, and often distracted moods. You two are most excellent individuals and I love you very much.

And to my siblings—Jerry, Joel, Janet, and Joyce—and my parents, Vivian and Orville Sullivan. It was growing up with you as my family that gave me confidence in myself and the knowledge that looks do not define a person.

Acknowledgments

This book would have been impossible to put together on my own. In writing it I have had the privilege to visit with and become friends with many terrific people. I thank each and every one of you for your assistance. These are just a few of the people who were so generous with their time and knowledge.

Karen and Richard Stimson were always very generous in supplying detailed information on all aspects of size acceptance.

Lee Martindale was a constant source of encouragement and guidance throughout all of my research.

Larry Woolwine gave me much laughter, a sense of perspective, and emotional support throughout.

Laura J. Bock, Carol Squires, Nancy Thomas, and Susan Williams of FAT LIP Readers Theatre generously allowed the use of some of the writings from their scripts.

Mary Armstrong shared a bit of her on-stage act.

Barbara Herrera allowed the use of her knowledge of Disney theme parks.

Philip Charles Barragan, Jr.; Ruby Blickenstorfer; Annette Bunnell; "Buttercup" Dee Davey; Laura Elijiak; William J. Fabrey; Pam Hollowich; Pamela Lynn; Lee Martindale; Susan Mason; Chris Molinari; Jody Muchnick; Janine Mueller; Carol Squires; Randy Sumner; Leslie Werner de Soliz; Yuri Vann; Larry D. Woolwine; and Rick Zakowich all shared their personal feelings and experiences.

Frances Berg, M.S.; Dean Edell, M.D.; Joanne P. Ikeda, M.A., R.D.; Pat Lyons, R.N., M.A.; and Ellyn Satter, M.S., R.D., M.S.S.W. shared their professional and personal thoughts.

Jim Davis and Kim Campbell at Paws, Inc. were gracious in allowing time for Garfield the cat to participate in an interview.

eluki bes shahar and Charlotte Abbott, my editors, and Avon Books saw the need for this book and published it.

Peter Lambert, Janice Koopman, and Samuella Rhoades enticed me away from my computer to watch peregrine falcons and white rainbows at Morro Rock and to calm my spirit.

Jayce Carson encouraged me to begin this project and to stick with it. His unfailing confidence in me and steadfast support was essential to its completion.

I thank you all.

Contents

x

Contents

Contents

First a Word About Words

Most of us who are above "normal" weight refer to ourselves as "fat" when talking to ourselves or close friends but we bristle at anyone else doing so. In interviewing for this book, I at first danced around terms, trying to avoid offending anyone. With an unerring ability always to guess wrong, I believe I managed to make everyone wonder where my head was. At first I stuck with the commonly used *overweight*. The response was often, "Over *whose* weight? I prefer to think of myself as fat. It's a short, simple, and descriptive term. Nothing more." An even bigger blunder was in falling back on the clinical term *obese*. Even those with medical backgrounds would say, "*Obese* is a medical term inferring illness. Just because a person is fat doesn't mean they are sick." Finally getting brave, I blurted out *fat* . . . to the wrong person. "What do you mean, fat? I'm just overweight. Besides . . . it's temporary."

At that point I decided that I might as well just toss all the choices into each conversation—*overweight, chubby, heavy, hefty, chunky, plump, calorically challenged, obese, stocky, zaftig, stout, corpulent, large, extralarge, husky, oversize, jumbo, big, roly-poly, tremendous, pudgy, rotund, heavyset, big-boned, great, fleshy, round*, and, for those of us with that certain European mystique . . . *en bon plump* (French for "person of plumpness" or "in good condition"). Why not just offend everyone and get it over with? But that wasn't really such a good idea and certainly not my intention.

Overwhelmingly the descriptive word of choice among individuals who have come to terms with being a larger-than-"normal" person is the word *fat*. It is time to decriminalize this word. I have chosen to use it on occasion throughout this book and mean no offense to anyone. Those of you who just don't care for the term should feel free to mentally change each occurrence of *fat* to whatever word you prefer. I won't be offended.

When I Lose Weight

When I lose weight, I'm going to . . .
  buy some new clothes
  take a vacation
  go back to school
  dance (in public)
  find the perfect job
  fall in love
  go to my kids' school events
  wear a swimsuit
  go anyplace I want
  learn a new sport
  take long walks
  leave an abusive relationship
  treat myself to a new hairstyle, a manicure, and a pedicure; and . . .
  like myself again.

Pick one. Or several. Feel free to add your own. The possibilities are endless. Most of us who are "overweight" have had our own plans for resuming life where we left off some thirty, fifty, one hundred, or more pounds ago. Losing weight is a difficult and long-term process at best. We have made the attempt to lose weight countless times, only to find ourselves at the same size—and often bigger—months later.

So what do we do in the meantime, while we wait for this magical moment when we are transformed into a "normal-sized" person?

I don't know about you, but I'm tired of watching the years go by and missing out on so much. I'm an intelligent, loving, productive, cuddly, witty, and friendly human being. I have many interests and a good sense of humor, am environmentally concerned, sometimes politically correct, and don't spit or make bodily noises in public. So, what's the problem?

Some days it can be hard to step out the front door. In our own homes, with people who love us, we're fine. Our families are like others . . . together we laugh, argue, watch television, prepare meals, cry, read, hug, juggle bills, celebrate holidays, and care about each other. But out in the rest of the world we sometimes encounter criticism, discrimination, discomfort, and humiliation because of our size. Not from everyone. But from enough people to make life pretty unpleasant at times. Fat people who don't have the comfort of supportive, loving families or friends can have a very difficult time of it.

We live in a society where it is no longer acceptable to make fun of, or legal to discriminate against, people because of their sex, race, religion, sexual preferences, or disabilities. The clod who utters remarks about someone based on any of these attributes is generally the one who looks bad, not the person at whom the comments are aimed. Not even the taunt "Your mother wears army boots!" has any impact today . . . Mother very well may be a member of the armed services. Discrimination and cruelty against people who are large, however, are still common. People who convey this attitude often feel justified in doing so.

The only "serious weight problem" I have is society's problem with serious weight.

Comedians take potshots at fat people regularly. David Letterman, even after battling his own increasing girth, seldom seems to make it through a show without a sight gag or remark putting down large people. True, Letterman's humor is often on the tart side on just about any subject, but this is exactly the kind of commentary that reinforces a very hurtful attitude. On the bright side, however, his rudeness toward fat people is increasingly met with silence or booing from his audience.

Letterman is hardly the only comedian to routinely insult fat people. Jay Leno is even worse. He recently appeared on his late-night show sporting a "fat suit" and playing into every fat stereotype he could, including shoveling food into his mouth by hand and smearing it all over his face and onto his clothing. Joan Rivers, Frank D'Amico (self-described king of fat jokes), Tim Allen, Andrew Clay, George Carlin . . . it isn't difficult at all to find comics who base at least part of their routines on body size remarks. Comedy club comedians are notorious for making barbed fat remarks or building entire routines on fat jokes. Woe be to any large person with the misfortune of sitting near the stage when one of these malicious bullies strides out. Is it humor if it advances stereotypes or is painful and humiliating to someone?

Self-righteous crusaders accost large-size people openly in public for a variety of "offenses"—from eating to taking up space. One woman, Cheryl, told me of being berated loudly by a woman in a grocery store as she did her weekly shopping. "You fat pig! How dare you eat like this? Don't you have any pride?" her attacker demanded. This incredibly uncivilized woman began removing items from Cheryl's cart and piling them on a shelf. A crowd gathered as a loaf of bread, a box of pancake mix, and a bag of potatoes were confiscated. Cheryl, completely embarrassed and unable to respond, burst into tears, took her five-year-old daughter by the hand, and ran from the store. When asked what she wished she had done, now that she was far enough removed to think it over, Cheryl replied, "I wish I had been calm enough to explain to her that I was shopping for my family also, none of whom are fat." It is sad to think that this perfectly lovely, shy, sweet woman thinks she has to explain herself at all to a very rude, malicious attacker.

Here's another example of stereotypes dying hard. A friend recently expressed frustration at eating with me. She said it was "a drag" because I eat so slowly and so little, obviously hiding my true habits from her. She just couldn't accept that I always eat slowly and am easily filled up by a couple of pieces of pizza. She seemed to expect me to eat like Beldar Conehead, consuming mass quantities of whatever food was handy. Yes, there are times when I overeat and times when I eat something outrageously high in calories. I enjoy food just like anyone else. But overeating is not the norm for me or most other people of substantial size.

The stereotypes held against fat people are awful (as are stereotypes in general). We are often perceived to be lazy, sloppy, stupid, immoral, mean, asexual/oversexed, jovial/angry, ugly, and gluttonous. And we all, of course, have been blessed with "such a pretty face." At various times in my life I have exhibited any or all of these qualities. Who hasn't? But I am none of these things normally.

Let's face it . . . fat people are often looked down on. Airlines, restaurants, theaters, and most places of entertainment generally provide seating that even average-size people find to be a tight fit at times. Decent clothing has, in the past, been next to impossible to find. And no matter how brilliant, charming, and witty we are at social gatherings, the Mel Gibsons of the world can be expected to go home with the 5'11", 115-pound bimbette.

In an article appearing in the *New England Journal of Medicine* in 1966, H. Canning and J. Mayer* concluded that even elite colleges and professional schools are less likely to accept fat applicants. Employers often refuse to hire fat people because "they don't fit our image" (Larkin, J. C., and Pines, H. A., 1979). Once employed, the large person generally makes less money and has fewer promotions (Rothblum, Esther D., et al., 1990). It has been estimated that businessmen give up $1,000 a year in salary for every pound they are "overweight" (Palmer, 1996).

Some doctors are disgusted by fat people and refuse to treat them. Others can't

---

*See the bibliography at the end of this book for complete citations on this and other references.

seem to treat a large patient for any medical condition without laying the blame for the problem on "obesity" (Maiman, Lois, et al., 1979). An orthopedic surgeon once refused to acknowledge a debilitating back injury of mine, brushing it aside by saying, "Fat women often exhibit back pains in an attempt to get their husbands' attention." This came after I had been in excruciating pain for three weeks. He sent me home after denying me any further pain medications so I would "get tired of this game and give it up." This is definitely not an isolated incident. Both in my personal life and in researching this book, this type of experience with doctors is a common complaint cited in the majority of conversations by fat people regarding health care.

A fat person can exhibit the exact same symptoms of flu as twenty other patients in a doctor's waiting room and be told, "If you'd lose some weight you'd feel a lot better." This goes far beyond embarrassment. Refusal by a physician to look at symptoms with an unprejudiced eye can result in misdiagnosis and improper treatment.

Discrimination and cruelty against fat people are so common that the majority of people in one survey of weight-loss surgery patients said they would rather have a leg amputated or be blind than be fat. The reasons given by these patients for this shocking preference have nothing to do with personal feelings about themselves but come from living with constant struggle in dealing with prejudice from all sides.

In a similar vein, Martin Seligman, Ph.D., author of *What You Can Change and What You Can't,* says that "American women pursue an unobtainable ideal of thinness. Throughout the world, in every culture that has this ideal of thinness, depression is twice as common for women as for men, and there are more incidences of eating disorders."

Is it only adults who are subjected to this discrimination and humiliation? Hardly. As difficult as life can be for adults dealing with a prejudiced culture, the most heartbreaking experiences are often what children must endure. Fat children are teased mercilessly on playgrounds and are left out of games. When these children turn to adults for help, they are told, "We'll put you on a diet, then it will be okay." As if the cruelty is their fault. Even within their own families, large children are often unaccepted and treated contemptuously.

According to the Centers for Disease Control and Prevention in Atlanta, 61 percent of girls had dieted in the year previous to the 1992 study. Twenty-eight percent of boys had attempted to lose weight (Berg, Frances M., 1992). What are we teaching our children about themselves? They will have to struggle with these "lessons" throughout their lives.

All of this must change. And changes are happening. There is a growing understanding in the medical community, and throughout the general population of the dynamics of body size and how size affects health and happiness. But before "overweight" people can demand acceptance from the rest of the world, we have to learn to love and accept ourselves. From that will come an end to size discrimination.

TOP TEN REASONS I AM FAT

10.   The dog ate my diet sheet.

9.   I lost my jogging shorts.

8.   I have to cook for my family.

7.   Dove Bars don't come in a no-fat, no-calorie version.

6.   Oprah said it was okay.

5.   Pritikin food tastes nasty.

4.   Girl Scout cookies.

3.   I wear this fat to keep the opposite sex away.

2.   I gain weight just by looking at pictures of food.

1.   Nobody doesn't like Sara Lee.

None of these things, of course, has anything whatsoever to do with being fat. We have been programmed to find excuses for our size . . . as if we have to apologize somehow for something we have little control over. Can having a piece of cake after dinner really cause excessive weight gain? Does the equation "3,500 calories = 1 pound of fat" tell the whole story? If it were all that simple, how many fat people would there be? The truth is, we don't really know what causes some people to become fat while others remain average-size. Some fat people get less exercise than some of their thinner counterparts . . . is that a result of, or a cause of, being large? Or does it have any significance at all? There are some very lazy average-size people out there and some very active fat people. Most of us—of all sizes—fall somewhere in between.

Recent studies show that fat people, in general, don't eat any more or have any worse eating habits than our thinner counterparts (Brody, Jane E., 1987). One study focused on people in an all-you-can-eat restaurant. Fat people took no more food than did other people; neither did they select foods of higher fat or sugar content. Of course, there are fat people who consume huge quantities of food. But so do many "average-size" (and many thin) people.

A friend of mine is as thin as a rail. He eats all day long . . . and we're not talking about carrot sticks and celery here. He consumes doughnuts, omelettes, french fries, buckets of fried chicken, cake . . . everything you could imagine. He exhibits the energy of a tree sloth and never participates in sports of any kind. I can't eat like that and have no desire to. I'm sure you know people of this type yourself.

People probably become fat because of a variety of influences—heredity, appetite, lack of daily farm work to do, metabolism, and so on. Most of us got to where we are through any combination of these and other as-yet-undiscovered reasons . . . often coupled with a heavy dose of dieting.

Despite all of the diet industry's efforts, our doctors' best advice, and our own multiple attempts at weight loss, we are a society of fat individuals. Even in this period of increased interest in physical fitness, the percentage of fat people is higher than it was even a decade ago. According to the latest, best guesses there are between 34 and 50 million adults and another 10 million children in the United States who are "overweight" by twenty pounds or more. That's just the ones they counted. You and I know there are lots more of us going about our lives and not participating in any fat census.

Anyone who believes losing weight is a simple matter of eating less and exercising more has either never been fat or is one of the fortunate few (3 to 10 percent) who have been successful in achieving and maintaining a significant weight loss. We have been presented with no-fat, sugar-free, taste-free, slide-right-through-you foods and still we gain weight. We are offered a "delicious, filling shake for breakfast and lunch followed by a sensible dinner" and we continue to overflow our overstuffed couches.

It seems that everybody is always on a diet, even though statistics tell us that over half of dieters will have regained the lost weight before a year is out. There is more at work here than a simple lack of willpower.

A panel of experts at the National Institutes of Health (NIH) conference in April 1992 concluded that 90 percent of dieters regain most or all of their lost weight within five years. Others place this rate at 95 percent or higher. This leaves just 5 to 10 percent of dieters who lose a substantial amount of weight and manage to keep it off for at least five years. Everyone who begins a diet thinks he or she is going to be in that lucky, but very small, percentage.

The panel stated that there was little doubt that excess weight increases risk for morbidity and mortality, but they did not find any evidence that losing weight reduces that increased risk. They did see weight loss as having a positive effect on the incidence and severity of noninsulin-dependent diabetes mellitus, hypertension, and the risk factors for cardiovascular disease. But, considering the high likelihood that lost weight will be regained, it was not determined whether or not any permanent benefits could be accomplished.

The NIH panel concluded that "the decision to lose weight should take into account the difficulty of the task as well as the potential adverse physical and psychological effects of weight loss regimens. These effects include the risk of poor nutrition, possible development of eating disorders, effects of weight cycling, and the sometimes serious psychological consequences of repeated failed attempts to lose weight."

There is even evidence of significant health drawbacks to dieting. Epidemiologist Steven N. Blair of the Cooper Institute for Aerobics Research in Dallas conducted a survey of 12,025 Harvard graduates. The average age of the men in the study was sixty-seven. They answered questions about weight-loss dieting, heart disease, hypertension, and diabetes and revealed that men who dieted to lose weight had a higher incidence of these diseases than men who never dieted. This was true even among the leanest respondents to the survey. Of those who said they were always dieting, 23.1 percent had heart disease, 38.3 percent suffered from hypertension, and 14.6 percent had diabetes. Comparatively, nondieters reported that 10.6 percent had heart disease, 23.4 percent had hypertension, and only 3 percent were diabetic.

The men in the survey were asked to indicate their body shape throughout their lives. Those whose shapes had varied more had higher incidents of disease than the men whose weight had remained relatively stable. Other studies bear this out.

Blair summarized, "The results appear to raise questions about research that has established obesity as a risk for heart disease. . . . One of the fundamental tenets of the weight-loss industry is if you get people to eat less, they'll lose weight. And if they lose weight, they'll be better off. And there is no evidence to support either one of these."

Blair presented his findings at the 1994 American Heart Association's annual epidemiology meeting. At the same meeting Dr. Stephen P. Fortmann, professor of medicine at Stanford Unversity, said, "In general, weight cycling has been hard to figure out. It is another reason not to diet."

This "dieting doesn't work" concept is not a new idea. In 1983 *Dieter's Dilemma* by Dr. William Bennett caught my eye. After a quick look at the introduction I put the book back on the shelf. I just wasn't ready to accept what Dr. Bennett was saying. To me it meant giving up on someday having that perfect body. I had heard of support groups for fat people, but to my mind these people were just looking for an excuse to give up. I was just temporarily overweight and next Monday I was going to start the diet that would finally work. Every Monday. For years.

Most of us want to live as long as we can and enjoy life to its fullest. There are ways to be healthier and more active, no matter what your size. *Fat* and *fit* are not mutually exclusive terms. But the decision of what (if anything) to "do about it" is yours entirely.

There are dozens of books on the shelf begging us to buy them and discover our innermost secrets and cravings . . . and offering yet another diet meant to "fix" us. Diet programs are available in every area of the country. If that's what you need, go for it! You must make your own decisions regarding your health. If losing weight is important to you, I certainly wish you every success. Everybody—fat or thin, tall or short—has to decide what is right for themselves. No matter what that decision, no matter what your size, you have every right to be treated with respect. By everyone . . . including yourself.

I no longer care why I am fat. I've wasted too much of my life wondering about it. Researchers and geneticists can figure it out for me and let me know when the verdict is in. What I do care about it is living in the here and now.

It took many years to come to accept that while I may want to look like Cindy Crawford and have a body *Playboy* magazine would beg to grace its centerfold (an offer which I would, of course, decline—yeah, right!), the best I may ever achieve is to be a Roseanne look-alike. And what is wrong with that? What I refuse to accept is the idea that because I am large I am not an important part of this world.

**Over WHOSE
weight?**

We owe apologies and excuses to no one. Not even to the doctors and weight-loss counselors who demand to know why their diets didn't work for us. We don't need to apologize to people who have their sensitivities offended by the sight of us or to the airlines because our ample hips overflow their ridiculously narrow seats. If anything, these people owe us apologies . . . for putting us on diets that seldom work long-term and often add to our health problems, for mean-spirited prejudice that causes a great deal of pain, and for humiliation over problems we didn't create.

Unfortunately, despite consistent findings in one study after another indicating that people have little control over their body size, society still pressures us to fit in.

Doctors continue to chastise us for our size and hand out the customary low-calorie diet sheets. Or, if they are really into it, they prescribe packets of powdered protein drink we are supposed to use to replace food in our lives. Despite the continued inability of the majority of dieters to lose weight and keep it off on any diet plan, diets are still the prescription of choice. Why is this? Is there a single other medical treatment besides low-calorie dieting with such a deplorably low success rate that is still being routinely prescribed? Outside of experimental therapies for the terminally ill, I don't believe so.

But it gets worse. The pressure to fit into the tiny mold society demands becomes so intense that some people endure potentially life-threatening surgical procedures in the hope of losing weight. Thousands of surgeries are performed yearly that staple, bend, fold, and mutilate our stomachs or intestines. The sad thing is, these surgeries have no better long-term effects than any other method of weight loss. The list of possible complications that goes along with these surgeries is staggering.

Those individuals who are most miserable and unable to cope with their feelings of shame and the lack of acceptance in their lives sometimes commit suicide. In the words of an infomercial diet cheerleader, "Stop the insanity!"

I've spent years counting calories. It doesn't do any good. It made me obsessive. I don't diet, but I've changed a lot of my eating habits. I'm not losing any weight, but I feel a lot better. I've done everything from diet pills again and again to trying every diet that has come out. I've had my jaws wired and I've fasted. I had my stomach stapled (a 97 percent exclusion) in 1982 and lost 130 pounds. I stuck to it. Then the weight loss slowed and I slowly began gaining. I was eating about 300 calories a day, starving myself, living on black coffee and water . . . and gaining weight.

—SUSAN MASON

Dieting should work! Take in less calories than you expend and the pounds should flow right off. It's just common sense. If the weight loss slows down, drop the number of calories again or increase the activity level. It seems so reasonable. For a very few, it does work, just as purchasing a lottery ticket is the answer to instant wealth for a lucky few. Even when we know the odds are stacked against us, we still diet. Each one of us believes that somehow we will fall into that elusive group of successful losers if we just find the right diet, begin at just the right moment, and find the strength of a prehaircut Samson within ourselves. It should be so simple.

One of the most difficult things in the world for me to accept has been the final, simple truth about dieting. It just doesn't work for the vast majority of people. After probably a hundred failed dieting attempts beginning at around age sixteen, including a stomach-stapling surgery in 1978, I still want the fault to be with me, not with the diets. If it had been my fault in the past . . . my own weaknesses each time . . . then it would still be possible for the right diet to come along that would "click" with me. I would finally be "normal-size." It almost felt like grieving to have to put aside the hope I have lived with for so long. But trying to lose weight seems like being in quicksand. The more you kick around and struggle, the deeper into it you sink.

Am I giving up? Yes. I am giving up hating myself for being fat. I am giving up accepting the type of prejudice heaped on fat people by those with no kindness and no understanding. I am giving up on the idea that I must be thin before I can have an enjoyable life. Oh . . . and one more thing. I am giving up supporting Jenny Craig, the Slim Fast company, and Weight Watchers' executives and group leaders. You may be very nice people, but I have better things to do with my money and my life. (For more information about the diet industry, please see Appendix A.)

Most of us have taken the pills, bought the diet books, joined Weight Watchers, been to at least one company like Jenny Craig, Inc., drunk the chocolate fiber shakes, had counseling, jazzercised, cried with Richard Simmons, followed diet sheets, learned biofeedback, tried twelve-step programs, stocked up on frozen diet dinners, and been on dozens of our own home-grown low-calorie diets. Some of us have had surgeries that do all sorts of strange things to our bodies, leaving us with complications and ugly scars; some people have even subjected themselves to shock treatments. We've lost hundreds of pounds in our individual dieting histories. And still we are fat. So now what?

We are told by our families, our friends, our doctors, complete strangers, and society in general that we must lose weight. How? If wishes and dreams, threats and cajoling, encouragement and rewards, humiliation and pain, starvation, hard work, and deprivation don't work, what does? Permanent weight loss is a possibility for a few. Improved health and fitness, however, are attainable by virtually everyone.

There are people who are in the business of catering to the large person's wants and needs. These are the people who should have our business. There are people, publications, and groups who work to end discrimination and enlighten the world as to the truth about the diet industry. These organizations and publications deserve our support.

Most importantly, we deserve to be treated with respect, understanding, and common decency, just as all others deserve to be treated. If anyone—family member, friend, caretaker, or businessperson—has a problem with that, he or she should not be a part of our lives. Certainly not a part we allow to influence us with negative attitudes about our own self-worth or whose pocketbook we enrich with our money.

That reminds me. This book is absolutely off-limits to anyone who cannot make a scale groan audibly or who doesn't love someone who can. The knowledge about to be entrusted to those of us graced with extra pounds will do others no good and may be more than they can handle. For everyone else, this book's purpose is to provide you with the information you need to be happier and more comfortable in this world.

Life is right now, no matter what your size. This day isn't coming back to you ever again and no one is going to regret its loss as much as you. Don't put off doing the things you truly want to do and don't let anyone make value judgments against you. Demand respect from those not giving it naturally. Sign up for that class you've been waiting to take. Buy a terrific wardrobe that fits you now. You deserve to look wonderful. Flirt! Try that new hairstyle! Join a softball team! Do what makes you happy . . . and don't wait any longer . . . do it today!

It's about liking yourself. You should never let size be an issue. You shouldn't wait till you are a certain weight in your life—going either way—to make your dreams come true.

—PHIL

How to Use This Book

Each chapter of this book provides the names and brief descriptions of companies, individuals, and organizations who have products or services to offer larger people. Unless otherwise indicated, the companies listed here offer catalogs or brochures of their products available through the mail. When you see something that interests you, turn to the back of the book for addresses, phone numbers, and, sometimes E-mail and Internet contact information.

Every effort has been made to insure that the information presented in this book is as up-to-date and accurate as possible. However, companies and publications commonly move, go out of business, and change policies. New resources pop up and old ones fade away. Any prices listed are approximate and are offered only to give an idea of general cost. Foreign prices are listed with an approximate conversion rate.

The majority of purchases made through mail order go off without a hitch, though it always pays to be an informed consumer and follow these tips:

- Choose your purchase carefully. Make sure you state the size, color, or any other pertinent information clearly.

- Know the company's policies regarding refunds, exchanges, and warranties. When in doubt, ask questions!

- Never send cash. Always pay by check, money order, or credit card so you have a record of the transaction.

- If there are any problems with the order, contact the company immediately.

If you have problems that cannot be resolved with a mail-order company there are several options available to you.

If you suspect fraud or misrepresentation, contact the National Fraud Information

Center. They maintain a fraud database. (See the resource list at the back of the book for information on how to contact this and the other organizations mentioned below.)

The U.S. Postal Inspection Service covers mail fraud, solicitations meant to look like government materials, and sexually offensive materials. Contact the chief postal inspector if you encounter a problem. For other postal service questions, talk with your local postmaster or the consumer advocate.

For the number of the Better Business Bureau nearest to the location of the offending company, call the Council of Better Business Bureaus.

For any other questions or help, contact your state consumer protection agency or the Direct Marketing Association or the Federal Trade Commission.

One last thing. If you find yourself on mailing or telephone lists you don't want to be on, contact the Direct Marketing Association, Mail Preference Service, or Telephone Preference Service. They can arrange to have your name taken off the lists of many companies.

Finally, no portion of the information in this book should take the place of sound, size-wise medical advice. Find a physician who treats you with respect and work closely with her or him regarding your health. Share the ideas and resources offered here with your doctor and others involved in your health care.

S I Z E
WISE

PERSONAL GLIMPSE:
CAROL

Carol has been a member of the performance troupe FAT LIP Readers Theatre (FLRT) for six years. She also works as an attendant for a disabled person, puts in twenty hours a week working for a parks and recreation department's art center, and works part-time at *Radiance* magazine as an editorial assistant. Carol's delightful sense of humor and insightful observations make for wonderful conversation.

About a year before I joined FLRT I had begun attending an exercise class for large women. I really love to dance. That's what got me to the class.

At first I didn't really look at myself. I would watch the teacher and other people, but not myself. Four or five months into the class I started to watch myself more. I hadn't lost much weight, even though I had been on a diet. I started to really become fascinated. I looked at the other women's bodies—how we moved and how we differed, our diversity and beauty. I certainly had never had any reason to see beauty in my own body before, unless it was above my chin and below my hair.

I attended a weekend retreat Alice Ansfield (publisher, *Radiance* magazine) put together, just a lot of large women coming together in a mountain resort. I remember feeling incredibly powerful when we were driving back. The first time we stopped at a gas station I went into the bathroom to wet down my T-shirt (it was so hot!) and there was this small-size woman there. I remember looking at her and thinking, "What is wrong with her?" All of a sudden I just started laughing, realizing she was the first thin woman I had seen in three days. It was one of those few classic times when the light bulb in my head went off.

Another epiphany came the second time (not the first) I heard someone say that

I

dieting doesn't work. Then it was, "Well, gosh, I've been doing this for twelve years and I'm fatter than I was when I began. Now, let me see . . ." Certainly you blame yourself, as a dieter, every time it doesn't work. That you didn't try hard enough, that you screwed up, that you went off the diet. Whatever. You're weak-willed. You're a slob. But you know, that's not who I am in the rest of my life. I'm a bit of a procrastinator at times, but why would it be in just this one area of my life when the rest of my life is fairly together?

The first time I saw FAT LIP Theatre was amazing. These women were up there talking about my life! They were talking about clothing, doctors, being called names on the street, relationship stuff, and hating yourself . . . but building toward a self-acceptance message in the end. They were advertising for people to come to an informational meeting and be interviewed to join them. That's how I got involved in FAT LIP.

We work from a feminist collective point of view, with consensus. What I've learned over the years is that every woman's voice is important and you should listen and not dismiss anybody. Maybe we can't find a compromise all of the time, but often-times we can find something that will work. Together, as a group of fat women, we are taking a message to the world about who we are. That includes both our diversity and our similarities.

We average ten to fifteen performances a year. Our scripts cover all ages of our lives from childhood, medical, social, and employment issues, and relationships. Planning the script depends on whether or not the audience is already on our side. We have done scripts for a particular audience, such as medical people. For instance, we might show them "this is what it's like to be a fat patient" or "what it's like to be a fat woman in this world and part of that is being your patient." We address things like access issues. For example, if all of the chairs in their waiting rooms have arms on them, what does that say to the fat patient who comes to them? Or if you are sitting there with a glass of Slim Fast on your desk, what are you, as a professional, saying to a patient? The audience just kind of sits there thinking, "Whoa! I never thought of that before!"

I get a lot of reinforcement from our performances. In fact, last week there were two times when I had to dance on-stage—solo—while a woman read a poem about a fat woman dancing. I was in this black one-piece body suit, clinging, and a short vest. I was up on stage, dancing in front of a group of predominately small- to medium-sized medical people. When I jiggle, I jiggle. When I shimmy, the flab on my arms, breasts, belly, and thighs really shakes. Someone called me a sex goddess afterward.

I like my body. It brings me a lot of pleasure . . . sex, dancing. I like the way my body moves. It has a wonderful sense of rhythm. Of course I have pains in my body, but I challenge a mid-size person to tell me she has never had pains in her body.

When I got out of college I wanted to be a photographer but kept putting it off. It was so ingrained in my head—"Let me lose weight and *then* they will hire me."

Now I say, "Go for it!" Get yourself dressed in the best thing in your wardrobe, get your résumé together, put down all the wonderful stuff you do, and put it under peoples' noses. Smile at them and say, "Here I am!" Your self-esteem may take a beating if people say no, but if you never try, you're always going to be stuck in one spot for the rest of your life.

"Dance Class"

Six years ago I started my last diet. This was to be the diet to end all diets. This time I would do it "right." Sensible, nutritious food on only 500 calories a day! And what would really make this the "perfect" diet was my newfound commitment to exercise. Now exercise as torture I had been through before, but this time I found a class especially designed for fat women. This was not just any old exercise class full of painfully remembered calisthenics, but it was a dance/exercise class. It was my personal dream come true!

I threw myself heart, soul, and body into my new program. Then something started to change and it wasn't my weight. I found myself really looking and listening to these women. For the first time I heard fat women say they were happy with their bodies, and they showed it as they bounced, jiggled, and strutted their way through each class. I heard these fat women question all the medical and social myths around weight. This was my first exposure to fat politics and I was fascinated.

But the most important change occurred during that first year. In the beginning, I hated to look at myself in the wall of mirrors we had to face, but gradually, from class to class, I started to really study the way my body moved. I watched the other women, noticing what our bodies had in common and how they differed. Where once I was repulsed, now I saw beauty in each step, in the clap of their hands, and in the swaying of their bellies.

And I was transformed. Where once stood a blob in leotards, now I saw an incredibly graceful fat body.

Segment of FAT LIP Readers Theatre script by Carol Squires.

1

IN GREAT SHAPE
WITH VITALITY

(Why Didn't We Try This First?)

Beginning a diet always involved a lot of planning for me. During the weekend before the all-important Monday of the last diet of my life I would draw up detailed food charts, prepare graphs with the planned number of pounds to be lost penciled in for weeks in advance, and set up daily eating schedules. Grocery lists would be made (four exactly six-ounce apples, one and a half three-ounce bananas, salad dressing with no more than seventeen calories per tablespoon—better put that fattening twenty-five-calories-per-tablespoon poison back). Talk about obsessing! And, of course, the inevitable exercise charts. Sunday nights would find me hurrying to get that last tasty morsel eaten before midnight. I'll bet more weight is gained on the Sunday night before diet day than in Christmas and Thanksgiving feasts. Working toward good health always had to be a combination of a low-calorie diet with aerobic exercise . . . together. The concept of being able to move toward being healthier without also having to go on a weight-loss diet was never offered as an option.

Our preoccupation with weight loss and our gullibility about the specious claims of the diet industry have to end. It is time to replace these attitudes with a love of ourselves and a healthy respect for moderation in all things.

The Canadian government program Vitality is a breath of fresh air. In acknowledging that beautiful, healthy bodies come in all sizes, the program addresses the issues

4

of staying healthy, not of conforming to health insurance size charts and societal pressures to lose weight.

The following is from the brochure provided by the Canadian government's health department:

Vitality—A Fresh Approach

Vitality. It's an approach to life that promotes the idea of personal choice—of taking charge of how you eat, how you can stay active daily and how you can feel good about yourself. Most of all, *Vitality* is about enjoying life....

A broad range of body weights and sizes can be "healthy." It depends on the individual. [We need] a broader view of well-being and healthy living. Hence, *Vitality* was born—a fresh approach to living that corresponds with enjoying eating well, being active and feeling good about yourself.

Eating well means choosing from a wide variety of foods that you enjoy. This includes emphasizing breads, other grain products, vegetables and fruit. It also includes lower-fat dairy products, leaner meats and foods prepared with little or no fat. If you eat a treat, balance it by staying active and eating a wide variety of foods for the rest of the day.

Enjoying being active, "your way, every day," is the key to "active living." This concept means finding ways to enjoy being active every day, at home, at work or within your community. It may be walking to the store, taking the kids to the park, mowing the lawn or going dancing with someone special. The only thing better than personal activity is sharing it with family and friends you care about.

Feeling good about yourself starts with accepting who you are and how you look. Healthy, good-looking bodies come in a broad range of sizes. Being proud of how your body looks and moves and believing in your own self-worth are more important than societal pressures to be perfect.

Vitality suggests taking charge of your life and enjoying time with family and friends. For further information, please call (613) 992-9204.

Reprinted with the permission of Health and Welfare Canada.

This work pointed out that "a broad range of body weights and sizes can be 'healthy.'" It stated, "Healthy, good-looking bodies come in a broad range of sizes." Read those sentences over again. And a third time. We have spent our lives having it pounded into our heads that the only way to be healthy and attractive is to weigh no more than insurance industry charts dictate.

The Vitality approach may seem too simplistic for those of us used to poring over calorie counters, keeping track of each gram of fat, and feeling guilty if we skip that boring aerobic workout. But look again at what it says. Good, basic common sense instead of fatphobia and discrimination applied to fat people. Wow! What a concept! Talk of accepting yourself as you are and making yourself healthy, not thin? This is stuff I can embrace and live with.

To find out more about the Vitality program, write to: Health and Welfare, Health Promotion Directorate, Fourth Floor, Jeanne Mance Building, Ottawa, Ontario Canada K1A 1B4; or call (613) 957-8328; or fax (613) 990-7097.

Enjoying ourselves? Feeling good about and accepting ourselves? Yes! It's about time.

Many of us tend to have that all-or-nothing attitude about our health. If we are "good," exercising and eating only seriously restricted amounts of the "right" foods, we are granted permission to feel good about ourselves. If we relax and eat and do whatever we feel like, we are "bad" and are made to feel guilty about straying. Who can blame us for struggling with this whole dilemma?

We've always been told that we need to be thin to be healthy and fit. We look to the medical community for facts about health, but in the past it has stuck its collective head in the sand and preached the gospel according to Saint Slender. Now the people who developed the Vitality program say to relax and realize that it's okay to be something other than a size 6. That good health and fitness can be achieved by people of all sizes. This is certainly a far healthier attitude and more realistic goal.

Can you stand some more good news? It's not just our Canadian friends who are finally seeing the light. The medical community in general may be slow to accept change, but strides are being made in the right direction by some terrific, influential people and organizations.

Nurses and dietitians seem to be the quickest to react to the latest research and what we, as patients, have been saying all along . . . weight-loss diets just don't work. Programs almost identical to Vitality are cropping up all around the United States, with activities we can love and look forward to participating in regularly, sensible eating habits that allow for personal tastes and foods we enjoy, and increased self-esteem replacing the negative attitudes and guilt-inducing sermons of the past.

The February 1994 issue of *Walking* magazine declared 1993 to be the year that diets were officially "dissed," encouraged people to throw their scales away and develop a "positive attitude about eating and exercise" and let bodies reach their naturally ideal weight through low-fat eating and regular exercise. "Thin doesn't necessarily mean healthy, and a heavier person who walks regularly can improve her health without necessarily seeing a difference on a scale." It was recommended you promise yourself "you'll be fitter and healthier and stronger than you are today—without dieting."

Counting calories is not higher math.

PLAYING

Remember when you were ten years old and thought you could fly? Just skip a little bit higher or with a slightly longer stride and you just knew you would take off? It was fun to run just for the sheer joy of it. Swimming meant cavorting and splashing like a playful sea otter. Riding a bike was the most wonderful form of transportation—the wind against your face as you raced along. Walking with a friend was a great time to share the day's events. Participating in a sport meant playing softball or tennis or basketball with your friends. Somewhere along the line exercise became a chore, something done in exact movements for a precise number of minutes. A punishment, of sorts, for the sin of being big. Okay, so maybe we couldn't really fly . . . maybe we still can't. But we can reclaim that joy of movement.

In thinking of becoming more active, forget those exercise tapes—unless you really enjoy them. Think about what you used to love to do. Or what you have always wanted to do. Or have been curious about.

I love horses. When my daughter, Elizabeth, was six years old and expressed interest in riding, I saw to it that she had lessons. For years I sat and visited with the other parents as our kids rode in never-ending circles. Eventually, as she proved her continuing interest and responsibility, I bought a horse for Elizabeth. She rode, groomed, fed, and cared for her horse. I sat and watched. As much as I would have loved to be the one riding, I held back, getting my enjoyment vicariously. I wasn't exactly active and limber anymore. Years of sitting on my rear between periods of Fondarobics had taken their toll. And there was the fear of being laughed at, of people staring. Watching was safer. And boring.

Then I met Calypso. Four months old, all gangly legs and energy, this beautiful Arabian colt came into my life. It was love at first sight, and I bought him for myself. Obviously he was too young to ride, but that didn't matter. In fact, it was better. Despite warnings against "treating him like a puppy," Calypso became my pet. It was so much fun to drive to the ranch where he was boarded, pull into the drive near his pasture, and yell out "Yo! Calypso!" He would perk up, whinny to me, and trot around excitedly, happy to see me. I would groom him, play with him, and take him for walks down a country road or around the property. Sometimes I would just visit with him in his pasture. He gave me a reason to get out of the house every day and do something that I loved doing. I didn't lose any weight, but it felt great to be active again. I started feeling good about myself for the first time in a long time. Calypso got me off my couch and moving again. It was the beginning I needed.

I don't know who or what your "Calypso" is. That's something you have to find inside yourself. (Hopefully yours won't have a $135-a-month pasture bill attached.)

A great mind in a great body!

So, what is your pleasure? The folks with the Vitality program recommend engaging in "physical movement in a variety of activities undertaken for the pleasure of participating and with the support of a positive environment." You and your doctor will have to determine what limitations, if any, you may have. Do you like to get outdoors? Maybe walking, boating, fishing, skating, or hiking is your thing. Perhaps gardening or golf. Swimming? Softball? Archery? Camping? Indoors there are a lot of choices too: bowling, volleyball (probably best not to do this in your living room), dancing, sex, martial arts, and weight training are just a few of the possibilities. The point is to find something fun that will get you moving. You don't have to be a fanatic to benefit from regular participation in exercise.

If you purchase only a few books this year, I highly recommend that one of them be *Great Shape: The First Fitness Guide for Large Women*, by Pat Lyons, R.N., M.A., and Debby Burgard (Bull Publishing, 1990). These two women have created a book with so much enthusiasm and love between its covers it practically leaps out, hugs you, takes you by the hand, and dances you merrily away to play. No "go for the burn" talk here. These ladies spark that love of movement and desire to play that we all have within ourselves. They show what I have long suspected to be true . . . inside every fat person there isn't a thin person struggling to get out; there is an energetic, happy person ready to have a good time.

Pat Lyons is a nurse, health educator, and author. *Great Shape* is about becoming active and healthy no matter what size you are. Through a program of the same name, Pat is working at Kaiser Permanente, Northern California Region, based in Oakland, and is leading the way in educating the medical community to improve care for fat patients.

I'm going to be forty-eight tomorrow. The thing I am celebrating most each year now is that all the things our culture tells us are bad about being a gray-haired fat lady just doesn't work on me. What I've really learned through the years is to value myself for who I am and to not accept all the stereotypes that are given by the world. That has been a real growth process and a struggle. For many years as I was growing up I identified being fat so strongly as the only characteristic I had. That being fat was bad and that I was a bad person because I couldn't do anything about it. I couldn't lose weight. It took me a lot of years to get over that kind of thinking.

I was very active in sports as a kid. But as the only fat kid on the tennis team at age fifteen I became too ashamed and uncomfortable, so I stopped playing. I basically went to the sidelines and stopped being active. I had a couple of spurts of skiing and playing tennis in my twenties, but for the most part was pretty sedentary. From fifteen to thirty I spent my time dieting, hating myself, smoking cigarettes, and seeing my weight go up and down several times. I was a classic depressed yo-yo dieter.

In my early thirties I spent a month with a friend who had just come back from India. She was practicing yoga every day, cooking healthy vegetarian foods, and exploring mind/body perspectives. I learned a lot from her. It was really my entry back to valuing my body and seeing that this connection between mind and body is really critical. We were in her home and she was teaching me so it wasn't like I was exposed in a public place. That was helpful. Most days we also baked bread. To this day, whenever I smell baking bread I connect it with yoga—and relax!

When I first started doing yoga I couldn't touch my toes. Sitting on the floor with my legs out straight I could only touch my knees. There is another move, the shoulder stand. I remember one day having my belly in my face and thinking, "Oh, God. This is so horrible. This horrible body of mine."

But I stuck with it. There was something important here that I could learn. By the end of a month of doing yoga every day I was able to not only touch my toes but put my face on my knees. So I saw a very different body in terms of flexibility, potential, and capacity. And with no change in weight. So the idea that my body was not capable just wasn't true. I saw that I was able to change my ability and flexibility in a very short period of time. After that I went back to playing tennis, began running, and have been active ever since. At 5'8" and 240 pounds I am still fat. But I'm fat and fit!

What I recognize now in working with women who are 300 or 400-plus pounds is that their reality can be very different from my reality. Furthermore, the needs of those who think they are fat compared with those who are fat are also different. But the sense of shame, depression, and wanting to commit suicide because of despair can still be very strong. One woman told me, "Your suicide weight is a lot higher than mine." I told her, "I don't have a 'suicide weight' anymore." But I knew what she meant.

Body loathing and body hatred affect women of all sizes. But there is a difference between someone who is my size saying, "I'll go out and just do it," versus someone who is much bigger or who has less background in activity or who has more mobility limitations. It's important to look at both physical reality and emotional needs. These two things go hand in hand when it comes to starting to be more active. But ability to take risk is also really tied to self-esteem.

I met a woman in my program who weighed 350 pounds and had very strong core self-esteem. She was always told by her family as she was growing up that she was a good person and deserved respect. She was the very fattest woman in the class, yet she was the most positive person there. What people get as children to build core self-esteem makes the biggest difference. If kids learn they are good people regardless of body size, they are better prepared to cope and deal with the discrimination that comes along later. But if they are criticized out in the world and are criticized at home they will have a much harder time.

For the past three years I have been doing programs based on Great Shape. We've been doing dance/exercise classes and support groups that are taught by large women for large women. Our definition of "large" is a woman who is over size 16. I've also been training instructors to role-model this idea of positive fitness and health regardless of size and to create a safe place where women can come and have fun and enjoy the camaraderie and the self-acceptance. The program is really based on physical activity and self-acceptance as the root to healing and well-being.

There is a definite professional trend to accepting the fact that diets don't work. Dietitians have probably been more vocal about that point than any of the other professions, although there are plenty of dietitians who don't want to believe it. As a profession, dietitians have made the strongest statements that diets don't work. They have taken a strong professional stand about some of the problems of dieting. Dietitians have experienced, probably most directly, the failure of dieting. They have seen people try really hard, lose weight, and then regain weight and feel worse than when they began.

Other professionals are becoming more aware as well. I spoke at a conference for nurse practitioners last fall. There were 550 practicing nurse practitioners, primarily ob-gyn and family practice nurse practitioners. A significant number of them (probably a third) were large women. When I talk with nurses I talk *about the stigma that fat nurses face with patients telling them, "What the hell do you know about health, you're fat," being discounted by their peers, being pressured to go on diets, all of those kinds of things. So I talk from the heart about how difficult that is. Then I talk about consumer rights. Basically that everybody has the right to be treated with respect. And I discuss the self-awareness movements. There are many health professionals who are really ready to hear this, both for themselves and their patients. They have experienced the failure of standard approaches to dieting and weight loss.*

Physicians are another group that I am working with. There are 3,500 physicians in our organization. We are encouraging them to focus on health, rather than weight, stressing three points—enjoying physical activity, feeling good about yourself, and eating well and not dieting. We are helping physicians see the value in a patient's feeling good about himself or herself via self-acceptance and size acceptance. We know that even people who have medical conditions like hypertension, diabetes, and heart disease have statistically been no more successful at losing weight than anyone else.

What we are talking about is a new paradigm about weight and health. We've done a teleconference to help physicians focus their encounters with people based on what people can do that is positive for them versus putting them through the same hoops of "lose weight/go on a diet." We presented information from the 1992 NIH (National Institutes of Health) Technology Assessment Conference that reported no matter what people have done to try to lose weight 90 to 98 percent are going to regain it within two to five years; that body fat distribution is much more significant in terms of linkages with health risks than absolute weight; and that upper body fat is associated with more risk than lower body fat. Small amounts of weight loss—even ten to twenty pounds—attained through moderate lifestyle changes are significant in improving health status. We wanted to give physicians something they can be effective in doing in long-term follow-up care. But it's going to be a long haul to change physician attitudes.

One of the issues I am very concerned about is the whole issue of medical care delivery and the numbers of people who avoid and delay medical care based on the way they have been treated in the past. If my goal is to be as healthy as I can be, I have to pay attention to getting preventive care like Pap smears, breast exams, and mammograms. One of the exercises we do in group education for large women is role-play what to say in a visit to the doctor so women can prepare emotionally to obtain care regardless of what the doctor says. We need to recognize that we large people have an equal right to respectful care just like anybody else.

And it's a two-way street. We have to recognize that what fat triggers for doctors is their sense of not knowing what to do. They are not in a clinical situation where they feel confident. Just like any of us, in a situation where we don't feel confident we may say and do things that are totally inappropriate. There are lots of physicians who are really at a loss about what to do to be helpful. That's why the education we are doing tries to teach physicians to focus on whatever the presenting complaint is. If that's the flu, to treat for the flu. Whatever the problem, to focus on that and to not give unsolicited advice to lose weight.

Oftentimes fat people feel targeted by a particular physician when, in fact, this physician may be rude to everybody. Physicians who are compassionate overall are physicians who are likely to be compassionate with fat people. Physicians who are abusive with fat people probably aren't any better with anybody else. What makes it so difficult with physicians is that when you are sick and in pain and you go to someone to be treated and are treated callously it can be so much more painful. It is absolutely devastating. Research by Dr. Jacklyn Packer in New York uncovered incredible abuse by physicians. One woman was taken to the hospital by the police after she was raped and was told by the examining doctor that she "really needed to lose weight." Some doctors only see fat. They don't see the human being and his or her needs.

People of all sizes get to the point of feeling it's all or nothing . . . this is what they have been told. That if you can't lose fifty to one hundred pounds, why bother. The medical literature doesn't back that up. For instance, the greatest health benefits from physical activity go to those who have been totally sedentary and become somewhat active. You don't have to become a jock to become healthier. One article that stands out in my mind went through all of the studies and described the health benefits of moderate weight loss. It showed how even ten to fifteen pounds for some people can help normalize blood sugar in diabetics and lower blood pressure. The weight loss is the result of these moderate lifestyle changes these people can maintain. It's not that they go on a fasting program and lose ten pounds in a month. That's not where the improvement happens; improvement happens as a result of behaviors maintained over time. Beginning to be more active for many people can start a whole process of moving on many other issues.

We have to ask: What does a vital, healthy lifestyle look like and feel like? How can we make that more accessible to people of all sizes? If someone has been too shamed to begin activity, we can create a safe environment for them to get started. The approach we took with Great Shape was to ask people to think about a time in life when they were doing something they enjoyed and to try to do that again. We encouraged people to do an activity for the pleasure of it, the enjoyment, exhilaration, and satisfaction rather than a "no pain/no gain" approach to exercise.

One of the major barriers people have to overcome are fears of humiliation and ridicule. I talk to people about getting a buddy so you can have some support. Sometimes the difficulty of that is when you get two or three big people together it becomes a bit of a "spectacle." It attracts attention and taunts. Then again, I'm in Oakland, California. I live a couple of blocks from Lake Merritt. Probably a quarter of the women who are walking around the lake are fat women. Fear of ridicule is difficult and I don't want to minimize that at all. But large women are becoming more and more visible. It really does come down to basics. Screw what other people think. What's more important, my life, my well-being, or what other people think?

It's really important for people to be prepared for public ridicule, however. It's like being prepared for anything else. You go for a job interview, you go through it in your mind. What's going to happen? How will I answer this question or that question? The same kind of preparation can be done for exercise. "Okay, if somebody hollers at me, what am I going to do?" I can holler back, ignore it, whatever.

But the most important thing is for people not to take ridicule on as "theirs." Get rid of it. Call a friend and get the justified anger out. Get the shame and sadness out; don't keep it inside. Don't own it. If a friend is not available, write about it. Get it out some way.

I was out with some fat friends several years ago. I'll never forget it. We were standing on the street and this guy comes by and looks right in my face and says, "Fat pigs! You're all disgusting!" I was so taken aback I was speechless. He walked away and kept turning around giving us dirty looks. I didn't even say anything. That can happen and is painful. On the other hand, he's a stranger. What the hell do I care about him?

I rarely experience fat criticism in my life now, professionally or personally. I have gotten to the point where I have educated all of the people around me to forget it . . . don't even try to bug me about my weight. I have also educated people around me, on the softer side, about increasing their compassion and caring for all people.

For some people it is just unconscious and they're surprised that what they are saying has such a negative effect on other people. There are many thin women who talk about their "saddlebags" or how fat they are and who see this as an identifying thing. "We're all in this together, we all have this problem." I have to stop them and say, "This is not a problem for me. If you have a problem with your weight, and your feelings about your weight I encourage you to look at ways you can learn to accept yourself. But I don't have a problem about my weight." I'll stop that kind of conversation right away, in a way that doesn't lay the blame on them and make them defensive but in a way that shows that I don't see weight as a problem in the way they do.

The brainwashing we have all had creates pain for all of us. The only way to stop the pain is for us to be compassionate and understanding with one another and supportive of each other.

There is a victim thing that people find very difficult to get out of. We have to be able to empower fat people in the same ways that we have empowered other people who have been victimized by social prejudices. We can be allies in overcoming social oppression, but nobody can do it for a victim. It is very difficult, but the victims have to get over the internalized feelings of shame and blame by themselves.

How do people deal with the discrimination in a lot of different sectors of their life? Discrimination is not likely to go away in the world. So, what are your choices? People can try to be able to live their lives the way they want, give themselves credit for trying, take small steps forward and believe in their right to self-respect and happiness. Love yourself regardless. Live life fully. That's my real message.

SPECIAL ITEMS

Activewear and Swimsuits

SOURCES:

Abundance—activewear (to size 26)

Bentley's—dancewear (Danskin Plus sizes 14–29)

Big Stitches by Jan—swimsuits (custom-made)

Lane Bryant—activewear, bras, dancewear, sweats, swimsuits (to 4X)

Danskin Plus—(to size 4x),

Fit to Be Tried—bike shorts, leotards, shorts, shirts (to 4X)

Full Bloom—T-shirts, sweats (to 9x)

L'Eggs Just My Size—dancewear, sweats (to 4X)

Making It Big—sportswear (to super-size)

Regalia—activewear, bras, swimsuits (to 4X)

Roaman's—activewear, bras, dance-wear, swimsuits (to 4X)

Silhouettes—sweats (to 4X)

Sue Brett—activewear, bras, dance-wear, sweats (to 2X)

Suits Me Swimwear (fits up to 250+ pounds)

Upscale Sweats—sweats (to supersize)

Women at Large—activewear (to Queen II, 72")

(See Chapter 3, "You Look Marvelous," the section titled "Swimsuits, T-shirts, and Activewear"), for more information.

Activewear and Swimsuit Patterns

Most pattern companies offer patterns up to size 2X, many run higher. The advantages to making your own include being able to resize the garment as you work and having a choice of material. $7–$15.

SOURCES:

Kwik-Sew—activewear (to 45" hips)

Great Fit Patterns—patterns (to size 60)

Besides these mail-order sources, check your fabric stores for Butterick (to 46" hips), McCall's (to 48" hips), Simplicity (to 50" hips), and Vogue (to 42" hips) patterns. (See also Chapter 3, "You Look Marvelous," for tips and patterns for sewing your own activewear.)

Athletic Shorts

SOURCES: Big & Bold—fleece or jersey (to size 5X), $16

Baseball Uniforms and Jackets

$35–$50.

SOURCES:

Big & Bold—jackets only (to size 8X)

Manny's Baseball Land—(up to size 4X in "full athletic cut")

J.C. Penney's "Simply for Sports"

Beach Umbrellas

SOURCES:

Basta Sole

Lillian Vernon extra-wide, in colorful stripes, $50+

Bicycle Seats

Remember, you are looking for a seat that supports your pelvic bones, not necessarily your size. Sometimes smaller is better.

The seat found in these sources is wider than most seats and is actually two separate pads with independent tilting action and large, foam-cushioned pads that fit on a regular seat support. $30–$50.

SOURCES:

Brookstone Hard-to-Find Tools

Hanover House (also carries sheepskin seat covers for this seat)

Bicycle Seat Pads
These gel pads won't break down, harden, or separate. Great shock absorber. $40.

SOURCES: Brookstone Hard-to-Find Tools

Bicycle Shorts
$30.

SOURCES:

Big Stitches

Fit to Be Tried

Bicycles
It's best to avoid shopping for a bike anywhere but at a reputable bicycle shop. Look for a sturdy frame (a mountain bike frame is an excellent choice), purchase tires with at least thirty-two spokes, buy extensions for your handlebars, if necessary, to allow the most comfortable posture for you, and be sure to find comfortable clothing. Sturdy shoes are very important for long rides.

Schwinn, probably the best-known of all bicycle makers, had this to say about the purchase of bicycles:

We do generally recommend our bicycle weight limit to 250 pounds. Most of our exercise equipment has a recommended weight limit of 300 pounds. However, it is usually the way a person uses the product that dictates whether that product will perform as it is intended by a manufacturer. A person weighing 100 pounds can do just as much damage to a bicycle or exerciser as a person of 400 pounds.

Boat ladders
Capacity to 400 pounds. $100–$170.

SOURCES:

Bart's

Defender

Boat Chairs

Folding yacht and fighting chair—26" wide. $120.

Baseless multipurpose fold-down seat—25" wide. $125.

Baseless multipurpose utility seat—24" wide. $100.

Baseless pilot seat—25" wide. $365.

Baseless standard seat—28" wide. $200.

SOURCES: Defender

Canoeing and Rafting Supplies
Inflatable rafts and canoes that support up to 1,000 pounds. $700–$7,000.

SOURCES: Wyoming River Raiders

Equestrian Attire
English and Western women's clothing in sizes up to 4X. Prices vary with item.

SOURCES: 1894—Arnot Mason Corporation

Equestrian Attire, Sew Your Own
Patterns for English and Western riding outfits, up to size 46 shirt for women and 48 coat for men. $7–$15.

SOURCES: SuitAbility

Exercise Mat
4' wide by 4', 5', or 6' long; this mat folds up into 2' sections. $200.

SOURCES: Enrichments

Fanny Floater
This U-shaped polyethylene-covered polyester seat is 25" wide and supports up to 275 pounds. $28.
SOURCES: Bart's

Football Fling
Toss a football back and forth on a long string with a partner. Strengthens arms. Can be used anywhere, even from a chair. $30.
SOURCES: Enrichments

Garden Weeder
Weed your yard and garden without bending. Trigger squeeze causes metal "jaws" to close on the offending plant, allowing you to remove it easily. $25.
SOURCES: Adaptability

Gardening Seat
The Scoot 'n Do, for those of you who like to garden but are uncomfortable working directly on the ground. This device holds up to 300 pounds. Seated almost a foot off the ground, you can scoot up and down garden rows, weeding, trimming, and picking as you go. $25–$60.
SOURCES:

Hanover House

Mellinger's Inc.

Gardening/Work Gloves
"Sized and designed to fit a woman's hand. Becomes more comfortable with wear. Ideal for gardening, carpentry, tradeswork and chores." You can even purchase a single glove if you have a problem with one wearing out. $20–$26.
SOURCES: Womanswork

Golf Clothes
Women's sizes up to 24. Prices vary by item.
SOURCES: Hot Off the Tour

Kneeling Pad
Extrawide, 21" (normal is 12" to 15"). Saves your knees when you are working in the garden or doing any kind of work (or play) that requires kneeling. $5.50.
SOURCES: Amplestuff

Kneeling/Sitting Cushion
There are many cushions for kneeling during gardening or housework, but few are all that sturdy or even very wide. This one is 22½" wide with a sturdy steel frame to help its user get up and down. It even doubles as a seat and folds flat for carrying and storage. Approximately $40.
SOURCES: Brookstone Hard-to-Find Tools

Lifejackets
Fitting chests up to 60", these vests are a must for water sports and boating. $50–$150.
SOURCES:

Bart's WaterSports

Defender Industries

Pedal Exercisers
Attach to or sit in front of your chair (depending on style you choose) and pedal away. $66–$200.
SOURCES: Enrichments

Pool Float
Hey, we can't be swimming laps all of the time! This float measures a generous 72" by 26" and is guaranteed to be un-sinkable. $145.
SOURCES: Preferred Living

Putter Finger
This handy golfing accessory is a 1½" attachment that fits over the handle end of a putter. It allows you to retrieve a golf ball without bending over. $4.
SOURCES: Miles Kimball

Physioball
A huge molded vinyl ball (16" to 37" in diameter) useful in all sorts of playtime activities. $21–$58.
SOURCES: Enrichments

Riding Boots
Custom-made. Call for pricing information.
SOURCES: The Dehner Company, Inc.

Rolls and Wedges
By Tumble Forms. Firm foam shapes to support your body during exercise. Price varies according to shape and size. $66–$122.
SOURCES: Enrichments

Shock Absorbers for Feet
They say walking or running causes an impact on your feet that is three to four times your body weight. Perhaps a little help would be appreciated. These shock absorbers were designed by a doctor. The claim is that they help prevent sore heels and knees, shin splints, heel spurs, and back pain caused by "heel strike." $9.
SOURCES: Miles Kimball

Shoes
Walking and running. Brands include Avia—(to women's size 11C, men's size 14EE); Brooks (to women's size 11D, men's size 15EE); Clark's (to women's size 10 wide, men's 13 wide); Easy Spirit (to women's size 10EE, men's 11EEE); Etonic (to women's 10D, men's 13EEEE); NaturalSport (to women's size 10 wide); New Balance (to women's size 11D, men's 14EEEE); Nike (to women's size 13D, men's 15EE); Reebok (to women's 12 wide, men's 15 wide); Rockport (to women's 10 extra wide; men's 13 extra wide); Saucony (to women's 11 wide). Costs vary by item.
SOURCES:

Coward Shoes (women's only)

The Comfort Corner

Friedman's Shoes (men's only)

Hersey Custom Shoe Company (custom men's and women's)

Maryland Square (women's only)

Massey's (women's only)

Miles Kimball

Shoe Express (women's only)

Wide World of MarLou (women's only)

Ski Chariot

Stand, sit, kneel, or crouch on this inflatable water toy as it is towed behind a boat, 36"-long by 24"-wide cockpit, 400 pounds maximum capacity. $140.

SOURCES: Bart's

Sleeping Bags

Oversize, extralong, and extrawide, 39" x 90" finished size. $100–$130.

SOURCES:

Cabela's

Campmor

Dunns

King-Size

Wyoming River Raiders (to 34½" wide)

Square Dance Patterns

For men and women. Skirts, dresses, vests, petticoats . . . everything you can imagine. $4–$10.

SOURCES: Shirley's Square Dance Shop— to size XXXL.

Sunglasses

Supersize, extralong frames. $30-$240.

SOURCES:

The King-Size Co.

SGD Merchandising

Sungold Enterprises

Woodmont Eyewear Fashions

Sweatshirts and Sweatpants

Up to size 8X. $20–$29.

SOURCES:

Big & Bold

Oh! Susanna

Thera-Bands

Wide (6") strips of rubber in a variety of colors and resistance strengths, attached to handles. For arm and leg strengthening. Approximately $8–$20.

SOURCES: Enrichments

Walking Sticks

Walking is really one of life's great pleasures. During the Victorian era, walking staffs were very popular. If you have trouble getting around, a walking stick may offer that little bit of extra help that keeps you mobile.

There is just something delightful about a hand-turned, wooden walking stick. And have I found a great place for you. The Poestenkill Hiking Staff Manufacturing Company (what a terrific name!) is owned by Albert Fromberger. Mr. Fromberger offers four designs, all painstaking reproductions of nineteenth-century sticks, each designed to be ideal for walking, hiking, backpacking, or just strolling. If you can't decide which of these beauties you want most, try choosing one by astrological sign. For instance, of the Scout model, the catalog says, ''The use of ash and black cherry (Sun + Venus) make this a strong feminine staff. Energywise well balanced and the counterpoint to the Forester staff. It is not a weak staff as the feminine influences of Venus are powered by the energy of the sun. This is a good staff for the confident male or female who will find it comfortable due to its balance, harmony and mellow energies it projects. In ancient times it would have been the staff of the Good

Sorceress or High Priestess.'' (Sounds like this one was designed for me!) $46–$60.

SOURCES: The Poestenkill Hiking Staff Manufacturing Company

Wet Suits

SOURCES:

Skin Diver Wetsuits—Custom-made to any size, $170. Free brochure.

Wyoming River Raiders—to size 2X.

CLOTHING

1-800-PRO-TEAM
Team wear for football, baseball, and hockey includes professional team items from the NFL, NHL, NBA, MLB, NCAA, and IHL, including jerseys, T-shirts, jackets, uniforms, and caps. Adult sizes from small to 2X on most items and to 3X on some; kids sizes S(8) to XL(20). You'll also find a few athletic shoes in up to 4E widths.

Bart's Watersports Catalog
Wet suits, swimwear, T-shirts (one shows a huge man on a wakeboard with the words ''Poetry in Motion''), to size 2X, life vests to size 3X; also inflatable rafts and boats.

Campmor
This catalog carries absolutely everything you can imagine for the outdoor enthusiast, from gaiters to winter boots, thermal underwear to snowshoes for people over 170 pounds. However, the clothing generally runs only to size 2X.

CURVES, Unltd.
Educational materials company advocating fitness for large-size exercisers. Call Gail Johnston for details, (510) 945-8891.

Defender
''America's Leading Discount Marine Outfitter Since 1938.'' Absolutely everything you can imagine for boating, including boats (inflatable and solid, supporting up to 8 persons, 2,800 pounds), survival gear and life vests (to sizes 2X), shoes and boots (to men's size 15M). Catalog $5.

Gander Mountain
A full line of hunting wear and camouflage wear in sizes to 6X, boots and shoes to size 13EE. (Where else can you find Rocky Corn Stalker Bear Claw Boots in mossy oak fall foliage?) Thermal underwear is available for both men and women to size tall 4X; silk underwear to size 2X.

Gilda Marx
Bike shorts, T-shirts, leggings, leotards, bra tops, and a full line of bodywear in sizes up to 3X.

J.C. Penney's Simply for Sports
General sportswear (including professional team attire) for men (sizes to 2X), women (sizes to 2X), and kids (sizes to XL).

MidWestern Sport Togs
Deerskin gloves, handbags, coats, moccasins, and accessories. Sizes up to 54 for men, 46 for women. Custom sizing is also available.

WalkUSA
Men's and women's walking clothing and activewear to size 2X.

NONDIET WORKSHOPS AND GROUPS

Nondiet workshops are springing up all over the country, many based on the programs listed below. Contact any of these groups for information on their programs, printed materials, and/or availability.

Abundia

Amity Associates

Body Trust

Diet/Weight Liberation

Fat and Fit Group Health Action (England)

Food and Nutrition Program (Australia)

G.U.I.D.E.

HUGS International, Inc. (Canadian, but has thirty affiliates in the United States)

Largely Positive

Size Acceptance Network (Australia)

Stop Dieting, Inc.

Weight Release Services

PUT A LITTLE ZIP IN YOUR LIFE . . .

DoubleXXRiders
This group in Colorado offers a newsletter offering moral support for full-figured riders plus tips on clothing and tack, etc. Send self-addressed, stamped envelope for information.

Potbelly Cycling Association
If you enjoy bicycling, have I got a group for you! This club, founded in 1995, will allow you to join if you don't have a potbelly, but you can only join as a wanna-be, an "Athletic Supporter."

Only if you have some substantial girth can you be a "Full" member. Joe Bruno, founder of the Potbelly Cycling Association, sees cycling as a fun way to get a little exercise and intends to continue enjoying it for the rest of his life. The $25 yearly membership fee includes a full subscription to the *Potbelly Cycling* newsletter and, for "Full" members, a personalized certificate, suitable for framing. "Athletic Supporters" receive valuable tips on how to achieve and maintain a potbelly.

EXERCISE CLASSES AND SPORTS INSTRUCTION (UNITED STATES)

Alaska

Women at Large, 907 East Dowling Road, Anchorage, AK 99518; (907) 562-6252

Arizona

Women at Large, 5140 West Peoria, Suite 5, Glendale, AZ 85301; (602) 486-2886

California

AbunDance (twice-weekly classes with certified aerobic instructor who is also a large woman), 3543 18th Street, San Francisco; (415) 337-6379

Big Moves, World Gym, 16th Street and Deharo, San Francisco; (415) 703-9650

The Big Splash, San Francisco; (415) 237-3978 or (415) 285-1769

Bodymoves Workout Studio, 1283 Camino Del Rio South, San Diego, 92108

Dance and Movement for Big Beautiful Bodies, Oakland YWCA, Oakland; (415) 531-9267

Great Shape Classes. These classes are co-sponsored by Kaiser Permanente Health Education departments, but you don't have to be a Kaiser health plan member to attend. If there are no classes listed in your area, but you would like to be on Great Shape's mailing list, call Yvonne Marshall at (510) 987-4560.

Fairfield, eight-week sessions, (707) 427-5777

Major Moves in Oakland, eight-week sessions, (510) 596-7858

Redwood City, eight-week sessions, (415) 299-2433

Vallejo, (707) 648-6272

Making Waves, 2423 Douglas Street, San Pablo, 94806; (415) 237-3978. Also Sundays from 11 A.M. to 1P.M. at Albany High School pool, sliding scale from $3 to $5; (510) 526-6206

Undeniably Me ("The fitness program for large women who want to have fun!"), San Francisco Bay Area, (415) 738-1221

Women at Large, 41899 Albrae Street, Fremont, 04538; (415) 490-1843

Women at Large, 1937 West 11th Street, Upland, CA 91786; (714) 949-1408

Colorado

Positively More, 6315 South University Boulevard, Littleton, CO 80121; (303) 798-2476

Women at Large, 690 West 84th Avenue, Thornton, CO 80221; (303) 426-6981

Connecticut

Women at Large, 167 Parkway North, Waterford, CT 06385; (203) 437-1301

Florida

Women at Large, 3690 East Bay Drive, Largo, FL 34641; (813) 536-2551

Georgia

Women at Large, 11235 Alpharetta Highway, Rosewell, GA 30076; (404) 751-9188

Idaho

Women at Large, Riverside Plaza, Blackfood, ID 83221; (208) 785-5292

Maryland

Women at Large, 18228 Flower Hill Way, Gaithersburg, MD 20879; (301) 670-1943

Massachusetts

Big Steppers, West Suburban YMCA, Newton, MA; (617) 244-6050

Michigan

Big In Sports ("Motivation, Education and Training for the Recreational Athlete"), Glenna Dunaway offers instruction in cross-country and alpine skiing, skating, and cycling with a special emphasis on working with large women, 2323 Mark Avenue, Lansing, MI 48915; (517) 485-0771

Minnesota

Dance Fun for Large Women, 5308 Chateau Place, Minneapolis, MN 55417; (612) 722-0722

Panda's, 11503 K-Tel Drive, Minnetonka, MN 55343; (612) 935-5354

Women at Large, 5340 Cedar Lake Road, St. Louis Park, MN 55416; (612) 541-0671

Women's Aerobics Plus, 4201 Minnetonka Boulevard, St. Louis Park, MN 55416; (612) 926-5149

Nevada

Women at Large, 1180 West 4th Street, Reno, NV 89503; (702) 323-3311

New York

Bourne Exercise Studio, One Chase Road, Scarsdale, NY 10583; (914) 472-4144

Fitness Designs, 501 East 85th Street, #2B, New York, NY 10028

The Smart Move, 131 West 72nd Street, New York, NY 10023; (212) 260-1520

North Carolina

Easy Does It, 1012 Oberlin Road, Raleigh, NC 27605; (919) 828-3205

Oregon

Ample Opportunity, 5370 North West Roanoke Lane, Portland, OR 97229; (503) 645-0497

Pennsylvania

Aerobics in Moderation, 2027 Chestnut Street, Philadelphia, PA 19103; (215) 564-3430

Big, Beautiful, and Fit, Arrott and Leiper streets, Philadelphia, PA 19124; (215) 831-9500

Women at Large, Greensburg Shopping Center, Greensburg, PA 15601; (412) 837-8103

Texas

Women at Large, 2215 North Midland, #4-D, Midland, TX 79707; (915) 697-5558

Women at Large, 1600 North Plano Road, #800, Richardson, TX 75081; (214) 644-2226

Virginia

Extrasize (call for class location), Norfolk, VA; (804) 473-8084

Washington

IDEA Fitness Consultant (call for class location), Chris Zagelow Patterson, Walla Walla, WA; (509) 327-6492

Water Women, a go-at-your-own-pace water exercise class with a hot therapy Jacuzzi pool available for use. Cost is based on ability to pay, from $3 to $5 per session. Class begins at 5:30. Fircrest Pool, 155th and 15th Northeast, Seattle, WA.

Women at Large, West 3330 Central, Spokane, WA 99204; (509) 327-6492

Women at Large, 1020 South 48th Street, Yakima, WA 98908; (509) 965-0115

Wisconsin

Women at Large, 4425 West Bradley, Brown Deer, WI 53223; (414) 354-2774

Women at Large is a franchise company with studios around the United States. Call Women at Large Systems, Inc., to see if there is a class near you.

EXERCISE CLASSES (BRITAIN)

Big Women Swim, Hackney Women's Centre, 20 Dalston Lane, London E9; (01) 986-0840

Want to Play Net Ball, Rounders, London; (01) 659-8843

EXERCISE CLASSES (CANADA)

Grand Size Fitness, Vancouver; (206) 574-5306

Women at Large:

#212 8915 51 Avenue, Edmonton, AB; (403) 465-2923

10114 175th Street, Edmonton, AB; (403) 484-9824

Box 3152, Edmonton, AB; (403) 986-5544

12-1425 Caribou Place, Kamloops, BC; (604) 828-1211

1044 Fort Street, Victoria, BC; (604) 389-1442

SPECIAL-INTEREST CLASSES

Model Mugging
A franchise organization teaching self-defense and empowerment to women of all sizes. Already in several locations throughout California and elsewhere. (Don't get your hopes up. I don't think this group lets you mug actual fashion models.) Call or write for information on classes in your area.

EXERCISE VIDEOS

As with most of the other resources listed, I am not in a position to recommend any of these videos in particular so far as the safety and effectiveness of the moves are concerned. Most were produced especially with the larger body in mind, though I have included several yoga videos with gentle stretching exercises.

•Low-Impact Aerobics•

Big on Fitness (Full Figure Aerobics). An exercise video by and for large-size women. Low-impact aerobics and stretching. The emphasis here is on positive attitudes and safe moves. This one will not exactly inspire you to greatness, though. These women look like they are stuck in a P.E. class. 45 minutes, VHS. $30.

SOURCES:

Amplestuff, Ltd.

West One Video

Breakout Low-impact aerobic videos from the chain of exercise studios named Women at Large. $35.

SOURCES: Women at Large Systems, Inc.

Great Changes: The Larger Woman's Workout Carnie Wilson and Idrea combine their talents to create this low-impact video. $15.

SOURCES: Warner Vision

HUGS Fun Fitness Video—Gentle Physical Activity Experience movement that leaves you feeling energized, not exhausted. Filmed in a natural outdoor setting, participants are "real" people, the movements are gentle. $25.

SOURCES: HUGS International, Inc.

I.Y.M. Low-impact aerobics 60-minute video designed for the full-figured woman, consisting of a warm-up, three cardiovascular workouts, stomach and leg exercises, and stretching. $20.

SOURCES: I.Y.M.

Idrea Says "Yes You Can"
This low-impact aerobics video comes highly recommended in *Great Shape*. $30.

SOURCES: Two Lipps Video

Just Move   Aerobic exercise in a rather uninspiring video. The message is right—exercise for the benefits of a more graceful, active life, not weight loss. I'd like to see the instructor of this one, Nellie Petersen, do another tape . . . with better technical support. $30.
SOURCES: D. P. Moves, Inc.

The Larger Woman's Workout   Low-impact aerobic workout for larger women. $25.
SOURCES: Two Lipps Company

In Grand Form with Jody Sandler   Low-impact aerobics. A beginner's video that teaches the basics (taking your pulse, proper attire, etc.). $30.
SOURCES: Grand Form Enterprises, Ltd.

Sharlyne Powell's 30 Minute Workout   This is a shorter version of Women at Large's low-impact aerobic *Breakout* tape. $30.
SOURCES: Women at Large Systems, Inc.

Richard Simmons Sweat & Shout   "Simmons meets Soul Train . . . a low-impact aerobics routine that's ideal for beginners." $20.
SOURCES: Collage Video

Richard Simmons Sweatin' to the Oldies I, II, III, and IV   Exercises with the ever-exuberant Richard Simmons, set to very upbeat songs from the 50s and 60s. $40 each.
SOURCES: Miles Kimball (tapes 2 and 3)

Richard Simmons Tone and Sweat & Disco Sweat   (Two tapes, sold as a kit.) Toning program utilizing rubber exercise tubing (comes with the tape) and low-impact aerobics. $40.
SOURCES: Collage Video

Weight Watchers' Easy Shape-Up   Particularly good for beginners, this three-video set features simple aerobics. $30.
SOURCES: Collage Video

Woman—Free Your Soul   Video is designed by an African American woman with stretches and dance movements. 22 minutes.
SOURCES: MPU, Inc.

• Walking •

Jane Fonda's Walkout Series   Instrumental music with occasional instructions from Ms. Fonda. Beginner and intermediate tapes. $20.
SOURCES: Collage Video

Look Who's Walking   Great video for any large person beginning a walking program. $30.

SOURCES: Orchid Leaf Productions

Praise Walk   Christian music, Christian vocals for inspirational walking. Beginner, intermediate, and advanced tapes. $20.
SOURCES: Collage Video

Richard Simmons's Classic Walk   Classical music combined with Richard's voice to keep you going. 60-minute cassettes, complete with warm-up and cool-down.

SOURCES: Collage Video

Sports Music Walking Tapes Walk to marches (Sousa, military, classical), party music ("In the Midnight Hour," "The Lion Sleeps Tonight," and so on.), or classical music (Vivaldi, Beethoven, and others). Available in beginner, intermediate, and advanced. $13.

SOURCES: Collage Video

•Stretching and Yoga•

Dixie Carter's Yoga for You: Unworkout II Simple, easy stretches and body-toning moves. 62 minutes, VHS. $20.

SOURCES: Video stores

Gentle Yoga with Naomi Rediscover enjoyable movement through yoga. The participants on this tape are average men and women of all shapes who are looking to balance their weight and treat themselves with respect. $34.

SOURCES: The Offner Team

Joan Collins: Personal Workout Joan Collins and her personal trainer demonstrate a sensible, easygoing routine of stretches and exercises for the legs, waist, and abdominals. Some light weights used. 50 minutes. $15.

SOURCES: Video stores

Lilias, Alive with Yoga Introduction to Hatha Yoga, adapted from the PBS program of the same name. Beginner and intermediate. $30.

SOURCES: Collage Video

Richard Hittleman's Yoga Course A serious instructional video. Beginner and intermediate tapes. $30.

SOURCES: Collage Video

Richard Simmons Stretchin' to the Classics Demonstrates healthful stretches set to classical music . . . with no talk. Beginner. $20.

SOURCES: Collage Video

Tai Chi Strength and Conditioning Fundamentals Video that allows you to set your own pace and work to tone all of your muscles. 50 minutes. $15.

SOURCES: (800) 745-1145

Warming Up: The Gentle Exercise Videotape for Formerly Inactive People

SOURCES: Portland Health Institute

Yoga for Round Bodies Five half-hour sessions at beginner and intermediate levels taught by "round-bodied instructors" Linda DeMarco, M.S., and Genia Pauli Haddon, D.Min., Ph.D., certified Kripalu Yoga teachers. $60 for both volumes; $30 for volume 1.

SOURCES: Plus Publications

Yoga Journal's Yoga for Beginners Introduction to Hatha Yoga. 56-page booklet included. $25.

SOURCES: Collage Video

•Special Needs•

Chair Dancing Exercises using a chair for balance and support. This video is excellent for people with knee problems or who have difficulty standing for exercise. Work up gradually through different fitness levels. All types and ages of people are used in this video. $20.

Sources: Collage Video

Custom-Made Exercise Video After a phone consultation to determine your individual needs, limitations, and goals, Kelly Bliss, M.Ed., puts together a video designed just for you. $50.

Sources: Work It Out, Inc.

Custom-Made Yoga/Stretch Tape Mara Lindsey-Nesbitt, a supersize woman, yoga/stretch instructor, and licensed massage therapist, designs your tape around your own strengths and weaknesses, teaching stretching, breathing, and relaxation. Ms. Nesbitt consulted with chiropractors, physical therapists, massage therapists, osteopaths, and other back care professionals to find moves best suited for the larger figure. Tapes run about 45 minutes each. $55.

Sit and Be Fit There are several tapes available in this series based on a television program of the same name. Almost all exercises are designed to be done in a chair. Video, $40; audio, $11.

Sources: Sit and Be Fit

BOOKS

Fitness the Dynamic Gardening Way Written by Jeffrey Restuccio, Balance of Nature Publishing, 1992. Turning your love of gardening into a pleasurable way to add healthful exercise to your life.

Great Shape: The First Fitness Guide for Large Women Written by Pat Lyons and Debby Burgard, Bull Publishing, 1990. An exercise guide for large women _by_ large women. Enjoy movement again and feel better about yourself with your improved flexibility. This is not your typical exercise book full of skinny models and exercises that would tax Jane Fonda. Pat and Debby address all of the issues that surround becoming

active again . . . from all of the excuses we use to avoid activity to finding the recreation you will love indulging in to tips on getting started. Very positive, fun, absolutely liberating.

There are people who will argue to the death that fat people cannot be healthy and fit, that the terms fat _and_ fit _are mutually exclusive. While experts will continue to disagree, even contradict one another on the actual health risks of fat, you need not wait for their consensus to become more fit and healthy regardless of your weight. There are definite things you can do to improve your_ health. *Most important is to define what health means to you and reach for that goal.*

Highly recommended.

Surviving Exercise Written by Judy Alter, Houghton Mifflin Company, 1990. Excellent resource for anyone about to begin or add to their exercise program. Full of safe exercises for any body type.

➡ If any data listed in this chapter need to be corrected, please let me know. If you know of a service or product useful to people of size, please write to me about it. The information may be made available to readers through the newsletter "Size Wise Update!," the Size Wise web site, or through possible future revisions of this book.

PERSONAL GLIMPSE:
RUBY

Ruby grew up in Alabama and Chicago, where she was an honor roll student and active in basketball, school politics, and cheerleading. She married young and raised her own three children and three of her younger siblings while dealing with a difficult marriage. Striking out on her own after her youngest graduated from high school, Ruby found her own strength and happiness while learning to love and accept herself.

When my first baby was born I went from 130 pounds to, six weeks later, exactly 180. I did not change my eating habits during that time and I certainly got enough exercise. My doctor put me on a diet. I could have only eight ounces of food a day, including water. And he gave me water pills. He said, "Water weighs too." I lost 50 pounds in no time. I gained back 60 in no time at all. This happened several times. I would get down to what he thought I should weigh, then would gain it right back. I eventually realized that unless I was coming off of a diet I did not overeat. I wasn't eating more than I had before; if anything, I was eating less.

A large part of the time I was dieting I was on Weight Watchers. In the past I had eaten when I was hungry and that was it. With Weight Watchers what I learned was to become obsessed with food. My whole life became centered around food—shopping, planning, cooking, and eating. In the morning, instead of worrying about my children being healthy or the deplorable state of my marriage, I would wake up wondering, "Was I good? Did I stick to my diet?" If I had stuck to my diet I felt very good about myself; if I hadn't, I beat up on myself.

I went from 130 pounds to 389 pounds and was dieting all the time except for brief intervals. In a week I could gain 7 or 8 pounds. I could gain 5 pounds in a weekend!

If you've dieted, you know that you are crazy when you diet. I used to black out, I'd be so hungry. And I was on Black Beauties . . . amphetamines. I did a lot of screaming and yelling. Since I couldn't yell at my husband, I yelled at my children. It was horrible.

I felt so guilty for putting on the weight. I would look around and realize I was not eating anywhere near as much as in the past. I wasn't eating any more than my thin sisters and brothers and friends. But I had no alternative to dieting. There was no one telling me, "Hey, just relax and let go. Quit this dieting and get on with life."

Society holds out this false promise . . . with the help of the diet industry. If you eat a low-fat, low-sugar diet and exercise a *lot*, you can be thinner. You are never going to get back down to a size 3—5—6—10—18. But you have everybody telling you that if only you will get yourself in control you can rejoin society and not be an outcast.

The hardest thing in the world for me to do was to quit dieting. Still today, if I find a dress that's just a little bit too small, I'll think, "I'm going to lose a few pounds and it will fit." Then I think, "What are you thinking about? It will fit for fifteen minutes!"

Not long after my divorce I was standing in line at the grocery store and saw this magazine that had a large-size woman on the cover. Its title was *BBW . . . Big Beautiful Woman*. I was really shocked. I didn't want anybody to see me reading this magazine and think I knew that I was big, so I shoved it underneath everything else in the cart. I remember when I went to check out the girl said, "Oh! *BBW magazine*! This is really great. I'll have to read this!" I'm looking at her, thinking, "Don't say that out loud, lady!"

I went to my apartment and, even though I lived alone, went all the way back to my bedroom and closed the door before I would read it. I was just amazed.

There were ads from men who wanted supersize women. Well, at 300-plus pounds I figured that I was supersize, so I answered about twenty ads. I waited and waited and waited but didn't get any answers. In two months I had only one reply.

I just had to find out what the situation was. All my fat life I'd been told that I have such a pretty face and then I find these men who want big women, so why didn't they answer me? I sat down and wrote them all again, asking, "Why didn't you answer my first letter? I'm certainly big and beautiful." Then I started getting answers . . . I wasn't big enough! It blew my mind! It was great. Here I could correspond with these men and send them pictures and have them write me back and tell me how beautiful I was. It was a wonderful period of healing.

That's when I started reading. But instead of reading diet books I read Dr. Bennett's *Dieter's Dilemma*, in which I read that I was fat because of my set-point, and dieting made me fatter. I knew that what he was saying was true because it was what had happened to me.

One of my correspondents, a guy from Chicago, turned me on to NAAFA. After a very short time I was president of the Chicago chapter of NAAFA, then I became chapter coordinator for four years. I was never going to get married again after what I had gone through, but in February of '82 I answered Conrad's letter; in July of '83 we met for the first time; in '84 I moved up here; on April 20, 1985, we got married.

When they talk about the negative side of being fat, it's always health. I'm 150 pounds heavier than when my knee started hurting me. One of my sisters has arthritis really bad in her back and in her ankle. My other sister, who is a nurse, has arthritis in her ankle, her wrist, and her back. They have never weighed more than 130 pounds.

I would not change my current life for my previous life (when I was thin) for anything in the whole world. I would be absolutely horrified at the idea. I spend hours in the pool exercising in the water. I also do exercises with weights, strengthening my muscles. Sometimes when I want to dance I think "Damnit! If I weren't so fat I could dance." Or I think, "What would happen if the house were on fire and I had to climb out a window?" But I have to stop and realize that the reason I am the size I am now is because of dieting. I know that is very very hard to believe. But it's true.

"Fourteen Ways to Better Health Right Now"

1. Stop dieting.
2. Treat your body with respect and love.
3. Toss your scale into the scrap metal bin on recycling day.
4. Reclaim the pleasure of eating and learn what foods—and how much—your body really needs and wants.
5. Go through your wardrobe and give away everything that doesn't fit to a homeless or battered women's shelter; then treat yourself to some classy new outfits that make you feel as great as you look!
6. Learn to appreciate the diversity of sizes and shapes human beings naturally come in and recognize the beauty, strength, and grace in ALL of them.
7. Make friends with the person you see in the mirror.
8. Get to know people of size who have learned to love themselves just the weigh they are: treat them as valued resources, role models, mentors . . . and friends.
9. Experience the joy in moving your body freely; find physical activities you love doing—dancing, swimming, gardening, bicycling, skiing, hiking, team sports, or anything else—and have fun playing!
10. Insist on size-blind, size-informed health care; if your caregivers aren't adequate to this basic requirement, find others who are.
11. Join a size esteem support group through your local community, health or women's center, church, or size rights organization; if no group exists, start one yourself!
12. Challenge size bigotry and fight size discrimination whenever and wherever you encounter it.
13. Pick something you've been putting off until you were the perfect size or shape, and go for it NOW—you are the perfect size and shape for YOU!
14. Make copies of these tips and send them to everyone you know!

From Largesse, the Network for Size Esteem.

2

IT HURTS WHEN I
DO THIS, DOC

When was the last time you went to a doctor for a checkup? You know, just the yearly check-under-the-hood to make sure everything is running all right? Do you go to the doctor when you have headaches or to find out why your back aches? Do you go in for anything short of a life-threatening emergency? Chances are good the answer is no. Most large people would probably rather not go near a doctor or hospital, not necessarily because we don't care about ourselves or our health.

Just about everybody interviewed for this book mentioned the frustration they felt in dealing with doctors, nurses, dietitians, dentists (yes, dentists), and other medical staff. Almost all had stories of going to see a physician with complaints having nothing to do with their size and being told to lose weight. Unfortunately, it is not unusual for a doctor to ignore completely the illness or problem and cut straight to talking about weight loss.

An unsolicited discourse about weight could perhaps be tolerated and chalked up to the doctor's not being educated on the subject if the lecture were accompanied by a serious look at the presenting condition. But most fat patients come away with less than satisfactory treatment for illnesses and injuries. Visiting a doctor can be expensive, intimidating, and frustrating; more so if you can't anticipate serious consideration of your problems. Beyond even the simple frustration is the very real possibility of improper diagnosis and treatment. You deserve much better!

As one of the doctors said at the AHELP (Association for the Health Enrichment of Large People) conference in San Francisco, "I cannot imagine not having my butt sued if this [dieting] were a drug with a success rate of only 2 to 5 percent and I prescribed it to someone." Yet every day doctors hand out dieting information.

When you diet and then gain back weight quickly, which is what happens to 98 percent of all dieters, you can build up plaque in the veins more quickly. When you lose weight the plaque doesn't go away. Maybe this is why fat people have more heart attacks.

There is no disease or problem a fat person has that thin people don't also have. How about dealing with the problem? Thin people have heart attacks, broken bones, back problems. To a fat person, however, doctors talk about complications brought on by additional weight and try to make a correlation between cause and effect. But you have no effect if you have a population where you can point to people of various sizes all the way from 100 to 500 pounds and they all have the same problem. Large women are much more likely to put off going to a doctor if they know they are going to be handed a diet.

My partner's sister is a large woman. Finally at the age of twenty-seven she decided to go have a Pap smear and exam. The doctor said he couldn't get the speculum in properly and couldn't do a Pap smear. He was just disgusted with the whole thing. He said he just couldn't do it; she was too fat. It had taken her three years just to get up the courage to go in. I suggested she go to a women's clinic where they see a lot more women.

—CAROL

You've probably heard this before (and possibly considered it to be a rumor) but I'm going to tell you again. Doctors are not gods. They don't have all the answers, they are capable of making mistakes, and they are prone to the same societal bigotry as everyone else. Then, to make matters worse, they have attended medical school.

Medical schools are beginning to teach the basics of nutrition and "obesity," but medical students are seldom given information that will truly be of use in treating fat patients.

This is where we, as consumers, come in. Just as no one's education is complete when the schoolroom is left behind, a medical provider's education is still full of weak spots when he or she graduates from medical school. I honestly believe that the majority of doctors are conscientious and concerned with providing proper treatment to all patients. If they are pushing low-calorie diets and are hung up on weight loss, it is most likely because they or their instructors haven't kept pace with the latest research. Working together, I believe that we can help educate most doctors about the futility of dieting and get them to begin to work with us toward better health at any size.

After a lifetime of experiencing the same frustrations most fat people face in searching for good medical care, I have struck gold. My physician treats me with respect, listens to my concerns, and addresses my health problems for what they are. Thanks to him and his staff I am getting healthier and feel as if I have someone to turn to when necessary. If you haven't found someone similar, keep looking.

When it comes right down to it, a doctor is running a business and providing a service. If your doctor can't see beyond his or her own prejudices and is unwilling to evaluate and treat your health problems just as he or she would those of other patients, find a doctor who can. You have every right to be taken seriously, to be treated with respect, and to leave a medical facility knowing your concerns have been addressed as well as possible. Anything less is unacceptable.

Dieting can be hazardous to your health.

I went to an eye doctor one day. After the exam he asked how much I weighed. I told him, "About 420." He kind of screwed up his face and sat back stroking his chin, looking at me. Finally he said, "That's too much." I said, "You're kidding!" He asks, "Does [your regular doctor] know about this?" I replied, "I've pretty much kept it to myself, but I had a feeling it might come up today so I mentioned it to him on my last visit."

But you know how it is. You go to a doctor with a sore throat and he will say, "Lose a few pounds and you'll feel better."

I eat between 1,500 and 2,000 calories a day. It's so frustrating because I can gain weight on that. I've had doctors tell me I am lying and I'm not dealing with reality. I refuse to take the abuse from health care professionals and people in general. There is no reason to get hostile or nasty. I refuse to accept their attitudes. I just tell them they are welcome to their opinions but I don't agree with them. This is my body and my life and until you are supportive of me, I don't want your input.

—SUSAN MASON

A CONVERSATION WITH DR. DEAN EDELL

Dr. Dean Edell, one of the first "media doctors," hosts the second most popular syndicated radio talk show in the country and can be seen weekly on the syndicated television program, *Hey, Dr. Dean.*

In the late 1980s, his program on NBC-TV, *Dr. Edell's Medical Journal*, received an award from, among others, the American Heart Association and the C. Everett Koop Media Awards competition. He has been nominated for numerous Emmy

Awards and received many other awards, including a recognition award from the American Cancer Society.

Dr. Edell is known for speaking out on controversial medical issues and translating complicated medical information into concise, down-to-earth information. He took time out to speak with me one day about dieting, health care, and size discrimination.

J: It is said that 98 percent of all diets fail to produce a sustained, substantial weight loss. What is your reaction to that?

DR. EDELL: Diets fail for a bunch of reasons. I don't know of any study that has ever shown that, taken as a group, fat people eat any more than anyone else. That has been tried many, many times. Yet the general public perception, the thing the diet industry builds upon, is that all fat people are gluttons, so we will fix them by not allowing them to eat everything they really want to eat and selling them a whole bunch of products and new books, and that will solve it. Well, it solves the problem of how to get money into their bank account, but it doesn't solve any other problems.

The major objection I have to the diet industry, from the worst to the best of it, is that it doesn't take into account that a significant percentage, if not most, of obesity problems have to do with genetics and metabolism. It's logical and makes common sense, but that doesn't seem to get through. Consequently, when we do studies all fat people are lumped together.

Certainly there are those who may be eating themselves fat. But, by the way, we're only beginning to learn that. Science is only now taking that claim seriously enough to try to prove that you can eat yourself fat, which tells you that we've never really proven it before. Otherwise why would we be doing the studies? Which are weird ones. For instance, they go to Africa and find that during some religious holiday some Masai warriors will gorge themselves and gain eighty pounds, then loose it right back down to their starting weight. Only when they do those studies are they figuring out, "Wow, you can eat yourself fat, but genetics are also keeping you at your normal weight."

When you lump everybody together and include those who eat themselves fat, you may see negative health statistics. What you don't know is, if you separated out those people who truly have metabolic and genetic problems, would you find any increase in health risk?

Diets don't work because sooner or later you are going to have to go off the diet. If someone says, "Here's a diet," the first question to ask is "How long do I go on this diet?" "Well, you go on this diet for two months." "Then what do I do at the end of two months?" "Well, em, er . . . we're not quite sure but we've got your money at that point and it doesn't matter because if you fail you go back on another diet and that keeps the industry going." The diet industry is a very healthy industry for that very reason. People keep losing . . . losing their money and not the weight, and we're right back where we started from.

If someone is going to make even a stab at losing weight, they have to say to themselves, "Whatever I'm going to do, if I can't do it for the rest of my life, be happy with myself, be happy with how I eat and be happy with my life, then forget it." It's a waste of time because the rhythm method of girth control isn't going to work and may have negative health consequences.

We live in one of the only societies in history that values the Twiggy stick figure. Biologically, of course, extra weight confers a great advantage in famine and in cold. That's the way nature meant it. At any time in the past, and in many places I can think of in the world today, pounds are positive. Fat was a valued thing. Obviously that has changed through the power of Madison Avenue and marketing. We've got everybody paranoid and trying to lose more weight than they even need to.

Studies show that if you ask the average woman what figure she thinks the average man prefers, she will guess something much much smaller and lighter than the average man actually prefers. Ask her to identify her own body shape on a chart and she'll miss there too; she'll think she's heavier than she actually is. She'll think she should be lighter and that society prefers a svelter figure than it really does. So we're all screwed up.

J: Even if we figure out that we shouldn't believe what the diet industry tells us, what do we do when former surgeon general Dr. C. Everett Koop comes out with his "Shape Up America" program . . . a program, by the way, financed heavily by Jenny Craig, Inc., Weight Watchers, NutriSystem, etcetera. Dr. Koop talks about how we need to diet and lose weight; he even discourages weight discrimination in the workplace. We're supposed to trust Dr. Koop.

DR. EDELL: Dr. Koop doesn't know everything. He buys into the same mythology that most doctors do. Here's how it comes down.

Dr. Koop sees a woman whom he judges to be overweight, and this woman is truly overweight. She gets up every morning. She walks. Eats no more food than Dr. Koop does. Okay?

What does Dr. Koop say to that person? What does Dr. Koop expect from that person? How dare Dr. Koop suggest there is something wrong with that person? Eats the same as he does, exercises as much as he does, and yet she is "fat." But he'll tell her to lose weight. Which means he thinks he is smarter than God, who made her, who gave her her genes and her metabolism.

Any time doctors think they are going to improve on the normal, healthy human body, look out! Because we have always been wrong. We have no right to speculate. To do something like that requires major, major evidence and major, major, major proof that we don't have.

You make a statement like, "Anyone who's overweight should adhere to this preposterous standard." Show me the proof! Just show me the proof. Well, we don't have it.

J: Do you think it's possible to be fat and fit?

DR. EDELL: Absolutely. Absolutely. Of course. Listen, you can look at something like osteoporosis, the big plague for thinner women. Osteoporosis is less common among overweight women. But let's suppose somebody went out there and absolutely proved that overweight people, whether genetically or through eating themselves fat, have worse health statistics. The question you have to ask is, "Okay, now can you prove you can change that?" We haven't done that.

We haven't shown that if you take a bunch of people and put them on a diet, put them on something you know doesn't work, that that's going to help. So, it's a house of cards built on a very weak foundation.

The first thing I'd like to see is somebody take a group of people who are metabolically overweight, separate them out, and see what their health is like. And then if their health is worse, so what? Can we change that? Lots of us have worse health because of our genetics. We are not all programmed to live the same length of time and have the same diseases. If medicine thinks they can change that, that's fine. But read my lips . . . prove it. Prove it.

We are so far from that. We cause so much psychic damage and hurt so many people. We discriminate and create such negative imagery in the whole process that it's an evil. It's an evil.

J: What are your feelings about weight-loss surgeries?

DR. EDELL: Weight-loss surgeries are way overutilized. Basically it is supply and demand, and the demand is there. People get desperate and are willing to lay their bodies down. They risk a major death rate on the table to have this surgery. And it fails. You can eat yourself through a stomach stapling easily. I've seen people do it all the time. I don't know that it brings happiness. The ultimate success rate is something we don't know. You hear about the disasters, and there are plenty of them.

J: One of the biggest problems fat people encounter is the inability to get good health care.

DR. EDELL: Alcoholics, drug addicts, cigarette smokers . . . all these kinds of people go to doctors and doctors never say a peep. Never even diagnose it simply because it's not obvious. When you are fat, it's obvious. It's easy for the doctor to pick on you, so to speak. Fat people are wearing a sign across their faces that says, "I am fat. Take a shot at me." It's real easy for the doctor to do, and they do it.

J: How do we change that?

DR. EDELL: Doctors are representative of society and are no different than any other group of people. Doctors can be sexist, fatist, and racist to the same degree as society as a whole is. It is unrealistic to expect something more from doctors than we expect from politicians, lawyers, and businessmen.

J: But we need so much more from doctors; we have to trust them with our health.

DR. EDELL: Yes, but they are just human beings, and we can't expect them to stand outside of society. If we live in a racist society, doctors will be racist. We're just college students who went on to medical school. Society needs to alter its view.

J: How does a person go about finding good health care?

DR. EDELL: You've got to ask questions. Go by instinct. That's something most people do pretty well. You know when you're being looked askance at, being denigrated. You have to use that sense. A person has to be aware these attitudes exist in medicine.

J: I've had women tell me of working up the courage to go to a doctor for a Pap smear only to be told, "You're too big, I can't possibly do a Pap smear."

DR. EDELL: I've heard the same stories. It's disgusting. You've got to nail a doctor when he does that. Send him a letter with copies to his employers. Most doctors are "employed" now, you know. Raise hell. I don't think it's going to change the doctor's mind. Is it the patient's job to raise the consciousness of these boobs? I don't know.

We can't worry about changing the world; all we can do is change ourselves. Readjust self-image. Start trying to like yourself. Start fighting all the negative stuff. It can be done. There are people who are members of ethnically abused groups who manage to raise kids with good self-esteem, who teach them to have pride in themselves. It's a tall order.

You know, Twiggy came out of the blue. It wasn't long ago that the idolized female form was fatter. I can easily see, next year some fashion designer comes out and all of a sudden having a few extra pounds will be in; over the course of a generation or two fat may come back as a beauty standard. These things are very trendy, very faddy. Anything is possible.

J: How is it that you understand what's going on?

DR. EDELL: I have an aunt, my age, who lived with us as my sister. My mother was on her case all the time to get her to lose weight so she could find a man. I lived through the pills, the depression, the suicide attempts, the whole deal with her. I remember her weight going up and down, up and down; seeing what it took for her to lose weight. I can eat huge amounts of food and not gain a pound. My father is the same way, my kids are the same way. She would have to eat nothing to lose weight. Today she has to be at least 300 pounds. She just had to let it go. She had five children, has led a productive life and is happy.

We doctors hear from people, "But doctor, I don't overeat." No one believes them. Well, then, why should anyone believe me when I tell you I do overeat and don't gain an ounce?

A Dr. Alfred Ferris once had seventy-seven weight-loss clinics throughout California. His program was probably as successful as any other of that ilk. You went in, got a diet, and got diet pills. You also had to go in every day for placebo shots. Having to go in every day is probably the support that people who lost the weight needed to lose it. They sure gained it back afterwards, though. Before I started doing radio, the transitional job I took was to work for him a couple of days a week. I would hit ten clinics and examine people to make sure they were healthy enough to go on these diets.

I went through diets with thousands and thousands of women. Not many doctors have that experience. I started to see through it all.

J: Did you ever see anyone maintain a significant weight loss?

DR. EDELL: Boy, I have to think hard. I can't say that I have. Anyone maintaining a loss was the average person who wanted to lose ten or fifteen pounds to get into a bathing suit . . . that kind of person.

I have no doubt people can fluctuate and throw their weight up and down ten or fifteen pounds. There may be the occasional person with an excessive eating habit who has eaten himself fat and then gets on top of his problem.

Let's put it this way. It would be inaccurate for me to say it doesn't happen just because I didn't see it. When these people left the clinic, or when I stopped working there, I don't know what happened. But I wouldn't be at all surprised if you could offer me evidence that says nobody kept it off, especially the major weight losses . . . like someone who had lost a hundred pounds.

Fat people are the last minority group in the country. I've proselytized on the air many times. Somehow everyone turns their backs on it. Everyone looks the other way. If it's the color of your skin, discrimination is illegal. If it's the amount of your skin, somehow that's okay. It is discriminatory. Society gets away with it.

If you just can't get up the nerve to talk to your doctor about this subject, feel free to give him a copy of this letter.

An Open Letter to Physicians

Dear Doctor:

Nothing personal, but few places are as unpleasant for a large person to visit than a medical office. It isn't the tests, the poking and prodding, the cold speculum, the needles, or even that heart-stopping bill that keeps us away. And it isn't that we don't care about our health. It's you, your staff, and those narrow seats in your waiting room. Let's start at the top:

When I place my health in your hands, it is my hope you will take my concerns seriously and will find some way to look past my size and beyond personal prejudices, if you have any. I am not asking you to marry me or even take me dancing . . . I am asking that you use your education to address any health problems I may be experiencing. Please listen to my concerns, then consider how you would test and treat these symptoms if I were not fat. Treat me with respect and I will return the favor.

I am aware that some diseases may be related to or aggravated by being large, and I want you to help me avoid or deal with those. But don't expect superhuman attempts at starving myself to achieve an impossible goal. Please be realistic. Diets don't work . . . ask me, I've tried them all.

Subscribe to publications like *Healthy Weight Journal* to help keep yourself up-to-date on the latest research and to *Radiance* or *Rump Parliament* to make yourself aware of issues I face that may affect my health. (Keep these magazines in your waiting room for the education of your patients and to show that you are size-friendly.) Request copies of informational brochures and other publications from Largesse or the National Association to Advance Fat Acceptance (of special interest are their pamphlets "Facts About Hypertension and the Fat Person," "How to Weigh Your Supersize Patients," and "Guidelines for Therapists Who Treat Fat Patients"). Join the Association of Health Enrichment for Large People (AHELP) and be a part of finding solutions to problems encountered by your large patients.

If I ask you for help controlling or changing my weight, offer your thoughts and suggestions. Alert me to health problems truly affected by weight . . . and be current with your information. Please don't hand me a low-calorie diet sheet and preach to me about self-control. Chances are good I've already heard it, tried it, and moved on. Unless you have good, solid evidence that a weight-loss treatment will work for me on a permanent basis, don't demand that I lose weight. You may become a part of my health problems by creating diet-induced diseases.

Please drop the terms "morbid obesity" and "gross obesity" from your vocabulary. They are offensive medical terms assuming disease. Not all fat people are sick . . . even fewer of us are morbid or gross. If you think I am either of these things, you are not the doctor for me.

Please don't demand that I be weighed unless absolutely necessary. If there is a compelling reason to weigh me, make sure your scale is in a private area. And please don't use this opportunity to humiliate me, thinking you can drive me to weight loss through shame. (There have been instances of doctors or their staff making mooing or oinking noises after weighing a large patient.) Record the information, use it when necessary, and please keep it confidential.

When prescribing medications, make adjustments for dosage if necessary. Consider not only weight but body mass index.

When taking my blood pressure, use the appropriate cuff. A standard cuff can be used for arms up to sixteen inches in circumference. Larger cuffs are available and should be kept handy. If those cuffs are too small, take the reading using my forearm.

Whatever you do, don't assume I am lying when we discuss my eating habits (or anything else). Some people who are fat have eating disorders and/or consume huge quantities of food. (Research shows most eating disorders appear in people of moderate, if not downright low, weight.) Most of us who are fat have lowered our metabolism through dieting to the point where even "normal" amounts of food can cause weight gain. Many people who are fat have been made to feel so guilty about eating anything beyond a dry salad they automatically admit to being "bad" when in truth they eat normally. Even fat people buy into some of the stereotypes. Recent studies have proven what fat patients have been saying all along . . . "I don't eat that much!"

Your staff: Just as you wouldn't allow your staff to snicker about the color of a person's skin or the lack of mobility of any individual with a disability, please make certain the same courtesy is extended to all your patients. Remarks are often overheard when a doctor, nurse, or assistant thinks the patient is out of earshot. Prejudice is born out of ignorance; educate your staff and insist upon a professional manner at all times.

Your office: Make your office comfortable, nonintimidating, and accessible. When choosing furniture, assume that many of your patients will be large . . . some may be more than 400 pounds. Choose sturdy chairs without arms. Make sure the cushions are firm and that the seat is not set too low to the floor. Few things are more embarrassing for the large person than trying to struggle up from a soft, low seat in front of others.

Examining tables should be braced to keep them from tipping. The steps up to the table should be wide and sturdy. (While you're at it, can you do something to warm up those metal tables?) Doors should be wide, allowing easy access to examining rooms, offices, and bathrooms.

Now . . . about those examination gowns. Get real! "Average"-size people struggle to keep themselves covered while wearing them. It is difficult to have a serious discussion about health concerns when my most pressing problem is an overexposed backside. Gowns that fit up to size 10X are available; please keep some handy. I suspect many of your other patients would appreciate them as well.

What I need from you is respect, professional concern, and your best medical advice. The very things all of your patients deserve. Given these conditions, I look forward to a long, healthy relationship with you.

Signed,
In Search of Good Health

A doctor at a medical convention asked, "How many of you see treating obesity as a major part of your practice?" Most of the hands in the audience went up. "How many of you are happy with the results that you get?" Only about three hands remained. They know it doesn't work. They have the same experience. They are seeing the same patient five years later at a heavier weight. Yet they still keep handing out diets. They are not trained to talk to this person and say, "Listen, I don't exactly know what's going on here."

—CAROL

When writing to your dentist, you can append the following:

Dear Dentist:

Visiting a dentist can be intimidating to a large person. The problem is often the furniture in a dentist's (and other health professional's) office, not just in the waiting room, but the chair the patient reclines in while having work done. Where in the world do these chairs come from? They are narrow and, at their most upright, are already in a semireclining position. Getting in and out of these chairs can be very difficult. Dental chairs come in different sizes, and while wider ones with more positions may be a bit more expensive, every office should have at least one. Then see to it that your larger patients are taken to the room with that chair.

Making patients comfortable takes some thought and planning, but is well worth it. Believe me, they will be more inclined to return if their needs are taken care of in a respectful, nonjudgmental manner.

We were in Germany and I had bronchitis and pneumonia at the same time and was so sick! I couldn't breathe. I went into this German doctor's office. He looked at me and said, "Frau Bush, you know you have to lose weight and you have to start walking three miles a day." I asked, "Can I wait until I can breathe?"

—CHRIS

HEALTH AND LIFE INSURANCE

Unless you are employed by a company that offers insurance as a benefit or you are a member of some organization that offers group insurance, chances are good that you are like so many other large-size people and have none at all. Even some group health insurance plans consider obesity to be a preexisting condition and refuse coverage to fat individuals. Few of us can buy health or life insurance, though some may be placed in high-risk pools and receive some coverage by paying high premiums. As an example, my Blue Cross health coverage premium costs $150 a month. It has a $400 yearly deductible and pays 80 percent of medical expenses up to $50,000 in a year or $500,000 in a lifetime.

Far and away the majority of people interviewed for this book carry no health or life insurance. The astronomical costs of health care can bankrupt a person faced with a long-term illness or hospital stay, but coverage often is not available or is unaffordable.

"Fit" and "Fat" are NOT mutually exclusive terms.

For information about the current state of health and life insurance, contact either the National Insurance Consumers Organization or your state insurance commissioner.

CONTINUING EDUCATION FOR MEDICAL PROFESSIONALS

Abundia
"Continuing education and training for professionals who are interested in (or at least curious about) promoting and implementing a nondieting, size-acceptance philosophy into their practices." Abundia works to examine treatment plans for large clients and helps medical professionals recognize and change personal prejudices and biases about weight, and sort through the contradictory research and media messages regarding weight.

The Association for the Health Enrichment of Large People (AHELP) Joe McVoy, Ph.D. A clinical organization dedicated to:

- Professional exchange that advances societal acceptance, personal empowerment, and appropriate professional treatment of fat people. A newsletter, the "AHELP Forum," is published quarterly, and a national conference is held yearly.

- Research that furthers the understanding of factors that both enhance and undermine the health of fat men, women, and children.
- Professional and societal education about the inappropriateness and health risks of weight-reduction dieting.

Healthy Weight Journal (formerly titled Obesity & Health) A bimonthly magazine dedicated to supplying its readers with the most up-to-date information regarding international research and the treatment of obesity. It also provides surgeon general's reports, fraud alerts, size acceptance features, news on upcoming conferences, and information on public policy and political issues, plus book reviews and editorials.

The mission statement of *Healthy Weight Journal* asserts, " . . . we are dedicated to the critical evaluation and reporting of obesity research and related issues. Realizing that weight is an easily exploitable health and social concern, we are also committed to exposing fraud and deception, and to reshaping detrimental attitudes toward size and weight."

Called "invaluable in preventive efforts" by the *Journal of the American Dietetic Association*, *Healthy Weight Journal* should be required reading for any health professional dealing with large-size patients at any level.

Francie Berg, M.S., L.N. (family social science, licensed nutritionist), adjunct professor at the University of North Dakota School of Medicine, is editor and publisher of *Healthy Weight Journal*.

Most of our subscribers are health professionals . . . doctors, dietitians, and medical libraries. We also have consumers, activist groups, and the media. The magazine is very readable for anyone. An interesting thing about obesity research is that all the different specialists are not reading each other's literature and don't know the jargon. We have fields like nutrition, medicine, psychology, and physical education involved in research and treatment. I try to bring this all together and make it readable for everyone. That's really my goal.

I've really made some attitude changes in the years I've been publishing Healthy Weight Journal. *I think our readers have made the changes too, right along with me. Actually, many leaders in the nondiet movement have been subscribers for many years. It makes me feel good to have provided some leadership in that area. When we first started I wasn't pro-diet, I was pro-healthy habits. I think people are really turning to that a lot more now, which is good to see. We are on the pivot of change. There is just so much rebellion against the whole bias toward dieting and thinness.*

—FRANCIE BERG

Melpomene Institute Educational materials on large women, self-esteem, and physical activity.

Size Acceptance Network (SAN) With a commitment to health at any size, SAN was initiated in November 1993 in response to feedback from both country and metropolitan health professionals.

SAN is comprised of health workers and organizations, linking them with up-to-date resources locally and overseas. Several yearly workshops are held and a newsletter is produced.

MEDICAL AIDS

Aneroid Sphygmomanometers In large adult and thigh cuff sizes.

SOURCES: Creative Health Products $142–$190.

Bariatric Treatment System
This bed is meant to be used in a hospital or clinical setting and has several important features. Built for supersize patients, it has a weight limit of 800 pounds. It adjusts from a fully flat position to an upright and/or reclining position and can also be situated to allow the patient to step easily onto and off the bed. There is an integrated scale system, fully powered lymphedema board, and siderails. An elevated radiolucent surface forms a pocket for an X-ray cassette, allowing X rays to be taken. $13,000 with scales, $12,000 without. A lease-to-own program is available.

SOURCES: Burke Mobility Products

Bath Seat Designed to fit the contours of a bathtub, this chair provides secure seating in the tub for people up to 650 pounds. $160.

SOURCES: Alimed

Bath Transfer Bench Holds up to 600 pounds. $500.

SOURCES: Alimed

Blood Pressure Units For those of you concerned with your blood pressure (that would include all parents), there are several do-it-yourself units available. The Omron Company of Japan makes a deluxe digital unit that has an LCD display that shows blood pressure and pulse rate. Its bands fit upper arms 8" to 17". $78.

SOURCES:

Amplestuff

J.C. Penney Special Needs

For the more traditional type cuff that requires a stethoscope, the standard cuff fits arms 10" to 16", with a large-size cuff for 13" to 19", and an even larger one for arms 17" to 26". $30–$60.

SOURCES:

Alimed

Amplestuff

Creative Health Products

AliMed

If arm units are inadequate for you, these are designed to be used on the wrist (fits up to 7¾" wrist) or fingers. Approximate cost: wrist, $140–$160; finger, $120.

SOURCES:

AdaptAbility (finger and arm monitor)

Bencone (wrist)

Sears (wrist)

J.C. Penney Special Needs

Body Belt
Helps support back and abdomen while improving posture. One size fits 36" to 56", Velcro closure. $15. (See also "Obesity Belt.")

SOURCES:

The King-Size Co.

Blair Shoppe

Cane Extra support for those with mobility problems.

SOURCES:

ConvaQuip offers one cane with a base of four slightly offset legs. It adjusts in height from 31" to 35" and supports up to 350 pounds. $70.

Commode Chair A sturdy replacement for shallow bedpans, this chair supports people up to 650 pounds. $516.

SOURCES:

Alimed

Gait/Transfer Belt Fits girth up to 66". $10.

SOURCES: Alimed

Heart Rate/Pulse Monitor For chests larger than 45". $42.

SOURCES: Creative Health Products

Hospital Gowns Take some of the trauma out of a doctor's visit or hospital stay with these gowns that fit up to a size 10X. Johnni's Treasures also offers custom sizes. $25–$30.

SOURCES:

NAAFA Feminist Caucus

Johnni's Treasures

Incontinence Protection Maxi Briefs and women's panty for minor bladder problems, fitting waists up to 55". $15–$20.

SOURCES:

Blair Shoppe

J.C. Penney Special Needs

Lift and Transfer System Designed to move the patient with mobility problems in and out of bed. Lifts patients up to 750 pounds. $1,500–$5,000.

SOURCES:

AliMed

Wheelchairs of Kansas

MRI System One of the most valuable hospital tools, the magnetic resonance imaging scan, often doesn't accommodate large people.

One system, the Philips Medical Systems's Gyroscan T5, is designed to handle patients of up to approximately 500 pounds and is in use in many hospitals around the country. Call Philips for more information and to locate the nearest hospital with this equipment.

There is also an open-sided MRI machine that is more widely available. This works well for the larger patient and for any who are claustrophobic.

Mercury Sphygmomanometers Thigh size. Call for pricing information.
SOURCES: Creative Health Products

Obesity Belt Lumbar and abdominal support for people with a 45" to 74" girth. $70.
SOURCES: Alimed

Rehabilitation Bed Designed to support a patient of up to 1,000 pounds. Full or semielectric beds available. Head and foot of bed raise and lower. $4,000.
SOURCES:
AliMed
Wheelchairs of Kansas

Scales Most scales weigh people up to 350 pounds. One manufacturer offers a digital scale that is said to have a capacity of over 600 pounds. This scale is portable with a 12" by 35" platform and a separate indicator unit. Call for pricing information.
SOURCES: Fairbanks Scales
Weights can be purchased from medical supply houses that allow you to weigh someone up to 100 pounds more than the amount listed on your balance beam scale. NAAFA has a pamphlet that gives instructions for other methods. Write to them for information.

Shower Chair, Folding The seat of this chair is made of the same material used for trampolines, which is rated at 300

pounds per square inch. It weighs just 7 pounds but holds up to 600 pounds. $200.
SOURCES: Alimed

Shower Chair, Wheeled Holds people up to 650 pounds. $600.
SOURCES: ConvaQuip

Shower/Commode Chair Holds up to 650 pounds, 20" to 26" wide. $200–$1,500.
SOURCES:
Alimed
Wheelchairs of Kansas
ConvaQuip

Socks, Nonbinding Perfect for people with circulation problems, swollen feet or toes. Also helps relieve the pain of cracked heels and heel spurs. Especially helpful for diabetics. $20 for package of 4 pair.
SOURCES: Blair Shoppe

Tub Transfer Bench Comfortable, cushioned seat on rustproof stainless steel frame. Fits over any tub. Holds up to 600 pounds. $500.
SOURCES:
Alimed
ConvaQuip

Urine Collecting Dish Holding a small plastic vial to collect a urine specimen is sometimes impossible for larger patients. These special holders fit onto the toilet bowl and are much easier to use.
SOURCES: Ableware

Walker Adjustable walkers certified to 650 pounds. $150–$250.

SOURCES:

Alimed

ConvaQuip

Watches With second hand and a band of expandable chrome with white enamel inlays, this watch is perfect for the larger wrists of medical personnel. $56.

SOURCES: NurseMates

Wheelchairs The average wheelchair has a seat width of 18", but more accommodating versions are available.

SOURCES:

Alimed's BCW 600 Wide Wheelchair is built to accommodate patients weighing up to 600 pounds. The chairs have seats anywhere from 24" wide and 18" deep to 30" wide and 22" deep. $2,000–$3,000.

Gendron, Inc. has a model with a 22"-wide seat that holds up to 350 pounds; also a model with a choice of three seat widths—26", 28", and 30"—with a capacity of up to 600 pounds. Call for pricing.

Sears Home Healthcare offers the average size, as well as models with 20"-, 22"-, and 24"-wide seats. The last one will hold people up to 410 pounds in everyday use. $800–$900.

Wheelchairs of Kansas offers several models with a variety of seat widths 18" to 30" with capacities to 600 pounds. Customizing is available. Two models recline. Call for pricing.

Wheelchair Ramp Sturdy ramp supports up to 750 pounds. $500.

SOURCES: Avenues Unlimited

Wheelchair Ramp One-piece, folding, 3' or 5' aluminum ramp for wheelchair or scooter built to support 600 pounds. $300.

SOURCES: AdaptAbility

Wheelchair Safety Seat Belt Attaches to any wheelchair frame, up to 60" from one side of wheelchair to the other (across the front of patient). $20.

SOURCES: Alimed

Wheelchair Van Ramp Supports up to 600 pounds. $325.

SOURCES: Avenues Unlimited

PROFESSIONAL UNIFORMS

Bencone Professional uniforms in sizes up to 5X, including some talls up to size 20T and petites to size 16.

Jasco Uniform Company Professional uniforms in sizes to 5X.

J.C. Penney Uniforms and Scrubs Name brand uniforms up to sizes 5X, including petites to size 32.

Johnni's Treasures Custom-made scrubs and uniforms of any size.

Mixables Uniforms in unlimited sizes at wholesale prices. Call for style sheets and swatches.

NurseMates Professional's Choice Uniforms in sizes to 3X (including a petite 3X in scrub pants), nurses' shoes to sizes 12EEE and 13E.

Nurses Station Professional uniforms up to size 2X.

Sweeter Measures Nursing uniforms, lab jackets, and scrub tops in all sizes.

Tafford "America's Best Uniform Manufacturer." Colorful, stylish scrubs, warm-up jackets, skirts, pants, and lab coats, most in sizes to 4X.

Uniform Connections "Uniforms for the medical profession." Uniforms to size 5X. Birkenstock footwear to women's size 13½; men's size 12½.

➡ If any data listed in this chapter need to be corrected, please let me know. If you know of a service or product useful to people of size, please write to me about it. The information may be made available to readers through the newsletter "Size Wise Update!," the Size Wise web site, or through possible future revisions of this book.

PERSONAL GLIMPSE:
JODY

Jody is a thirty-four-year-old fashion designer, ex-*Playboy* model, and owner of her own large-size clothing business, Myles Ahead.

I have always been fat, ever since I was a small child. I also have a wonderful family I am very close to. That's a very important aspect of my life. My parents instilled a lot of confidence and a sense of responsibility in me. My size was somehow always okay. I think the more okay it is for you, the more people accept you for who you are.

High school was tough for me. I have memories of being called "Fatty," "Chubs," and other names. But I haven't allowed that to happen too much since. If someone says something to me now I just say to them, "I don't know where you came from, but where I grew up that's considered rude." There just came a time where I started feeling really good about myself and decided not to put up with it.

I love spending time in the city . . . enjoying different shows at the museums, dining in good restaurants. I work very hard and enjoy having someone wait on me for a change. There are so many things I'd love to do, but it's hard to find the time.

I love to travel and have been to London several times and to Italy. Italy is wonderful! A few of my large-size friends went and said the same thing. The men there love larger women.

I've had a lot of very good men in my life. I've been very lucky in that respect. My family wonders why I'm not married. I've had proposals, but it just has never happened. I'm at the point where it would be nice to share my life with someone and have children. Maybe that's just ego. But there is so much I have to do in the next few years, I can't imagine having that responsibility. Where will I find the time? I would like to have a dog or plants, but I don't even have the time for that.

I did full-figure modeling for five years and was working for a modeling agency in Manhattan when *Playboy* magazine came in saying they wanted to do a pictorial on large sizes. The agency showed them pictures of me and some other women. I was a size 16 at the time, about 160 pounds. The largest woman they selected was about an 18 or 20. It was a good experience, a lot of fun, and a real confidence booster. They certainly made me feel beautiful, and I loved every moment of it.

About three years ago I started designing clothing for plus- and supersize women. In the beginning I was mainly interested in just starting my own business. The more I became involved in the plus/supersize clothing industry the more I realized that supersizes are very much discriminated against. There were virtually just a handful of designers in the world who design for that size. I just couldn't understand how there could be millions of supersize women and nobody was making anything for them to wear. I still don't understand why. So I have dedicated my life to making these women feel more beautiful and self-confident. I can't believe there are companies that sell large-size clothing and use thin women as models. I hear that from people all the time. I can't imagine putting out a catalog and having size 8 models. How could it be? My catalog will have my clients and friends as models. No matter what size you are you can look beautiful.

Most of my designs come from me, what I'd like to see. I also work with a very talented designer. We keep an eye on what the styles and fabrics are for the rest of the world. And I listen to my clients . . . what they need, what's comfortable, what works.

My clients have had so few choices in the past. I help them first by finding the perfect size. Something that fits and feels good. From there we coordinate their pieces so that instead of having to buy twenty different outfits a year, we build a wardrobe of mix-and-match. A lot of versatile pieces that work. I appreciate what my clients look like. It's such a thrill after I design something to see it on someone, to see it come to life. It overwhelms me at times to see somebody wearing something I've designed and looking spectacular. I love to make my clients look good. If they look good, they feel good. I get an unbelievable amount of satisfaction from my work. It can be very stressful at times, but I've never been happier. I love to work, work, and work. I wake up with an idea and see it finished by the end of the evening. Everything in my life revolves around my business.

I consider myself to be very attractive. I don't diet because diets don't work. I just want to be healthy. You have to make your own happiness. And you know what? Being thin isn't the answer. Society says it is, but the last time I heard, the majority of women—some 75 percent—were over size 16. We are the majority. Larger people make up the world.

"They Told Me I Was Fat"

They told me I was fat:

Not considering me for the lead in *Sound of Music*

Not making jeans big enough to fit me

Saying to me, "You are a wonderful person, but I'm not attracted to large women."

Saying, "You have such a pretty face, it's too bad you can't lose that weight."

I told myself I was fat:

Not asking the boys to dance when they didn't ask me

Accepting verbal abuse on the street

Dieting

Wearing dark, ill-fitting clothes

I am finished listening to that.

I am fat

I can be the leading lady

I am an attractive woman

I will ask the boys (and girls) to dance

I will not accept verbal abuse

They told me I was fat

I am fat—so what?

Segment of FAT LIP Readers Theatre script by Susan Williams.

3

YOU LOOK
MARVELOUS!

For the last twenty years—ever since I passed size 18 for the last time—shopping for new clothing has been a depressing, demoralizing ordeal. Other women may shop for fun or to cheer themselves up; I would only go shopping on a last-minute-absolutely-have-to-find-something-right-now basis.

Twenty years ago there were no stores selling attractive fashions in comfortable, pretty fabrics in sizes over 16. All that was available were dresses, blouses, and pants in the dreaded, bulletproof, shiny polyester. The prints looked like bedsheet or curtain designs. Shopping in catalogs was little better . . . low-quality, dumpy fashions seemingly meant to shame me for having every figure flaw known to women's magazine editors.

Shopping for new clothes meant being reminded that I was different, that I didn't fit or belong. It was never a matter of finding something I loved (or even liked). Shopping was just an attempt to find something I could stand to wear without too much embarrassment. Fortunately, I could sew. Many of the things I wore were handmade. But most patterns for home sewing stopped at size 16 or 18. I always had to add inches and hope for the best.

I've longed to wear neatly tailored dresses, lacy bras, and long, romantic skirts. Many times I have found myself pointing to a dress in a catalog and telling my daughter, "If I were thin, this is what I would wear," as if showing her what I am really like, what an attractive, classy mother she has but just can't see.

Boy, have things changed! In 1985 a store in New York, the Forgotten Woman, began offering designer clothing for women. A beaded Bob Mackie gown could be purchased there (for $12,000) in a size 22. Since then several famous name designers have created styles for large women. Many designers are now making careers of creating fashions just for plus- and supersize people. It isn't that being fat is now "in" in the fashion industry, but at least large consumers are seen as a market worth designing for. While I was researching this book it seemed as if a new fashion resource opened up daily.

Plus-size clothing stores and catalogs now carry beautiful clothing in the same fabrics and styles you see in other clothing lines. Even the old standbys like Lane Bryant have updated their lines to include many very nice selections. The home shopping networks often offer some fashions for men, as well as women in sizes up to 6X.

Men overall haven't fared as well as the ladies in this trend. As one man said to me, "Unless I want to dress like a lumberjack, I have very few choices." I've found his complaint to be a valid one. But then, women have always had a wider selection when it comes to fashion. (Well, not counting Liberace and Elton John.) Some sharp entrepreneur should jump on this void. However, while men don't have as wide a choice as women, they should find plenty of clothing to take them through work, play, and formal occasions.

Today we can all be well-groomed and well-dressed. All of the companies listed in this chapter offer their products through mail order unless otherwise specified. Check out all the possibilities.

A BONE TO PICK

I find it insulting to see a clothing catalog or store window aimed at selling to plus- and supersize customers using size 8 models or mannequins.

Not just another pretty face

Ever the curious one, I wrote to some of the companies that use small models to sell large-size clothing and asked about their reasoning. The responses were: ". . . we have found that the large-size customer identifies with larger-size models, although she does not purchase this way . . ." and ". . . we are selling a dream and an image . . ."

The statements that large women don't buy clothing shown on large models doesn't hold water. John Nordstrom, co-chairman of the Nordstrom Company, tells me, "You are right on—we have had tremendous success in using models that actually wear Encore [Nordstrom's line of plus-size fashions] clothing rather than, as you say, 'selling a dream.' Our Encore departments are having tremendous success right now, and our advertising certainly is a part of that success."

Many other designers and suppliers report the same success. These are not models you have to look at closely to see if they are borderline large or borderline small. They are big women. And they look wonderful. It's inspiring.

All I can say to companies who don't use models the same size as the clothing they are selling is that I have a lot of choices now, and my decision is to buy from merchandisers who are not ashamed to have me as a customer.

I don't buy from the Lane Bryant catalog because it's clothing for fat women modeled by really anorexic types. I even wrote and said, "Know what? I would buy from you if you featured your clothing on people who look more like me." They wrote back, "Well, our research indicates that our customers prefer these models." I thought, "Well who the———have you been asking? Jenny Craig? My mother? Who?

• **Plus-Size Clothes on Plus-Size Models** **•**

They think we're stupid! They think we think: If I order that dress, I'm going to look like that wasp-waisted model on page 28. Honest to God, putting fat women's clothing on skinny women! Can you imagine a catalog with African Kente cloth clothing modeled by, say, Regis and Kathie Lee? "Oh! Doesn't Cody look cute in that pillbox hat?"

—MARY ARMSTRONG

FINDING YOUR SIZE

There are, quite literally, thousands of stores that carry items up to the size equivalent of XL. They are common, and you can find them easily on your own. For this book, I have included only companies that carry sizes up to 2X (or equivalent), at least.

There isn't space here to list each company's or each designer's sizing chart. Below is a very general index. Be sure to check with each company's sizing chart before ordering.

WOMEN'S SIZE CHART

Bust	Waist	Hips	X Size
40–46	33–38	42–48	1X
46–52	38–44	48–54	2X
52–58	44–50	54–60	3X
58–64	50–56	60–66	4X
64–70	56–62	66–72	5X
70–76	62–68	72–78	6X
76–82	68–74	78–84	7X
82–88	74–80	84–90	8X
		90–95	9X
		95–100	10X

MEN'S SIZE CHART

Neck	Chest	Waist	X Sizes
17–17½	46–48	42–44	1X
18–18½	49–52	45–48	2X
19–19½	53–56	49–52	3X
20–21	57–60	53–56	4X
21–22	61–64	57–60	5X
23–24	65–68	61–64	6X
25–26	70–72	65–68	7X
27–28	73–76	69–72	8X
		90–95	9X
		95–100	10X

Again, keep in mind that these charts are very general. Be sure to check sizing in each catalog as you shop.

MEN'S CLOTHING

Flight Jackets Several varieties of nylon or handcrafted leather in sizes up to 3X. $75–$400.
SOURCES: Preferred Living

Hats Larger sizes, several styles. $20–$30.
SOURCES: King Size

Levi's 501 Jeans Button front, heavy-duty denim that fits (after shrinkage) waists up to 60". $30.
SOURCES:
Rocky Mountain Connection
Drysdales, Inc.

Levi Strauss & Company has begun a new program: custom-fit jeans, made to measure to fit any figure. After a custom fitting, your new jeans should be on your ample hips within three weeks. Generally, this service should cost about $15 more than the price of regular jeans. Contact your local jeans stores to see if they offer this service yet.

American View Casual clothing, not exclusively for large-size men, but some items up to size 4X.

America's Shirt Catalog Two-ply 100 percent cotton blended pima and pinpoint Oxford shirts in sizes up to 22" neck, 38" sleeve.

Big Men's/Stout Men's Shop Guaranteeing to offer customers extra care and "extra mile" service, Big Men's offers a wide selection of clothing (in sizes up to 12X). You'll find everything from pajamas to dress suits, with a wide selection of casual wear.

Cahall's Brown Duck Catalog "The Finest in Outdoor Work and Sports Clothing." In sizes small up to 4X. Brand names include Carhartt, Levi, Osh-Kosh, Rocky, La Crosse, Wolverine, and Danner.

Casual Male Big & Tall Reasonable prices for casual and career wear in sizes up to 6X. Brand names include Harbor Boy, Grade A Jeans, Himalaya Outfitters, Pure Sweat, and Alexander Lloyd.

Drysdales, Inc. Casual men's western wear in sizes up to 60" waist jeans, 3X T-shirts, and 2X shirts.

Frederick Shirt Company Beautiful dress shirts in many styles and fabrics up to 18" collar, 36" sleeve. Great selection.

G & L Clothing Jeans up to 66" waist (Levi's relaxed fit up to 60" waist); Dockers relaxed fit up to 54" waist; wrinkle-free cotton slacks (Haggar, Farah, Dockers, and Long Haul) up to 66" waist; shirts up to 8X; blazers up to 70" chest; flannel shirts, work clothing, and more. No catalog, call for information.

Imperial Wear The finest names in American and European design for men's clothing in sizes up to 64 regular and 56 extralong. Accessories, activewear, coats, belts, casualwear, jeans, shirts, robes, tuxedos, raincoats, formalwear, suits, and shoes (up to size 15EEE). Nice selection at reasonable prices.

International Male Men's clothing for guys who "dare to question the standards of style" in sizes up to 4X. There really are some wonderful fashions here. Unfortunately, the majority of them only go up to XL. Bigger men will find some worthwhile items, however. Cotton jerseys, shirts (banded collar, cord, twill, Oxford, grid, tux, worker's and long-sleeve henley, pirate), athletic shorts, and shoes (up to size 13EE).

J.C. Penney for Men/Big & Extra Tall/ Workwear/Shirt and Tie Required Wide selection of men's clothing in sizes regular up to extratall 4X. Men's dress shoes up to sizes 13EEE and 16M.

Jenny Gapp (JG:2) "Men's Fine Furnishings." Silky nylon luxury underwear up to size 2X already made, with custom sizes to fit any need.

King Size Company Clothing for tall and big men up to sizes 9X, though most items go up to 6X, many up to 8X. A wide selection of shirts, pants, vests, jackets (including professional sports jackets), coveralls, sweats, underwear, robes, and shoes up to 16EEE. King Size has a good selection of colors in a T-shirt that goes up to 9X and costs only about $11 each. Supersize sunglasses, thongs (up to size 16, M[D] width), watches (bands that stretch up to 12"), belts (dress and casual up to waist size 72"), fanny pack (fits up to waist size 68"), hats (up to head size 4X [26½"]), ties sized to length and proportion for big guys (63" long and almost 4" wide), and a supersize towel (40" x 65").

Kishu's East-West Fashions Custom-made suits. "Our head fitter from Hong Kong travels across the United States three or four times a year to meet with clients. If you would like to meet with him for a fitting (suit—$350, tuxedo—$450), please write to us via E-mail." The fitter takes over forty precise measurements to assure the final product will fit your body perfectly. You can select the fabric of your choice from a selection of over 2,000 different choices, from herringbone to houndstooth. Your suit will arrive four to six weeks after the fitting.

Lebow Brothers—Clothing for Men and Boys Good selection of suits, slacks, dress shirts, and evening wear in sizes 36 up to 52 (including extrashort, stout, and portly), boys' sizes 11 up to 20 (young men's and husky).

Mansour's Mens Wear Name-brand men's dress and work wear, most in sizes up to 6X, some up to 8X. There is also a nice selection of briefs, boxer shorts, and thermal underwear in sizes up to 13.

One Bad Bear "Bears are our thing and we've got lots of fun Bear wear." T-shirts, sweatshirts, and polo shirts, all available with or without the One Bad Bear logo in sizes up to 10X. You'll also find bear jewelry, mugs, steins, mouse pads, hats, ties, suspenders, and cards.

Phoenix Big and Tall Men's clothing in sizes up to 6X. Blazers, shirts, suits, pants, jeans, shorts, jackets, swim trunks, and robes. Belts up to 56" waist, ties 61" long.

Poley's Big and Tall Levi, Gant, Izod, Palm Beach, Sebago, and Jockey brands in sizes LT up to 4XT and 1X up to 8X. Also suits and sports coats in sizes 42XL up to 72 portly.

Preferred Living Polo shirts and flight jackets up to 2X.

Quinn's Shirt Shop Arrow irregular dress shirts in big and tall sizes.

Repp, Ltd/Big & Tall Very nice selection of men's sporty, casual, and dress clothing in sizes regular 1X up to 8X and extra tall large through 5X. Jackets, shirts, sweaters, pants, vests, suits, underwear, and sweats. They also carry thermal underwear (up to 5X) and extra wide socks (12 through 16XL).

Rochester Big and Tall Good selection of basic clothing, both casual and dress, up to size 4X in a variety of prices.

Sears Big & Tall Wide range of selections from dressy to casual in sizes up to 4X. Belts up to 72" waist and shoes up to EEE width.

Sexy Fat Boys Casual sportswear includes shirts, tank tops, T-shirts, cardigans, sweat pants, and shorts in sizes 1X up to 6X.

Short Sizes, Inc. "Distinctive apparel for the shorter man" in sizes up to 50 for individuals up to 5'8". Sweats, jackets, shirts, pants, suits, pajamas, robes, and sweaters.

I. Spiewak Men's sport outerwear in sizes up to 6X. Jackets, parkas, snorkels, pea coats, baseball jackets, leather cossack and taslan jackets.

Stout Men's Shop Casual and career wear along with some swimwear in sizes up to supersize.

Undergear Men's fitness fashions and undergarments up to size 4X. Most are up to XL, but there is a small selection of larger sizes. You'll find all sorts of stuff to sweat in, including muscle pants, cotton jerseys, athletic shorts, and pant liners.

WorldWide Outfitters Work gloves of several types in large sizes, work aprons (mechanics, rubber, PVC, and leather) up to 35" by 50", coveralls up to 2X, work boots up to EEEE widths, work shirts up to 5X, heavy-duty pants up to 66" waist, jackets up to 5X, and Sara Glove safety products.

WOMEN'S CLOTHING

Belts Adjustable leather, stretch, metal, and braided belts in "Plus-Sizes."
SOURCES: Jus-Lin Belts

Sleevebands These ingenious little bands in black, silvertone, or goldtone allow you to shorten your long or three-quarter sleeves and hold them in place comfortably. $5 a pair.
SOURCES: Making It Big

Socks Queen-size anklets, crew, knee-highs in wool or cotton. $4 to $10.
SOURCES: Vermont Country Store

A & E Apparel Casual knit fashions in mix-and-match designs up to size 26.

A Personal Touch Casual tops, skirts, and tunics up to size 5X.

Abigail Starr Llama Group dress and casual fashions up to size 26. Some custom sizes available.

Above and Beyond Wonderful selection of women's dress and casual pants for all sizes, including custom-made supersizes. Materials include rayon, gabardine, denim, and cotton/poly twill.

Adini En Plus Dresses and sportswear in sizes 1X up to 3X in prints, solids, and natural fibers.

Amazon Designs Under the label "Amazon Originals," Amazon Designs creates housecoats, jackets, pants, shorts, tank tops, shirts, tunics, and cardigans for women over 5'10" tall and over size 22. You choose the article of clothing and then choose the fabric you want it made in. According to one satisfied customer, "I've never subscribed to the idea that we 'can't' wear certain colors or certain prints. If it looks good and makes me feel good, I wear it! It's not like we can hide the fact that we are a large presence, so it's important to have clothes that fit well and make us feel good about ourselves." Amazon Designs creates a pattern specifically for you, then sees to it that you have clothing you love.

Adaptations with Attitude Very nice collection of dressy designer merchandise from Designers Unlimited in sizes 14 up to 8X in the catalog, custom sizes available.

Ambassador Value Showcase Though not a clothing catalog per se, you will find several items (casual shirts, skirts, a cardigan, and more) in sizes up to 3X. They also carry nightgowns up to size 6X, bras up to 50DD, panties up to 62" hips, and girdles up to size 7X.

Anthony Richards Conservative designs from career and formalwear to dresses and lingerie in sizes up to 3X. Bras are available up to size 52DD.

Apples & Pears Women's casuals in sizes 2X up to 8X. Sweatshirts, coats, tunics, and hats. Most of the tops have embroidered designs.

Astarte Woman Special-occasion fashions and lingerie in sizes 14 up to 32.

August Max Woman ". . . luscious lingerie, sleepwear and spring separates exclusively for sizes 14 up to 26 . . ." Both casual and dress fashions.

Avon Casual and officewear dresses, skirts, blouses, and jackets, with some items up to size 4X.

Back to Basics Soft-Wear No, this isn't for your computer. The items in this catalog are made of natural fibers that are soft against your deserving body. Danskin shorts, pants, tights, leggings, scoop-neck bra tops, and tees up to size 4X. Also panties up to a 52" hip.

Barbara Stone Designs ". . . washable silks for the plus-sized woman who demands style and quality." Dress and casual pants, T-shirts, tank tops, skirts, jackets, vests, shorts, and dresses to fit up to 2X.

Big, Bad, & Beautiful Women's casual fashions in sizes 12 up to 5X supersize. Mix-and-match skirts, pants, tops, vests, and dresses.

Big, Bold and Beautiful Casual and officewear dresses, plus sportswear and lingerie in sizes 14 up to 2X.

Big Dreams Sweatshirts, T-shirts, polo shirts, and denim shirts in sizes up to 8X.

Botero Wonderful, exotic-looking women's blazers, vests, and dresses for both dress and casual occasions, plus nightgowns and flannel pajamas up to 5X, all modeled on large, lovely models. Nice selection of accessories also.

Brownstone Woman Classic women's fashions, casual to officewear to evening wear, in sizes 1X up to 3X.

Carole Little II Collection Denim jackets, sportswear, tunics, jumpers, vests, crepe blouses, and dresses for all occasions in sizes 1X and 2X.

Cathy O Elegant and soft, these women's fashions are made of fabrics that look and feel like silk and rayon yet are completely washable. Lovely, flattering shapes and colors modeled by elegant, large ladies. Sizes up to 5X.

Cello "Every Woman Deserves Quality, Style and Comfort." Dress and casual plus and supersize fashions.

Chadwick's of Boston, Ltd. Classic dress and officewear women's clothing, most items in sizes up to 2X.

Classics Skirts, tops, dresses for both dress and casual occasions, up to size 4X. Call for information.

Color Me Big Casual hand-decorated clothing in sizes 1X up to 4X and custom sizes.

Cotton Threads Clothing Casual 100 percent cotton clothing from petite to tall, up to size 6X and custom sizes. The selection is small, but this cottage industry company will work with you in creating just the right size for you in pants, caftans, skirts, shirts, and tunics.

Coy Very nice dress and casual knits in sizes 14 up to 2X with some supersizes available. Also some jewelry.

Cynthia Rae for Well-Rounded Women "Timeless, good quality classics that will give well-rounded women confidence in dressing." Pants, dresses, blazers, dusters, and coats in sizes 14 up to 3X and custom sizes.

DJ's Plus Sizes Dressy to casual clothing in sizes 1x up to 3X.

Dallas Fashion Nice dresses, suits, and sportswear up to size 3X.

Daphne Though essentially a New York City boutique, Daphne is happy to work with customers through mail order. Dressy fashions and officewear are available in sizes 1X up to 5X "off the rack," also custom sizes.

Desert Rain Hand-decorated casual clothing in sizes 1X up to 5X, also some jewelry.

Designs by Elba Manfredi Tuxedo, rayon, and chambray shirts only up to size 1X; fleece cardigans and pullovers up to size 5X. All pieces have Ultrasuede designs.

Dion-Jones Sportswear to evening gowns, sizes 14 up to 5X, plus custom sizes. Dion-Jones usually sells through stores but also offers mail order. Be sure to check this supplier for hard-to-find petite and tall sizes.

Distinctions Dresses, evening gowns, and sportswear in sizes 12 up to 3X. (See also "Clothing Video Catalogs.")

E Style, the Fashion Catalog for African-American Women "Style That Speaks Your Body's Language." This catalog was created by *Ebony* magazine and Spiegel. Beautiful formalwear and casualwear, swimsuits, and lingerie, generally up to size XL but many up to 2X.

Elegance at Large Clothing for just about any occasion in sizes up to 6X with custom sizes available. Careerwear, activewear, outerwear, and loungewear.

Elianna "Clothes for the Woman." Tunics, formalwear, dusters, and daytime dresses in sizes 16W up to 32W; tall, petite, and custom sizes.

Encore Blouses, dresses, leather coats, tunics, wide-leg pants, cardigan jackets, leggings, shirts, romantic lace skirts, T-shirts, blazers, swimsuits, warm-ups, underwear, and nightgowns in sizes mostly up to 3X, some up to 4X.

Entrance Beautiful dresses and separates for work, home, or formal occasions in chiffon, rayons, and some crinkle fabrics. Sizes 14 up to 36, some supersizes.

Essence "The Original Catalog for Today's African-American Woman." Many of the styles in this catalog have an obvious African influence—and they are beautiful. Lovely clothes in beautiful colors and exciting styles in sizes 6 up to 26. The most fun part of this catalog, to me, is the large selection of hats! Check it out.

Estar Fashions Plus Women's "beautiful, natural fiber clothing." Very nice separates, dresses, jackets, and coats up to size 5X. Many of the items offered by Estar can be customized through changes in hem lengths, neckline styles, embellishments, and shoulder pads for an additional charge. Estar offers a cotton knit belt in a variety of colors custom-made to your waist size and fleece coats in several styles. Fashions are depicted through drawings rather than photos, and sample swatches are included.

Ethnic Attitudes Afro-Centric designs in contemporary Euro-American styles in sizes 3 up to 8X, with petite and custom sizes available. The fabrics are imported from Senegal, West Africa.

Ethnicity "Afrocentric Fashions and Gifts. . . . Ethnicity was born out of the frustration of searching for African-American products in Connecticut." Made from cloth shipped from Senegal, these fashions include tops, shorts, harem pants, jumpers, and vests in sizes up to bust 48, waist 40, hips 50.

Exotica International Blazers, sportswear, camisoles, blouses, pants, dusters, and cocktail dresses up to size 26.

Fairy Godmother at Large New and used dress and casual clothing, sizes 14 up to super.

Far & Wide Source Guide This Canadian company offers undergarments and imaginative casual fashions in sizes up to 8X.

Fashion Galaxy "The Outlet Store That Comes to You." Clothing up to size 5X. Sweaters, bodysuits, dresses, shirts, tunics, rompers, pajamas, and tights in sizes up to 4X. Not a large selection, but the items are inexpensive.

Fingerhut Lingerie, pant sets, rompers, jackets, underwear, and dresses mostly up to size 3X, a few pieces up to 5X.

The Forgotten Woman Career to casualwear, suits, and coats in sizes 14W up to 24W.

Full Figure Design Company Career and casualwear in mid through super sizes.

Great Discoveries Women's casual and dress knit jackets, skirts, shells, pants, and tunics up to size 28W.

Great Changes Boutique Dress and casual clothing and lingerie in sizes 1X up to 3X.

Greater Woman Classic casual and dress fashions in sizes 14 up to 8X.

Harriet Carter Casual garments or loungewear. Lightweight, cool, sleeveless in assorted colored stripes, some in seersucker, in sizes medium up to 3X.

Heart's Delight Romantic, feminine pants, skirts, jumpers, dresses, tops, shirts, tunics, and other items up to size 4X. These clothes are cut very generously and are made using beautiful materials.

Hovland Mfg./Hovis Jeans Three styles of jeans for tall and large sizes up to 60" waist; jean jackets, a duster, and blazers up to size 6X.

J.C. Penney Full line of fashions up to size 32WP (women's petite) and 32W (women's), and junior plus 1X up to 3X.

J.C. Penney Especially for Talls Casual and dress fashions for women 5'8" to 6'2" in sizes 8 up to 2X.

J. Jill, Ltd. Women's knits, sweaters, suits, blouses, dresses, and pants in subdued colors and classic lines. Casual to office. In sizes up to 3X, 30W, and some 16 petite.

J. W. Ramàge (used to be Nightlines Plus) Lingerie and daywear, sizes 14 through supersizes. Nightshirts, pull-on pants, vests, tops, dresses . . . a little bit of everything in beautiful, comfortable fabrics. Particularly nice is their poncho style jacket with pockets, push-up sleeves, and a zipper front.

Jalon Enterprises Suede and leather tunics, dresses, shirts, trousers, smocks, and skirts in sizes 14W up to 36W.

John Sun Silks Silk designs in separates and solids, some signed and numbered originals, in sizes up to 6X, plus custom sizes.

Jozell Fashions Plus Swimsuits year-round, great accessories, and a full selection of name-brand clothing up to size 4X or 52.

Junonia "Dedicated to the Active Lives of Women Size 14 and Up." Swimsuits, leotards, T-shirts, leggings, bras, jackets, shorts, and shirts in sizes up to 4X. There is one very nice lace detail T-shirt that is available up to size 6X.

Just My Size Though Just My Size specializes in major name-brand stockings and undergarments, they also carry a full line of casualwear up to size 4X, including tunics, dresses, pants, and dresses. BBW brand socks fit up to size 3X (up to 400 pounds). Bali, Just My Size, and Playtex control panties, briefs, and girdles are available up to size 8X, bras up to 50DDD; Just My Size cotton and nylon panties fit up to hip size 60". Hanes brand "Fitting Pretty" hosiery is available up to size 5X, and BBW hosiery up to size 7X.

Just Right! Appleseed's women's fashions for sizes 14 up to 26, some petites. Bright colors, lots of sporty casualwear, nice dresses, jackets, shells, cardigan sweaters, a few elegant dresses, underwear, and loungewear.

L. A. Designs Activewear, jogging sets, executive designs in sizes 1X up to 4X.

LBW (a division of L. Bates) Casual and officewear dresses, blouses, pants, tunics, jumpers, blazers, and jumpsuits in sizes 4 up to 4X.

La Costa Spa Women's casual clothing in sizes up to 3X.

Lane Bryant Probably the largest and oldest mail-order house for women's large-size fashions, Lane Bryant still uses small models to sell to big women. However, they have recently hired two larger models—Kim Coles of the television show "Living Single," and Anna Nicole Smith. The selection is diverse and in sizes 14 up to 56 and women's petite up to size 34. Shoes up to size 12EEE.

Large Lovely Lady Beautiful dresses and suits for both day and evening in sizes 14 up to 36. Interesting detailing on many of the items.

The Lerner Woman Full line of misses' sizes 12 up to 24 and women's sizes 34 up to 54.

Make It Big This shop in New Zealand offers comfortable casual clothing in sizes 18 through supersizes.

Making It Big "Natural fiber clothing for large and supersize women." A wonderful catalog, full of exciting, contemporary women's clothing. The sizing at MIB is a bit different. From size 1 (36" bust, 31" waist, 40" hips) up to size 4 (71" bust, 72" waist, 75" hips). Several fashions are available in petite sizing. Each catalog includes a few jewelry items, socks, and usually slippers.

Cynthia Riggs, president of MIB, says, "Every woman has the right to express herself through fashionable clothing and deserves accessibility to a contemporary wardrobe. We sell to women like ourselves, so we know what our customers want. . . ." Each catalog includes a newsletter with updates on fashions, cyberspace, publications, activism, and customers.

Marketplace—Handwork of India The majority of the fashions run up to only 1X, but a recently introduced line for full-figured women includes a Kota top and a hand-block batiked Anjana dress with delicate embroidery in sizes up to 3X.

Mature Wisdom Women's casual and dress caftans, dresses, blouses, and pants. Some up to size 3X, a few items up to 5X.

Michelle's Jumpers, dresses, T-shirts, and casualwear in sizes up to 8X.

Myles Ahead Beautiful swing coats, pants, dresses, and big shirts for all occasions in sizes 16 up to 24 plus supersizes.

Nadina Plus Casual fashions in 100 percent natural fibers.

Nakazawa One-of-a-kind fashions, both casual and dress, in sizes up to 6X.

National Casualwear, sportswear, and nightgowns in sizes 12½ up to 24 with a few items up to 2X.

New Look from Sharon J Sportswear to dressy outfits in tall sizes up to 3X.

Newport News Casual and officewear dresses, sportswear, and lingerie in sizes up to 4X.

Nicole Summers Designs "A spirited style all your own." Women's dress and casual fashions in sizes up to 4X, including petite sizes up to 16.

Old Pueblo Traders Women's clothing up to sizes 3X. These clothes have a more classic, tailored look. Hush Puppies and boots in hard-to-find sizes.

PF 147 "America's newest fashion line for stylish women in sizes 14 through 32." Paula Wise casual and dress.

PFI Fashions Office and casual separates, dresses, and sleepwear in sizes 1X up to 6X.

Paradigm Casual to dressy in sizes 2X up to 8X.

Parsinen Design Features 100 percent cotton casual separates in sizes 1X up to 4X.

Pastille Sportswear and special-occassion dresses in sizes up to 3X.

Peaches Sweaters in 100 percent cotton—plain, tweeds, or beautifully embellished—in sizes 1X up to 5X. Wholesale prices for sweaters sold in stores around the country.

Peacock Clothes "A Unique New Concept in Large Women's Clothing." Catsuits, T-shirts, tie-dyes, casual and careerwear, raincoats, skirts, vests, and dresses up to supersizes.

Peggy Lutz for Lutes Design Specializing in supersizes (including the very-difficult-to-find supersize petite), quality dresses, blazers, "upscale sweats," skirts, and pants. This company is a small, women-owned San Francisco–based enterprise. There is also a Peggy Lutz Plus Size Outlet in Sebastopol, California. Call ahead for hours.

Plus Woman Cardigans, sweaters, pants, and leggings, most up to size 8X. Very nice selection.

QVC (and other cable shopping channels) These regularly offer clothing up to at least size 3X. The models are all sizes and the quality is generally very good.

Queentex Caftans in both dressy and casual styles in sizes 38 up to 52.

Rainy County Knit Wear Sweaters and vests in wool, mohair, acrylic, or mercerized cotton in custom sizes.

Regalia Women's fashions, both dress and casual, sizes 14 up to 4X. The usual items plus dazzling party blouses and dresses, lace shells, a very cozy-looking blanket coat, fake fur, and festive holiday styles.

Roaman's Another old standby, Roaman's offers the usual women's items in sizes 14 up to 4x. Their selection is extensive, including both dress and casual items.

Rocky Mountain Clothing Casual jeans and blouses in sizes 16W up to 30W.

RogersWear "Super Size Career Clothing." Clothing for women who are "weary of the dowdy, tired of the slipshod and bored with the mundane." Dresses, capes, pants, shirts, and jackets up to size 8X.

Roselyn "Oakland's Fashion Stop for the Fuller Figure." Specializes in supersizes and larger sizes. Dresses up to size 56, suits up to size 54, bras up to 48H and 56DD, pantyhose up to 7X, girdles up to 56" waist, slips up to size 6X, panties up to size 18, Lycra activewear up to size 4X.

SW's Full Figure Designs Dresses and suits for office and dress occasions in sizes 24W up to 34W.

Saks Fifth Avenue Just as you would expect from Saks, these styles are elegant, refined, and on the expensive side. Sweaters, tunics, knit suits, jackets, and eveningwear up to sizes 3X.

Sandi Kent Absolutely gorgeous designs; lacy and romantic tunics, blouses, dresses, and skirts. The most generously cut styles fit up to 3X. This is a small but delightful catalog.

Sandra Williams' Full Figure Designs Petite and tall lingerie, skirts, and pants in crinkle silks and failles up to size 9X, with custom sizes available.

Says Who? Simple, fun styles; casual clothing in sizes up to 4X. Two retail stores and mail-order brochure.

Scarlet Crane "Quality Clothing for Large Size Women." A very nice collection of casual, comfortable, cozy-looking clothing in denim, flannel, and brushed cotton twill. Shirts, pants, jackets, and skirts in sizes 18 up to 36 (cut large) . . . these are the classic items you can live in and explore the world in. I have my eye on a chamois shirt described as "A shirt that's soft and warm, that becomes softer and warmer the longer you wear it. . . . We promise it will keep you snuggly warm on your moonlight walks or clam digs at Bodega Bay."

Sears Woman's View Complete selection of women's casual and dress fashions in sizes 14 up to 52.

Sharon Philips Careerwear and dress suits, blazers, and coats up to size 7X.

Sharon J's Women's dress and casual shirts, simple shells, pants, skirts, tops, and jackets in cotton/poly knits, rayons, and poly failles up to size 5X.

Silhouettes Women's contemporary fashions for career, casual, and special occasions in sizes 14W up to 32W, some petites.

Spiegel Spiegel has two catalogs, "For You" and "World Class," that offer a wide selection of dresses, blouses, and other clothing in sizes 14 up to 4X, some petites.

Sue Brett I hesitated to include this company, since according to their size chart their fashions go up only to a size 1X, but their 1X seems to run big. Owned by the same company as Lerner, Roaman's, and Lane Bryant. Wide selection of inexpensive careerwear and casual items.

Sweet Cheeks Designs Quality casual, career, and romantic styles cut to your own measurements. Custom sizing available. Brochure and fabric swatches.

Sweeter Measures Lots of variety here, from elegant dresses to Western prairie dresses, jackets, and swimsuits in sizes up to 8X. The fashions are depicted through drawings; samples of materials are attached to the catalog. It's very nice to be able to sample this way. Sweeter Measures has recently added "nursing essentials"—pullover tops, pants, lab jackets, and scrub tops.

T-Cole Designs Simple blouses appropriate for both career and casualwear, cut full and extralong in sizes large through 3X.

The Tog Shop Dresses, sweatshirts, tunic tops, pants, and loungewear up to size 3X. Most of this catalog carries items up to only 1X, but there are quite a few larger items.

Ulla Popken "New Classics." Casual and sportswear in sizes 12 up to 30, with some petites. Dresses, T-shirts, sweaters, skirts, and suits in cottons, rayons, denim, velvet, and linen.

Uniquity Plus Casual and careerwear, custom-dyed clothing in all-natural fibers, in sizes up to 5X.

Unlimited Concepts Custom women's clothing at very reasonable prices in sizes up to 5X. Jumpsuits, swing tops, short sets, jackets, shirts, suits. Short of mak-

ing your own, I don't know how you could work any more closely in designing your wardrobe. Sharrell, Sandy, and Lynn work together with you in choosing contours, materials, decorative touches, and color to create a look that is you.

Vagabond Imports Mostly loose-cut cotton gauze and poplin shirts with a few dresses, jackets, and skirts. This is a small catalog with about 100 selections, but the products are different from anything in the other catalogs.

The Very Thing "A wardrobe for elegant living." A wide selection of fashions, from dresses to resortwear, most up to XL, some up to 3X, petite sizes up to 16.

Wendy Dale Pajamas, smocks, health care nightgowns (back opening), dusters, shifts, and aprons; most up to 2X, some up to 4X. These styles tend toward the basic old-fashioned, simple look.

Woman Catalog Petite, tall, plus and supersize casual sportswear, dresses, stirrups, and sweaters.

Women Size Shop Career and maternity wear in sizes 14 up to 70.

MEN'S AND WOMEN'S CLOTHING

Aprons and Smocks Cobbler, long-sleeve smock, and butcher block unisex styles in sizes up to 2X. $28.

SOURCES:
Amplestuff
Chock

Professional, attractive aprons, hats, jackets, and vests to fit chefs up to 6'6" tall, 390 pounds. There are even baseball caps, toques, and berets to match. You choose the fabric and styles.

SOURCES: Chefwear, U.S.A.

Bib Overalls   Made in sizes fitting up to a 66" midsection. $18–$24.

SOURCES:

Key Industries

Joe Sugar

Fanny Pack   Those handy little packs you see slender folks wearing to carry their cash, credit cards, and NutraSweet packets in. Now you can have one too. These are made a little larger than the ones made for those "other" people, so they look good on the larger body. Most of these fit up to a 92" waist. $20–$38.

SOURCES:

Amplestuff

King Size

Worldesigns Incorporated

Sunglasses   Extralarge-size frames flatter and protect better. $25 and up.

SOURCES:

Hidalgo

King Size

SGD Merchandising

Sungold Enterprises

Woodmont Eyewear

Tams   Beautiful knit hats "are a great solution for comfortably topping off one's outfit. They are the answer to easy dressing for men or women, all year 'round, gracefully framing the face.'' Custom sizing available. $18.

Sources: Keltic Kate's Tams

Chock Men's and women's underwear from thirty-three manufacturers, including Hanes (up to 5X), Jockey (up to 5X), and Berkshire (up to 6X).

Deva Lifewear Beautiful natural fabrics (cottons and silks) and shapes cut to allow plenty of ease of movement in sizes up to 2X (a roomy 2X). Romantic shirts and loungewear for men; dresses, shirts, pants, flowing suits, and slips for women; and unisex shirts. This cottage industry clothing company puts out a beautiful catalog with models appropriate to all sizes of clothing.

The Disney Catalog T-shirts, henley shirts, nightshirts, sweatshirts, shorts, and jackets; most up to 2X, some up to 3X, all with Disney designs.

Eddie Bauer Men's and women's classic casual styles. Lots of denim, plaids, cotton knits, and wools. Jeans, pants, jackets, turtlenecks, shoes, and more. Some in sizes up to XXL for men, XL for women.

Gypsy Moon "Transformative" clothing that moves and swirls with you in sizes small to "bountiful." Custom sizing is always available, so call with your measurements. This is a beautiful, very unique catalog with a strong Gypsy/fairy-tale feel. The clothing is romantic, feminine, and very flattering for those of us with a bit of Gypsy spirit. Fabrics include silk velvets, rayon jersey, and suede. I particularly love the hooded, floor-length cloak in silk velvet and the "Juli" skirt, a "witchy gypsy skirt, that looks as if it could be made of cobwebs and stardust." Men's clothing includes a Highwayman shirt . . . "Also for thieves, rogues, and beggarly rascals," leggings, pants, shirts, and vests.

It's a Revolution African-inspired prints and designs for casual and officewear in sizes up to 5X.

J.C. Penney Workwear Men's overalls, work shirts and pants, jackets, tool belts, and jumpsuits up to size 2X and 2XLT; work boots and shoes up to size 14EEE.

Lands' End Classic, casual styles, excellent quality. Some of the men's items run up to size 3X; women's only up to XL and petite XL.

L. L. Bean Men's and women's classic casual styles—very warm, cozy, high-quality garments in fabrics from silk to Gore-Tex at reasonable prices. Now only if we could convince them to offer larger sizes. You'll also find a large selection of boots and hiking shoes up to size 14EE, slippers and socks up to XL. Clothing in sizes up to 2X for men, including some tall XXLs; women's up to only XL, and children's up to XL (18-20).

J.C. Penney Fashion Influences Fashions with an African-American influence in sizes 8 up to 3X and, interestingly, sportswear and T-shirts for men with Negro League Baseball logos in sizes L up to 2X, jackets and sweatshirts with Black university logos in sizes L up to 2X, and knit shirts with a logo from the Hoop Dreams Scholarship Fund. Also, a vest, casual shirts, pants, and jackets for men in sizes regular-medium up to 2X and 3XT.

Johnni's Treasures Sweatshirts and T-shirts through supersize with custom sizes available.

Luskey's "Texas's Leading Western Store Since 1919." Dress and casual jackets, vests, shirts, jeans, dusters, coats, blouses, chaps, and skirts up to men's size XXL, women's size XL. Boots of all sorts up to men's size 13E and women's size 9 wide.

Northstyle This is a beautiful catalog with some gorgeous items . . . especially if you are into wolves, frogs, eagles, and other wilderness inhabitants. The sweatshirts, sweaters, and shirts are available in sizes up to 2X.

Pendleton Maker of fine wool products, Pendleton offers a nice line of beautiful, classic, durable fashions for both men (up to 2X) and women (unfortunately, only up to size XL), and petite women (only up to size L). Despite the limited number of items available for the fuller figure, this is an excellent source of plaid wool scarves, mufflers, neckties, caps, and scuffs.

Richman Cotton Company Issuing one catalog a year, the Richman Cotton Company offers comfortable men's and women's clothing made with the closest

to 100 percent pure cotton/chemical-free fabrics available at reasonable prices. You can purchase the materials by the yard or buy clothing in sizes up to 3X. You'll find long johns, shirts, sweats, parkas (up to size 4X), a men's shirt, and some cozy-looking skirts and dresses. Oh . . . and a few costume items . . . a drawstring blouse, bodice, and smithy shirt.

Sankofa "A world where Afrika meets America in the world of designer fabrics and fashionable creations." African-motif styles in silk and natural fibers in sizes up to 34W. Both dress and casual.

Scotch House Ladies' dress and casual sweaters, skirts, and trousers from Scotland, up to size 48, men's sizes up to size 52. Custom size ordering is available.

Sears Sears has pretty much stopped their "shop-at-home service," but they still handle specialty catalogs. Call and request their ladies' or men's big and tall catalog. The selection covers just about everything and runs up to sizes 4X for women, up to 9X for men. I have to hand it to Sears . . . they have many unexpected items. For instance, four wildlife design T-shirts in sizes up to 8x, fanny packs that fit up to size 72" waists, supersize sunglasses, hats up to 27" head size, shorts up to 8X . . . pretty much the same stuff you find in their "regular" catalogs but in sizes we can wear. Most of Sears's large-size line is handled through King Size (men's) and Silhouettes (women's).

Shepler's Western Wear Men's and women's casual clothing with a definite Western feel in sizes up to 3X (bust up to 51", waist up to 43", hips up to 52") for women, 2X (chest up to 50", waist up to 46") for men. You'll find whip-stitched tops, denim dresses, ruffled blouses and skirts, hand-decorated clothing and accessories along with jeans, hats, and boots. Men are offered a wide selection of shirts, jeans, belts, and hats. I want a pair of those Tony Lama turquoise handcrafted boots!

Sizable Difference Stadium jackets (up to 8X), fleece cardigans (up to 6X), team or rodeo satin jackets (up to size 8X), pocket T-shirts (up to 5X), cotton T-shirts (up to 5X), cotton briefs (up to 5X), boxer shorts (up to 5X), and sweats (up to 6X).

Spiegel A wide selection of quality dress and casual fashions for men (up to size 2X) and women (up to size 3X) with some XLTs.

Tilley Endurables "The best travel and adventure clothing in the world." A wide selection of shorts, pants, vests, and jackets, most through size 3X.

Vermont Country Store This very unique catalog carries some "old-fash-ioned" items—cola syrup (for upset tummies), liquid peppermint soap, and hassock fans (I love those!). It also has men's madras robes, nightshirts, grand-father shirts, and underwear, most up to sizes 3X. Ladies will find scoop-neck floats, cotton Oxford-style shirts, wrap skirts, jumpers, culottes, embroidered cotton sweaters, A-line tent dresses, and muumuus, most up to size 3X.

Wearguard Uniforms and work gar-ments for men and women up to size 5X. There are some short sizes (5'4"–5'7") up to XL. Also some sports-wear, jackets, and heavy-duty work shoes up to men's size 13 wide and women's size 10 wide.

SWIMSUITS, T-SHIRTS, AND ACTIVEWEAR

AHT Designs A T-shirt in only one de-sign ("I'm Not Pregnant—I'm Fat") and one color (pink on white), but it's cer-tainly original.

All Texas T's Cotton/poly T-shirts in assorted colors and sizes 2X through 10X.

America's T-shirt Catalog Button-down shirts and T-shirts up to size 2X.

Anne Terrie Designs "Fashion Swim-wear for all generations of Plus Size Women" in sizes up to 24W.

Art-Wear I love the shirts in this cata-log. The designs on many of the T-shirts have a theme . . . the animals in the place of humans and vice versa. My fa-vorite is of two deer at a taxidermy shop, the hunter mounted and ready for the den. On the more serious—but equally festive—side are some beautiful

Christmas sweatshirts. Most items are available in up to size 4X.

Big Ass Sportswear While not exactly politically correct, I suppose the name of this company is at least descriptive. T-shirts in 100 percent preshrunk cotton, sweatshirts and sweatpants of 50/50 poly-cotton-blend fleece, and night-shirts, all in sizes 2X up to 10X. Be forewarned . . . every item of clothing has a logo . . . "BIG" with buttocks attached. All items are the same price, no matter what your size. This is a small, home-grown company. They request you phone for information after six P.M. Central time. (No longer in business.)

Big & Bold "Casual, Comfortable Clothing for Men and Women." Offering T-shirts, sweatshirts, sweatpants, jack-ets, and shorts in sizes up to 8X. Big & Bold offers "over 5,000 designs available to suit your hobbies and interests," including dogs, flowers, horses, Native American graphics, sports, religious, and humorous sayings.

Big Day at the Beach Swimwear in sizes up to 10X.

Big Stitches by Jan Custom-made swimsuits in any size. Choose from several styles and fabrics, send your measurements, and two to four weeks later you will receive a swimsuit created just for you. Also available are poolside wraps, bicycle shorts, and T-shirts. Custom artwork is also available for just $35 more . . . just let Big Stitches know what you have in mind and/or send along a drawing or picture. A basic suit runs around $70. Extra features, additional $20; special fabrics, additional $20; matching swim cap, $6. Send self-addressed, stamped envelope for brochure and ordering information.

Blue Sky Designs "Fashions to Paint or Ready to Wear." In sizes small through 5X. Men's and women's T-shirts, sweats, and jackets, some in "splatterwear."

Body Image Task Force This informational/support organization sells "All Women Are Beautiful" T-shirts in sizes small up to 10X.

By Ro! "Our swimwear line is designed for the voluptuous, large-sized woman with flattering lines, contemporary styles and the great fit you need." Made with four-way stretch nylon/spandex and double lined, in customized colors, up to size 5X plus custom sizes.

California Rainbow Tie Dye Tie-dyed shirts up to size 3X.

Carol's Creative Corner Fun, brightly colored T-shirts and nightshirts in adult sizes small up to 10X.

Carolina Made Heavy cotton T-shirts in sizes up to 5X. Also available are jackets (up to 3X), golf shirts (up to 3X), sweatshirts and sweatpants (up to 2X), and denim shirts (up to 2X). This company sells only wholesale, but will sell to groups also.

Castles Direct "Princess Laurel" and "Fair Maiden Cynthia" are waiting eagerly to set you up with activewear and accessories up to size 4X. T-shirts ("I've got big bones" and "If this were the 1500s I'd be a Goddess"), sweatshirts, and health-related books.

Coca-Cola Catalog The Coca-Cola Company has a catalog of all sorts of items with their trademark stamped on them. They also have T-shirts and sweaters, most up to size 1X, some up to 2X.

Colorado Coyote Ribbed nightshirts, hooded T-shirts, golf shirts, cardigan jackets, and jersey nightshirts in sizes up to 6X, T-shirts and sweatshirts up to size 8X. Excellent choice of colors and a cute assortment of animal/nature designs.

The Company of Women Though most of the clothing items in this catalog go up to only size XL, there are a few that are larger. This company is a subsidiary of a shelter for abused women, and the profits help provide the shelter with the monies it needs.

Country Store "Country Gifts for Country Folks." Can't say I'm "country folk," but I find a lot of the items in this catalog to my liking. Besides all the country cookbooks, homey decorations, and useful gadgets, you'll also find T-shirts and sweaters with beautiful nature scenes in sizes up to 4X.

DJ's Positive Images T-shirts and greeting cards with creative, fun, size-positive images up to sizes 8X. I loved the fat lady in the embrace of a handsome vampire with the words "Bite Me." Fat ladies flying kites, scuba diving, and dancing at Stonehenge, plus more. Something else interesting with this catalog . . . shirts featuring famous women from history: George Sand, Harriet Tubman, Bessie Smith, Margaret Sanger, Mourning Dove, Elizabeth Gurley Flynn, Diane Fossey, Helen Keller, and Sappho.

Desert Rain Mercantile Company
". . . celebrates the Spirit of the West and Southwest clothing and handcrafted jewelry." Beautiful T-shirts in sizes 1X to 5X, sweatshirts in sizes 1X to 4X.

Dvora Dreams Original hand-painted T-shirts up to 2X (custom orders also). These shirts all have a fantasy theme with designs like castles, butterflies, unicorns, Pegasus, winged cats, and mermaids. You choose a design and a quote (from the list supplied, or your own).

Fit to Be Tried Activewear in sizes 1X to 4X. Oversize T-shirts, shorts, unitards, sport bras, swimsuits, bicycle pants, and leotards. A generously cut terry wrap is available, as is a pool/beach terry robe. Very colorful stuff.

Full Bloom "Imprinted Sportswear for the Fuller Figure." T-shirts with your choice of slogan or design on the front, sizes 1X up to 12X. You can even send in a photo to be reproduced in full color on a white shirt. Full Bloom has recently begun making dresses and loungers from any of the shirt styles. Men's shirts are cut with wider shoulders and no flare at the hips. Will send fabric swatches.

Full Fitness by Jazel Activewear in sizes 14 up to 24.

Good Vibrations Tees and sweats, up to size 4X, featuring oversize designs, lifelike detail in designs of cats and dogs (120 breeds available).

Hep Cat If you love cats, this catalog is for you. Featuring T-shirts with adorable cat designs, Hep Cat offers 100 percent cotton long-sleeve shirts, short-sleeve T-shirts, sweaters, and nightshirts in sizes up to 2X. Anna Grupke, the owner of Hep Cat, says she is working on finding good-quality tees in 3X and 4X. These are beautiful designs sure to give warm, cuddly feelings to cat lovers everywhere. I particularly loved the snow leopard and Socks, the White House Cat . . . ("Finally . . . an Independent in the White House!").

Holy Cow, Inc. For those of you who adore those black-and-white cows of Woody Johnson, this is the catalog for you. Just about everything you can imagine has cows on it . . . cookie jars, stationery, towels, cups, address books, wallets . . . you get the idea. There are a few T-shirts up to size 2X, but the majority go only up to XL.

Intimate Appeal Loungewear and swimwear in sizes up to 6X.

Jozell Fashions Plus Sweatshirts, T-shirts, hand-painted and beaded tops in plus and supersizes.

Just Big Sportswear Serious discount merchandise here . . . basic tees (up to size 8X) at $9 apiece (prices noted here are for the largest size), pocket tees (up to 6X) at $9.50 apiece, jersey shorts (up to 6X) at $9.50 apiece, heavyweight sweats (up to 8X) at $25 a pair, and poplin jackets (up to 8X) at $39. Most items must be purchased in lots of a dozen.

Lefty LaRue Handprinted T-shirts, sizes 2X to 8X. All shirts here are one price, $20, and are appropriate for both men and women.

Living Epistles "The best witness you can wear." Some very interesting, high-quality T-shirts in sizes up to 4X. From the more traditional "Lily of the Valley" and "The Lord is my Shepherd" to "Eternity Your Choice: Smoking or Non-Smoking" and "Practice safe sex . . . get married and be faithful (or just abstain)."

Manny's Baseball Land "America's Finest All Sports Catalog." Team jackets, shirts, hats, jerseys, and shorts from all professional teams, all professional sports, in sizes up to 4XL.

Marlene's Craft & Design Sweatshirts, jackets, and T-shirts in sizes up to 4X.

Me Being Free T-shirts and nightshirts in sizes 2X up to 10X, featuring big, beautiful people.

Mour to Dri Here's a unique, very welcome catalog. Men's and women's beach/bath cover-ups in large, luscious sizes. Robes, wash mitts, cover-ups, beach towels, and wraps. Towels come in three styles. The original Mour to Dri body towel is a full 45" wide and 8½' long. The pocket towel has a pocket added for carrying beach items. The beach party blanket towel unfolds to a 7½' width and is 8½' long. All of the wearable items are 90" in circumference but can be custom made and/or monogrammed. Very nice stuff, Mour to Dri!

Naturally Yours Leggings in 90 percent cotton/10 percent spandex, available in a dozen colors in sizes up to 4X.

Needle in a Haystack Solid-color 100 percent cotton T-shirts in sizes 1X up to 5X.

Northern Sun Merchandising T-shirts in heavyweight, 100 percent cotton up to size 3X. One of particular interest says, "GOD is comin' and she is FAT!"

Not So Subtle Tees . . . and more Feminist themes on T-shirts and sweatshirts up to size 3X. "Feminism is the radical notion that women are people," "Straight But Not Narrow," "Outrageous Older Woman!"

Original Jo's Features 100 percent cotton tees up to size 8X in a wide range of colors. Transfers include several Southwest designs, animals, and a few humorous commentaries ("If they can put one man on the moon . . . why not ALL of them?"). This is a new business with plans to expand with more designs and a line of gauze separates.

Pango Pango Swimwear Women's very skimpy swimsuits that fit up to 47" hips. Most of these suits are bikinis. The tops run up to an F cup with bands cut to your measurements.

Parsinen Design Contemporary, fashionable, dress and casual dresses, pants, tunics, shells, T-shirts, vests, skirts, jackets, and kimonos. A sample sheet of materials available is enclosed with information sheets on all fashions.

Prescription Sportswear Pocket T-shirts up to sizes regular 6X and tall 4X with wildlife designs, including whitetail deer, wild turkeys, and wild boars.

Queen of Hearts Swimwear in sizes 18 up to 24.

Rainbow Tees T-shirts up to 5X, sweatshirts up to 2X.

Sandy's Wearable Art T-shirts in sizes up to 5X.

Snake & Snake Productions 100% cotton T-shirts in sizes up to 6X. This women-owned and -operated business produces T-shirts, jackets, sweatshirts, and shorts for both men and women. Designs include polar bears, the Peace Tree, new moon, night tree, cave wall drawings, goddesses dancing, Indian warrior goddess, "Venus envy," Queen Nefertiti, and many more.

Vermont Country Store A wide selection of men's and women's fleece, chamois, and broadcloth nightwear, slips, bras, dresses, pants, and skirts in sizes S through 3X. You'll also find hats, boots, gloves, and slippers up to 3X. This catalog

is unusual in its old-fashioned look and selection of items. The Christmas catalog offers sleds, lace table runners, crystal icicles, Glass Wax stencils, hardwood alphabet blocks, penny candy kaleidoscopes, wooden fiddlestix, powdered vanilla extract, Goo Goo Clusters, peppermint pigs (complete with a red velvet bag and steel hammer for smashing), and cream filberts (just to name a few items). A fascinating trip down memory lane.

What on Earth Not exactly a T-shirt catalog, What on Earth offers a "collection of fun wear and delightful diversions." You will discover all sorts of unusual items (this is really a fun catalog), including some unique, clever T-shirts up to size XXL. I hesitated to include this catalog because there are so few items above XL, but what they have is unique and of good quality.

Willow Moon Regular T-shirts up to size 5X, long-sleeve T-shirts up to size 2X, and jockey underwear up to size 11. Shirt designs celebrate the goddess with "titles" like "Moon Dance," "Forest Womyn," "Grove Womyn," "Mother Tree," and "Wild Womyn." Shorts and leggings will be available soon.

Wireless Some catalogs are that full of fun stuff. This one is great for all kinds of items to brighten your day, from a Felix the Cat mug to a delightful baby gargoyle. The proceeds go to support public radio. There are lots of colorful, witty shirts and sweatshirts. Some only go up to size 1X, but many go up to 2X.

Womanswork This catalog mainly offers gloves of all sorts designed to fit women's hands, but they also offer nice heavyweight T-shirts (both long- and short-sleeved), a sweatshirt, and a zipper sweatshirt, all with the Womanswork logo, only up to size 2X.

Women at Large Activewear in sizes to fit women up to 6' tall, 450 pounds.

XL's "Cotton tees and sweatshirts with great designs in larger sizes for women and men." Absolutely gorgeous designs on these shirts . . . especially for the nature lover. Blank tees are also available. Sizes up to 5X.

Zala Design Activewear and leotards in sizes up to 7X.

Zenobie F. Creations Beautiful swimwear in sizes 2X up to 6X.

CLOTHING VIDEO CATALOGS

So far all of the videos I have viewed offer only women's clothing. Perhaps if you men make enough noise . . .

Astárte: Woman by Design A wonderful collection offering a wide variety of fashions presented in an easy-to-follow format. Clothing for all occasions—

work, fun, and special occasions—in sizes up to 4X. Astárte also offers handmade jewelry and accessories. Jennifer and Nanette choose their best-selling designs from their store in Torrance, California, to offer at-home shoppers. Call for video price.

Distinctions Leisure, daytime, and special-occasion wear. These fashions are the same as ones sold in the San Diego Distinctions stores. Modeled by big, beautiful models (sizes from 14 up to 24, five of them professionals, two store employees). Each video presents approximately fifty outfits, most up to 4X, some up to 6X. $5.

Enchanted Collection, Ltd. This video catalog offers lingerie up to size 3X. $20.

For Play Boudoir lingerie up to sizes 4X. $15.

Greater Woman "We've selected unique hard-to-find quality clothing, gathered information on fabric, fit and care, and videotaped the whole experience." With this introduction Darcy Beck invites you to "grab a cup of coffee, get comfortable and let's go shopping!" She offers beautiful selections from Japanese Weekend, Elianna, Parsinen, House of Ross, Janet Terri Designs, Calise by Accuventure, CitiCulture II, LBW by L. Bates, T. D. Sanders, Back Porch Ivy, Lourie' Collection, Terry Town, Fine & Fancy Lingerie, Faye, and a personal favorite of mine, Myles Ahead. I *love* the red-and-black swing coat and matching dress. Beautiful pieces at surprisingly reasonable prices. Tapes arrive every three months. $10.

Large and Lovely Bridal Center Video of absolutely gorgeous gowns starting at size 20! Dresses are available up to size 46 with custom sizing available. Very reasonable prices for your once-in-a-lifetime gown. 30 minutes. $13.

JEWELRY AND ACCESSORIES

Ankle Bracelet Plus size in blue, white, and gold glass beads with a sun charm. Perfect for sandals or bare feet days. 10" to 11" lengths. $18.

SOURCES: Fit to Be Tried

Austrian Crystal Necklaces and Bracelets, adjustable $25–$35.

SOURCES: C. Flaherty

Bangles 8", 9", and 10" silver- or gold-plated in three styles—plain, rope, and Celtic. $9 (silver), $24 (gold).

SOURCES: Amplestuff

Choke Necklaces Made for the larger woman. Write for pricing information.

SOURCES: Barb's Abundant Jewels

Jewelry Clasp Clamp You know how it is next to impossible to hold on to one end of a bracelet clasp while trying to work the other end into it? This little gadget allows you to hold on to one end comfortably with the hand the bracelet is on while you fasten the clasp. $4–$12.

SOURCES:

Miles Kimball

Amplestuff

Necklace Extenders In gold- or silver-tone and 3", 4½", and 6" lengths. One set of each length. $3.

SOURCES:

Miles Kimball

Robin Barr Enterprises

Silver Bangle Bracelets 8", 9", or 10" silver-plated bangles. Five for $40. Photo postcard, $1.

SOURCES: COY

Venus II Pendant The Venus of Willendorf pendant in black, cobalt blue, jade green, light blue, or clear Pyrex, approximately 2" high, on extralong cord. $15–$20.

SOURCES: Ample Shopper

Cherokee Designs by Judy Native American–made jewelry in many styles. All one-of-a-kind in custom sizes.

Desert Rain Mercantile Beautiful silver and turquoise Native American necklaces (38" strands).

Fashion Touches Belts up to any length, leather or covered in any material you provide, and covered buttons.

J. Lumarel Corporation Necklaces and bracelets in 14K gold in longer lengths for greater comfort.

Just*4*U Jewelry One-of-a-kind beaded necklaces and earrings custom designed to your specifications. Choose your own color scheme, length, and focal beads.

Custom bridal party necklaces also available. $10–$30.

Majestic Mountain Art Jewelry Large and long styles and custom designs.

The Right Touch Accessories catalog featuring plus-size accessories only. Find those belts, shoulder bags, capes, scarves, necklaces, bracelets, and watches. The jewelry is both costume and better quality. "Accessories have always been the individual's signature, it creates a mood, changes the look of a dress . . ."

Robin Barr Enterprises Jewelry extenders for watches, chokers, bracelets, and anklets made of 24K gold or sterling silver plate.

Sign of the Unicorn Hand-wrought sterling silver and 14K jewelry. Rare and unusual semiprecious stones, mythic and abstract themes. Everything available in large sizes.

Star River Productions (also Nancy Blair, Great Goddess Collection) Goddess pendants, earrings, necklaces, and more.

Votta's Wearable Art Beautiful bracelets, earrings, and pins designed by a talented group of artists. Bracelets can be made to your size (instructions for measuring your wrist correctly for each type of bracelet are included) and are very reasonably priced. Especially amusing was the "I'll never go hungry again!" bracelet, a circle of clear tubing filled with multicolored beans capped with a tube of sterling silver.

Xtras "Accessories for Women of Size." Fine jewelry and accessories in sterling silver and 14K gold customized to fit larger women. (I have a real fondness for silver, just in case any of you are starting your Christmas shopping early.)

LINGERIE AND LOUNGEWEAR

Why is it that girdles and "controllers" are always modeled by women who can't find an ounce of flabby tissue on their bodies, let alone have to worry about girding and controlling it? Ah, well.

Measuring for a bra: While there is no foolproof way to measure for a comfortable-fitting bra (sometimes you just have to try them on), there are two ways to determine what is most likely to be right for you, both of which work best if you are wearing a bra while measuring.

1. Wrap a tape measure under your arms and above your bust. Hold the tape firmly but not too tightly.
2. Wrap a tape measure directly under your breasts (at the bottom of your bra). Again, hold the tape firmly but not too tightly. Add five inches to the number indicated.

To determine cup size, measure around the fullest part of your bust. If that number is the same as or one inch larger than the chest wall measurement, your cup size is A. If it is one to two inches larger, your cup size is B; two to three inches larger is a C, and so on. Each inch generally indicates the next cup size.

It is difficult to determine panty size . . . there is so much variation from manufacturer to manufacturer. Be certain to check the size charts included with each catalog.

•Items (and one organization) of Special Interest•

Bra Extenders Two-, three-, or four-hook extenders. You can pick these up at just about any fabric store or through some mail-order houses. Set of 2 for $2 to $3.

SOURCES:
Miles Kimball

Women of Size
Comfortably Yours

Chafe Shields These shields are designed to fit against the insides of your thighs from the crotch to above the knee to prevent soreness. Fits up to size 2X. $30.

SOURCES: Ambassador Value Showcase

Bra Strap Cushions These cushions slip right over your bra straps and keep them from digging into your shoulders. Set of two pairs, $3.50.
SOURCES: Miles Kimball

Fat Fannie Pantyhose up to size 5X. $4 per pair.
SOURCES: Andrew Barry Associates

Pambra's "Absorbs perspiration under and between breasts AND adds comfort to underwire bras." Sizes 38 to 50. Package of three for $10 to $13.
SOURCES:
  Amplestuff
  Baby Becoming
  Barely Nothings
  Bruce Medical Supply
  Far & Wide
  Pambra's Inc.
  Vermont Country Store

Shoulder Pads Specially designed to fit sizes L up to 3XL. $10.
SOURCES: The Competition Group

Tops Top-heavy ladies can write to this London company to receive practical hints and advice in dealing with problems associated with having large breasts. A newsletter is also available upon request.

Torso extenders Snap-on extenders for crotch opening of teddies add four to six inches to length of garment. $15.

SOURCES: Tropical Adventure

Tummy Uplifter Support for tummies up to 50". $25.
SOURCES: J.C. Penney Special Needs

Alice's Undercover World Custom-fit bras in any size . . . all the way up to 64Z. You'll find foundations by Active, Airway, Amoena, Bali, Camp, Carina, Carnival, Discrene, Exquisite Form, Goddess, Henson, Jezebel, Jobst, Jodee, Lou, Olga, Rago, Spenco, Va Bien, Vanity Fair, and Youthcraft. Alice's also offers prostheses up to size 12.

Armands Nice variety of panties, hips 48" through 71", sizes 13 up to 18.

Attitudes and Lace Lingerie in sizes 1X up to 4X.

Barely Nothings Lingerie and more in sizes up to 4X. A very nice catalog. Gowns, peignoirs, robes, Scantihose, teddies, baby dolls, body stockings, bustiers, lace gloves, kimono robes, pettipants, bras, stockings, Marabou slippers, feather boas, panties, Pambra's, garter belts, Danskin Plus activewear, and even things for men. (Does the man in your life need some sheer black boxers or maybe Velcro-sided tear-away briefs?) There are also some very nice robes, including one gorgeous black one with a tiger on the back. Be sure to join the Birthday Club when you order.

Body Webs Catsuits, leotards, and casualwear in sizes 1X up to 3X.

Bra Lady Custom-fit bras.

The Bust Stop Huge selection of bras in sizes 26A up to 6OOO.

Colesce Couture Not exactly a catalog company, Colesce Couture is marketed through home fashion shows. Sizes run up to 2X.

Champagne & Lace Boutique Beautiful lingerie catalog and store with sizes up to 4X. This store is owned by Carol Doda, a very well-known (and well-endowed) stripper from San Francisco's North Beach area. Be sure to check out the glow in the dark panties.

Comfortably Yours Bras (up to size 48D), foundation garments (most up to XL, some up to 6X), hosiery, slips (up to size 2X), garter belts, foot care products, mastectomy bras and forms, and cosmetics. Most in sizes up to XL.

Damart Thermal underwear and socks for men and women, sizes up to XL for most items, XXL on some. This is also a great source for extralarge gloves and back supports (available in up to 3X). Excellent quality.

Decent Exposures "100% cotton comfort designed by women for women." Custom-designed "unbras" up to size 55K, soft and cozy nightshirts up to size 24, and underpants up to size 12.

Designs by Norvell Bras up to size MM cup.

Exclusive Appeal Lingerie and French silk up to sizes 4X.

Exquisite Form Bras, band sizes up to 48, cup sizes up to FF.

Extra Emphasis A beautiful selection of bras in sizes 32 up to 56.

Fine & Fancy Lingerie Company "Beautiful women come in all sizes." A small but very attractive collection of camp shirts, nightgowns, kimono jackets, poet's shirts, camisoles, panties, bodysuits, and bustiers up to size 5X.

Fit to Be Tried Bras, sizes up to 44DD. Sports bras up to 4X.

For Play Boudoir lingerie in sizes up to 4X.

Frederick's of Hollywood Lingerie and undergarments in sizes up to 3X.

Full Figure Woman's Lingerie Full line of teddies, bustiers, baby dolls, sleep shirts, long gowns, chemises, and poets' shirts in sizes 1X up to 4X.

Grace's Underworld Bras, sizes up to 60JJ; prostheses.

Goddesses Lingerie up to size 3X.

Hanes/L'Eggs/Bali/Playtex Discount catalog for bras, loungewear, and hosiery in sizes 1X up to 4X.

Heinz Gift Shop Intimate apparel in sizes 1X up to 4X.

High Places Victorian-style corsets, bustiers, and lingerie in sizes 18 up to 26, 1X to 3X. Satin, lace, leather, and feathers. Catalogs vary in price and content: European Victorian Corsets (fit 20" to 42" waists); Plus Size Contemporary Lingerie, sizes 18 to 26; and Plus Size Vogue Leather Lingerie, sizes 18 to 24.

Intimate Appeal Everything from a playful Mickey Mouse sleep shirt and bras to palazzo jumpsuits and embroidered lace cotton gowns, most up to size 3X.

Intimate Attitudes Beautiful, very slick catalog filled with every kind of lingerie you can imagine in gorgeous, rich colors. Most items run up to size 4X. Be sure to check out the maid's outfit. (We're assuming no one expects actual housework to be done here.)

Intimate Encounters Foundation garments and lingerie in sizes up to 4X.

It's a Secret Plus Lingerie up to size 6X plus body paints, gels, glitter, and assorted creams and oils. There are also a few sexy items for men.

JaneEtte Bras in sizes up to 72ZZ and support garments—sold at parties, from personal consultants who come to your home, or through the mail if there is no representative in your area.

J.C. Penney After Surgery Inner Fashions Postmastectomy bras and a line of full-figure support bras up to size 48DD.

Jeunique Bras, sizes up to 46MM and N.

Lady Grace Intimate apparel from many big-name manufacturers, including Bali, Olga, Carnival, Wondermaid, Playtex, Exquisite Form, Formfit, CustomMaid, and Leading Lady. Bra sizes up to 52, cup sizes up to I. Girdles and half-slips up to 9X, some nightgowns up to size 3X. Telephone operators are available to help you with sizing.

Laughing Sisters "Like a hug you can wear!" 100 percent cotton double-napped flannel nightgowns or lightweight cotton in sizes 14 up to 36 through custom supersizes. These are wonderful, high-quality gowns with a generous cut. Some of the gowns are made especially for nursing mothers. Available in solid pastels, dark colors (red and green), and floral prints. Laughing Sisters has recently begun offering pettipants made to your measurements. For a brochure, send a large SASE.

Lillian Lavergne Designs Egyptian cotton or Victorian eyelet half-slips and camisoles.

Lingerie Elegance Romantic lingerie in sizes 1X up to 3X.

The Lingerie Warehouse Big Gals "Fashion and Comfort for Plus Sizes." Bras in sizes up to 52DD, support briefs from large up to 6X.

Lovable Company Bras, sizes up to 48DD.

Madame X Lingerie Sexy lingerie in sizes up to 4X.

Magnolia Lingerie Lingerie in sizes 1X up to 4X.

Marcus & Wiesen Girdles and other foundation items up to size 42.

Missouri Mail Order, Inc. Specializing in bras up to size 46E and girdles up to size 6X. Brand names include Exquisite Form's Ful-ly and Big Gals bras and Lose It! and Magic Lady controllers and Ful-ly Hour After Hour All-in-One.

My Mother's Star Bras (sizes 38A up to 60JJ) and foundations.

Nadina Plus Intimate apparel made in natural fibers in sizes 12 up to 32.

Oh! Such Style "Intimate Apparel for the Full Figured Woman." Sizes up to 4X. Nice assortment, including a fun bunny set for a playful evening.

Pamper Me "Sensuous, Glamorous Lingerie Customized for Beautiful Full Figure Voluptuous Women." Your first request for a catalog yields a small brochure of about a dozen items. When you place your first order, they will send along a catalog with all of their available items.

Perfect Comfort Control briefs, mid-thigh shapers, knee-length shapers, and capri-length leggings. Most up to size 6X, some up to 13X.

Playtex Bras, sizes up to 50DD.

The Primary Layer "Next-to-the Skin Comfort." Sizes up to XL for most items, up to 3X for some; 100 percent cotton nightgowns, chenille robes, and pajamas for men and women.

Provocative Lady Three catalogs are available: Intimate Attitudes (up to 4X), Especially Yours (up to 3X), and XTC Leather "Twice as Sexy" (up to 3X). The first two catalogs are, as hinted, provocative lingerie. XTC Leather offers leather lingerie with chains and buckles.

Queen of Hearts Foundations, sexy sleepwear, garters, and more.

RJ's Apparel African-inspired loungewear in sizes from 1X up to 9X.

Romantic Interludes "Elegant Lingerie Fashions." Sizes up to 4X. Beautiful materials, classic lines, and gorgeous, big women for models. If these creations don't make your lover's heart race, call the paramedics (or the coroner) immediately.

Romantic Notions Bustiers, unique garter teddies, and more in sizes 1X up to 4X.

Roselyn Bras, sizes up to 56H.

S. Johnson Naughty-but-nice lingerie in sizes up to 4X.

Sally's Place Wow! What can I say? This selection is wild. Garter belts, musical g-strings, temporary tattoos, bustiers, pasties (even special ones for the blushing bride), fingerless gloves, and costumes that will definitely command attention. And body shells. Did I mention the hats? A great, must-see catalog. Sizes up to 4X. (Oh! You *have* to check out the "Pin the Macho on the Man" party game!)

Sarah's Bare Necessities   Lingerie parties at home complete with games, adult toys, and body oils. Lingerie up to size 4X.

Secret Pleasures   Intimate apparel in sizes up to 4X.

Sheer Mahogany   Corsets, stockings, and garter belts up to size 5X; bras up to size 60JJ.

Soft Sensations   Nightshirts in unique styles.

Support Plus   Bras (up to size 48DD), support garments (up to size 3X), housecoats (up to 2X), and some thermal underwear (up to size XL).

Suzanne Henri, Inc.   A special measuring system makes this bra company unique. Before ordering a bra you request the fitting system (with their exclusive "fitting crowns") for $6. Use the fitting system to determine your proper size and return it with your order. Sizes from 28C up to 60JJ. Nursing bras available.

Sweet Dreams Intimates, Inc.   Bras and undergarments (sizes 34B up to 60H), lingerie and bridal sets (up to size 6X), teddies, and bathing suits (up to size 32).

Tropical Adventure   Exotic lingerie in sizes 1X up to 4X. (Be sure to request the "big and beautiful" catalog.)

Vanity Fair   Bras, sizes up to 50DDD.

Women of Size   Quality lingerie for sizes up to 4X. All of the usual plus a wide selection of panties and garter belts. This catalog also offers some men's clothing—robes, boxers, kimonos, pants, briefs, and thongs. Be sure to specify that you want the catalog for large-size women. (They also have one for those less well blessed, stuck in sizes S, M, and L.)

Yellow Creek Originals   Briefs, half-slips, full slips, and camisoles cut from a pattern made specifically for you. Custom-fitted lingerie is also available . . . all at very reasonable prices. In fact, your first pair of briefs is free.

WEDDING FASHIONS AND FORMALWEAR

The majority of these companies don't offer a catalog, preferring to work directly with the customer to find the gown of your dreams.

Above & Beyond   Formal attire and wedding gowns in sizes 16 up to 32. Brochure available.

Alfred Angelo   Gowns in sizes 20 up to 44.

Ange D' Amour Wedding gowns up to size 20.

Bianchi Gowns up to size 20.

Bridal Originals Gowns up to size 30.

Bridal Veil Bridal gowns, bridal party gowns, and mothers' dresses custom-made up to any size. Gowns can be duplicated from photos or magazines.

Carmi Couture Gowns up to size 20.

Chilbert's Tuxedos "A Formalwear World at Your Fingertips." For the big man, whether you are tall or short. Trousers (up to size 60), blazers (up to size 60), tuxedos (up to size 60), and cumerbunds (up to 56" waist).

Christos, Inc. Designer bridal fashions made up to any size, and accessories.

Elianna Wedding fashions, including a beautifully detailed princess jacket and bridal gown in iridescent organza over tulle and taffeta with organza roses and bow loops, and feminine dresses for the bridal party in sizes 16W up to 32W; also tall, petite, and custom sizes.

Diamond Collection Gowns up to size 20.

Eden Gowns in sizes 20 to 32.

Essence by Esther Gowns up to size 44.

Eve of Milady Gowns up to size 20.

Fink Gowns up to size 20.

Galina Gowns up to size 20.

Ginza Collection Gowns up to size 42.

Ilissa Gowns up to size 20.

Impression Bridal Designer wedding gowns cut to any size, also headpieces and veils.

J.C. Penney Bridal Collection Wedding gowns and bridal party fashions up to size 28W.

Large and Lovely Bridal Center Absolutely gorgeous gowns starting at size 20! Dresses are available up to size 46, with custom sizing available. Very reasonable prices for your once-in-a-lifetime gown. See also "Clothing Video Catalogs."

Large Lovely Lady Traditional wedding gowns in sizes up to 3X, and beautiful eveningwear available in 2X up to supersizes.

The J—Western Division "Gowns for the Entire Bridal Party." To size 28W. Trains, maternity, and bridal suits are also available.

Jasmine Gowns up to size 44.

Jessica McClintock, Inc. This small catalog presents just a few gowns and several dresses, but they are all lovely. If you are planning a less-formal wedding, many of the dresses will serve the purpose quite nicely for around $200 to $300.

Jim Hjelm Gowns up to size 20.

Lili Gowns up to size 26.

Mary's Gowns up to size 30.

Mon Cherie Gowns up to sizes 20 and 44.

Moonlight Design, Inc. Designer bridal fashions.

Mori Lee Gowns up to size 42.

San-Martin Bridals Designer bridal fashions.

Sweetheart Gowns up to size 44.

T. C. Originals, Inc. Original bridal fashions in any size.

Wedding Web This Internet site will be useful to people planning to make a for-malwear purchase in (so far) Los Angeles, San Francisco, New York, Dallas, or southern Florida. Some of the retailers listed do mail order and custom sizes, however, so this might be worth checking out.

MATERNITY WEAR

For photocopies of *Big Beautiful Woman* (BBW) magazine's 1993 series of articles on pregnancy and the big beautiful woman, send $2 to BBW Moms at BBW magazine.

Bellybra Pregnancy support garment up to size 2X. $42.
SOURCES: Basic Comforts

Baby Becoming Nursing bras and maternity clothing in sizes 1X to 8X. Tops, shirts, tunics, nightgowns, leggings, and dresses. Charlotte Bradley, owner of Baby Becoming, says she is open to ideas for items you are interested in and would love to hear from you.

Betsy & Company Mix-and-match co-ordinates up to size 3X.

Bosom Buddies Nursing bras in sizes up to 46I.

Cyberbaby Nursing bras in band sizes up to 46, cup sizes up to G.

Fit for Two Two styles of pants in sizes up to 3X.

From Here to Maternity Sizes up to 24. No catalog but will mail.

Glori-Us Maternity briefs up to 52" hips; nursing bras up to 46DD.

J.C. Penney Baby & You A wide selection of maternity and nursing fashions in sizes up to 3X.

Julianna's "Generously Sized Clothing for the Large & Tall Expectant Mother."

Maternity dresses, shirts, T-shirt dresses, shirts, shorts, pants and straight skirts, tank tops, and short sets up to size 28. Swatch samples included with catalog.

Playtex Nursing bras up to 42DD.

Special Delivery Plus Maternity fashions in sizes up to 3X.

SEW YOUR OWN

If you are handy with fabric and sewing machine, making your own items of clothing can be an alternate path to a gorgeous wardrobe. Most of these catalogs specialize in costumes, business suits, and sportswear. If you are looking for patterns for lingerie or wedding dresses, check catalogs such as Vogue and Simplicity, found at fabric stores. There are several books available that detail how to enlarge patterns, if necessary.

Extralong Measuring Tape These measure 100" to 120" and have lots of wonderful uses above and beyond measuring ample hips. $2.

SOURCES:

Hancock Fabrics

Amplestuff

Nancy's Notions (120")

Clotilde (120")

Beautiful Babes Patterns simple enough for the beginning seamstress in sizes up to approximately 5X. You'll find a pretty complete wardrobe here.

Bellamy Manufacturing Skirts, pants, and dresses (with some maternity) in sizes up to approximately 5X.

Clotilde "25 Years of Sewing Notions." Patterns up to size 2X (including a Western duster, jackets, skirts, and

vests) and several excellent books to help in making pattern adjustments.

Creative Square Dancer (Shirley's Shoppe) If you love to scoot back, allemande left, and do-si-do but can't find the duds to sashay in, this place is for

you. Men's and women's square dance attire, sizes up to 42" chest, 34" waist, 44" hips.

Fashion Fit Pattern Service Computer-fitted patterns (over 100 to choose from) made especially for you. This is an on-line service. You can also have the piece made for you after you choose the pattern and materials and supply the measurements.

Great Fit Patterns Patterns for women's tops, skirts, lingerie, and dresses in sizes 38 to 60.

The Green Pepper This is a fascinating catalog of unusual items . . . you'll find all sorts of sporting wear—jackets, vests, overalls, jogging suits, windbreakers, bicycle shorts, mittens, caps, and jumpsuits. The patterns only go up to size XL, but they are easily modified. Beyond clothing, Green Pepper also offers designs for windsocks, packs, sleeping bags, garment bags, bicycle handlebar bags, horse blankets, and carries all the zippers and assorted hardware you need to complete your projects.

Harriett's Tailoring Men's and women's period patterns, costumes, and uniforms custom-made. Beautiful Revolutionary War, Colonial period, and Civil War fashions from a woman who has created pieces for many museums, historic sites, and movies.

Heidi Marsh Beautiful, authentic reproductions of Civil War costumes in sizes up to 52" bust, 46" waist, 54" hips for

women; 54" chest, 52" waist, and 55" hips for men.

Joan Bartram Designs Patterns for women's knitted sweaters and vests, sizes up to 52. Also carries some plus-size patterns for kids up to size 30.

Krüh Knits An extensive collection of books and patterns for machine-knitting sweaters, pullovers, cardigans, vests, coats, and other apparel for both men and women (up to size 3X).

Mary Maxim Christmas sweater and sweatshirt kits—appliqué, beads, knit, and cutwork in sizes up to 2X. Also sweaters to crochet with other themes or that are just plain pretty in sizes up to 3X.

McCall's Some patterns up to size 50 for women (54" chest, 49" waist, and 56" hips). Men's patterns run up to size 56 (48" chest, 44" waist). Available through retail stores.

Nancy's Notions Great Fit Patterns, sizes 38 to 60, include dresses, pants, skirts, jackets, and tops. Nancy's also carries a video on enlarging patterns.

Newark Dressmaker Supply Folkwear patterns (Australian drover's coat up to size 22, kilts in all sizes, Kinsale cloak), Great Fit Patterns, and books. This catalog is a real treasure trove of supplies for all sorts of sewing and crafts work.

Northwest Traders Patterns include frontier pants, shirts, war shirts, trousers, leggings, dresses, waistcoat vests, and capotes (long, usually hooded cloaks or coats) in several styles and lengths. Capotes are unusual coats and are made of colorful blankets. After you choose the blanket, the item can be handsewn for you or you can purchase a kit and complete it yourself. Styles include long hunter, voyageur, meti's, nor'wester, old tailor, frontiersman, canoe jacket, and fringed. Sizes run up to 2X. Patterns cost approximately $5.75 each; capote kits between $134 and $179.

Past Patterns ''Meticulous Patterns of Fashion Rages between the Victorian and Supersonic Ages . . . Patterns for Clothing Worn Between 1830 and 1939.'' These patterns include gowns, chemises, petticoats, bustles, stays, riding habits, wedding gowns, sunbonnets, and nightgowns for women up to size 20; drawers, shirts, and trousers for men up to size 50'' chest. These sizes aren't very big, but I have included them because it is so easy to make adjustments while cutting and sewing.

S.E.S. Patterns Nice selection of custom-made patterns to fit you perfectly.

Suitability Riding attire, English and Western, for women up to size 46 blouse and men up to size 48 shirt. Not only will you find all the basic habits, riding skirts, breeches, hunt coats, jodhpurs, and riding jeans in this catalog, there are plenty of items for your horse. As long as you are treating yourself to a new hunt coat, sew some matching saddlebags or ankle boots for your mount.

Unique Patterns Design Limited Custom-fit patterns for women of all sizes. You purchase the Home Measuring Kit, which consists of a training video, a measuring manual, a tape measure, and registration forms. After selecting a pattern from a catalog of over 100 designs, you return a registration form with your order. The company then creates the pattern within approximately forty-eight hours exactly to your measurements. Unlimited sizes. $35 for Home Measuring Kit; patterns range from $7.50 to $20.50.

Vibrant Handknits USA High-quality art sweaters; hand-knitted, signed, and numbered; up to size 28 and custom sizes.

Vogue Most women's patterns available up to size 22, but a few go up to 24 (46" bust, 39" waist, and 48" hips). Men's up to XL. Available through retail stores.

Zen Home Stitchery Clothing, cushions, and accessories for meditation. Custom-made and patterns.

If you have access to E-mail, Mary Wilson maintains an excellent list of commercially available patterns for big men. Write to her for details.

BOOKS AND COMPUTER PROGRAMS OF INTEREST TO THE SEAMSTRESS (THESE ARE FOR YOU MEN, TOO)

Altering Men's Ready-to-Wear Written by Mary Roehr. Excellent resource for making your clothing purchases more comfortable and attractive.

SOURCES: Clotilde

Altering Women's Ready-to-Wear Written by Mary Roehr. Excellent resource for making your clothing purchases more comfortable and attractive.

SOURCES: Clotilde

Astárte/Woman, "Style Is Not a Size, It's an Attitude!" This quarterly newsletter is published by the folks at Astárte/Woman by Design. Basically a fashion newsletter, it touches on other issues of interest. For instance, the spring 1995 issue discussed battered women's shelters and their need for donations of large-size clothing.

SOURCES: Astárte/Woman by Design

Big Knits and ***Great Big Knits*** Written by Dawn French and Sylvie Soudan. Patterns in a wide variety of stitches and designs created especially for large-size women.

SOURCES: Trafalgar Square Publishing

Burda Fashions for the Fuller Figure Magazine Patterns up to size 34W.

SOURCES: GLP International

Dress Shop 2.0 Step into the latest in patterns for home sewing . . . this is a computer program that lets you choose items (skirts, pants, dresses, shirts, vests, suits), enter your measurements, and then print out the pattern. "Whatever your size or shape, Dress Shop 2.0 guarantees a custom fit." For IBM or Macintosh. $130. Order from LivingSoft or look for this program in software and fabric stores.

Elizabethan Costuming (1550–1580) Easy-to-follow instructions for creating beautiful Elizabethan-era costumes in any size. Other Times Productions.

Get Physical, by Stretch & Sew Book to help you create activewear.

SOURCES: Stretch & Sew

Pants for Any Body Written by Paty Palmer and Susan Pletsch. Help in altering pants patterns.

SOURCES: Clotilde

Plus-Size Sewing Listing Updated regularly; compiled by Freda Rosenberg. This list of catalogs that carry plus-size patterns offers a wide variety of fashions, sewing accessories, books, and videos.

SOURCES: Freda Rosenberg

Sew Big: The Fashion Guide for the Fuller Figure Written by Marilyn Thelen; published in 1991 by Palmer/Pletsch Associates. Marilyn Thelen has written this fashion guide for large-size people. Help with selecting fabrics, choosing patterns, and adapting those patterns for your figure.

SOURCES: Amplestuff

Sew Splashy, by Stretch & Sew Book to help you make your own swimsuits.

SOURCES: Stretch & Sew

Sew You're Not a Size 12, by Stretch & Sew Book to help you create activewear.

SOURCES: Stretch & Sew

Sewing Activewear Put out by Nancy's Notions. Great video guide to making your own exercise, dance, and swim- wear. $38 to purchase; $20 to rent for two weeks.

SOURCES: Nancy's Notions

Shortcuts to a Perfect Sewing Pattern An invaluable book to help with altering patterns to fit you perfectly.

SOURCES: Newark Dressmaker Supply

Victorian Costuming, Volume 1 (1840–1865) Easy-to-follow instructions for making Victorian costumes in any size. Other Times Productions. $12.

SHOES, BOOTS, AND STOCKINGS

Grips Overshoes Used by U.S. Postal Service letter carriers, policemen, and security personnel for maximum traction on slick surfaces. Available to men's size 12½ and women's size 14½. $39–$44.

SOURCES: Preferred Living

Leggings Features 90 percent cotton/ 10 percent spandex leggings in black, pink, white, turquoise, lilac, royal, jade, purple, forest green, navy, burgundy, and brown up to size 4X. $31 per pair.

SOURCES: Naturally Yours

Large-Sized Socks "For extra-wide feet and ample ankles." These black or white socks are 100 percent cotton and perfect for both summer and winter wear. For women and men. $9 a pair.

SOURCES: Amplestuff

Scantihose An alternative to panty hose, they fit up to 50" waists. Scanti- hose are two separate stockings held up by a belt, similar to the standard garter and stockings, except this belt holds the stockings up on the side and inside of the leg, not the front and back. Ideal for anyone who has trouble putting on panty hose. Can be worn throughout a pregnancy. $8 per pair.

SOURCES:

Limited Editions

Bruce Medical Supply

Shoe Horn 23" long, to let you slip into your shoes without bending or using a support for your foot. Can also be used to help in taking off your shoes and socks. $13.

SOURCES:

AdaptAbility

AbleWare

Amplestuff

Can-Do Products

Brookstone Hard-to-Find Tools

Shoe Stretcher   This is a spray for your shoes, wherever they pinch. $3.
SOURCES: Amplestuff

Shoe Stretcher, Adjustable   This wooden insert slips into your shoes and can be adjusted to stretch parts of the shoe that pinch your foot. $6.
SOURCES: Miles Kimball

Sock-Aid Installer   This device can help you slip your socks on without bending over. $15.
SOURCES:
  Ableware
  AdaptAbility
  Amplestuff
  Bruce Medical Supply
  Can-Do Products
  Enrichments

Sock Pull/Shoehorn Combination   In either 12" or 18" lengths. Helps with putting on socks and shoes. $8–$9.
SOURCES: Enrichments

Tights, Ribbed and Opaque   In sizes 1Queen (5' to 5'5", 150 to 200 pounds), 2Queen (5'5" to 5'10", 175 to 220 pounds), and 3Queen (5'7" to 6', 220 to 260 pounds). $15.
SOURCES: J. Jill, Ltd.

Active Soles   Dress, casual and athletic women's shoes in sizes up to 13EEE.

Andrew Barry Associates   Panty hose and knee-highs up to size 5X.

Aussie Connection   Wonderful fleece sheepskin slippers, boots and scuffs for men and women. Sizes up to 15.

B. A. Mason   Large selection of men's and women's shoes in sizes up to 16EEEE.

BBW Panty Hose   Support and regular up to size 7X.

Bencone Casuals   Women's shoes. Sandals, dress casual, dress comfort and walking shoes. Sizes up to 12EE.

Birkenstock   "The original comfort shoe." Custom-fit sandals, clogs and shoes for men and women.

Cartan's   Women's shoes. Sizes up to 13EE.

Church's English Shoes   Custom-made women's and men's shoes. Up to size 14EEE.

Clover Nursing Shoe Company   Sizes up to 12EE.

The Comfort Corner   "Where Comfort Is Guaranteed." Soft Spots women's casual, dress, and sport shoes and boots up to size 12EEE. The catalog comes with a special customized sizing chart.

Coward Shoes   Women's shoes up to size 12EEE, 13WW and half sizes. Every style you can imagine, from sandals and slip-ons to boots and heels.

D&M Enterprises   BBW panty hose in sizes up to 7X.

Danskin Plus Panty Hose Leggings, panty hose, and tights up to size 4X.

Fit for a Queen Leotards up to 64" hips, tights up to 72" hips, panty hose up to 80" hips.

Friedman's Shoes Men's shoes in sizes from 7 up to 20. Every style of men's shoe you can imagine is in this catalog, from fine Italian dress shoes to beach sandals.

Gloria Vanderbilt Panty hose up to 60"-plus hips.

Hitchcock Shoes, Inc. Men's shoes in sizes up to 13, EEE to EEEEEE widths.

Hersey Custom Shoe Company Men's and women's shoes. This is a pricey running or walking shoe, but it is made exactly to your specifications, including different size shoes for different size feet, totally nonleather shoes for people who object to animal materials, adjustments for orthotic inserts, and special built-up spots anywhere your feet need them. Expect to pay $130 to $200. Once you have ordered a pair of shoes, your records are kept on file, ready to use at any time.

Johansen Brothers Shoe Company, Inc. Wide selection of ladies' shoes in more than 130 different sizes up to 12EE and 13D.

Lori Alexandre Boots for wide calves (15" to 25") in sizes 5 up to 13.

Lorrini, Inc. of Montreal "Stylish boots for wide calves." Equestrian look, over the knee, Western, flats, heels . . . a very nice selection of quality boots up to 13 wide with a calf measurement up to 24".

Maryland Square All types of shoes, some up to EE width.

Masseys An excellent selection of women's shoes in sizes up to 14EE or 10EEEE. I can't imagine a type of shoe that isn't represented here . . . there are over 1,000 styles in each catalog.

McB's Shoes for Women "McB's caters to special women with widths as narrow as AAAAA, as wide as EE, and sizes up to 13."

Marietta Hosiery Designer-quality queen-size panty hose at discount prices.

Mitzi Baker Footwear Women's shoes. Sizes up to 13 medium.

Shoe Express Ladies' big and wide shoes in sizes up to 15AAAAA and WW.

Support Plus "Specialists in Support Hosiery." Men's (up to size 11–13/XL, up to 20" calf) and women's (up to size 4X) support hosiery.

Wide World of Mar-Lou Brand-name footwear up to WW width, some size 15 shoes.

Zala Design Leotards and leggings up to size 7X.

SPECIALTY ITEMS

Ana's Accoutremonts Ana's motto: "We Fit Every Body." A unique idea in costuming . . . you pick a pattern from the brochure, fill out the measurement chart, purchase your own material, then send everything to Ana's. Size makes no difference. You are charged for labor, and the completed costume is returned to you by a guaranteed shipping date. Costumes include Renaissance, Medieval, Roman, Byzantine, Tudor, Pirate, Civil War, Future Fantasy, Cavalier, Mideastern, Norman, Samurai, and Mongol.

Arctic Sheepskin Outlet Beautiful hats (up to 3X), slippers, rugs, mittens (up to size 2X), and headbands.

Arthur M. Rein Custom-fit furs, proper fit absolutely guaranteed. Call for price quotes and further information.

Celtic Costumes Fine woolen cloaks and costumes fitted to your specifications.

Distant Caravans Black leather cavalier gloves up to sizes XL. $30.

Elizabethan Costuming (See the "Books and Computer Programs of Interest to the Seamstress" section.)

Fabulous Fakes "The Luxurious Alternative to Animal Fur." Absolutely beautiful, authentic-looking fake furs, fun furs, and "fabu-leather" in sizes up to 2X. These coats come in either ready-made or in sew-it-yourself kits and are surprisingly affordable.

The Horse's Mouth Historical clothiers for reenactions, weddings, and theater. Custom-tailored, made-to-order period clothing.

Hy Fishman Furs Plus sizes from 14 to 26. The catalog has beautiful furs modeled by gorgeous, large women.

Hinsdale Furriers Always a few items in stock up to size 50. Hinsdale will custom-make furs for any size.

Jalon Enterprises Leather, suede, and silk coats, jackets, and shirts (some with mink or fox collars) in sizes 1X up to 5X.

Jamin' Leathers Leather jackets and pants designed for bikers up to size 64T.

J.C. Penney Scouts Adult Girl Scout uniforms in sizes up to 3X.

Johnni's Treasures Halloween costumes for both adults and children in custom sizes.

Julen Furs Faux fur coats, each individually designed, many fur types, accessories, and styles in sizes through 28. Brochure and fur samples available.

Langlitz Leathers Gorgeous, thick leather jackets, pants, vests . . . even T-shirts and caps . . . made to order. Send them your measurements and they will carefully craft clothing and accessories that you will wear for many years.

Lonely Mountain Forge Quality armor and art metalwork, custom made, for your knight in shining armor. Excellent for battle recreations, Renaissance fairs, or just plain rescuing the damsel or prince of your dreams.

Merlyn Custom Costuming Renaissance clothing, including hooded cloaks, shirts, tunics, Tudor dresses, buccaneer shirts, and Italian Renaissance overdresses in sizes only up to XL. However, Merlyn's is happy to custom-make clothing in any size for both men and women.

Park's Fantasyland Costume Co. Peasant, middle class, nobility. Hats, doublets, breeches, skirts, dirndls, chemises, and more. Sizes 1 up to 54 for adults and children. Custom orders also. If you have a costume sketch, send it to the people at Park's and they will give you an estimate. Rentals and sales.

Quartermaster Military, security/police, fire, EMT and EMS uniforms, T-shirts, jackets, and rain parkas. Most up to size XL, some up to XXL.

Renaissance Dancewear Excellent quality dancewear in sizes up to 2X with custom sizing available. The cotton-Lycra material this company uses is wonderful . . . soft, thick, and stretchy and sure to last for a long time. This dancewear is used by theater, opera, and ballet companies around the country.

Sodhoppers Medieval boots and shoes custom-designed and custom-fit. ("Delivered with haste!")

The Stallari Armory Custom-fit armor for all your Renaissance military occasions. Helmets, breastplates, gauntlets, and leg and arm harnesses in several periods and styles.

Vanson Leathers "At Vanson, leather is an attitude." Hand-cut, double-stitched leather jackets, pants, vests, chaps, greatcoats, and accessories in custom sizes.

Windwalker Moccasins Custom-fit two- or three-button moccasins, perfect for Renaissance fair participation. With toe cap, heel guard, domed top, and rolled leather edging, these are not cheap . . . approximately $200 per pair. Any size foot and leg can be accommodated with their special "Fit Yourself Kit," included in the price.

PERSONAL CARE ITEMS

Ample Hygiene for Ample People Twenty-page booklet written by Nancy Summer with straight talk about cleanliness for large people. Ms. Summer addresses chafing, odor, irritations, and other concerns and presents simple, easy-to-handle solutions. Excellent resource. $5.
SOURCES: Amplestuff

Bath Brush and Sponges Supersoft, extralong-handled. $7.

SOURCES:

AdaptAbility

Harriet Carter

Comfort House

Smith & Nephew

Beauty Salon Capes Plus through custom sizes. $30.

SOURCES: Johnni's Treasures

Betadine Skin Cleanser This is the most effective cleanser for killing the bacteria that thrives in warm, damp places. $8.

SOURCES:

Amplestuff

most local pharmacies

Bidet For those with difficulty using toilet paper or who just want that extra bit of personal cleanliness, these bidets are easy to operate, attach to your toilet seat easily, and use warm air and water. $500.

SOURCES:

AdaptAbility

Hepp Industries

Sanlex International, Inc.

Bidet, Portable A smaller, less-expensive version of the above bidets, these (there are two sizes) are still effective and easy to take with you on trips. $27.

SOURCES: Amplestuff

Booby Bibs (I don't name 'em, I just report 'em.) A handy little device for those of us who are well-endowed.

These clear plastic bibs are perfect for keeping your clothing clean while eating messy foods. $6 for a package of 6.

SOURCES: Liz McGee

Brush/Comb on Handle 20" handle helps with grooming. $35.

SOURCES:

Ableware

Comfort House

Smith & Nephew

ChafeGuard Antifriction cream for use between thighs, under breasts, and wherever you need it. Coming in a form much like solid deodorants, ChafeGuard contains lubricants to prevent chafing and aloe to help heal. $6.

SOURCES:

Support Plus

Mature Wisdom

Foot Brush 24" handle and brush for scrubbing your feet. Also useful when applying medicines. $15.

SOURCES:

Ableware

Avenues Unlimited

AdaptAbility

Enrichments

Sears Home Healthcare

Smith & Nephew

Foot Scrubber This little device attaches to the tile wall inside your shower stall with suction cups. You can rub your feet against it for a comforting massage and cleaning. $14.

SOURCES: Vermont Country Store

Foot Sponge Thin, soft sponge positioned at the end of a 30" handle makes cleaning between your toes easy. $18.
SOURCES: Comfort House

Garment Bag Supersize, 32" × 55", 5" gusset, black. $70.
SOURCES: King Size

Hangers and Hanger Covers Extralarge to securely care for your wardrobe . . . 18" to 21" wide. Price varies according to type and size, from 6 for $6 to 3 for $10.
SOURCES:
 Amplestuff
 Laughing Sisters
 Preferred Living

Incontinence Panty Panties with special leakproof pouches, in sizes up to 3X. $13. Liners: set of 3 for $10.
SOURCES:
 Ambassador Showcase
 Comfort House

Joint Warmers Made of lamb's wool to keep arthritic joints warm (or just for winter wear). Fits up to 20" knee and 11" ankles. $4–$10.
SOURCES: Vermont Country Store

Loofah Back Scrubber Approximately 12" long and 3" wide. Terry cloth backing with rope handles; makes scrubbing your back and other hard-to-reach places easier. $20.

SOURCES:
 Brookstone Hard-to-Find Tools
 Miles Kimball

Lotion Applicator Long-handled applicator with foam pads that hold and distribute lotion and ointments to your back and other hard-to-reach areas. $10.
SOURCES:
 AdaptAbility
 Country Store

Massager This deep massager doesn't fool around when it comes to relieving the ache in tired muscles or improving circulation. Used by professional massage therapists. $94.
SOURCES:
 Amplestuff
 Sears Home Healthcare

Men's Support Brief Back and tummy support in sizes up to 2X. Zipper front. $15.
SOURCES: Ambassador Showcase

Personal Cleanliness Travel Kit A 12" bag of all the items you need to stay shower-fresh while away from home . . . this kit even includes the Ample Hygiene booklet. $27.
SOURCES: Amplestuff

Posture Corrector Crisscrossing your back and shoulders with wide, comfortable bands to help correct upper back posture. $22.
SOURCES: Ambassador Showcase

Posture Support Band Firm support to both stomach and back. Fits from 26" up to 54" waist. These are great for relieving back strain. $13.

SOURCES: Ambassador Showcase

Sanitary Panty Crotch of panty has a flexible plastic shield between layers of cotton knit. In sizes up to 2X. Package of 3 for $15.

SOURCES: Ambassador Showcase

Scrub Sponges (long-handled) A variety of sponges and soap holders to make overall hygiene easier. $3–$9.

SOURCES:
Ableware
AdaptAbility
Amplestuff
Enrichments
Sears Home Healthcare

Socks, Men's Support, running, walking, dress, and cotton tube socks in sizes 12 up to 16. $6–$10.

SOURCES: King Size

Toenail Clipper This clipper has a long handle (18") and a pistol grip to make a much shorter reach of this job. $13.

SOURCES:
Ablewear
Comfort House

Toe Washer Soft sponge mounted on a 30" handle, making cleaning between your toes an easy-to-reach task. $10–$14.

SOURCES:
Ableware
Smith and Nephew

Toilet Paper Tongs Important for maintaining personal hygiene if you just aren't as flexible as you would like to be. $30.

SOURCES:
Ableware
AdaptAbility
Amplestuff
Enrichments
Smith & Nephew

You might also consider using sturdy back scratchers for this job. Stores like Pier 1 Imports sell nice wooden ones for around a dollar apiece. Plastic-coated tongs can also work.

Towels, Extralong Wrap yourself up in these big, fluffy towels. Average 102" long. $38–$50.

SOURCES:
Amplestuff
King Size
Mour to Dri

Tummy Band Girdle Special straps adjust with a wide band of Velcro, giving you control over how much support you use. In sizes up to 44" waist. $17.

SOURCES: Ambassador Showcase

Umbrellas Extralarge umbrellas are great for people with more to protect from the rain. $25–$75.

SOURCES:

Basta Sole

Making It Big

Uncle Sam Umbrella Shop

Watches Extralong bands fit wrists up to 12". $45.
SOURCES: King Size

Water Shoes Rubber-soled with Velcro closure straps and elastic drawcords, adjust to a comfortable fit. $30.
SOURCES: King Size

Wearable Napkins Proportioned for the larger person and available in two designs. $18.
SOURCES: Amplestuff

Wigs Not all wigs fit the same. These mail-order companies have beautiful wigs in large and adjustable sizes. The selection is really excellent; these wigs look nothing like the ones of twenty years ago. The styles are modern and very realistic looking. Prices vary, generally $35 to $125.
SOURCES: Beauty Trends

Wonder Buttons These little buttons work with the collar button on your blouse or shirt and increase the collar by half a size. $2 each; set of 2 for $3.50.
SOURCES:

Clotilde

Harriet Carter

Vermont Country Store

BOOKS, FASHION GUIDES, MAGAZINES, AND IMAGE CONSULTANTS

BBW (*Big Beautiful Woman Magazine*)

BBW is the original fashion magazine for plus-size women. One-year subscription: $10 in the United States, $20 foreign.

Beauty comes in all sizes.

Belle Quarterly fashion/lifestyle magazine for African-American women of size. One-year subscription: $13.

The Big Beauty Book: Glamour for the Fuller-Figure Woman Written by Ann

Harper (Holt, Rinehart, & Winston, 1983).

Big Clothes for Big Men Updated regularly; written by Freda Rosenberg. Sources of outerwear, officewear, work clothes, casuals, shoes, underwear, and more.
SOURCES: Freda Rosenberg

Breaking All the Rules Written by Nancy Roberts (Viking Press, 1987). With an emphasis on exercise for feeling better, not for weight loss, this book tells of one woman's struggle with self-acceptance. The chapters on clothing were especially good.

There has been so much nonsense written about what big women should and should not wear that I hardly know where to start. All of the so-called rules of "fat dressing" are based on the premise that we should be trying to make ourselves look slimmer. I am always infuriated when I read some article aimed at big women, or see in some catalogue for outsize clothes, descriptions of clothes that tell you how much thinner they make your arms look or how they flatter you by fitting loosely and covering up a "protruding tum."

Highly recommended.

Emerging Visions Enterprises (EVE) Catherine Schuller (plus-size model, writer, and spokesperson) and Suzan Nanfeldt (image consultant, writer, and speaker) share this consulting venture. They teach image improvement for plus-size women through workshops, speaking engagements, and writing. They offer computerized ten-page body proportion/style analysis, fashion consulting, and information on the ins and outs of plus-size modeling. Lately, department stores and other fashion outlets are using EVE's services to learn how to provide for their larger customers.

Freda's Secrets Written by Freda Rosenberg; updated regularly. Guide to large women's fashions.
SOURCES: Freda Rosenberg

Full Style: Style and Fashion for the Fuller Figure Written by Karen Jackson (self-published, 1993). This book actually falls somewhere between book and newsletter. Ms. Jackson, who used to sell clothing through her mail-order business, gives tips on finding and choosing clothing and accessories, working with a tailor or dressmaker, and makeup.
SOURCES: K. S. Jackson

Nothing in Moderation Small newsletter from the owner of a store by the same name in Oak Park, Illinois. This is mostly a sales circular, but there are also some interesting updates on size acceptance. Write for subscription information.

P.S. Style This bimonthly newsletter's mission is to "identify resources and provide counsel to help plus-size women look their best." This excellent resource gives you real help in dealing with all sorts of figures in all sizes. For up-to-date news on designers, the newest fashions, and the right look for you, check this one out. Fashions are modeled by plus-size women, generally sizes 14 to 16. One-year subscription: $30.

Plus Style: The Plus Size Guide to Looking Great Written by Suzan Nanfeldt (Plume Books, 1996). Humorous, down-to-earth instructions for improved self-esteem and increased confidence in selecting clothing, makeup, and hairstyles that best suit your personality and body. This book doesn't teach you how to look thinner . . . it does better than that. It teaches you how to look your best at any size.

Style Is Not a Size—Looking and Feeling Great in the Body You Have Written by Hara Estroff Marano (Bantam Books, 1991). Practical clothing tips.

Yarnome Full Figure Woman "Plus-size women now have a fresh, new resource on how to look good and feel great every other month." (Yarnome is the name of the daughter of the founders of this publication.) Keeping tabs on who's who in the large-size fashion industry, *Yarnome Full Figure Woman* is an ambitious production. Look for issues that cover plus-size models and designers, mail-order fashions, holiday shopping, intimate apparel, and accessories. Published bimonthly. Two-year subscription: $9.95.

PHOTOGRAPHERS

Big, Beautiful Images Boudoir, portrait, glamour, and model portfolios for the big, beautiful woman.

Big in Pictures Makeover photography in your own home. This company, based in England, is run by a pair of big, beautiful photographers who understand your concerns.

Bob Abrams Photography "I specialize in fashion portfolios for the full-figured woman."

Enlargements Glamour makeover and photo session for large women with a wardrobe provided by the photographer, Ed Harn.

Specialty Photography by Laurice Makeover and photo sessions for large women.

PAGEANTS

Large Lovely Lady Beauty Pageant For eighteen-plus-year-old, size 14-plus ladies. The event features modeling workshops and receptions and is attended by model scouts. Prizes are offered, and the winner receives $1,000, a modeling contract, cosmetics, jewelry, and television appearances. The tenth annual pageant was held in late April 1994. Sponsored by Dimensions (the organization, not the magazine).

Miss Plus USA Pageant and Convention Produced by Dimensions Plus-Size Models, Marshall Field's Department Stores, and Carole Little II Dresses, this event is celebrating its twelfth year and is held in conjunction with the annual Miss Windy City Pageant. Prizes have included cruises, cash, modeling contracts, cosmetics, jewelry, gift certificates, and television appearances. Contact Dimensions Plus Models.

Ms. U.S. Plus U.S. Plus Pageants, Inc. produces local and national pageants for contestants from age fourteen and size 14. The national pageant, Ms. U.S. Plus, was first held in April 1996 and may be entered at the state level (if a pageant is held in your state) or at the national level. The winner received the official crown, a trophy, sash, cash award, and sponsorship awards. Categories included Best Photogenic and Congeniality.

MODELING OPPORTUNITIES

Aria Uses models between 5'8" and 5'10" tall, sizes 12 to 16. Send pictures or go to open call on Wednesdays at 5:00 P.M. in Chicago, Illinois.

BBW The magazine conducts yearly model searches. Check the fall issue for information. Fifty models are selected, one to represent each state. Their photos are featured in the magazine and each receives a prize. In 1996 the four first-place winners received a five-day cruise, on which they participated in fashion shows and photography sessions.

Beautiful Women's Collection Model Search Yearly search for new catalog models, open to all women ages eighteen and up; $25 entry fee. Contact: Heinz Gift Shop (send a self-addressed, stamped envelope for information each year).

Big, Bold & Beautiful Uses models 5'8" and over, sizes 12 to 20. Send photos with self-addressed, stamped envelope.

Bizon Uses models 5'7" and over, sizes 14 to 18. Send photos (professional only).

Casablanca Uses models 5'8" and over, sizes 14 and up. Send photos with SASE or call for an appointment in Atlanta, Georgia.

Chic Full Figure Fashion Expo Always on the lookout for runway models—men, women, and children—for fall expo in Chicago. All sizes considered. Models chosen will be required to attend a six-week training session. Contact: Chic Full Figure Fashion.

Chic Full Figure Fashion Newspaper Calendar Model Search Submit a photo of yourself for consideration. Models chosen will appear in CFFF's newsletter/calendar. Must be eighteen or older. Contact Chic Full Figure Fashion.

Clothz Biz Women sizes 14 to 32 for catalog and national advertising. No experience necessary.

Cunningham, Escott, Dipine (CED) Uses models 5'8" and over, sizes 10 to 18. Send photos with SASE or call and ask about next open call in Los Angeles, California.

David & Lee Model Agency Uses models 5'8" and up, sizes 14 up to 18. Send photos.

Dimensions Plus-Size Model Agency Uses models 5'8" and up, sizes 14 up to

24. Send photos and SASE. Dimensions holds a Large Lovely Lady Beauty Pageant in Chicago every April.

Elite Model Management Uses models 5'8" to 5'10", sizes 14 up to 16. Phone for appointment in Chicago, Ilinois, or send photos with SASE.

Extra! This women's magazine is always looking for models.

Fontaine Agency Uses models 5'8" and up, sizes 12 up to 18.

Ford 12+/Big Beauties Uses models 5'9" and up, sizes 12 up to 16.

Greater Woman Model Search Models for fashion videos, sizes 14 up to supersize; mature models 40 years and older; petite plus models under 5'4".

Helen Wells Agency Uses models 5'8" and up, sizes 16 up to 24, ages 18 up to 50. Send photos with self-addressed, stamped envelope.

Kim Dawson Agency Call ahead to see what current requirements are or send photos with SASE.

Look Uses models 5'8" to 5'10", sizes 12 to 16, any age. Send photos and self-addressed, stamped envelope or attend open call on Wednesdays at 2:00 P.M. in San Francisco, California.

Lynell's World of Difference Production Company Full-figured fashion shows and models.

Michelle Pommier Uses models 5'8" and up, sizes 14 to 18. Send photos with self-addressed, stamped envelope.

Mitchell Management Uses models 5'8" and up, sizes 14 to 20. Send photos with self-addressed, stamped envelope or attend open call on Wednesdays at 1:30 P.M. in San Francisco, California.

Next Management Uses models 5'8" and up, sizes 14 to 18, twenty-one years of age and over. Attend open call, Monday through Friday, 11:00 A.M. in West Hollywood, California.

Obelisk Modeling and Talent Agency Uses models of any size.

oooO Baby Baby Productions Models for advertising, fashion shows, magazines, and glamour assignments. If you are poised and self-assured, over size 14, and up to size 26/28, please send both a close-up snapshot and a full-length pose for consideration. Include the following information: height, weight, dress size, availability (days or only weekends). Tell them why and what types of modeling you are interested in and about any prior modeling experience you have. Include a self-addressed, stamped envelope for return of photographs.

Plus Models Management Ltd. Uses models 5'8" and up, sizes 12 to 20; also handles plus petites, 5'2", sizes 16 to 18. Open calls on Tuesday and Thursday in New York. Send or bring photos.

Radiance Magazine publishes annual Radiant Readers photo spread and other modeling needs.

SMLA Modeling Agency Uses models 5'8" to 5'11", sizes 10 to 22. Hair must be shoulder-length or shorter. Send your portfolio (required) and call for an appointment in Los Angeles, California.

Specialty Models Considers models of all sizes. Send photos with self-addressed, stamped envelope.

Stars, the Agency Uses models 5'9" and up, sizes 12 to 18. Send photos with self-addressed, stamped envelope.

Stars Casting Uses models 5'8" and up, sizes 16 to 22, any age. Phone for information on next open call in Washington, D.C.

Suzanne's Uses models 5'9" to 5'10", sizes 12 to 18, any age. Send photos with self-addressed, stamped envelope or call for information on next open call in Chicago, Illinois.

T.H.E. Uses models 5'9" and up, sizes 16 to 18, any age. Attend open call on Wednesdays at 10:00 A.M. in Washington, D.C.

Three West Casting Uses models 5'8" to 5'11", sizes 16 to 20, any age. Send photos with SASE; phone for information about next open call in Baltimore, Maryland.

Wilhelmina Uses models 5'9" and up, sizes 10 to 18. Also uses some plus petite, 5'4" and under, sizes 14 to 18. Send photos with SASE.

If you are interested in pursuing a career in modeling, be sure and check out *The Ultimate Guide for Plus-Size Modeling*, a book by Catherine Schuller and Susan Nanfeldt of Emerging Visions Enterprises. It's full of excellent information that may just give you the edge you need to succeed.

➡ If any data listed in this chapter need to be corrected, please let me know. If you know of a service or product useful to people of size, please write to me about it. The information may be made available to readers through the newsletter "Size Wise Update!," the Size Wise web site, or through possible future revisions of this book.

PERSONAL GLIMPSE:
RANDY

Randy is a thirty-seven-year-old writer for a large corporation.
Big even as a child, he dieted often and sometimes achieved
"normal" weight. Eventually he came to realize that not only
did he not accept the pressure to be thin, he *wanted* to be
big. With that realization, he gave up dieting for good.

I've dieted ever since I can remember breathing, but never with any real success until junior high school. I got down to 165 and kept it off through college. It wasn't what I wanted or expected it to be. I gained the weight back again. I've been a lot happier now that I have thought it through for myself.

I went through several years as a "normal-sized" person, expecting my life to change. Really, it didn't. At least not in the ways I had expected. I had expected more career success, I expected to be more attractive to more people, I expected to feel better. The interesting thing is I actually felt worse. It didn't make me feel more active or more energetic. I was surprised at that. I had thought feeling lighter would mean I could do more or would want to do more. But that really wasn't the case. I didn't feel like a whole person. I didn't feel like the me I had always known. I felt ordinary and as if my personal power had been reduced. When I say "power" it's not physical power. It's more of a completion; like I'm more fully expressed.

Not only was I not happy being thin, it was strange. It was almost like losing a part of me. Something was missing. It also seemed like my personality had changed. I wasn't able to express my inner self as fully as I could as a fat person. I hadn't lost the weight for me; I was motivated by outside forces and opinions. Once I realized I had bought into a belief system that really wasn't my own, the process of feeling better began. I look at myself now and remember when I was a little kid. I'd see pictures of people I wanted to look like, and I find that I have pretty much gotten there. I'm what I had always thought I would be or wanted to be.

My parents had a book about human potentials/norms. One section talked about the biggest and smallest, thinnest and fattest. That kind of thing. There were some pictures of pygmies and a sumo wrestler, and I wanted to look like the wrestler. I was getting all of the negative reinforcements saying, "No, that's bad," but on the inside was saying, "No, that's not bad at all." I still have that dichotomy. I don't know if we ever are able to totally feel one way or the other. When people say something painful it still affects me, but I don't have so much of a problem because it's their judgment, their value system.

I am absolutely comfortable talking about being fat. I never shy away from the "f" word . . . ever. In fact, I got a wonderful comment from a woman I work with who is quite large and was shocked when I first came to the department because she had never heard anyone use the "f" word in public and be so open and positive about it. She told her therapist that she was just so blown away by it. Over the course of months she grew to consider me her sort of role model. It's one of the reasons I am so vocal about it. It's not that I throw it in people's faces and challenge them. It's not meant to be argumentative, it's meant to ease the way, to bring it out in the open. To have to pretend I'm not fat is ludicrous. You'd be surprised how many people still say, "Oh, no you're not! You're not fat!" It's insulting. I think what they are trying to say is, "Yeah, you're fat but it's okay on you."

I get the usual comments from people, but, surprisingly, the more open I am about being fat and the older I get and the more positive I become, the less crap I get about being fat. To me, we are all different and we all have different likes and dislikes. I don't ever hear people say, "Gee, you're blond! You're disgusting." Why would it be okay to say, "Fat people make me sick"? We are so trained to believe what they are telling us. Even inside we are wondering, "Well, how do I feel about being fat? Maybe I *am* a disgusting pig."

When at a restaurant or other public place, if some of the chairs have arms on them and some don't, I think nothing of asking for the one without. Or trading or moving the chairs around. I'll just tell people it's not comfortable for me to sit in a booth. It doesn't embarrass me anymore. I'm not pushy about it, but I don't ask in an apologetic way. I am large, and I expect to be treated in an accommodating way. I went to a movie theater here in the Bay Area recently. The seating was atrocious. By the time I got out of there I was bruised on both thighs. Even the chairs at work, I've noticed, make the sides of my legs sore.

I hate clothes shopping. I wish I could wear certain clothes and they would look the way I see them in my mind. The choices are limited, very unflattering nine times out of ten, and expensive. It's not that I think clothes look better on thin people; they have more choices and more ways to find things that flatter them as individuals than we have. For men, unless you like wearing those god-awful safari shirts, you can be hard-pressed to find something.

There is no reason for being fat to stop you from doing anything. It's never been hampering in my career. I really think you need to look within yourself and determine what your own real feelings are . . . on this or any other issue in your life. I don't find [being fat] ugly in myself, so I don't know what it's like to be fat and totally repulsed. A lot of that comes from outside. You should live your life according to how you see fit.

We are all here and we are all given a unique personality, mind, and body. We have to explore the universe in our own unique ways. A lot of the lessons we have to learn may be unpleasant, but they're still learning experiences. You just have to make the best of them you can. We are all valid just the way we are.

"... Straight for the Wicker"

Being fat is like being a member of a different race. Being an alien. Being sick. People are fatophobic. They are petrified that obesity is contagious. They are scared shitless that they will somehow catch your fatness. That if you move into their neighborhood, they will stop exercising, stop eating properly, and begin to look like you.

You think people treat us fatties differently. You invite us over to your house, never for dinner, and when you answer the door, you say, "Come on in and sit on this concrete sofa." Or, "Try our new steel-reinforced chair."

I always head straight for the wicker.

From Goodbye Jumbo, Hello Cruel World, *by Louie Anderson.*

4

IT'S A SMALL WORLD AFTER ALL!

The more a person deviates from average size, the more difficult it becomes to find comfortable, secure accommodations. All sorts of situations present the potential for embarrassment and discomfort. Going to restaurants, theaters, medical offices, amusement parks, or even using public transportation presents the potential for a humiliating experience, to say nothing of being unable to enjoy being out in the world with others.

One car manufacturer mentioned to me that cars are designed for the "95 percent man." That leaves 5 percent of the population in this country who just don't fit behind the wheel of a car. An even larger number may fit but they sure aren't comfortable . . . or safe.

I recently had to wait at a Midas Muffler shop for over two hours while having some work done. There were several chairs in the waiting area, all exactly the same—metal with very uncomfortable arms that bruised my hips. Is it asking so much that businesses provide armless seating? This certainly has not been my only experience with inadequate seating. Of course, if a company just simply has too much business, perhaps it can afford to alienate one third of the adult population. But it seems like bad policy to me.

It can be difficult to get the rest of the world to satisfy our needs. Unfortunately, many people withdraw as they gain weight, staying home rather than risking embarrassment. Leading a life of seclusion and missing out on experiences just because of poor accommodations is a terrible waste. It is possible to furnish your home with seating that fits both your lifestyle and your hips. We can also work on improving public accommodations. Read on.

This chapter offers tips for buying sturdy, attractive furniture and ways to make your home safer and more comfortable, to find roomy transportation, and to locate comfortable hotels, restaurants, and theater and recreation possibilities. And it ends in the same place life does . . . the funeral home.

•
Built for Comfort, Not for Speed
•

GENERAL HOUSEHOLD HELPS

Door Hinge
By Duromatic, this hinge adds two inches to any doorway. Installation is simple, requiring only screws and a screwdriver. $22.
SOURCES:
  Accessibility
  AdaptAbility
  Sears Home Healthcare

Dust Pan and Brush, Long-handled Allows easier pickup of items and dirt from the floor without bending. $14.
SOURCES:
  AdaptAbility
  Enrichments

Dusters, Long Reach 80" long handles eliminate the need for climbing to dust hard-to-reach areas. $23/$35.
SOURCES: Enrichments

Elevators If climbing stairs has become impossible for you, you don't have to be limited to one story of your home. An in-home elevator with a capacity of up to 750 pounds is available. The price on these units varies considerably, affected by style, size, and the structure you intend to put it into.
SOURCES:
  Cheney
  Inclinator

Grabbers/Reachers There are a lot of grabbers out there—these items extend your reach to help you pick things up off the floor or off high shelves. Some of the posts are solid, some extendible; there is some difference in length also. Handles vary, and the devices on the end that do the actual picking up range from simple tongs to more complicated spring systems. $25–$30.
SOURCES:
  Ableware (big variety)
  Accessibility
  AdaptAbility
  Amplestuff

Avenues Unlimited

Brookstone Hard-to-Find Tools

Bruce Medical Supply

CME Medical Equipment

Can-Do Products

Comfort House

Enrichments (has one with a locking grip)

Independent Living Aids

J.C. Penney Special Needs

MailHawk Mfg. Company (this reacher was designed for daily use by rural mail carriers and comes in three lengths—20", 28", and 42"). Under $15.

Sears Home Healthcare

Support Plus

Hammocks According to Swings 'N Things, a well-built hammock can support up to 500 or 1,000 pounds, depending on the style you choose. Write to them for a brochure explaining the construction, support, and comfort of a hammock. Other catalogs offering hammocks generally mention a weight capacity of around 500 pounds. $100 (stands extra).

SOURCES:

L.L. Bean

Brookstone

Hangouts

Preferred Living

Swings 'N Things

Wyoming River Rafters

Ladders, Rescue This is an item we hope to never need, but if ever there is a fire in your home it may just save your family's lives. Rated to hold up to 700 pounds, these ladders come in two-, three-, and five-story lengths. $50–$150.

SOURCES: Preferred Living

Lift Chair With a 27" wide seat, this chair is equipped to comfortably support someone of up to 800 pounds and assist in lifting from a sitting to a standing position. $700–$900.

SOURCES: Air Physics

Lift Seat This portable seat can lift a person of up to 400 pounds and can be of enormous assistance if you have back problems or other difficulties in getting up from a sitting position. $500–$900.

SOURCES: Air Physics

Light Bulb Changer, Long-handled If you feel unsafe climbing up on stools or chairs to change ceiling light bulbs, here is a great help. The shaft of this tool is 48" long, allowing you to reach just about any bulb. $10.

SOURCES: AdaptAbility

Rolling Workseat With an 18" seat height and heavy-duty frame (400-pound capacity), this sturdy little seat on wheels can be pretty helpful for many tasks. $90.

SOURCES: Preferred Living

Standing Stool These are great for support while doing dishes or cooking meals.

The sturdiest I was able to find says it will support up to 300 pounds. $90.

SOURCES:

Can-Do Products

Enrichments

Mature Wisdom

Step Stool   A good, sturdy step stool is invaluable. The Levenger model is made for use in a library but is lightweight (15 pounds) and can be used anywhere. Made of solid hardwood, it should last a lifetime. $180. Chef's World has a step stool that supports up to 500 pounds. $50.

SOURCES:

Levenger

Chef's World

Vacuum Cleaner Extended Reach   Add twenty feet of crushproof hose to upright and canister-type vacuums, allowing you to easily clean stairs. $30. A 6' sturdy wand will help you vacuum ceiling debris. $30.

SOURCES: AdaptAbility

UPHOLSTERED FURNITURE

When purchasing upholstered furniture it can be difficult to tell exactly what you are getting. With a little luck you might happen upon a salesperson who not only knows what he is talking about but who is also honest enough to steer you right. Don't judge a piece by looks or price tag. Go shopping armed with a little knowledge, be ready to do some testing, and you will end up with sturdy, durable, lovely pieces.

Look for frames made of 3/4" (minimum) kiln-dried hardwood boards (such as oak, maple, and ash) in all of the critical areas. Hardwoods are not only sturdier but hold fasteners more securely and are less likely to warp. Softer woods are acceptable in less-important structural areas.

There should be plenty of reinforcements at high-stress points. It is a good idea to tip your old couch or chair over and see where it has worn out. This will help you evaluate new pieces. Look for a combination of glue, wood dowels, bolts, screws, and corner braces holding the frame together. Makers of cheap furniture often scrimp. The strongest furniture is double or triple doweled. You aren't likely to find extra braces and doweling except in the more expensive lines.

If you are purchasing a couch, consider models that have a platform base (no legs). If you are looking at one with legs, look for a center leg on the frame for additional support.

Ask the salesperson to remove the dust cover on the underside of the piece to allow you to check the springs. The springs of the sofa or chair should be thick, coiled, spaced no more than five inches apart, and held together by tie wires.

Always sit on a chair or sofa before purchasing it. You are looking not only for fit and comfort, but for any odd squeaks, groans, or movements. If it feels unstable, pass it by. Bounce up and down, wiggle it, lift up one end by the arm. If it doesn't feel rigid or if it creaks, look elsewhere.

Cushions are filled with foam that comes in varying densities. The denser the cushion, the longer-lasting you can expect it to be. Furniture manufacturers generally offer a statement about the expected lifetime of a cushion. Ask to see it. Never settle for shredded foam cushions. They tend to become lumpy and lose their shape quickly. Make sure the cushions are of uniform size, are identical on both sides (so you can reverse them), and have zippers (so they can be cleaned easily). The purchase of an extra set of cushions will greatly extend the life of your new couch.

Lift Chairs/Cushions There are several devices to help a person get out of chairs, from cushions with springs that push up when a lever is pressed to motorized chairs that lift entirely up and forward. (I see a Chevy Chase comedy routine in here somewhere.) The problem is that most of them are designed with a top weight limit of around 200 to 300 pounds.

SOURCES: Sears Home Healthcare offers one recliner with a 20" seat and a 350-pound weight capacity ($1,700), and another with a 24.5" seat and a 350-pound weight capacity ($2,500).

J.C. Penney's Flexsteel lift recliner has a weight capacity of 300 pounds. $900.

Recliner Franklin Big Man's—with extra lumbar support pad, hardwood and plywood frames, and cowled, glued, and stapled construction. Seat is 40" wide by 43" deep.

SOURCES: J.C. Penney Special Needs. $550.

FURNITURE BY MAIL

The following companies offer handcrafted and/or custom-made, sturdy furniture through mail order and are worth checking into.

Bartley Collection Kits for building your own solid wood (cherry or mahogany) reproduction furniture.

Butcher Block & More Furniture Solid oak furniture.

Classic Country Chairs Handcrafted Adirondack chairs, wonderful for relaxing in your yard.

Concepts in Comfort Custom-designed and -built furniture.

Cornucopia Early American and primitive-style chairs, handmade. This company carries some beautiful rocking chairs.

Crossroads Country Store Assemble your own kits of solid pine furniture.

E. T. Moore Company Custom pine furniture.

Earnest Thompson Handcrafted Southwestern-style furniture.

Franklin Custom Furniture Custom-built sofas and chairs.

Frontier Furniture Handmade log furniture. Not exactly for a formal dining room, this practical furniture will nonetheless appeal to many.

Furniture Makers Guild King-size chairs for the king-size person. Highly recommended.

Homestead Furniture Handcrafted oak, cherry, and pine country furniture.

Hunt Galleries, Inc. Custom-made chairs, sofas, and benches.

Karl's Woodworking Mill Handcrafted solid wood furniture.

Klein Design, Inc. Solid oak rockers, chairs, and sofas.

Mack and Rodel Cabinet Makers Custom hardwood furniture with old-world craftsmanship.

Olde Mill House Shoppe Handcrafted country-style furniture.

River Bend Chair Company Handmade Windsor chairs.

Sawtooth Valley Woodcrafts Custom-made beds, chairs, and couches.

This End Up Wonderful, sturdy, comfortable couches, chairs, beds, futons, and outdoor furniture. This company has stores all over the country but also offers mail-order service. Classy and very reasonably priced. Highly recommended.

Walpole Woodworkers Handcrafted natural cedar furniture.

William James Roth Handcrafted period reproductions and custom-made furnishings.

MATTRESSES AND BEDS

Comfort, comfort, comfort. You spend a third of your life in bed, and the time you spend there is very important. A good night's sleep makes a world of difference in how the next day goes. Choose a good solid frame, a mattress that supports your body well, and settle in with a cozy pile of blankets and pillows for a rejuvenating rest.

This is no time for shyness. If you are going to purchase a mattress, you have to try it out. Go to the showroom and lie down. Make yourself comfortable. If you have a sleeping buddy, shop together.

Always buy the mattress and box springs as a set. They work as a team. Innerspring mattresses are the most popular choice. The more coils the better (there should be at least 375 in a queen mattress, 450 for a king).

Bed Wedge Gives a gradual lift to your shoulders and head to provide more comfort. $18.

SOURCES: AdaptAbility

Amish Country Collection Early American–look rustic bedroom furniture.

Bartley Collection Kits for building your own hardwood beds.

Brass Beds Direct Custom-made solid-brass beds.

Country Bed Shop Specializes in custom work, seventeenth- and eighteenth-century beds and other furnishings.

Craftmatic Comfort Mfg. Adjustable beds.

18th Century Woodworks Handmade Colonial-style beds.

Electropedic Products Adjustable beds.

Lisa Victoria Beds Custom-designed brass beds.

Wonderbed Mfg. Adjustable beds.

BATHROOMS

To my way of thinking, the ultimate luxury in life is a big, deep bathtub with whirlpool jets. Companies listed here provide some wonderful choices.

Kohler Company Whirlpool baths up to 64" wide and 24" deep. Pure heaven. If you would like to design a more comfortable, practical shower, they offer several shower alternatives and components for creating shower stalls in different shapes and sizes.

Ole Fashion Things Beautiful, big, old-style claw-foot bathtubs.

Tennessee Tub, Inc. Restored antique claw-foot bathtubs.

SPECIAL ITEMS

Bathtub Grab Bar
Makes getting in and out of the bath a lot safer. Several styles are available, including vertical and horizontal bars. Some clamp onto the side of your tub, others attach to the wall. $15–$50.

SOURCES:

Ableware

AdaptAbility

Avenues Unlimited

Brookstone Hard-to-Find Tools

Bruce Medical Supply

Can-Do Products

Comfort House

Enrichments

Hanover House

Independent Living Aids

Miles Kimball

Sears Home Healthcare

Support Plus

Bath Seats Tubular frames designed to fit within a standard bathtub, these are perfect for sitting while bathing or showering. $200–$300.

SOURCES: ConvaQuip offers three versions, each designed to support up to 650 pounds.

Bath Transfer Benches For assistance getting into the bathtub without the worry of stumbling, this bench supports up to 650 pounds. $550. Benches with lower weight limits are available from any of the sources listed under "Bathtub Grab Bars."

SOURCES: ConvaQuip

Bathtub Scrubbers 24" to 35" handles make scrubbing the tub easier. $6.

SOURCES:

AdaptAbility

Miles Kimball

Hanover House

Commode Chairs There are several types of commode chairs with a variety of sizes. Some have two arms, others are designed with the right or left arm missing or are completely armless. They range from one version that has 24" between the arms and is certified to sup-

port up to 850 pounds to one that is 36" wide, weight certified up to 1,500 pounds. $570–$750.

SOURCES: ConvaQuip

Shower Chair Wheeled for easy transport into shower stalls, these chairs provide a comfortable place to sit. $300–$740.

SOURCES: ConvaQuip offers three models, from one with a 22" width between arms, designed to support up to 250 pounds, to one with a 26" width between arms, supporting up to 650 lbs.

Shower Spray, Hand-Held Makes it easy to wash all parts of your body, allowing you to get all-over clean. These devices can be found at most home improvement centers or through catalogs. The people at Amplestuff recommend one in particular, the Super Saver. $30.

SOURCES: Amplestuff

Toilet Seats As with every other product designed to support humans, toilet seats sometimes are just not up to the challenge of providing a long-lasting place of comfort in our lives. The most common problem involves the little rubber feet on the underside of the seat. These often flatten or split. According to the *Ample Shopper*, issue #5, models are available that have four, not the more standard two, bumpers. They recommend that you search out the Sanderson company's Magnolia 200WB or 3100TM (elongated) seat, carried by Wal-Mart, True Value, Ace Hardware, and other home supply stores.

OUTDOOR FURNITURE

Adirondack Designs Redwood chairs and love seats.

Bench Manufacturing Cast-iron and wood benches.

Canterbury Designs, Inc. Cast-iron and aluminum benches.

Classic Country Chairs Teak, mahogany, and birch Adirondack chairs.

Kenneth D. Lynch & Sons Cast-iron, wrought-iron, stone, concrete, and wood benches.

Lyon-Shaw Wrought-iron gliders.

Dan Wilson & Company Custom-made mahogany garden furniture.

OFFICE ENVIRONMENT

•Office Chairs•

If you are one of those thousands of people who spend eight hours a day sitting at a desk, I don't have to tell you how important and how difficult it is to find a comfortable, durable chair. If it is time to replace the chair you currently use, keep the following considerations in mind.

Adjustability is of prime importance when selecting a chair. The more modifications you are able to make for your own body's needs, the better. Some chairs conform automatically to a person's weight distribution. Others depend on levers and knobs that are adjusted manually. You should at the very least be able to align the seat's height and the degree of tilt to the back of the chair. Look for a chair that allows you to sit with your heels comfortably resting on the floor.

Casters on a chair will help you move about more easily. This may be important when moving into or out of a chair or in turning from one area of work to another. Keep in mind, however, that casters are often the weakest part of a chair and can break or bend. Chairs with casters generally have a smaller footprint, making them a bit less stable.

Armrests can be helpful if you must hold your arms in the same position for a long period of time, but they limit the seat size. If you want armrests, be sure to sit in the chair for a period of time to make sure there is plenty of hip room.

The foam padding in the seat of a chair needs to be firm. Stand by the chair and press down hard with your hands. You shouldn't be able to readily feel the frame of the chair. Ask the salesclerk what filling is used. Progressive density molded polyurethane foam is the best. Slab foam over rubber webbing is also acceptable.

AliMed This company offers several office chairs designed for people 250 to 650 pounds. $650+.

Global Business Furniture There are several pieces of sturdy, comfortable furniture in this catalog, including some with adjustable arms that can be moved from side to side as well as removed completely. Of particular interest are an executive seat with a 23.5" wide by 21" deep seat and the "Excalibur" chair, with a 32" wide by 30" deep seat; each supports up to 500 pounds and has a six-prong, extrasturdy base.

K-Log Company of Illinois Has a chair with a seat depth of 21", width 23". It comes with a five-year warranty guaranteed for people up to 500 pounds. Are you sitting down? This chair lists at $1,175 (but can be purchased through their catalog for about $735).

Mormax The BioFit+ Size chair looks especially sturdy and comfortable. The chair seat is 26" wide x 16.5" deep with a 3"-thick dense foam seat pad over a heavy-duty multiple hardwood, steel-reinforced seat board. The seat back has adjustable lumbar support. The chair is supported on a base of 1.5"-diameter steel tubing with a 30" leg span, giving it excellent balance. Sounds like a real workhorse, and it is. But not only is it sturdy, it is also attractive. It is designed to comfortably hold someone up to 650 pounds and comes with a warranty of ten years . . . even on the pneumatic seat height control. Each chair is custom built, requiring a wait of about four to six weeks. You can choose from fourteen colors of cloth upholstery and eleven colors of vinyl upholstery. The chair is available with arms and/or casters if you like. $600 without casters; $735 with casters. Arms $70 additional.

This same company offers two other chairs, one designed for people weighing between 200 and 350 pounds and another for those under 200 pounds. Mormax is also interested in designing and distributing other items of use to large people. Any suggestions for them?

Therapeutic Gloves For those of us who spend hours typing (or sewing, quilting, or anything else that exercises the hands), these magic gloves fit snugly over the wrist to just below the fingers, giving support and gentle massage. Sizes 2 to 5 (there is a measurement chart in the catalog). $16.

SOURCES: Clotilde

TRANSPORTATION

•Automobiles•

It is difficult to say which cars will "fit" and which won't. So many variables come into play. Not only body size, but body shape is important. Short people with ample tummies have a different problem than do their long-legged, evenly proportioned but large counterparts.

In the end, you are just going to have to try on the car. Don't be shy, no matter how many people are hovering around. This is a major purchase, and you not only have every right to be satisfied with it, your safety could be at stake. When you have located a car that seems right, it may be smart to rent one exactly like it for a few days, just to see how comfortable with it you will be.

Here are some things to consider when shopping for a car.

- Tilt steering wheels give you more room, not only when driving but also when getting in and out of the car.
- As a general rule, two-door cars allow easier access (to the front seats anyway).
- The height of a car is important. Some are really low-slung, and getting out of them can be a problem. Some of the taller cars look as if a ladder is needed for climbing in and out.
- Driver seats that adjust electrically are very convenient, but they can also cut the amount of space available by quite a bit . . . sometimes an inch or more.
- Bucket seats are generally less roomy than bench seats.
- Be sure to try the seat belt. Its angle may cut into you uncomfortably. Also, the clasp end that sticks out from the seat may dig into your leg.
- Is the control panel laid out comfortably for you? Can you reach the radio . . . heater . . . wipers, and other controls without driving the car off the road?

It is possible to have some features customized at a body shop if you can't find something suitable. A smaller steering wheel can replace the standard one (though this is definitely not recommended in cars equipped with a driver's-side air bag), front seat tracks can be welded to a position farther back (only helpful if your legs are long enough to reach the pedals), special wooden pedal blocks can be purchased to extend their reach, longer seat belts can be installed, and seat belt extenders are available through your car dealership (ask before you purchase a car—some manufacturers don't make these available and you may have to pay extra to have a longer belt installed). State laws vary, so be sure to check before purchasing a car with plans to make adjustments. Above all, get everything in writing before signing any contracts. Don't get stuck with a car that doesn't fit.

Accu-Back Back Support Orthopedic back support that adjusts in seconds. $37.
Sources: Amplestuff

Car Slide This clever device helps you slide easily in and out of car seats. Made of denim and vinyl, it folds easily to take along with you. $72.
Sources: Ableware

Steering Wheel This 10" wheel is about 5" smaller than the average steering wheel, giving the driver more space. People who use these tell me it doesn't take long at all to adjust to the new "feel" of driving. Either you or your mechanic can install it. Make sure your state allows the use of smaller steering wheels. $34. (Adapter kit is available and is required. $22.)

SOURCES: Amplestuff

Swivel Cushion Helps with getting in and out of cars. Turns 360 degrees, supports up to 600 pounds. $30.

SOURCES:

Ableware

AdaptAbility

Ambassador (cushion supports up to 300 pounds)

Bruce Medical Supply

Harriet Carter

J.C. Penney Special Needs

Mature Wisdom

Sears Home Healthcare

Support Plus

These 1996 cars, based on leg and head room, are considered to be . . .

Very Roomy

Acura TL

Audi A6

Lexus LS400

Mazda 626 and Millenia

Mitsubishi Galant

Nissan Maxima

Toyota Avalon and Celica

Volkswagen Passat

Roomy

Buick Park Avenue

Chrysler Sebring/Dodge Avenger

Dodge/Plymouth Neon

Ford Crown Victoria and Taurus

Geo Metro

Honda Accord and Civic

Hyundai Elantra and Sonata

Infiniti Q45

Lexus GS300 and SC300/400

Lincoln Town Car

Mazda MX-6

Mercury Grand Marquis and Sable

Mitsubishi Diamante

Mitsubishi Mirage

Nissan Altima

Oldsmobile 98

Pontiac Bonneville

Saab 900

Saturn SL/SW

Subaru Impreza, Legacy and SVX

Suzuki Swift

Toyota Camry

Volkswagen Golf/Jetta

Average:

Acura Integra

Buick Century, LeSabre, Regal, Riviera, Roadmaster, and Skylark

Cadillac DeVille, Eldorado, Fleetwood, and Seville

Chevrolet Astro/GMC Safari, Beretta/ Corsica, Caprice/Impala, Cavalier, and Lumina

Chrysler Cirrus/Dodge Stratus/Plymouth Breeze, Concorde, and Town and Country

Dodge Caravan, Intrepid

Eagle Summit, Summit Wagon, Talon, and Vision

Ford Aerostar, Contour, Mustang, Probe, Thunderbird, and Windstar

Honda Odyssey and Prelude

Hyundai Accent

Infiniti G20

Isuzu Oasis

Kia Sephia

Lexus ES300

Lincoln Continental and Mark VII

Mazda 929, MPV, MX-3, and Protégé

Mercury Cougar and Mystique

Mitsubishi Eclipse

Nissan 240SX and Sentra

Oldsmobile 88

Oldsmobile Achieva, Aurora, Ciera, and Cutlass Supreme

Plymouth Voyager

Pontiac Grand Am

Suzuki Esteem

Toyota Corolla

Volvo 850

Cramped

Audi A4

BMW 3-series

Chevrolet Camaro, Lumina Minivan, and Monte Carlo

Ford Aspire and Escort

Geo Prism

Mazda Miata

Mercury Tracer and Villager

Nissan Quest

Oldsmobile Silhouette

Pontiac Firebird, Grand Prix, Sunfire, and Trans Sport

Saab 9000

Saturn SC

Toyota Previa and Tercel

Very cramped:

Chrysler LHS/New Yorker

Honda del Sol

Infiniti J30

Mercedes-Benz C-class and E-class

Toyota Paseo

Volvo 900 series

For those of you interested in a Jaguar, I don't have any specific model recommendations, but I can tell you that all of the 1993 and 1994 MY sedans are fitted with ten-way adjustable power seats and tilt steering wheels. The "easy entry" switch on these cars moves the driver's seat back, making it easier to get in and out. Jaguar will install longer seat belts if requested.

If you are lusting after a Porsche, the 944/968 models offer a bit more legroom (44.5" compared with 43" in the 911s and 928s) and a longer seat track (9" compared to 7"). Porsche cautions against replacing the steering wheel under any circumstances with a smaller model because of driver's-side air bags.

The people at Mercedes-Benz recommend you consider their S-class line, stating it was designed "with the knowledge that human beings are generally larger now than they were just ten years ago." Referring to the interior as "cavernous," they point out that the front seats offer "infinite adjustability" with a lower cushion that can be adjusted forward and backward independently from the rest of the seat. The new C-class will also offer these options.

For what it's worth, I drive a Ford Taurus and find it to be very comfortable. It all comes down to personal fit. Bodies come in all sizes and shapes, as we well know, and the car that seems perfect for one 300-pound person may be uncomfortable for another. Also take into consideration any passengers you may be traveling with.

With regard to car safety tests, test dummies range in size from a child to the "95 percent man." The "50 percent man" represents the "average" male. (I'll withhold social commentary here.) The smallest adult dummy is the "5 percent woman." In other words, car safety features haven't been tested for the 5 percent of people at either end of the size spectrum.

• Airlines •

Here we have it . . . the most problematic mode of travel for people of almost any size, but especially we larger angels. Flying.

Which airline CEO was it who first uttered the immortal line, "You can never be too rich or too thin"? The airlines may love their wide-bodied planes, but they sure don't have any respect for their similarly shaped passengers.

Who is to blame for the very small seats? Go straight to each airline's headquarters to point the finger. There may be some limitations due to emergency exits and cabin dimensions of a plane's design, but the airline still decides how many seats to install and how closely to space the rows. Your level of comfort in an airline seat is determined by several factors, including seat pitch (front-to-rear spacing of seat rows), seat width, and the configuration of seats.

Airline seats vary from 18.5" to 23" wide, often depending on the aircraft and its configuration. If you have the option, travel on a DC-9 or MD (series 80) with a 2/2 configuration (two seats on each side of the aisle). These seats are 23" wide. The 727s, 737s, and 757s have a 3/3 configuration with 19" seats. Airlines with 3/3/3 or 3/4/3 configurations use an 18.5" seat. These are usually the A300 series, DC-10s, MD-11s, or L-1011s.

Wherever you are flying and whatever airline you end up on, there are ways to give yourself a bit more room. Ask the person arranging your ticket to check the door and exit rows on the seating chart for your plane. They may be configured in such a way as to allow a more comfortable pitch, more legroom, or wider seats. Bear in mind that you may be denied a seat on the exit row because FAA regulations allow only people who would be able to help evacuate the plane in an emergency to sit there. Bulkhead seats allow more legroom, but the armrests generally don't go up and the tray tables swing out from the armrests, allowing very little room. Window and aisle seats also offer a bit more space.

Speaking of armrests, raise them when you sit down. If the person next to you complains (which isn't likely), quietly explain that you need the extra room. Most people are understanding.

Try to travel during the off rush hours, when there is a better chance of having an empty seat next to you.

When making reservations, request that the seat next to you remain empty if at all possible. Of course, the airline isn't going to pass up another fare if they can get it, but it's worth trying.

Seat belt extensions are available on all airlines. If you need one, ask before boarding. I've heard at least one story of a stewardess stopping in the middle of her safety speech to reprimand a passenger for not being properly buckled in, and then holding everyone up while she searched for the extension. This little incident didn't exactly get the traveler's vacation off to a great beginning.

Some people purchase the seat next to them to assure comfort (an expensive option, but worth it to some). If you have done this, make sure you remind the stewardess when you board the plane. If things become crowded, she may try to fill the seat. Some airlines now require larger passengers to purchase a second seat. Ask while making flight arrangements and seriously consider another airline if at all possible.

Modern airports are often spread out, and the walk between connecting flights may be lengthy. Be sure to allow plenty of time.

And last but not least . . . the rest rooms on planes are terribly small. Even getting to them can be impossible, what with climbing over other passengers and navigating narrow aisles past carts of drinks and meals. If at all possible, go to the bathroom right before boarding the plane. Some flights have handicapped accessible bathrooms, but don't plan on those being all that much larger.

According to the Consumer Reports Travel Letter (CRTL) of September 1991, this is how the airlines stack up in considering passenger comfort.

The Best

Midwest Express (serves Milwaukee and major cities in the East)

MGM Grand (direct flights between Los Angeles and New York offer deluxe coach)

Alaska (highest minimum comfort score of any of the larger U.S. airlines)

The Worst

Delta (seems to be the big "winner" here). CRTL gave Delta "Special Mention" for its "disdain of the comfort of its Coach passengers" and for installing "ultra-tight, charter-style" seating in its MD-11s and similar seating in its long-range L-1011-500s.

Northwest (installed 19" seats in new A320s even though there was space for 21" seats with no decrease in number of passengers)

El Al (Israel), Martinair, and SAS (these three install seats at "extremely tight pitch")

Air Canada, Air New Zealand, Canadian International, El Al (Israel), and Qantas (have installed narrower than necessary seats)

I had decided to go to Chicago for a NAAFA conference with two other girlfriends. We boarded a plane in Los Angeles headed for Arizona, where we were due to transfer to another plane to take us on to Chicago.

In Arizona we walked from one terminal to another to get to the new plane. I always ask to preboard to give me a minute or two to get on the plane, get a seat belt extender, etc. When I asked to preboard, the airline representative asked, "Why are you asking to do that?" I explained the situation, then my friends and I stepped aside to wait to board.

Out of nowhere came two supervisors. They pulled me aside and informed me, in a very public way, that I was not allowed to get on this plane unless I bought a second seat. They didn't say anything to my friends. We were all 250 to 300-plus pounds. This was in a very crowded terminal. There were hundreds of people milling about.

At first I was in disbelief. Then I started saying, "Wait a minute. I just got off the same type of plane with the same airline. There was no problem before. Why all of a sudden am I now too fat to fly on your airline?"

We asked, "Where is it written? Show me where it says you have a right to do this? On my ticket it says one pass to get on the plane. It doesn't say you have to be under 200 pounds."

We asked them to explain why they were taking me out of line and humiliating me in public. They wouldn't give me a definitive answer. They said if I did not buy a second seat I was not going to be allowed on the plane, even though I had a ticket to ride. They even threatened to get security.

We tried to reason with them. We had flown with some unaccompanied children on the previous flight who were continuing on. I offered to sit next to them and put up the armrest. The representatives refused. They then turned to my friends and told them they would have to board now, separating us. Once I saw myself standing totally alone, I felt I had no choices left. I didn't want to be stranded in Arizona and didn't want to be by myself. I was crying profusely. It was very demoralizing. Everyone knew the fat person was the problem; the fat person was holding up the plane. Luckily, I had a credit card and was able to charge another ticket.

They didn't start this in L.A. They didn't say, "Excuse me, you're too fat to fly on this airline," where I would have had the choice of getting my bags off the plane and going home. They did it where I had no options.

What they did to me was very wrong. I was discriminated against. They took away my human rights. I'm terrified now of flying, of getting on a plane and then being forced off.

—Pam

You have every right to be on these planes. If you are treated badly or have an unpleasant experience, write or call the airline headquarters and the Federal Aviation Administration: Office of Public Affairs, Federal Aviation Administration, Department of Transportation, 800 Independence Avenue SW, Washington, D.C.

• Trains •

Years ago I rode with my grandmother on a train from Kansas City, Missouri, to Wichita, Kansas. I haven't been on a train since, but the memory of that trip has stayed with me to this day. There is something special about watching the changing scenery from a train as it winds its way through areas where highways don't go, through tunnels that burrow into mountains, and past tiny towns that are sometimes not even dots on maps. Train travel is a way to see the country that is both nostalgic and relaxing. However, like most public transportation, it is not exactly for the claustrophobic. Space is limited, and the seating is often little better than airline accommodations. If you have any concerns about being able to be comfortable, call ahead and talk to the special services desk at Amtrak.

Following are descriptions of accommodations on the three major passenger lines.

Superliner (western long-distance)

Family bedrooms are designed to accommodate two adults and two children. They are equipped with a sofa and two child seats, two adult berths, and two short berths. Rest rooms are just outside the room.

Room—5'2" long by 9'5" wide

Lower berths—adults: 6'4" long by 3'2" wide

children: 4'9" long by 2' wide

Upper berths—adults (ladder access): 6'2" long by 2' wide

children (ladder access): 4'9" long by 2' wide

Special bedrooms offer ample space throughout, including the toilet. They are equipped with two facing reclining seats, upper and lower sleeping berths, and a sink, vanity, and toilet with a curtain for privacy. Food and beverages can be delivered to your room.

Room—9'5" long by 6'6" wide

Lower berths—6'6" long by 2'4" wide

Upper berths—(steps access): 6'2" long by 2' wide

Deluxe bedrooms are located on the upper level. These rooms have a sofa and armchair by day, an upper berth and wide lower berth by night, and are equipped with a sink, vanity, and private toilet facilities, including a shower.

Many deluxe bedrooms are separated by a folding partition that can be opened to form a four-bed suite.

Room—6'6" long by 7'6" wide

Lower berths—6'6" long by 3'4" wide

Upper berth—(ladder access): 6'2" long by 2' wide

Economy bedrooms are located on both upper and lower levels and have two reclining seats that convert to a bed and an upper berth. Rest rooms are outside the room.

Room—6'6" long by 3'6" wide

Lower berth—6'2" long by 2'4" wide

Upper berth—(steps access): 6'2" long by 2' wide

Heritage (eastern long-distance)
Some rooms are specially designed to accommodate passengers with mobility problems and have a toilet and sink. Food service is provided.

Room—11'6" long by 3'6" wide

Berth—6' long by 2'11" wide

Double slumber coaches provide accommodations for two adults, including rest room facilities.

Room—6' long by 3'7" wide

Lower berth—6' long by 2' wide

Upper berth—(built-in step): 6' long by 2' wide

Single slumber coaches provide one reclining chair and one berth that folds down from the wall.

Room—6'2" long by 3'7" wide

Berth—6'2" long by 2' wide

Bedrooms are equipped with either two chair seats or a long sofa and rest room facilities. Some of these rooms are divided by a partition that can be opened to create a four-person suite.

Room—7'6" long by 5'4" wide

Lower berth—6' long by 2'11" wide

Upper berth—6' long by 2'11" wide

Rooms are designed for use by one adult and offer one easy chair and one berth that folds out of the wall.

Room—6'6" long by 3'6" wide

Berth—6' long by 2'11" wide

If you find the dining areas uncomfortable and are booking a sleeper compartment, stewards are generally able to bring meals to you. Bathrooms are often quite small, so it might be a good idea to ask to see if a handicapped or family room is available. The bathrooms in these compartments are relatively roomy. If you have any concerns about your comfort, call Amtrak for reservations and information about any special arrangements that need to be made.

• Hotels •

There are many things that go into making a hotel desirable, including location, noise level, friendliness, cleanliness, price, comfort, and accessibility. When making reservations for a room in a hotel be sure to make any of your special needs known to the guest services manager. If you have mobility issues, be specific in asking how these will be addressed. Most staff members are happy to cooperate in making your stay comfortable in any way available to them.

•Dining Out•

Below is a list of some of the largest restaurant chains in the country. The main office for each was contacted and asked to supply a description of their general seating accommodations. Not all chose to respond to letters or phone calls, so random samplings have been used to give you an idea of what to expect.

Within each chain there is some variety from location to location. This is generally due to the pattern of growth of the company. Bear in mind that some have been in business for fifty or more years.

This is a service industry, so most companies are interested in customer concerns. If you have a problem with seating or accessibility in any restaurant you visit or would like to frequent, contact the store manager or the head office and express your needs. If the problem isn't addressed satisfactorily, how you handle your complaint from that point is up to you. Your choices are many—from squeezing yourself into the inadequate seating and suffering in silence all the way to picketing the national headquarters. The address listed next to each restaurant is the main office.

Because of the Americans with Disabilities Act (ADA), requirements that took effect in September 1992, all restaurants must have at least one aisle that is 36" wide and rest rooms that are wheelchair accessible. This is a boon to larger-size customers as well.

Seating in most restaurants tends to be on the "cozy" side. I have tried to provide some basic information here to give you an idea of what you are likely to encounter in these establishments. Measure your own dining room chairs to get an idea of what is comfortable, then compare that information to what is given here.

Generally the most troublesome aspect of restaurant seating is encountering narrow booths. Again, sit at your own table, then measure the distance between the back of your chair and the edge of the table to see how much space you require. If a restaurant offers only chairs with arms or booths that will likely be too small for you, call ahead and ask if an armless, sturdy chair can be made available.

Never be afraid to ask for comfortable, safe accommodations. It isn't your fault if the seating provided is too small. If any particular establishment doesn't fit your needs and you really want to dine there regularly, contact their main office and voice your concerns.

The Black-Eyed Pea 8115 Preston Road, LB#7, Dallas, TX 75225; (214) 363-9513

Seating: Both draw leaf tables and stationary booths are available. Chairs are 15" square, armless, and sturdy. Aisles are generally 4' wide.

Company comment: "To our restaurant company, sitting down to a meal should be an enjoyable experience, and it is our desire for all of our customers to be completely comfortable when dining in our restaurants. Rudeness and discrimination toward any of our customers are unthinkable and never tolerated."

Blimpie 1775 The Exchange, Suite 215, Atlanta, GA 30339; (800) 447-6256 or (404) 984-2707

Seating: Stiff, upright, armless chairs are available; they measure 16" by 16". Tables are movable.

Company comment: "We train all of our franchisees to treat customers as if they are guests in their own home. If a customer has an unpleasant experience, we encourage them to call the main office."

Blue Boar P.O. Box 169001, Louisville, KY 40256-9001; (502) 776-2481

Seating: Chairs are upholstered, sturdy, and armless, measuring 16.5" by 16"; tables and booths. Booths are 18" deep.

Company comment: "If there is ever a problem, the customer should ask for the manager."

Bob Evans Farms 3776 South High Street, P.O. Box 07863, Columbus, OH 43207-0863; (614) 491-2225

Seating: Fixed booths and counter seats are available, with 16" from booth seat to table. Movable tables and armless chairs are also available with a seat width of 17".

Burger King P.O. Box 520783 GMF, Miami, FL 33152; (800) 937-1800

Seating (random sampling): We found the booths and fixed seating at these restaurants to be quite tight—16" from the edge of the table to the back of the seat—but there were movable

tables and moderately sturdy chairs available.

Carl's Jr. 1216 North Harbor Boulevard, Anaheim, CA 93845; (800) 422-4141

Seating (random sampling): Mostly booths with 17.5" space between table edge and seat back. There were some bar stools, placed tightly to the cabinet, and a few moderately sturdy movable chairs.

Casa Bonita 8115 Preston Road, LB#7, Dallas, TX 75225; (214) 363-9513. See information on the Black-eyed Pea; this restaurant is owned by the same company.

Chesapeake Bay Seafood House 8027 Leesburg Pike, Suite 506, Vienna, VA 22182; (703) 827-0320

Seating: Both fixed booths and movable tables are available. Distance from back of booth seat to table edge is 18". Chairs have 18" circular seats.

Company comment: "As far as I know, we have never had a problem in any of our restaurants concerning a large-size customer being discriminated against. All we are concerned about is that our customers (of any size, shape, color, etc.) are happy with the service and the food they receive."

Chick-fil-A 5200 Buffington Road, Atlanta, GA 30349; (404) 765-8015

Seating: Chairs are armless, with widths from 16" to 18"; typical cluster-style seating with fixed seats ranges from 20" to 22" from table to seat back. Booths and loose seats are adjustable. Booths are generally movable.

Company comment: "Our goal is to 'WOW' our customers rather than just satisfy them. Therefore, those with special needs provide us with a great opportunity to show our gratefulness for their business."

Crystal's 8115 Preston Road, LB#7, Dallas, TX 75225; (214) 363-9513. See information on the Black-eyed Pea; this restaurant is owned by the same company.

Denny's Flagstar Corp., 203 East Main Street, Spartanburg, SC 29319; (800) 733-6697

Seating (random sampling): Mostly booths with 16" distance between seat back and table edge. There are sometimes movable chairs and/or tables available. The chair that is brought when a customer asks for one has arms and is not much roomier than the booths.

Dairy Queen, Inc. 7505 Metro Boulevard, P.O. Box 39286, Minneapolis, MN 55439-0286; (612) 830-0200

Seating: Varies from store to store (each store is individually owned).

Comment: "All stores that offer indoor seating must have at least 5 percent handicapped-accessible seating."

El Chico Restaurants, Inc. 12200 Stemmons Freeway, Suite 100, Dallas, TX 75234; (214) 241-5500

Seating: New restaurants have booths with arm and side chairs. Variations in older restaurants make it difficult to respond in more detail.

Comment: "With the different seating options we provide, we should be capable of comfortably seating most every person coming into our restaurants."

International House of Pancakes 25020 Avenue Stanford, Unit 170, Valencia, CA 91355; (805) 294-8877

Seating (random sampling): Fixed booths with 16" space between table edge and chair back. There are some moderately sturdy armed chairs available with a seat width of 19".

Jack-in-the-Box 100 North Barranaca Avenue, Suite 200, West Covina, CA 91791-1600; (818) 858-0668

Seating (random sampling): Fixed tables and chairs with 16.5" between table edge and chair back. Lots of moderately sturdy chairs available.

Kentucky Fried Chicken P.O. Box 32070, Louisville, KY 40232-2070; (502) 456-8300

Seating (random sampling): The majority of stores use loose tables and chairs with some fixed booths. The chairs have no arms and are 16" in width.

Long John Silver's 101 Jerico Drive, P.O. Box 11988, Lexington, KY 40579; (606) 263-6000

Seating: Booths and movable tables are available; the chairs are 18" wide.

McDonald's Corporation 21300 Victory Boulevard, #800, Woodland Hills, CA 91367; (818) 594-0525

Seating (random sampling): All booths or tables with attached chairs with 17" between table edge and chair back. Chair seats are 16" wide.

Marie Callender's 1100 Town & Country, Suite 1300, Orange, CA 92668; (714) 542-3355

Seating: There is considerable variation from restaurant to restaurant.

Company comment: ". . . we train our staff to be courteous and hospitable to all of our guests. We strive to provide each guest with a great dining experience . . ."

The Nut Tree Nut Tree, CA 95696; (707) 448-4111

Seating: Seats measure 16" at the base and 19" arm to arm and are available even at booths. All tables are movable. Booths measure 15"-16" from back of cushion to the table.

Company comment: "Guest satisfaction is very important to us. If guests have an unpleasant experience, they should immediately bring it to the attention of the manager on duty. If they do not feel comfortable doing this, they should either call or write to let us know what happened."

The Old Spaghetti Factory International, Inc. 0715 SW Bancroft, Portland, OR 97201; (503) 225-0433

Seating: Both booths and tables are available. The tables are movable. Most of the chairs are armless and quite sturdy. Seats are approximately 17.5" wide. Aisles are spacious.

Company comment: "All of our employees are trained to be sensitive to our guests and to treat every guest with courtesy and respect."

Pizza Hut, Inc. Attn: Consumer Affairs Department, P.O. Box 428, Wichita, KS 67201; (316) 681-9602

Seating: There is a wide variety of seating from store to store. Current company-built, dine-in restaurants have both booth seating and open tables. The armless chairs have 17" seats.

Company comment: "Our goal at Pizza Hut is to make each Pizza Hut occasion a pleasant experience by always providing 100 percent customer satisfaction."

Red Lobster 5900 Lake Ellenor Drive, P.O. Box 593330, Orlando, FL 32859-3330; (407) 851-0370

Seating: Freestanding tables are available, as are booths with fixed seats and tables. Chairs have arms, seats are 20" wide by 15" deep.

Company comment: "Our guest-first service ensures that we do not discriminate against any of our guests."

Taco Bell 17901 Von Karman Avenue, Irvine, CA 92714; (800) 822-6235

Seating (random sampling): All booths with a 17" clearance between the table edge and chair back.

Taco Bueno 8115 Preston Road, LB#7, Dallas, TX 75225; (214) 363-9513. See information on the Black-eyed Pea; this restaurant is owned by the same company.

Village Inn 400 West 48th Avenue, Denver, CO 80216; (303) 296-2121

Seating: Fixed booths with 16" clearance from booth seat to table. Movable tables and armless chairs are also available.

Comment: "Our staffs are made up of genuine, caring individuals."

I was at a café, sitting in this little white chair on a tiled outdoor patio. When I first sat in the chair, I felt the back give a little. I thought, "This is kind of fun. A little bit of a shock absorber." At the end of breakfast I leaned back. The two back legs just gave way and I fell. I was stuck because the chair had arms on it and the two front legs didn't give. My roommate was there; he stopped at mid-slice in his pancake and just stared at me. I said, "Please help me. I can't get up by myself." He was so shocked he just stared at me there on the floor. So I had to wiggle and roll off the side of this chair onto the floor to get up. People weren't laughing. I don't think they knew how to react.

I was mortified! I thought, "Oh, my god, I broke a chair!" Then I thought, "Hey! I broke a chair!" I started laughing. I was trying to roll myself over to get up; I couldn't do anything else but laugh. It was a milestone for me, my first broken chair. It was a very funny experience.

—PHIL

• Theaters •

Is there a person of size alive who hasn't had the experience of panicking when faced with the notoriously narrow seats of a theater? This is one of the most often mentioned problems confronting large people. Most people love going out to a movie. Unfortunately, most theater seats don't love our ample hips. What is it with theater designers?

•
My Body Is Not
"Too Wide" . . .
the Seats Are
Too Narrow
•

I wrote to each of the offices listed below to inquire about seating within each company's theaters. Few of them chose to share specific information with us. In all fairness, diversity due to the varying age of theaters within a chain can make it difficult to publish data. However, it seems that a service agency whose main "product" is seating would have a head office that is very much aware of such basic information as seat size and aisle width.

The average seat width seems to be 21", with a depth of 21" and a row measurement of 38" from seat back to seat back. Some theaters offer seating of varying widths, staggered to accommodate each patron's view of the screen. Some offer at least a few seats with armrests that lift up. There are seats that have holders, seats that rock, seats that recline, and even couch seats.

As in all situations you are unsure of, it's best to call ahead and talk to the manager. He will be able to direct you to wider seats in the theater, if any are available. If you have a problem while visiting a theater, talk to the manager—and don't hesitate to contact the home office if you don't get satisfaction. Everybody has a higher up, except the owner. And the owner's interest is profit. Which brings us back to you. They want your money. Let them know how they can get it.

AMC Theaters has recently announced it will be providing seats with armrests that retract, making a 45" seat, in all of its new theaters. These seats will also have higher backs and more room between rows. Excellent news!

AMC Entertainment 106 West 14th Street, Kansas City, MO 64105-1914

Carmike Cinemas 1301 1st Avenue, Columbus, GA 31901-2109

Chakeres Theaters 19 South Fountain Avenue, Springfield, OH 45502-1205

Cineplex Odeon Corp. 70 East Lake Street, #1600, Chicago, IL 60601-5907

R. C. Cobb, Inc. 924 Montclair Road, Birmingham, AL 35213-0000

Consolidated Theaters 1130 East 3rd Street, #490, Charlotte, NC 28204-2624

Eastern Federal Corp. 513 South Tryon Street, Charlotte, NC 28202-1898

Floyd Theatres, Inc. 4226 Old Highway 37, Lakeland, FL 33813-0000

General Cinema Corp. 27 Boylston Street, Chestnut Hill, MA 02167-1700

Jack Loeks Theaters 1400 28th Street SW, Grand Rapids, MI 49509-2785

Mann Theaters, Inc. 704 Hennepin Avenue, Minneapolis, MN 55403-1811

Mann Theaters 9200 Sunset Boulevard, #200, Los Angeles, CA 90069-3584

Marcus Theatres Corp. 212 West Wisconsin Avenue, Milwaukee, WI 53203-2380

National Amusements 200 Elm Street, Dedham, MA 02026-4536

Neighborhood Entertainment 1510 East Ridge Road, Richmond, VA 23229-0000

Pacific Theaters 120 North Robertson Boulevard, Los Angeles, CA 90048-3102

Trans-Lux Corporation 110 Richards Avenue, Norwalk, CT 96854-1692

United Artists 5619 DTC Parkway, Englewood, CO 80111-3000

United Artists Theater 1400 Old Country Road, Westbury, NY 11590-5129

VACATIONS

•Theme Parks•

Theme parks are extremely popular vacation destinations that offer the potential for embarrassment or disappointment for larger visitors. Most are spread out over a fairly large parcel of land with lots of walking required to get from one attraction to another. Long lines sometimes lead to rides or shows with too-small seating. As in most matters of "fit," it isn't weight so much as shape.

If you are planning a visit to a park, call ahead and ask for any brochures or maps that can be mailed to you. Talk to a customer relations manager to address any specific problems you anticipate. While in a park, don't be shy about requesting information and/or help.

This quick rundown of the rides and attractions at Disney parks (courtesy of Barbara Herrera, an admitted Disney park addict) gives a good idea of what to consider.

All of the parks have plenty of wheelchair parking available with trams moving throughout the parking lots to take passengers to the park entrance. Wheelchairs (both electric and standard) are available for rental at park entrances and are wonderful for those with difficulty walking considerable distances. Don't worry about having to pass through narrow turnstiles . . . all of the parks have gates that swing open. If you need any other assistance just ask. These are friendly people.

Magic Kingdom

ADVENTURELAND:

Enchanted Tiki Room is a show with bench-type seating.

Pirates of the Carribean is a boat ride with bench-type seating that moves pretty smoothly except for a short drop down a waterfall. Not wheelchair accessible.

Swiss Family Treehouse is an attraction involving uphill and downhill walking.

FANTASYLAND:

Carousel Horses is a gently moving ride offering both bench seats and, of course, carousel horses.

Dumbo Flying Elephants is a gently moving children's ride with low bars across the lap and tight seating.

Grand Prix Raceway is a gently moving ride with bench-type seating. Spacing is tight on this ride.

It's a Small World is a gently moving ride with bench-type seating. No wheelchair access.

Legend of the Lion King is a show with theater-type seating.

Mr. Toad's Wild Ride really isn't all that wild, and it offers bench-type seating with high bars for gripping.

The Skyway is a gently moving ride with bench seating and a 700-pound limit.

Tea Cups is a twirling ride (not for those of us suseptible to motion sickness!) with bench-type seating that is a bit tight.

FRONTIERLAND:

Big Thunder Mountain is a roller coaster with tight spacing and a low bar across the lap.

Country Bear Jamboree is a show with bench-type seating.

Jungle Cruise is a gently moving boat ride with bench-type seating.

Railroad Ride is a gently moving ride with bench-type seating.

Splash Mountain is a roller coaster with tight spacing and a low bar across the lap.

MAIN STREET:

Main Street Cinema is a movie with theater-type seating.

TOMORROWLAND:

Astro Orbiter is a simulator ride with jerky movements. Seating is theater type with low bars across the lap.

Carousel of Progress is a show with theater-type seating.

Delta Dream Flight is a gently moving ride with roomy seating and a high bar in front for gripping.

Space Mountain is a roller coaster with close seating and low bars across the lap.

Time Keeper is a movie presentation with no seating.

Wedway People Mover is a gently moving ride with bench seats and a high bar in front for gripping. No wheelchair access.

TOWN SQUARE:

Hall of Presidents is a show with theater-type seating.

Haunted Mansion is a gently moving ride with bench-type seating with a high bar for gripping. Getting on the ride portion of this attraction is a bit tricky as you have to move quickly. Not wheelchair accessible.

Mike Fink Keel Boats is a gently moving ride with bench-type seating.

Tom Sawyer's Island is an attraction with no seating.

Epcot Center

FUTURE WORLD:

Body Wars is a flight simulator with jumpy movements. It has theater-type seats with low bars.

Cranium Command is a show with bench-type seating.

Journey to Imagination is an attraction with a variety of activities. The seating is theater type with low bars across the lap.

The Land is a gently moving boat ride with bench-type seating. It is not wheelchair accessible.

Living Seas is a gently moving ride with bench-type seating and quite a bit of walking.

Making of Me is a movie with bench-type seating.

Universe of Energy is a gently moving ride with bench-type seating.

Wonders of Life is a gently moving ride with rather tight seating with low bars across the lap.

WORLD SHOWCASE:

Canada is a movie with no seating.

China is a show with no seating.

France is a movie with no seating.

Mexico is a gently moving ride with bench-type seating and high bars for gripping. It is not wheelchair accessible.

Norway is a rather spirited boat ride with bench seating and low bars across the lap.

United States is a show with limited theater-style seating.

MGM:

Backstage Tour is a tram ride with bench-type seating.

Beauty and the Beast is a show with bench-type seating.

Great Movie Rides is a show with bench-type seating.

Hunchback of Notre Dame is a show with bench-type seating.

Indiana Jones Spectacular is a show with bench-type seating.

Little Mermaid is a show with theater-type seating.

Magic of Disney Animation is a demonstration with no seating.

Monster Sound Show has theater-type seating.

Muppet Show has theater-type seating.

Star Tours is a simulator with jumpy movements. It has theater-type seating and a low bar across the lap.

Tower of Terror is a thirteen-story drop ride with bench-type seating and high bars for gripping.

HIKING, CAMPING, AND CATTLE DRIVING

If nature is your thing but you have stopped exploring the great outdoors because you just aren't sure what conditions you are going to find in any given park or wilderness area, lace up your hiking boots and let's get going. There are 357 areas covering over 80 million acres in the United States waiting for your arrival. To determine which parks are right for you, write to the National Park Service. They will be happy to send you a booklet detailing each park in the system.

Look through the parks in the area you are thinking of visiting, then request specific information on issues of particular concern to you. Write to: National Park Service, Office of Public Affairs, U.S. Department of the Interior, Washington, D.C. 20402 for the booklet.

If you are really itching to get into some outdoor adventures, contact Wilderness Inquiry. This group "provides outdoor adventures for people of all ages and abilities. Program offerings include canoe, kayak, and dogsled adventures throughout North America." You may call their office for the current schedule.

You don't have to be an experienced horse person to enjoy a taste of the Old West. Some dude ranches and guest cattle drives offer bare-bones excitement; others offer luxuries you might not expect . . . even showers. Contact American Wilderness Experience for information on outfits throughout the United States.

RECREATIONAL VEHICLES

If you don't want to deal with the hassles of airports, small airline seats, and hotel beds, perhaps vacationing in a recreational vehicle is for you. Motorhomes can be quite luxurious, designed to your specifications, and as comfortable as your own living room. With a queen-size bed, color television, and built-in shower, you can travel in style. For more information about custom-designed motorhomes, contact Born Free Motorcoach, Inc., Monaco Coach Corporation, or check your yellow pages under "Recreational Vehicles, Custom."

CAMPING SUPPLIES AND CLOTHING

All of the following companies carry a wide variety of clothing (up to size 4X in most cases) and supplies (all carry extrawide and extralong sleeping bags) to make camping out a lot more fun and comfortable than it used to be. The mail-order catalogs are quite comprehensive from all of these stores. You can outfit an entire trip without stepping out the door.

Bass Pro Shops   I've been to this store, in Springfield, Missouri . . . it's *huge* and even has a monstrous fish tank (with monstrous fish) with live shows featuring a diver who goes in to feed fish as big as he is. Very interesting place to visit, even if you aren't into hunting, camping, or fishing. The catalog offers basically the same things as the store (minus the fish show) in sizes to 3X. Catalog $3.

Cabela's   "World's Foremost Outfitter of Hunting, Fishing, and Outdoor Gear." In sizes up to men's 3X, women's XL/30W. You can outfit an army here . . . complete with guns. Parkas, shirts, pants, vests, hunters' bibs, gloves, hats, coats, thermal underwear, and boots. An amazing selection.

Cahall's   "The Finest in Outdoor Work and Sports Clothing." In sizes up to 4X for men, XL for women. Thermal lined pants, jackets, hoods, vests, gloves, and coveralls; jeans, sweatshirts, overalls, and jackets by famous name makers— Osh-Kosh, Levi's, Carhatt, and Key. Boots and work shoes up to men's size 15 and women's size 11.

Campmor   Outdoor work clothing and sportswear up to women's size XL and men's size 3X. Parkas, pants, jackets, hoods, thermal underwear, socks, and shoes up to men's size 13, women's size 11.

Dunn's   Similar to the other stores listed here, but many of the items have a more Western flair and some are European style. Very nice selection of men's items up to size 3X.

Gander Mountain   Outdoor and sportswear, most to size 3X, some to size 6X. Excellent selection of rugged shoes and boots up to size 13EE.

Wyoming River Raiders Canoeing and rafting supplies, including boats, gear, wetsuits, clothing (up to size 2X), and sandals (up to men's size 15, women's size 11).

CRUISES

The height of luxury, taking a cruise seems to be the dream vacation. If you shop carefully through a good travel agent—especially an agency that specializes in cruises—you can find a size-friendly atmosphere and destination perfect for you. Some agencies even offer cruise packages designed specifically for the larger passenger. Most of us tend to think of the Love Boat, with its instant romances and parade of slim bodies when we think of cruises. Don't let those images keep you from what may be a wonderful experience, providing memories you will always cherish.

Each cruise line (and sometimes each ship within a fleet) has its own atmosphere. Ranging from the very formal, with elegant dinners and dances, to ships filled with children rollerblading and working on their very own shipboard television news show, there seems to be something for everyone. If you're into it, you can even cruise with Richard Simmons on Carnival Lines' "Cruise to Lose."

Sylvia Ponti of Cruise World Representatives was kind enough to offer these suggestions to help make taking a cruise more enjoyable:

It's true that ships' cabins don't compare with hotel rooms. You won't find two double beds in a cabin, but you will find two twin beds that push together to make a queen. I don't recommend an extremely large person going into an upper berth, but the lower bed will easily hold someone in the 250+ range. A good idea is to reserve a stateroom with a double bed and maybe an upper berth. In the case of two people traveling together, request a cabin that would accommodate a third person—in case you want to bring your mother at the last moment, if her health permits. You'll get a cabin that will accommodate three or four without paying anything extra. Check on the configuration of the beds to make sure that two of them will push together.

A lot of the newer ships have wide aisles but smaller cabins. Some of the smaller cabins can be found on the largest ships. An extremely large person might request a wheelchair-accessible cabin. These provide larger bathrooms and a more spacious room.

Sylvia notes that some of the public areas have chairs that are small by most standards, but there are always comfortable couches available. Being a large person, she considers herself to be a good test case for size and says she has always found spacious accommodations in the lounges, showrooms, and most of the theaters.

Listing just some of the activities available—talent shows, parties, children's programs, movies, midnight buffets, gambling, court sports, wine tastings, bingo, ice-carving demonstrations, cooking classes, and much more—Sylvia says, "After dark there's nothing more romantic than a ship. Stars flash like neon in the sky. Dance floors shimmer with colorful sights and sounds. The casino is awhirl with winners dancing to the sounds of coins falling from nearby slot machines . . . and big, splashy Broadway-style shows light up the night. The fun never stops till you do."

Your clothing depends on where you are traveling . . . shorts, bathing suits, and tennis shoes for the Caribbean; layered clothing for Alaska. One cocktail dress or tuxedo is needed for formal evenings. (See chapter 3, "You Look Marvelous!" for clothing sources.)

Cruise World Representatives Sylvia Ponti, contact.

Le Grande Weekend Luxury weekends in England designed for pampering large ladies.

Radiance Tours Alice Ansfield of *Radiance Magazine*, contact. Call to be put on the mailing list for information about cruises and tours specifically for big, fun-seeking women. You'll make some great friends as you cruise the Greek Isles, tour Hawaii, or check out the fall foliage on the East Coast.

The Travel Shoppe Juanita Sanford, contact. "Specializing in Fat Friendly Service Meeting All Your Needs."

Thomas Cook and King Size Co. Thomas Cook and a leading mail-order cataloger for big men's clothing have teamed up to "give them [big men] the best advice and information available" for enjoyable vacations.

AND WHEN I DIE . . .

I prefer to think that I, my family, all of my readers, and everyone I know possess the gifts of good health and immortality. But, on the off chance that this is an incorrect assumption, here is what I've learned.

Most people need only concern themselves with a few religious and esthetic decisions when choosing a casket for a loved one. Carolyn Hirschman, in an article for *Business First* magazine, wrote, "Caskets are a lot like cars. Some are stripped down; some are souped up. They can cost a little or a lot. Styles, sizes, and colors vary. Almost everyone needs one sooner or later. Like cars, they get you where you are going." I don't know, Carolyn. I don't think I care how long it takes for this particular vehicle to go from 0 to 60 miles per hour or if it has driver's-side air bags. A really good CD player and cruise control would be nice, though.

Wood or metal, pink or sky blue, full or half couch (this indicates how much of the lid is open for viewing), embroidered or ruffled fabrics, velvet or silk, pad or innerspring mattress . . . there are a lot of decisions to be made, and the final cost can run into thousands of dollars. Our concern, even in death, is size.

Standard casket widths vary from 21" to 27.75", which beats the heck out of the standard 19" theater and airline seats, but often is still not roomy enough. Oversize caskets are available to funeral homes but must be special-ordered from their suppliers. This may cause a slight delay in funeral services. The oversize caskets also have limited choices in materials, color, and selection.

Cemeteries today are laid out in a very structured manner, with burial plots planned quite close to one another. When purchasing a burial plot, a significantly larger person may be forced to purchase two. (Holy Airlines, Batman!) Well, in this case I suppose it's more understandable. Cemeteries are, after all, a real estate business. One funeral director I spoke with suggested that sometimes it's possible to purchase a plot near a corner or edge of a development where extra space may be available. If your interment is to be in a vault, arrangements can also be made for oversize spaces.

Prearranged funerals are becoming more common and may be something to consider if you anticipate the need for a larger-than-usual casket and/or burial plot.

I just couldn't end this chapter on such a somber note . . .

JUST FOR THE FUN OF IT

Think Big
Everything in this catalog is supersize. For instance, there's a cookie jar that looks exactly like an Oreo cookie . . . almost a foot across. There's also a 68" tall pencil, a 38" tall baby bottle, and a 26" bandage. My mother collects refrigerator magnets. I wonder what she would think of a 17" by 15" magnetized piece of toast? My personal favorite is the 13" coffee cup and saucer.

➡ If any data listed in this chapter need to be corrected, please let me know. If you know of a service or product useful to people of size, please write to me about it. The information may be made available to readers through the newsletter "Size Wise Update!," the Size Wise web site, or through possible future revisions of this book.

PERSONAL GLIMPSE:
CHRIS

Chris is a successful real estate agent, foreclosure counselor, and financial adviser. Like so many women, she began gaining weight during her first pregnancy and has been a big, beautiful woman ever since.

Fat or thin, I don't know what it is, but I have a lot of men friends. I have never gone out looking for men. My current boyfriend walked into my real estate office. We've been together for five years. He is forty-one, very attractive, and just loves me to death. He won't even look at other women. I couldn't get rid of him if I wanted to. He won't go. He has me to cuddle up to at night and he's not going anywhere. He calls me his queen. And I am. When we first got together he said he had never gone out with a woman who was overweight. Now he says, "Boy, if we ever broke up, I wouldn't want a skinny girl anymore." He's been spoiled. A woman can be overweight and have whatever she wants. She can find a man who loves her.

Men open the door for me . . . they do things for me. The other day a friend, Bob, said, "You know, you are a well-taken-care-of woman." I said, "Well, I deserve it. And it better stay like this."

One of my favorite lines from a movie is from *Body Heat*. William Hurt and Kathleen Turner were walking down this promenade at a carnival or something. He said something really inane. She said, "You're not very bright, are you? I like that in a man." I like that. Just make me happy, please me, and I'll take care of the rest.

I read an article once about how people describe themselves in personals ads. Of course, an overweight woman is "rubenesque" or "queen-size." A man is a "teddy bear" or a "John Madden type." Okay, so you're fat, blond, and stupid. The men will stipulate "no overweight women," "gorgeous and attractive only." Please! The

143

guy probably looks like Woody Allen. People really see themselves in some kind of fantasy life. Men especially.

What I hate the most is that sign in the back of pickup trucks that says "No fat chicks." Most of the guys who have those signs are ugly Bubbas with their butt cracks hanging out and a gun rack on the back window. Who would go out with them anyway? No woman with two brain cells would. It's a cosmic joke. Most of the fat women I know are pretty intelligent women and, honey, you should be bowing at our feet, kissing the hem of our skirts!

I've dieted halfheartedly, hating every minute of it, feeling mad and angry at the unfairness of it all. When I just let it happen, it happens better. I'm not going to ever say I'm on a diet. What I'm doing now is just trying to be healthy. If I want pie or anything else, I'm going to have it.

In 1988 I did a firewalk, and after I did that the little things didn't bother me anymore. If I can walk on fire, I can do about any damn thing I want to do. When I'm ready to lose weight, it will just happen. I think it's just a matter of letting go, not letting it be an issue.

The people who are bothered by overweight are not sensitive people. They really aren't worth worrying about, and I have to feel sorry for them. We are all really beautiful people. We have a lot to offer. Other people need to recognize that. There are things I can do that others can't do. When people first meet me, I win them over. Being overweight becomes a nonissue. I show them I am powerful, I'm important, and if you don't like me you are losing a lot. That is just kind of my general attitude. Your fat is really not who you are. Weight is just a number. Who you are is in your heart.

So What!

So what!
So what that I'm almost 50 and acting 14.
No, it's not immaturity. It is not menopause.
How could it be second adolescence when I never had the first?
And that's the point.

I was a fat kid, a fat teen—ridiculed, ignored—never dated, never kissed, never went to dances (tho' I taught all my girlfriends how to dance so they could impress their dates), never flirted, never desired—did dream, did fantasize, never hoped.
I was the mature daughter, the best friend, the good student, helpful, supportive, nurturing, amusing—sobbing inside.
Now I want everything I missed:
I want flirting & dating & necking at drive-ins.
I want picnics & dances & parties, more than I can count.
I want to be romanced & courted and wooed and
I want flowers & candy & love notes & surprises just for me
I want to sit by the phone in agony—wondering & hoping
I want to be giddy when it finally rings.
I want to giggle with my girlfriends comparing suitors.
I want to spend all afternoon deciding what to wear for a date
I want the excitement & butterflies just before the doorbell sounds.
I want my head to swim when I'm kissed
I want to be breathless & scared & thrilled with all the attention.
I want what my thin girlfriends had & what I read about in *Seventeen magazine*.
Well, guess what . . . I'm having it all, and if I'm acting 14
So what!

Segment of FAT LIP Readers Theatre script by Laura J. Bock.

5

GETTING TO KNOW YOU

During 1993, a music video was aired frequently on MTV that showed a beautiful, chubby little girl dressed in a colorful bee costume, complete with antenna. She does a happy little dance at a school function of some sort. The other dancers are all dressed alike in standard ballerina style. Their dance is stiff, boring, and regimental; the little bee girl twirls and bobs and smiles for anyone who will watch. But everyone she dances for just stares at her, unsmiling, not understanding her or her happiness.

Perplexed and rejected, she dances her little heart out for everyone she encounters until, discouraged and hurt, she runs away.

Imagine her excitement at finding a group of people dancing and cavorting in a field of wildflowers, obviously enjoying themselves . . . all dressed in an array of colorful costumes. She runs to join them, her dance even wilder and freer. She has found her element; a group of people who are like her, who accept, understand, and welcome her. She can be herself.

Do I think we should seek out only people who are like us? No, I don't. But everyone needs support and acceptance. If you aren't finding it in your current group of friends, perhaps it's time to build a new group.

We all crave friendship, love, and acceptance. But finding friends and lovers can be difficult for anyone. In this time of global overpopulation, people seem more isolated than ever. Large urban areas with millions of people packed close together can be the worst possible places for finding new friends. Neighbors no longer know each other's names unless there is some sort of conflict. Every time you go shopping the faces you encounter are almost always those of strangers. Even if someone were to seem friendly, who can you trust anymore?

These problems certainly aren't limited to big cities, however. Meeting people can be difficult everywhere. When we do see someone we'd like to get to know better it's often not easy to approach. We think if we could just lose weight, we'd have lots of dates. Think about it. This is true for all kinds of people, not just people who are large. Look at all of the "average"-size people you know who are sitting at home, complaining about there being no one good left. As in so many instances, we automatically blame the problem on our weight. True, there are lots of people in this world who would never even consider dating a large-size person. Forget them. That attitude is their problem, not yours.

> *I've been drawing fat women since I was in elementary school. I started watching* Designing Women *because of Delta Burke. She's very pretty and probably doesn't even realize it. My favorite TV actress was Wendie Jo Sperber.*
>
> *I like strong women. I think that's one of the main reasons men don't like fat women. You have much more control over little ladies. I love chubby cheeks. I love somebody you can talk with.*
>
> *The one problem I see with fat women so often is the lack of self-esteem. They often will do things that degrade themselves. They often act more desperate to get a man. I'm looking for that one woman who cares enough about herself not to do those things.*
>
> *I've never been out with a skinny woman. I figure, why should I lie? People are going to be talking about me and that used to bother me. It doesn't now. Now I tell people my preferences. I'll tell the whole world now. Why would you live for someone else's image? Why make yourself miserable to look good to someone else?*
>
> —Yuri

There are lots of men and women who honestly care a lot more about the kind of person you are than about how you look. There are people who are very much attracted only to larger companions and mates, just as some people prefer redheads, muscular physiques, or tall companions. But you have to get out there and meet them. They are not likely going to come to your door and beg you to show them your dazzling personality. Do you think you came this far only to sit at home with a bowl of popcorn waiting to see who's on Letterman tonight? I think not.

First, let's start with the obvious. What do you like to do? What are your interests? Do you like to bowl? Love the theater? Dying for a look at a blue heron walking through a salt marsh early in the morning? Join a league. Buy season passes. Join a bird-watchers' club and then go on the outings and to the meetings. Not only will you be out doing something of interest to you, but you just might meet someone special who shares those interests.

Built for comfort . . . not for speed

If the only person who shows interest in you is the person hiding shyly behind the binoculars with a passion for the mating habits of tall birds, don't knock it! Behind those binoculars you may find just the person you've waited for all your life. Or someone who is an interesting new friend.

Take some chances and choose not only long-held interests but something new. How about a class at the local college? Or the line dancing group that meets at the city center every Wednesday night? The point is, you have to get out there. You've heard all of this before, but you've made one excuse after another not to participate. No more. Stop hiding. Make plans now to expand your circle of friends. Keep an open mind and use your imagination. Here are some further possibilities.

Pen Pals

Pen-A-Friend

Stacy Alberts, president. Looking for a pen pal? Find someone special to correspond with through this service. For $4 you can acquire the name and address of one "Large & Lovely" pen pal. For $10 your name can be placed in a special cross-country listing that goes out to others. Pen-A-Friend also offers four booklets of interest: *Sex Appeal Secrets for Full Figured Ladies, Full Figured Woman's Guide to Happiness, Full Figured Woman's Guide to Sexuality,* and *Building Big Beautiful Self-Esteem.*

Write Weight International pen pal program.

> *I had asked this guy to dance and he had turned me down. That same song, he was dancing with somebody else. I walked up to him and said, "Did you turn me down because of my weight?" He looked at me and said, "No, I turned you down because you're a better dancer than me."*
>
> *It blew my mind! I had to laugh. I said, "Please, I would really like to dance with you." And we did fine.*
>
> —ANNETTE

Social Clubs and Organizations for Both Women and Men

• California •

BABES! Todd Douglas, founder. "Where Big Is Beautiful." Dances, dinners, and other social activities in the Ventura area.

The Big Difference Pamela Lynn, director. The Big Difference, located in the Los Angeles area, is a big, busy club. There seems to always be some event coming up . . . dances seem to be the big favorite. But Pam certainly doesn't stop there. On top of dances for virtually every holiday, she puts together fashion shows, a formal open house, and Cinco de Mayo, Mardi Gras, and pool parties. Give the Big Difference a call and get your name on their mailing list. By the way, the events newsletter contains a personals section.

Big Stuff Dances "For culturally diverse, big, beautiful singles and those who love them!" Monthly dances at good hotels in the San Francisco area. Cash bar, door prizes, lingerie fashion shows.

The Dinner Group Here's something a little different . . . this Long Beach group is for those who are interested in gaining weight or encouraging weight gain.

Fat and Terrific (FAT) San Francisco Bay Area group with movies, picnics, and various other outings. Dinner meetings are held the third Saturday of each month.

More 2 Luv Dance parties and other social events, including yard sales and casual backyard parties, in the Los Angeles area.

Movers and Shakers San Francisco Bay Area dinner club meets once a month.

oooO Baby Baby Special events for BBWs and their admirers in the San Francisco Bay Area.

• Florida •

Livin' Large South Florida dances.

Rubenesque/Full Figured Dances Howard Green, sponsor. Call for information on singles dances in the Fort Lauderdale area for "Rubenesque/Full Figured People and Those Who Admire Us."

• Indiana •

Livin' and Lovin' Large Social functions for full-figured ladies and their admirers on a bimonthly basis, for folks in the Fort Wayne area.

• Georgia •

Southeast Super Singles Social events and a bimonthly newsletter with personal ads for people in the Atlanta area.

• Massachusetts •

Big Sensations Monthly dance parties and social occasions for big, beautiful people and their admirers in Massachusetts.

Fat and Happy Club Formed in 1993 in Somerset with the goal to provide an organization with a newsletter, social events, a clothing line, and social meetings at regional, state, and national levels.

Sensations Monthly dance parties for big men and women and their admirers in Massachusetts.

• Missouri •

Chub Club Social club for large-size people and their admirers in the Saint Louis area.

Midwest XXXtras Size acceptance group in the Kansas City area with social functions.

• New Jersey •

Ample Awakenings Dance parties and socials in the South Jersey and Philadelphia areas for people of size and their admirers.

• New York •

Goddesses Dance parties in the New York City area for big, beautiful women and the men who love them. Call or write for more information and a sample newsletter or just show up for one of the dances. Thursday nights ($10): Stars, 381 Jericho Turnpike, Floral Park, NY; (516) 437-8590. Or every other Saturday ($20): Café 44, 315 West 44th Street, NYC; (212) 582-3080.

Goddesses also arranges lingerie shows. Talk to Nancy for more information.

Large Encounters Dance parties held weekly at various locations in New York and New Jersey. $10 to $15 per person.

Personality Plus Dance parties for large people and their admirers in the Pearl River area.

• North Carolina •

Extra Dimensions Dances and other social events in the Raleigh area. "There is always a festive, friendly, and fun atmosphere as well as entertainment, food, and dancing." Subscribe to Extra Dimensions' newsletter to keep abreast of all special day, weekend, and week-long trips planned.

• Pennsylvania •

At Large Social club with dances, swim parties, workshops, and weekend getaways. Newsletter for members.

• Rhode Island •

The Well-Rounded Club Diane Ilic, founder. Dances and other social events for "Big beautiful gals and the men who prefer them!" in Rhode Island, Massachusetts, and Connecticut.

• Texas •

People of Size Social Club "Created especially for big folks and friends. Where your pants or dress size doesn't matter, but your attitude does!" This Dallas organization offers dances, raffles, personals, and a bimonthly newsletter.

• Virginia •

The Wide Appeal Social Club Dances, trips, hobby clubs, pool parties, pen pals, and parties for large people and their admirers. Single members may participate in a matchmaking service. Bimonthly newsletter.

• National •

National Association to Advance Fat Acceptance (NAAFA) Conventions offer workshops, fashion shows, swim parties, special interest group meetings, guest speakers, discussion sessions, sight-seeing trips, and talent shows. Of special interest is the annual Fat Woman's Gathering, held in the fall each year and hosted by NAAFA's Feminist Caucus.

• Canada •

People At Large (PAL) Social and support network "to promote size acceptance, self-esteem and social integration" in Etobicoke, Ontario.

• England •

Planet Big Girl Club in London for large women and their admirers, open on the first Thursday of each month.

Social Clubs and Organizations for Women

• California •

Club 14 Plus A Los Angeles–based social and educational organization for big women.

• Massachusetts •

Abundance: Full Lives for Large Women Support group for women of size in the Newton Center area.

Social Clubs and Organizations for Men

• The Brotherhood of Girth •

Ottawa, Ontario–based men's group dedicated to improving the lives of fat people everywhere. While not a gay men's group, gays are welcome to participate. Social and political activities, information databases, and charity events benefiting various causes are available.

Social Clubs and Organizations for Gays and Lesbians

• California •

Let It All Hang Out (LIAHO) This fat lesbian group sponsors dances and other fund-raisers in the Oakland area for a float in the Lesbian/Gay/Bisexual Freedom Day Parade, held yearly in San Francisco.

• National •

Affiliated Big Men's Clubs, Inc. A gay men's organization that serves as a clearinghouse for information regarding big men's clubs all over the country and in Europe. There are clubs in New York; Chicago; Atlanta; Houston; Seattle; San Francisco; Denver; Washington, D.C.; Fort Lauderdale; Naples; Los Angeles; San Diego; Daly City; London; Milan; and in Belgium, with new locations opening regularly.

• France •

Amigros France Gay men's organization similar to Girth and Mirth.

• International •

Girth and Mirth These gay men's clubs are found throughout the United States and Europe. They are formed for the benefit of big men and their admirers to provide an accepting atmosphere and social opportunities free of prejudice. Girth and Mirth holds yearly conferences, called Convergence. In 1993 they met in Washington, D.C., and in 1994 in New York City. See Affiliated Big Men's Clubs (above) for a listing of clubs currently operating. New ones are being formed every year.

I love to meet people, dance, party, go out and have a really good time. When I created the Big Difference, my purpose was to establish an atmosphere where people would feel comfortable no matter what their size. I wanted to see lots of people having a good time. I started my club with the hope we could have lots of people coming in, meeting new people and bringing that kind of energy home with them.

My girlfriend and I came up with the name . . . the Big Difference. It has so many different connotations. Big people, making a big difference in your life, a different kind of club. All positive. August 7, 1992, was our first event. We had about 200 people, probably 60 percent women. For a club like this that seemed to be a great ratio. We seem to draw new and exciting quality men and women. We have hostesses to make people comfortable. We try to give the extra touch, the feeling that you belong.

Rubens had GREAT taste in women.

Every dance is totally unique. There are some regulars and always some new and exciting people to meet. We like trying different things. We do party dances right now. We had one at a bed-and-breakfast that was very successful. We're looking into a hot tub party this summer. We have located a place in San Dimas with a hot tub that holds twenty to thirty people.

We have people who fly in for events or drive for four hours to get here. One woman has flown in from Colorado for ten dances now. There is nothing available where she is. She could fly to New York or elsewhere if she chose to, but she comes to us.

What I would like for people to get from the Big Difference is "Wow, I'm having a great time! Man, I feel good. I made myself look great and people responded in a positive way." Or "I felt positive about myself." Take that home with yourself. Incorporate good feelings and confidence like this into your life. No one should question us living life to the fullest.

—PAMELA LYNN

Dating Services

• California •

Pudgy Love "Pudgy Love is a dating service for hefty, hardy, singles, age eighteen and older and those that wish to date hefty people." This service in Burbank sends a short questionnaire and then uses your responses to match you to others for possible correspondence, dating, and/or marriage. You pay $60 for ten introductions.

• New York •

Full of Life Judy Nisbett and Phyllis Saunders, founders. "Full of Life is a computer dating service that promotes self-acceptance for those who are rich in body and their admirers who join us in the realization that Beauty Comes in All Sizes."

You fill out a questionnaire and mail it in along with a check or money order (one to three introductions, $35; three to nine introductions, $75; six to eighteen introductions, $100; twelve to twenty-four introductions, $120). Your information is entered into Full of Life's database, and the computer matches you up. Each month they send you the profiles, first names, and phone numbers of up to three matches. The same people get your profile. It's up to you to take it from there.

Operating in the Mamaroneck area, Full of Life also sponsors events . . . a jazz tea and lingerie show, game nights, dances, Sunday brunches, and safe sex workshops . . . and publishes a quarterly newsletter listing upcoming events, articles of interest, and stories of successful matches.

• Pennsylvania •

Big But Beautiful (BBB) Joye Asta, founder and manager. BBB operates mainly in the Philadelphia area, serving as matchmaker for the "tall and/or full-figured." Prospective dates are personally selected from information you supply through a questionnaire. A list of first names and phone numbers is mailed to you; what you do from there is up to you. BBB has been operating since 1987, and Ms. Asta estimates she has served more than 12,000 clients.

BBB has a yearly newsletter that is mailed to clients informing them of "Happenings"—media attention, engagements, weddings, births, and so forth.

Chubby Connections This service serves people in the Philadelphia area.

• England •

Chubby Companions Based in the Lancashire area, this company offers unlimited introductions and competitive rates to those interested in romance of a larger nature.

Plump Partners Dating Agency A national dating agency in England.

PERSONALS PUBLICATIONS, MATCHMAKERS, AND CHAT LINES

We've all seen the ads:

> *DWM, 45; 6'1", 170 lbs; Lee Majors type; enjoys romantic evenings and quiet talks. Athletic and sociable. Sensitive. Seeking pretty, slender SWF, 18–25 for fun and possible relationship.*
>
> *(Reality translation: Divorced white male, 55, 5'10", 250 lbs; my mother says I'm handsome; football games by the soft glow of the TV tube [Keep it down, would you? This is an important play.] I bowl with my buddies. I know all about that PMS nonsense. No fatties.)*

Forget those losers. Here are some personals ads services created especially for large-size people and their admirers.

BBW Express "The magazine of personal classified ads for BBWs (Big Beautiful Women) and the men who love BBWs." Published by the people at *BBW* magazine. No 900 number; all ads have a code number. If someone interests you, you write to them via the code listed in the magazine. Subscription: approximately $20 for 12 issues.

Beautiful Girls German personals magazine. Subscription: approximately $10 (U.S.), 15 DM.

Big Ad International personals for large gay men. *Big Ad* offers fiction, articles on pertinent issues, and personal ads, many with pictures. Each month four men are featured, complete with three pages of photos for each man. Published bimonthly. $6.95 per issue or $38 for a one-year subscription (which allows you to place one free 50-word ad); $40 in Canada, $75 international.

Big Ad Personals Big gay men and their admirers. Call this line to leave a message of your own or to listen to and respond to other ads. A service of *Big Ad* magazine. $1.29 per minute.

Dimensions "The lifestyle magazine for men who prefer large, radiant women." Lots of personals ads with some photos. Adult material. Bimonthly. Subscription: $24 for 6 issues.

Dimensions Personals "For big women and their admirers." You may call this number to leave a message of your own, listen to and respond to other ads, or respond to many of the ads that are listed in *Dimensions* magazine. $1.49 per minute.

The Grande Connection Personals service for large-size people and their admirers. This service offers a couple of items not found on other lines. From the menu you can choose to hear a calendar of size-positive events, arranged by area code; browse through a collection of goods and services available from many sources (if you have something to offer, be sure to place an ad); or listen to ads placed by women looking for men or men looking for women. $1.49 a minute.

Large Encounters Personals Newsletter and Chat Line Personal ad newsletter for big, beautiful women and the men who love them. $1.50 a minute for chat line.

Love Handles Singles publication for large people and their admirers. Send a self-addressed stamped envelope for subscription information.

Love Handles For large people and their admirers. $1.49 a minute.

Loving You Large Dateline Personals and interactive forums on issues affecting large-size women and their admirers. $1.98 a minute.

NAAFA-Date Talking Personals "Go ahead. Flirt a little." $1.49 a minute.

oooO Baby Baby Talking Personals Place an ad on the 800 number, then call back later on the 900 number to pick up messages. The 900 line also carries information about events across the country. $1.49 per minute.

The Romance Line "The place to meet men who adore big women." $1.99 a minute.

Larry Woolwine, publisher of *Big Ad* magazine, is an attractive, cuddly-looking, 6' tall, 310-pound, thirty-nine-year-old gay man who moved to San Francisco from Atlanta in 1980. His voice and manner reflect a friendly, open, and intelligent conversationalist. Larry grew up in West Virginia, the son of a coal miner, and worked in the hotel industry until recently.

In 1976 I moved to Atlanta, Georgia. In 1980 I met someone through a personal ad. I moved to San Francisco and I lived with this person for seven years. At that time I weighed around 240 to 250 pounds. We had a good relationship. The main thing was he thought he could change me as far as my build and body size went. The whole six years he constantly hounded me about losing weight. He would tell me, "You're such a good-looking man. All you need to do is lose a few pounds and you can have anybody you want." Basically he didn't realize I didn't want "anyone." I wanted to be settled down in a monogamous relationship.

In the six years when I was in that relationship, constantly being hounded about my weight, my weight constantly fluctuated. Ten pounds down, ten pounds up. Or ten pounds down, twenty pounds up is the way it usually goes. As soon as I ended that relationship and accepted myself for who I was and where I felt comfortable my weight stabilized.

In 1987 I ended that relationship and found myself a single, large male thrown out into the gay community with AIDS on the rise. I really didn't know how to deal with it. I had been with someone for such a long time. A couple of friends got me involved with a small group in the Bay Area called Round-About, which was for large gay men and their admirers. They helped me open my eyes as far as seeing that it was okay to be a large man. We were still discriminated against, pretty much laughed at, and not accepted in the Castro Area (the large gay community here). We were more accepted in the south-of-Market area, where the leather-type guys hang out.

The bar scene wasn't my scene. Dating wasn't something I looked forward to. So I turned to running personal ads in local gay and lesbian papers. I was very honest and up-front that I was 6'2", 280 pounds, not a bodybuilder. I would talk to people on the phone; they would think I was pleasant and cordial. I would try to explain to them that I was a husky-built-type man. They would say, "I would like to meet you." So I'd go out for dinner and drinks, thinking all along that the conversation and the meeting were going very well. At the end of the evening I would get very bold and ask how they felt things were going. They would reply, "Well, you are just a little bigger than I thought you were going to be." It was like being hit by a Mack truck. I went through a lot of those.

In 1990 I decided this was not what I wanted, that there had to be a different avenue. I had compiled a list of names of one hundred people who were either large-size men or admirers of large-size men. I contacted a number of them asking if a personals magazine for large-size people was something they would be interested in. I got a positive response from a little over two thirds, so we proceeded. In January of 1990 we mailed out the first issue of Big Ad. *It was a total of four 8½" by 11" pages folded in the middle with twenty-five personal ads. We charged $1 apiece. Within a year's time I would say we had about three hundred people who were writing back and forth to each other. The magazine was now about ten pages, folded, photocopied on the Xerox machine and put together on a friend's dining room table.*

In February of 1992 a friend of mine said, "Why don't you try and put these in a gay bookstore?" The first store we contacted was A Different Light Books here in San Francisco in the Castro Area. They took fifteen magazines and called two weeks later saying they needed to get fifteen more. At this point the magazine was paying for itself . . . postage and printing. The labor was a labor of love. It continued growing as one store after another was contacted or contacted me.

In the 1993 June/July issue, we went to an 8½" by 11", forty-four-page, full-glossy, professional, offset-printed format. We are now printing four thousand copies with over five hundred personal ads and photographs. There are men from all over the world . . . Australia, New Zealand, Africa, Mexico. Ten percent of our subscribers are outside the United States. In each magazine we feature four men. We try to do a smaller man who is attracted to large men; a medium-size large man, what we call a "teddy-bear"–type guy; and we try to do a full-framed man, which can be anywhere from three hundred to five hundred pounds. Also, at the end of the year we do a magazine called Special Edition *that is nothing but photographs, generally about fifty pages, of models from the prior year.*

In February of 1992 we went on-line with the first 900 number exclusively for large-size men and women . . . straight, gay, and lesbian. It is advertised all across the United States in magazines like Dimensions, *gay and lesbian newsletters, and NAAFA newsletters. We average one hundred and twenty-six calls a day, and the average is about five minutes per call.*

I know of probably forty couples who are together because of ads placed in Big Ad. *I had a call just a few minutes ago from a man, Ray, who had been one of our "featured" men in a regular edition and then had been on the cover and the centerfold of* Special Edition *last year. Ray had gone down to pick up two friends of his who were coming in from New Orleans to our yearly confer-*

ence, called Convergence, for big men. They had a third associate with them who asked who was picking them up at the airport. They told him that it was Ray and who Ray was. This guy couldn't believe that there was a real person named Ray. He thought we had just hired someone to "be" Ray, to do those ads. He had literally been in awe of Ray. He was astounded when Ray picked them up at the airport. Now they are happily living together here in the Bay Area and have been for six months. I think the majority of people who advertise in Big Ad, probably 90 percent, are looking for a long-time commitment.

There is so much vulnerability in the large community . . . both gay and straight. We don't monitor our calls on our 900 number that often, but our service bureau does. They gave me a call about three weeks ago saying there was a message I really needed to listen to. It was from a large, black, straight female living in, I think, Chicago. She had gone onto the straight men's side to leave a message for the women to listen to. She was warning about someone on the 900 line she had corresponded with. Besides running up a considerable phone bill, she ended up in Nashville, Tennessee, in a motel at her expense. Then the guy spent little or no time with her in a four-day weekend. She was warning people to be careful of him and asking them to leave her a message telling her of similar incidents. She said she would pass the information on to the owners of the 900 service so that we could screen our users better. I had to delete the message, but I did leave her a message explaining that there is no way we can screen our users for that sort of problem.

People write to me monthly complaining they have written to someone and not received a reply. They want me to suspend that person's subscription. I can't go to these people's homes and make them write letters. And I can't tell you if someone is telling you the truth on the phone. You have to know that yourself and not be so vulnerable. A lot of large people feel they are lonely and what they need out of life is someone. But you will only end up being hurt even more if you aren't careful. It's hard, so far as trying to meet someone and finding out what they are really like.

I don't consider myself different from anyone else. I live basically a heterosexual lifestyle, but my partner is male. We have a three-bedroom, two-bath home and a dog. One of us cooks dinner; one cleans. I think because of the AIDS epidemic more gays are coming together in a more monogamous, heterosexual-type life.

We really try to promote the use of condoms. I do a lot of trade shows and stuff for the magazine. I think the majority of the 900 numbers are promoted as sex lines. We wanted to promote that this was not a sex line. It's a personals, introductory service. Basically, it is just voice mail. At the trade shows, my giveaway for the magazine is condoms. Of course, being the chubby community, most are disappointed when it isn't candy! When we went to NAAFA we gave a piece of candy and a condom.

There was an article in the Advocate *about a woman who said, "If you are large there is a very good percentage you are HIV negative." That is scary because that is, under no circumstances, true. And that goes for straight or gay. The virus doesn't care how many fat cells you have. I've had friends who have passed away (from AIDS) who still weighed 220 pounds. It attacks people in different ways. I'm afraid if the large community feels that as long as you are fat, as long as you've got some weight on you, you're healthy. It's just not true. I think the gay community, among large-size individuals, is more knowledgeable about that. It scares me that people don't use protection.*

FRIENDSHIP AND ROMANCE ON THE INFORMATION SUPERHIGHWAY

Computers have become a major part of our lives in a very short time. We can use them to keep us organized, play games, and work. But are you aware of the social possibilities? With the addition of a terminal program and a modem, you can talk to people across town, in another city, and all over the world through on-line services or bulletin board services (BBSs).

Most communities have at least a few local boards; most large cities have hundreds. For information on how to contact these boards, call the store where you purchased your modem. They should be able to point you to a listing of all that is available locally. Boards may be of general interest or geared to specific topics such as computing, role-playing games, science fiction, home schooling, religion, parenting, chess, large people, writing, sex, matchmaking, alternate lifestyles, and others. The possibilities are as varied as the people who use them. Users are all ages, professions, and interests.

Some boards have only message bases; some have chat areas. Messages are posted and can be read by anyone who comes along later. In chat areas you talk with someone else who has also called the board at that time . . . the talk is "real time." Depending on the number of lines the BBS has, you may have just one or two other people to talk with at a time—or there may be fifty others on-line. The bigger services, like CompuServe and America Online, can have hundreds of people in chat areas at one time.

Most of the people you talk with on-line will just be acquaintances. Some will become close friends. A few may become best friends you don't know how you ever got along without. But these friendships don't have to stay on the computer. It's not unusual to take the computer friendships off-line by talking on the telephone, exchanging photos, meeting for group parties, or just meeting one-to-one. Friendships deepen, romances bloom, and some people even marry other people they met on-line. The point is, you can interact with others on an intellectual level without having judgments made based on looks.

It is entirely possible to make business contacts, find a job, go shopping, keep in touch with family across the country, make friends, fall in love, and even get engaged (not recommended, but I've seen it happen) without leaving the comfort of your home. I have become involved in business deals through on-line contacts and have made friends with publishers and other writers who have helped my career. I work in my home and transmit articles I have written to publishers all over the country via my modem. The possibilities are endless.

• E-mail •

E-mail is the main form of communication for most on-line service users. When you sign onto a service you will have your very own E-mail address. From there you can send and receive E-mail with people on the system you use and, almost always, on other systems throughout the world. There is generally no charge for this service (though some systems charge after a certain number of pieces are sent), and your message is usually sent and received within minutes. E-mail can be sent via Internet to many of the people, organizations, and services listed in this book. Check their listings for on-line contact information.

And Ye Shall Be Known As . . . In most chat areas you choose an alias. Some people use their own names or a variation of them (DonnaM, ~*~David~*~). Most seem to enjoy being a bit more creative, choosing a name that tells something about themselves (Pilot, Happy Husband) or their interests (Sky Diver, ChessMaster). Others love being able to express a part of their personality (Shy Guy, PixieHeart) or show a certain heavenly glamour (Star Fire, Angel's Delight). Choosing an alias is a lot like picking personalized license plates for your trip down the information superhighway. Your on-line name adds to the perception people have of you, so choose carefully and have fun.

Donna was thirty-one years old, divorced, and weighed over 300 pounds. She lived in Phoenix, had a good enough job, her own car (paid for), a few friends, and a dog. She used a computer at work and would often access a major on-line service to conduct research for her boss. At night she used the same service to talk with people from all over the world. On-line she was known as *SweetChild*. Donna was shy and quiet. As *SweetChild*, however, she was confident and bold, the life of the party. Always quick with a clever comment and friendly to everyone, she was well-liked and sought after for conversations.

It wasn't long before *SweetChild* had made several good friends. *Merry Maid* (who lived in Denver), *En Vogue* (from New York), *KnightMe* (from Sacramento), and she were all particularly close. They would meet on-line every night at eight. They would tell each other about their days. *En Vogue* had a new baby and *SweetChild* loved to hear about the baby's little progresses.

PuppyDoc, a veterinarian, often joined their group and shared stories about her patients.

SweetChild soon developed a special liking for *KnightMe*. They spent hours chatting each week, both with the others and alone. He delighted in her sense of humor and often told her what a wonderful friend she was. She loved his kindness and obvious concern for her. They told each other everything . . . past and present . . . and shared their dreams. When *SweetChild* was home with the flu for three days, *KnightMe* stayed on-line and amused her. From that point on, they were almost always seen on-line together.

About six months after Donna had met Mark (*KnightMe*'s real name) on-line, he suggested they meet in "real life." Donna was nervous as can be, afraid that Mark wouldn't like her. She had told him she was a big woman and even exchanged photos, but she was still nervous. Mark persisted and they did get together. The friendship turned into far more.

It took a lot of planning and some big changes, but almost a year to the day after first talking on-line, Mark and Donna were married. She moved to Sacramento; they found a house just outside of town. Donna plans to buy a couple of horses before long. They both still keep in touch with *Merry Maid*, *PuppyDoc*, and *En Vogue*.

Mark tells me he had never really thought about dating fat women before and it's unlikely he would have been attracted to Donna if they had met the old-fashioned way. But he and Donna had become so close on-line . . . well, he just didn't care about size. He says he fell in love with her sense of humor, intelligence, and compassion and now is very much attracted to all of her.

(This story is true; names and aliases have been changed. Any duplication of an on-line alias is purely coincidental.)

Of course, not everybody who goes on-line finds true love. But everyone can find friends. Most of the people in the on-line community are friendly, honest, intelligent, and sensitive. There are also con men (and women), oddballs, and crude people. As in all of life, you have to use common sense and good judgment.

Generally, you pay a monthly fee and receive a limited number of hours on-line. For instance, on CompuServe you are billed $9.95 a month. For this you receive five hours of on-line time; subsequent hours are billed at $2.95 each. Other options are available. There is some variation in prices from system to system, but this is pretty general. Local systems seldom charge anything, but some do. You just have to check around to find the right board for you.

Following is a listing of the major national systems that have chat areas and smaller boards that are either built around larger users or have areas devoted to fat issues. Please keep in mind that rates change often and services come and go.

•BBSs of Special Interest•

The Amazon Arena "We have the largest selection of big, powerful, and Amazonicly proportioned women of any BBS in the world." The co-sysop here is said to be 6'3", 250+ pounds, with 32" thighs. You can download gifs (computerized pictures) of this woman and others. Adult files and gifs. Registration: $45 a year, $50 for credit card users. Use registration form found on-line.

The Big Picture "The best in pro-fat." This BBS offers free limited access; you can increase the amount of time alloted daily by making a donation to the board; you pay long-distance charges. Conferences include these topics and more: Big Men's Conference, the Personals, Large Clothing, and Health and Fat Issues. Like most BBSs, the user base is 85 percent male. No real-time chat.

Centerville BBS Featuring FAT (Fat Activists Together). Centerville BBS offers an open forum for discussion of size rights activism. Except for long-distance charges, there is no fee to access.

Electronic Erotica BBS "Your best Pro-Fat on-line source." Over 2,000 BBW pictures available for download plus contacts for singles and couples.

Paul's Waka Waka BBS "Serving gay and bi chubbies from all over the world." Paul Casey, the sysop, has been running this system since 1989 and has more than 500 users. Though the BBS is based in Washington, most of Paul's users are from out of state. Access is free with limited daily time, but donations are always accepted and give you an increase in the amount of time allowed.

The Rotunda "This is a Pagan, pro-fat BBS of an adult nature." Interesting, if somewhat eclectic, combination of topics. This very friendly board offers access to two Internet newsgroups of interest, alt.support.bigfolk and alt.fat.sex. The sysop, John Halbig, is a writer, photographer, and admirer of large ladies.

The Snack Bar Fat-friendly BBS aimed mostly at FAs (fat admirers). Gifs, text stories, and forums.

•International Systems (The Really Big Guys)•

America Online (AOL), CompuServe (CIS), Delphi, and GEnie All have real-time chat areas. Most offer supportive, message-based forums for large people, such as CompuServe's Ample Opportu-nity forum. On these services you can interact with people from all over the world. If your Internet provider offers Internet Relay Chat (IRC) be sure to join one of the many BBS chat channels.

•Something a Little Different•

Matchmaker "The Electronic Pen Pal Network." This system is run on E-mail. You fill out a matchmaker questionnaire as you sign on. The system then matches you up with others and gives you their names and E-mail addresses. You can browse the personal information of those selected for you and determine if you are interested in corresponding with them. Only first names are used, so you have a good deal of anonymity.

Local dial-ups are available in Houston; San Antonio; Dallas; Austin; Santa Clara, California; Denver; New York; San Diego; Tampa; Los Angeles; Washington, D.C.; and Anchorage. Dial the main number with your modem for further information and numbers for other cities.

USENET NEWSGROUPS

Using your computer you can also access newsgroups, each dedicated to a specific subject. These are accessible and participated in by people from around the world. Some of the usenet newsgroups that may be of interest to you on the Internet are listed in Appendix B.

MAILING LISTS

Mailing lists are essentially the same as special interest newsgroups but are carried on through E-mail to a list of subscribers. This is a benefit in that the owner of the list can remove users who are a problem and can also control the content of messages posted. Many people prefer mailing lists to newsgroups, feeling the added privacy allows them to be more open with their feelings. Mailing lists are available to people from all over the world. See Appendix B for lists especially for big folks.

WORLD WIDE WEB SITES

Web sites are accessible through a system referred to as world wide web. They are information sites, most often used for advertising a service or company. They run the gamut from simple text information to state-of-the-art graphics and live movie camera shots. A friend told me of a web site where you can watch a bridge being built . . . live. Many of the businesses listed in this book have web sites. Check them out! Appendix B at the end of the book contains the addresses of many sites of interest to large people.

➡ If any data listed in this chapter need to be corrected, please let me know. If you know of a service or product useful to people of size, please write to me about it. The information may be made available to readers through the newsletter "Size Wise Update!," the Size Wise web site, or through possible future revisions of this book.

PERSONAL GLIMPSE:
"BUTTERCUP"

During the week Karen is a thirty-year-old assistant director of sales. She says that, as the only woman in the division, the men spoil her. I suspect they enjoy the task immensely. On weekends she transforms herself into the wildly delightful hostess of a popular local cable access show. Her soft, whispery voice combined with her unusual inflections and forthright manner are reminiscent of the movie legend she models herself after, Marilyn Monroe. In either persona, Karen is delightful, full of fun, and sure to bring a warm smile.

My partner, Billy, and I had a weekly cable access show. We were the number-one show on our station. It was wild. I went by the name of Buttercup. Buttercup was this big blonde with a lot of hair, lots of makeup, and big false eyelashes. Buttercup basically came across as this blond bubblehead who sees the world through rose-colored glasses. But she had a real wild side to her that she exposed every time there was a real good-looking guy on the show.

We would have three guests—one "normal" person and two really off-the-wall people. We'd have a really tacky Elvis impersonator, then maybe a nymphomaniac and a cemetery owner. We'd sit in this big round pink booth. Naturally, we would make the conversation go toward sex. Before you knew it, people would forget they were on camera because it was such a relaxed setting. You'd be surprised at the things people want to tell you. We just kept the questions and laughter flowing.

We're both overweight, and we constantly joked about food and diets. Billy is totally relaxed, and every week he would talk about it, saying, "Oh well, I didn't diet this week but there's always next week. Big deal."

We also did talent shows and community things for charity. We got tons of fan mail. People would write in asking, "Do you wear underwear?" and "Are you and Billy having an affair?" They asked for my autograph all the time. I enjoyed giving autographs with lipstick. I'd carry a bunch of cheap tubes of lipstick and make the men take off their shirts so I could write a big *B* on their chests. People gave me presents every week. They'd act like I was this big star. It was great fun. We were forever getting into trouble. We had church women calling all the time and complaining. That's how we knew we were so popular. I never went out with men who wrote to me at the show. They liked Buttercup . . . the character.

Billy is also a hairdresser. He tells me all the time that women who are thin and really gorgeous will ask, "How can I meet men?" Here they are a perfect size 6 with big boobs and natural blond hair and they are sitting at home on a Saturday night. That makes me feel really good when he tells me things like that.

The last time I weighed myself . . . well, I shouldn't say the last time. Basically, the last time I like to remember, I weighed 155. So that's what I tell people. I have a problem with numbers. I'm a size 24. I don't mind saying the size because as a woman you know what a 22-24 is. I accept myself for who I am and love myself. I do have physical limitations—I can't go up three flights of stairs without huffing and puffing. But being overweight isn't going to stop me from going out on a Saturday night. I think of myself as a bigger version of Marilyn Monroe.

I admit I'd be a little happier if I was thinner, but I don't let it worry me. I'd like to lose weight for health reasons. When Oprah went on Optifast, I went on Optifast. I did Optifast for eighty-seven days straight and never cheated once. I lost ninety-five pounds. I got really thin, but then I also got real sick and lost a lot of my hair.

I'm a real goal achiever. I set a goal and achieve that goal no matter what. I do it perfectly, but once it's over I'm back to my old ways. I don't think diets work. You spend so much money on Jenny Craig, and once you finish eating those little packets of food you go back to your own food. Now I basically try to eat healthier because I realize I'm going to have this problem for the rest of my life. So I make choices. I believe in trying to live a healthy lifestyle. That's the important thing.

I think that basically no matter what size I am, I'm the same person. I take every day as it comes. I'm not going to let that four-letter word (*diet*) ruin my life. That's how I got so heavy, because of the damned diets. Every time I went on one I'd gain the weight back and more.

I was on the *Jerry Springer Show* one time. I asked him, "What do you think I should do, sit home all the time wearing black and not leaving my house?" It really upsets me when I find people are not living life to the fullest because they are overweight. God knows you may wake up tomorrow with regrets. Sure, there are physical limitations. We're not going to go bungee jumping, but heck, we can go out and do whatever else we want.

I went to get my driver's license renewed not too long ago. The guy says, "Is there anything you want to change on here?" He's looking at me, and I know he's making some kind of comment about my weight. He says, "Well, you know there's something on here that's not right." I say to him, "Well, okay, so I'm not a natural blond. But keep it."

He just started laughing and said, "Get out of here."

"Fat Lady Blues"

I've been on a diet ever since I was sixteen,
Trying hard to fit the image of your basic beauty queen,
You know . . . tits the size of teacups and a waist no one can find,
From Atkins down to Scarsdale, I tread the trail to thin,
Dreaming of designer jeans to pour my svelte self in,
Counting carbohydrates ain't exactly higher math,
Courting malnutrition on the diet path.

Lane Bryant, I swore solemnly, had seen the end of me,
I had my eye on Jordache huggin' hips size skinny three,
When suddenly it hit me like a bolt out of the blue,
That I did not want a bra size thirty-two.

A pipecleaner figure doesn't fill my heart with joy,
How sexy is the figure of a twelve-year-old boy?
If the perfect ten's Bo Derek then the logic seems to be,
That I'm at least a twenty 'cause there's twice as much of me.

Never say "Diet"; bring on the chocolate cake,
The way the Good Lord packaged me is what you'll have to take,
I'm a very sexy lady because I choose to be,
If it was good enough for Rubens, it's good enough for me.

I'm a very sexy lady because it's what I choose,
And you can bet my better assets . . . I won't lose.
I've been on a diet ever since I was sixteen
Trying hard to fit the image of your basic beauty queen.
You know . . . tits the size of teacups and a waist no one can find
And God forbid I should have a behind.

6

LET ME ENTERTAIN YOU!

(Television, Movies, and Songs—Oh My!)

It is a fact of life that we as a society are heavily influenced by the media. What we see and hear on television and in the movies shapes our lives to a great extent. The people who make decisions about how the world is presented to us in these formats have enormous control over attitudes, lifestyles, and state of mind.

Politicians quickly learned the importance of presenting the proper "look" to the eye of the camera. A scruffy, gaunt-looking Richard Nixon found out the hard way what it was like to go up against the handsome, well-groomed, youthful John F. Kennedy during the presidential debates of 1960. One has to wonder how William Taft, at 6', 335 pounds, or Grover Cleveland, at 5'11", 280 pounds, would fare if stumping for votes today. Of course, in their time large men were seen as prosperous and successful. President Clinton, who hovers around 225, seems to feel the need to make amends, as it were, by being seen jogging with troops of reporters and Secret Service agents in tow. David Letterman has a running gag, complete with visual aids, about President Clinton's love of fast-food french fries and makes frequent reference to the president's size. The wise politician keeps a slender profile and smiles big for the camera as he jogs by.

TELEVISION

The typical American adult spends about three hours a day watching news programs, sitcoms, and movies on television; children average even more time. In many homes the television is turned on whenever someone is home . . . sometimes even when no one is home.

So it stands to reason that television plays an important role in defining how we see ourselves and others. Not only does it reflect society's attitudes, it wields incredible power in creating them. A report released by the National Commission on Working Women and reported in the November 26, 1990, issue of *U.S. News & World Report* shows us a television world populated by women who are "young, white, beautiful, and scantily dressed."

There are virtually no Asians or Hispanics or fat people on TV. Most women work as housewives or secretaries and apparently drop off the face of the earth by age forty. The commission blamed this distortion on the lack of women in decision-making positions behind the scenes and "praises the introduction of flawed women like Roseanne as antidotes to the idealized glamour of prime time." ("Flawed women"???)

I love my body . . . every gorgeous inch!

There are relatively few successful fat actors and actresses in television or the movies. For every Roseanne and John Goodman there are hundreds of Holly Hunters and Baldwin men (how many of those guys are there, anyway?) populating our screens.

In the past such wonderful actors as Francis Bavier (the lady who played Aunt Bea on Andy Griffith's show; Dan Blocker (*Bonanza*) and his look-alike son, Dirk Blocker; Andy Devine (Roy Rogers's shows and other westerns); Carroll O'Connor (*All in the Family*); Sally Struthers (also of *All in the Family*); Sebastian Cabot (Mr. French on *Family Affair*); Raymond Burr (*Ironside*); Vivian Vance (*I Love Lucy*); and William Conrad (*Jake and the Fatman, Cannon*, and many movies, including *Body and Soul, Sorry, Wrong Number, East Side, West Side*, and *The Road Back*) have graced the screen. And who can forget Alan Hale, Jr., the skipper on *Gilligan's Island*?

More recently, Wendy Jo Sperber (you may remember her from the sitcom with Tom Hanks and Peter Scolari, *Bosom Buddies*), Susan Peretz and Leslie Boone made history in 1990 with their short-lived but ground breaking show, *Babes*. The women played large-figured sisters who shared an apartment and large figures. Though it leaned a bit too heavily on fat jokes, the show presented fat women as real people with jobs, romances, and the same problems everyone else encounters.

On *Cheers* George Wendt kept us in belly laughs for many years as Norm, the barfly and perfect foil for Cliff, the mailman. Another beloved figure is Charles Kuralt, recently retired, who was a wonderful, calming influence on *Sunday Morning*. Before that he brought us picture postcards from *On the Road*.

Conchetta Farrell, a favorite of mine for years, appeared regularly on *L.A. Law*. Arsenio Hall, a big man even when he's thin, goes up and down in weight but always looks great. His late-night talk show was a success for several years. Gailard Sartain was visible on *Hee Haw* and in the "Ernest" movies. Dana Elcar appeared regularly on *MacGyver*. Nell Carter entertained us for years both with her beautiful singing voice and on *Gimme a Break*. Charles Durning appeared in *Evening Shade* and countless movies. Thea Vidale's short-lived show, *Thea,* presented a fat woman as a strong, loving, competent head of the family.

Delta Burke deserves a tip of the hat for her portrayal of Suzanne Sugarbaker in the long-running series *Designing Women*. The world watched as Delta went from a slender actress playing an ex-beauty queen who considered herself to be the ultimate man bait to a large, alluring actress sharing her frustration and pain at being treated differently because of her increasing size. One episode addressed these issues and was handled with humor, dignity, and compassion. As a woman of ample size, Ms. Burke is still gorgeous and beautifully dressed (with her own line of clothing now in the stores).

More current shows have given us Roseanne on her namesake program (who was once quoted as saying she was a "dyslexic anorexic" . . . she never thought she was fat enough), John Goodman (rock steady and cuddly on *Roseanne*), Marsha Warfield (a strong, intelligent presence on *Night Court* for years, then a regular on *Empty Nest*), Dennis Franz (*NYPD Blue*), Al Roker and Willard Scott (morning weathermen who bring us smiles no matter what the weather), Jackeé (the voluptuous bombshell à la Marilyn Monroe on *Sister, Sister)*, Jane Abbott (*Evening Shade*), Della Reese (*Touched by an Angel*), Liz Torres (nominated for an Emmy for her work on *The John Larouquette Show*), Nell Carter (*Hangin' with Mr. Cooper*), Louie Anderson (*The Louie Show* and countless appearances on comedy club shows), Elaine Miles (the beautiful, dignified, always calm Native American Marilyn, from *Northern Exposure*), along with many cast members of varying large sizes, Yvette Freeman (nurse Haleh Adams on *ER*), Shirley Knight (*Law and Order*), Michael Moore (*TV Nation*), Reginald VelJohnson (Carl on *Family Matters*), David Schram (Roy on *Wings*), Darlene Conley (Sally Spectra on *The Bold and the Beautiful*), and Dave Thomas (Wendy's hamburger chain founder and commercial spokesman). Speaking of commercials, the Snapple lady, Wendy Kaufman, added her own unique flavor while selling us fruit drinks, and I miss her presence.

Then there is always Rush Limbaugh . . . well, enough said.

Still, with few exceptions, the majority of parts available for larger actors are characters who *fit* the fat person stereotypes—lazy, sloppy, unkempt, mean, and/or stupid—or, on the other side of the coin, jolly.

Some television shows are absolutely horrible when it comes to their treatment of fat people. David Letterman cannot seem to resist taking a jab at the occasional large audience member or guest. (Zsa Zsa should consider slapping him instead of policemen when she appears on his show!) Jay Leno is even worse. *Home Improvement*'s lead character, Tim Allen, makes frequent jokes about Al's never-seen fat mother. And the always politically incorrect *Married with Children* is notorious for its jokes about Peg's fat mother and Al's fat women customers.

Picket Fences had the perfect opportunity but blew its chance to make a statement about the discrimination large people face when the show hired actress Darlene Cates for an episode in the 1994 season. Her character's husband dies. An autopsy indicates he was murdered by suffocation. The show ends with tearful apologies from Ms. Cates for being so fat and accidentally smothering her husband as they both slept. While it was stressed that the husband had been quite devoted and loved his wife dearly, overall the show used the fat lady to reinforce negative stereotypes (how many of us have really smothered unsuspecting partners in bed?) and did nothing to present fat people in a positive light. (Ms. Cates, by the way, did a wonderful job playing the mother in the movie *What's Eating Gilbert Grape*.)

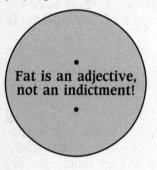

Fat is an adjective, not an indictment!

On the other hand, *Picket Fences* scored points for one of its regular cast members, Zelda Rubenstein. Size was never an issue, and she was treated just like anyone else on the show, even though Ms. Rubenstein is both fat and a little person. This delightful actress played her part with humor and dignity.

Even the news programs are loosening up on their tradition of plastic Barbie and Ken anchors and other on-air personnel. In 1981 Christine Craft was demoted from her position as anchor to reporter at KMBC-TV in Kansas City, Missouri, for being, according to her, "too old, too ugly, and not deferential to men." (She won the first courtroom battle but lost on appeal.) Her problem wasn't size, it was looksism. But today news viewers can watch the talented Candy Crowly (a large woman whose reports on CNN covering the Senator Packwood debate were concise and well-presented) and several other newswomen over age forty-five in key, very visible positions. Star Jones is a gorgeous, big woman who was prominently featured on several talk/news programs during the O. J. Simpson trial. Slow but sure progress.

Speaking of the news programs (the print media and radio are just as much at fault here) . . . it's a shame that John Candy's death was blamed repeatedly in the press on his large size (6'3" and 350+ lbs). While his weight may have been a contributing factor, seldom were his family history of early deaths to heart disease, his yo-yo dieting, his lack of physical activity, his two-pack-a-day addiction to cigarettes, or his recent seventy-pound weight loss (all now believed to play a much more important role in heart problems than body size) discussed. Why did his weight have to be mentioned at all during tributes to him? He was a much-loved, admired, and talented actor with many friends and fans who will miss him. His size did not define him or his contributions.

Many media stars go up and down in size . . . Elizabeth Taylor and Oprah are the two who catch the most flack from the press when their weight goes up. Oprah seems to lead the country on a wild roller coaster weight-loss/gain ride. One person told me, "When Oprah diets, I diet. When she gets thin, I get thin." Such is the influence of people in the media. I congratulate Oprah on her recent lifestyle changes that have given her improved health (and, as a by-product, a smaller body). Now, will she loan me her personal cook and trainer? I hope Oprah's most recent weight loss (and accompanying fat bashing) won't send thousands of people back to dangerous low-calorie diets in an attempt to emulate her success.

On the other hand, cable channel ESPN2 offers *The Fabulous SportsBabe*, a big, high-spirited, very popular and knowledgeable woman who seems to have no shortage of her own fans.

CAN WE TALK?

Talk shows are a whole breed of entertainment unto themselves. Some shows are informative, some amusing; most seem to be confrontational—which is exactly what the producers of those shows want. Ratings are what counts, and the viewing public seems to be looking for a good fight. Don't be fooled for one minute that the average talk show producer invites large people on to discuss the issues with some hope of finding solutions or ending discrimination. Hosts' attitudes often flip-flop with each program, one day being sympathetic and seeming to understand size acceptance, the next day helping to pitch the latest low-calorie diet. The bottom line is ratings, and what makes ratings soar is controversy.

Almost every talk show producer planning a "fat theme" invites an "expert" (usually someone hawking the latest diet book) to appear on the panel to chastise the large participants into dieting or being ashamed of themselves. Often there are people planted in the audience to argue every point made or to ridicule the guests.

If you have something to say to the producers or hosts of a talk show about a topic or the treatment of a subject or guest, by all means speak up! Write and let them know your feelings . . . both positive and negative. Your opinion may make a difference. Most shows list contact information as they hit the halfway point or at the end of the program.

Things may be looking up on the talk show front. The *Rosie O'Donnell Show* became an instant hit when it premiered in July 1996. Rosie tells America to grow up about body size and accept that people come in all sizes. She doesn't apologize for her size, has no plans to ever diet again, and seems quite secure with herself. The best part is she doesn't take comments about her weight lightly, as Donny Osmond found out after suggesting a helicopter might not be able to carry her. Donny found himself back on the show a few weeks later begging forgiveness while singing "Puppy Love" in a dog costume. Rosie made her point while America chuckled and cheered. Her overall success with a format of variety acts and celebrity guests may well change the look of daytime TV.

Lee Martindale, the editor of the size-positive magazine *Rump Parliament*, was astounded one night at the behavior she witnessed on a television program on PBS featuring Covert Baily. Mr. Baily was pushing his latest diet book. It wasn't the message that bothered Lee so much as the fat-bashing used to goad people into buying. Within the first ten minutes a fat man was referred to as "El Grosso," viewers were told that "lazyfatperson" is all one word, fat people were portrayed as ignorant overeaters and slobs, and negative stereotypes—that fat people lack willpower and are gluttons—were reinforced. This on PBS, the station run supposedly by and for enlightened, intelligent people.

As Lee pointed out, "It's like funding a positive presentation of the Ku Klux Klan with money donated by African Americans, or using funds donated by Jewish organizations to finance a pro-Nazi program. There is no difference." She immediately complained to her local affiliate and began organizing a boycott.

You can let television stations and producers know when they have participated in this type of bigotry through letters. The FCC requires that all letters be saved for review when licenses are being renewed. Below are the addresses of the major networks; direct your letters to the Audience Relations Department.

For information on how to reach the office of the producer of any show you view, you can also contact the local affiliate or your cable company.

ABC 1330 Avenue of the Americas, New York, NY 10019; (212) 456-1000

Arts & Entertainment 555 Fifth Avenue, New York, NY 10017; (212) 661-4500

CBS 51 West 52nd Street, New York, NY 10019; (212) 975-4321

Cinemax 1100 Avenue of the Americas, New York, NY 10036; (212) 512-1000

CNN 1050 Techwood Drive North West, Atlanta, GA 30318; (404) 827-1500

FOX Network 10201 West Pico Boulevard, Los Angeles, CA 90035; (213) 856-1000

HBO 1100 Avenue of the Americas, New York, NY 10036; (212) 512-1000

MTV 75 Rockefeller Plaza, New York, NY 10019; (212) 258-8000

NBC 30 Rockefeller Plaza, New York, NY 10020; (212) 664-4444

Nickelodeon 75 Rockefeller Plaza, New York, NY 10019; (212) 258-7500

PBS 1320 Braddock Place, Alexandria, VA 22314; (703) 739-5000

Showtime 1633 Broadway, New York, NY 10019; (212) 708-1600

USA Network 1230 Avenue of the Americas, New York, NY 10020; (718) 488-1800

TNT 1050 Techwood Drive Northwest, Atlanta, GA 30318; (408) 827-1647

MOVIES

Every film from Columbia Pictures begins with a lady in a tunic striding forward through the clouds, right arm upstretched and holding a torch. At her inception in 1924 Lady Columbia was voluptuous and curvy, in keeping with the tastes of the day. Over the years she has had a few changes—mostly in hair style and dress. In 1993 Lady Columbia was thinned down considerably and now looks positively skinny. Poor Lady Columbia—gone from looking like a goddess to appearing to be a hungry waif. (In a slightly different area, women engraved on U.S. coins have become decidedly smaller over the years. Women immortalized in coin were, for 128 years, big women. Beginning with what was commonly known as the "Flapper" coin, produced in 1921, models have reflected the growing obsession with thinness in our society.)

Movie stars of the past—like Marilyn Monroe (large by today's standards for a sex symbol), Mae West, and Lillian Russell (both of whom weighed around 220 pounds at different times in their careers)—were loved, admired, and lusted after. Peter Ustinov, Broderick Crawford, Jackie Coogan, and Orson Welles all had distinguished careers as larger-than-life movie stars. Buddy Hackett, W. C. Fields, Lou Costello, Curly Howard, and Oliver Hardy have brought laughter and many smiles to moviegoers.

More recently, large people have been represented in movies by actors and actresses like Rosie O'Donnell (*Sleepless in Seattle, A League of Their Own, Exit to Eden,* and *The Flintstones*), Kathy Bates (brilliant in *Fried Green Tomatoes*), Jonathan Winters, James Earl Jones (what an incredible voice!), Dom DeLuise (*Fatso* and many others), Ned Beatty (*Deliverance*), Danny DeVito, Bette Midler (always bold and delightful), Kathy Najimy (*Sister Act I* and *II* and a wonderful performance in the television special *In Search of Dr. Seuss,* plus dozens of other roles), John Belushi and Dan Aykroyd (originally of *Saturday Night Live*), Marianne Sagebrecht (*Baghdad Cafe*), John Candy, Ricki Lake, (*Hairspray, Cry Baby,* and *Babycakes*), Paul Sorvino, Marlon Brando (the ultimate *Godfather*), James Coco, George Dzundza (*The Butcher's Wife, Fatal Attraction*), Brian Dennehy (*Cocoon*), Pat Corley (*Against All Odds, Night Shift,* and *The Black Marble*), Ritch Brinkley (*Cabin Boy Captain, The Man with One Red Shoe*), Bob Hoskins (*Roger Rabbit*), Zero Mostel (*A Funny Thing Happened on the Way to the Forum*), Victor Buono (*What Ever Happened to Baby Jane?*), Walter Olkewicz (*Making the Grade, Jimmy the Kid*), Edward G. Robinson, Denis Burkley (*Son-In-Law, Stop or My Mom Will Shoot, Suburban Commando, Murphy's Ro-*

mance, No Way Out), Michael G. Hagerty (*Wayne's World, Overboard, Red Heat*), Divine (*Hairspray*), and countless character actors. And I adore Harvey Fierstein. Harvey has had a very successful career playing some of the most unusual and touching roles written for stage, screen, and television.

Ken Tipton, a character actor on television and in movies (he's in *The Flintstones* movie as one of Fred's Water Buffalo buddies), tells me that there are advantages to being a large actor, the main one being lack of competition. Hollywood and New York are teeming with pretty boys. When he goes up for parts requiring a more "real look" or a person of size there aren't that many people reading for the director.

Camryn Manheim, who appeared as Virginia in *The Road to Wellville*, wrote and starred in a one-woman off-Broadway production, *Wake Up, I'm Fat!*, a very well received look at her struggle for self-acceptance that touched people dealing with all sorts of issues in their lives, not just weight.

There is no shortage of talented, large people for the entertainment industry . . . just a serious lack of parts that aren't denigrating and negative. It's time for Hollywood to recognize that people of all sizes can be sexy, glamorous, exciting, and entertaining. If you have a yearning for the sound of "Lights! Camera! Action!" go for it! Don't you dare let your size keep you from anything, not even stardom.

THEATER GROUPS AND PERFORMANCE ARTISTS

Diane Amos
You may remember this charming lady from the Pine Sol commercials, but she does so much more than sell cleaning products. Ms. Amos is available for stand-up comedy for all types of conventions, group gatherings, and seminars. Not only do children love her (she does career days), but their teachers seem to also (she gives seminars about adding humor to teaching). Contact her agent, Amy Glin, for these types of appearances. She also does television, movies, commercials, and voice-overs. Contact Stars, the Agency for these assignments.

Mary Armstrong
Upbeat, witty, and thought-provoking, this take-no-prisoners comedienne is available for comedy performances, workshops, and conferences.

Fat Chance Theater
Mimi Orner, contact. Fat performance theater.

FAT LIP Readers Theatre
Carol Squires, contact. Separating several of the chapters of this book you will find excerpts from the master script of FAT LIP Readers Theatre. This group of fifteen "fat, feisty women" is a wonderful example of activism that doesn't involve picket lines . . . there are all kinds of ways to make a point. "We come together from varied cultural backgrounds and are not afraid or ashamed of the way that we look or what we need to say. We fight discrimination against fat

people by presenting our ideas in a theatrical way." Taking the advice of Mary Poppins, these wonderfully creative women use a spoonful of sugar in the form of humor, music, dance, and skits to get their very important message of size acceptance across.

Formed in March 1981, FAT LIP Readers Theatre is available for performances on stages and television and at conferences and workshops. Sponsored by the San Francisco Women's Building/Women's Centers (a nonprofit group), FAT LIP Readers Theatre uses its own unique brand of political theater to help change society's attitude about fat people. A thirty-minute video, *Nothing to Lose*, is available for approximately $35.

The Fatimas
This well-known troupe of belly dancers has been performing for several years and has been seen on national television many times. Call for information about or to arrange performances in the Southern California area.

I've been involved in the Fatimas for about four years. We're a group of large-size women who bellydance. I got involved chiefly for the exercise, then found that I was performing. The first performance I participated in was in front of a crowd of average-size people at a party. We were there to entertain. It was really difficult trying to put myself in the mind-set that I was a dancer. I've never fooled myself in my own head that we're professional dancers; the most you could say is that we are a novelty act. But we do try to ap-

proach it seriously. We got out there and did our thing and got it over with. All I could think about was, "What am I doing here?" It's just really hard when you have tried to hide all of your life to suddenly get up in front of a group like that.

Some people laugh when they see us, but some people really do admire us. It's almost as if we are making a political statement. We're flying in the face of convention. That's why sometimes when I'm thinking, "This is a hassle . . . I'm hot and sweaty," I still go on.

—DEE

Frankly Carmen
Self-described "America's Most Wanted Comic at Large," this comedienne's unique style and sharp wit cover topics of interest to women of all sizes—from the unusual vantage point of one of six fat wives of a polygamist Mormon.

Susan Mason
Comedienne, actress, model, artist, and singer extraordinaire. Susan has appeared on numerous television programs and at comedy clubs and size-acceptance gatherings. Look for her artwork on greeting cards and T-shirts.

Kari Ann Owen
Modern dancer whose choreography honors the larger figure. This creative artist is available for performances in the San Francisco Bay Area.

Deb Parks-Satterfield
Comedienne, chief cook and bottle washer for the now-defunct comedy

group 4 Big Girls, and workshop leader. Available for workshops addressing the issues of "taking up space," self-love/self-hatred, and taking care of ourselves.

SAFFIR (Seattle Area Fat Feminists Inspiration and Rage)
Diana Mackin, contact. Collection of per-

formers from the Seattle NOW Body Image Task Force educates the public through size-positive theater.

Wry Crips
Pandoura Carpenter, contact. Disability and size-positive awareness performance group.

SINGERS AND SONGS

No one in the field of music is bigger than Elvis . . . so to speak. He's the King. The Queen of Soul, Aretha Franklin, demanded respect—and got it. Talented, beautiful, and big, she takes command of a stage with a voice known throughout the world. Until his death in 1995, Jerry Garcia could still fill stadiums with Dead Heads, aging hippies, yuppies, and an entire new generation of fans. I don't remember a time when he didn't resemble a chubby teddy bear. (You just have to admire a man who has an ice cream like Cherry Garcia named after him.)

Tricia Yearwood and Garth Brooks both seem to go up and down a bit. Wynonna Judd proves a person can be gorgeous and talented at any size.

Jennifer Holliday, an awesome lady with an awesome voice, dazzled audiences with the Tony-winning *Dreamgirls* in the early 1980s before losing a reported 150 pounds. She dazzles at any size.

Burl Ives was a classic, with a voice that could melt icicles in Alaska. Dolly Parton was just as successful when she weighed 150 pounds (at 5'1") as she is now, trimmed down to 110. Barry White's incredible, sexy voice has warmed many a night and many hearts. I seriously doubt if anyone listening cares about his size.

Many of us remember Mama Cass Elliot (who, by the way, did not choke to death on a ham sandwich) and her amazing voice. Kate Smith's voice was strong, optimistic, and stirred patriotism for the entire country during World War II. She will always be one of this country's most beloved singers.

There have been many big, beautiful gospel singers. Perhaps most prominent today is Bernice Reagon. Her incredible voice has also stirred souls in jazz, folk, and rhythm-and-blues as she performs with the group Sweet Honey in the Rock. (Ms. Reagon is also a history professor at American University in Washington, D.C., and has been curator emeritus at the Smithsonian Institution for twenty-three years. She recently produced a twenty-six-part series on black gospel music for National Public Radio.)

Those fortunate enough to be able to pick up the Canadian channel CBC have been treated to *Rita and Friends*, a program highlighting Rita MacNeil. She has been named "Female Vocalist of the Year" at the Canadian version of the Grammys and has many gold albums. Not only is she a big woman, her voice is incredible. Check out any of her albums for size-positive attitudes.

These are just a few of the very talented, successful, and larger-than-size-14 performers known and loved the world over. That's not to say the music world doesn't have its prejudices also. In 1994, C&C Music Factory released a CD and accompanying video; the beat was eminently danceable, the voice incredible. However, the woman "singing" on the video was actually lip-synching (Holy Milli Vanilli, Batman!) to words sung by Martha Wash . . . a woman C&C considered to be too fat to fit the image they wanted. Ms. Wash sued and received acknowledgment for her work.

A little more difficult to find than big performers are size-positive songs. Many of these were suggested by participants in the on-line newsgroups alt.support.big folks and soc.support.fat-acceptance. Often lyrics, titles, and/or performers were remembered but I was unable to locate an album or other source for the song. Those songs have been included in the list in hopes someone may know where to find them. By all means, if you know the sources or know of other size-positive songs, let me know.

"39-21-46," by the Showmen.

"All of Me," by Jamie Anderson. From the album *Center of Balance*.

"Angel in the House," by The Story. From the album *Angel in the House.*

"Another Fat Song," by Uncle Bonsai. From the albums *The (In)Complete Bonsai* and *Myn and Wymyn*. (A spoof of liposuction)

"Art Is Calling For Me (The Prima Donna Song)," by Victor Herbert. From the operetta *The Enchantress.*

"Baby Got Back," by Sir Mix-A-Lot. From the album *Mack Daddy*. A "salute to women who are curvy" according to Sir Mix-A-Lot. This rap was number one on Billboard's pop singles chart for four weeks. With lines like "I like big butts and I cannot lie," Mix-A-Lot has come under fire from groups accusing him of sexism. He says, "I was tired of seeing a lot of women starving themselves and trying to look like what *Vogue* wants." The song's video received a lot of complaints and requests when it was played on MTV, quickly becoming one of the most polarizing videos ever.

"Bicycle Race," by Queen. From the *Greatest Hits* album.

"Big Beautiful Spoon," by Poi Dog Pondering. From the *Wishing Like A Mountain* album.

"Big Bess," by Louis Jordan and his Tympany Five. From the *Just Say Moe! Mo' of the Best of Louis Jordan* album.

"Big Big Woman," by Rashida Jokha Oji. From the album *Big, Big Woman.*

"Big-Boned Gal," by k.d. lang. From the album *Absolute Torch and Twang.*

"Big Bottom," by Spinal Tap. From the album *This Is Spinal Tap.*

"Big Fat Funky Booty," by the Spin Doctors. From the album *Turn It Up-Side Down.*

"Big Fat Mamas Are Back in Style," by Buster Poindexter. From the *Buster's Happy Hour* album.

"Big Girls," by Alix Dobkin. From the album *These Women/Never Been Better*.

"Big Italian Rose," by Fred Small from the album *No Limit*.

"Big Legged Mommas Are Back in Style," by Taj Mahal. From the album *Like Never Before*.

"Big Legged Woman," by the Righteous Mothers. From the album *All the Rage and None of the Calories*.

"Big Mama Candye's Blues," by Candye Kane. From the album *Home Cookin'*.

"Kiss of Life," by Peter Gabriel. From the album *Security*.

"Booty and The Beast," by Poppa Chubby (Ted Horowitz). From the album *Booty and The Beast*. Other size-friendly songs on the album include "Sweet Goddess of Love & Beer," "Secret Chubby," and "Chubby's Goodnight."

"Built for Comfort (Not For Speed)," by Dianne Davidson. From the *Breaking All The Rules* album. Earlier recordings by Howlin' Wolf and by Merl Saunders on the *It's in the Air* album.

"Cholly," by Fishbone, from the album *In Your Face* (1986).

"Davy the Fat Boy," by Randy Newman. From the *Live and Self Titled* album.

"Eat If You Want To," by Spare Tyre.

"Fat," by Weird Al Yankovic (parody of "Bad," by Michael Jackson). From the album *Fat*.

"Fat-Bottomed Girls," by Queen. From the *Jazz* album (1987). Rock anthem performed with great enthusiasm by one of my all-time favorite groups.

"Fat Boy," by Billy Stewart. From the album *One More Time/The Chess Year*.

"Fat Boys," by Uncle Bonsai. From the album *Boys Want Sex In The Morning*.

"Fat Boy Rag," by Bob Wills. From *The Essential Bob Wills* album.

"Fat Girl," by Max Airborne, recorded by The BuckTooth Varmints.

"Fatso," by The Story. From the album *Angel In The House*.

"Fatty," love song by Morrissey.

"Full Woman," by Rachel Bagby. From the album *Full*.

"Grow Mrs. Goldfarb" (unknown artist).

"Hand Me Down My Jogging Shoes," by Ronnie Gilbert.

"How Could Anyone . . . ," by Libby Roderick. From the album *If You See a Dream*.

"Huggin' and Chalkin'," by Cab Calloway. The singer of the song tells lovingly of his woman, so fat that to hug her he marks his progress with chalk.

"I Don't Want to Be Thin," by Sophie Tucker.

"I Like 'Em Fat Like That," by Louis Jordan. From the album *Five Guys Named Moe*.

"I'm Not Too Fat," by Susan Graetz. From the album *Somewhere Between.*

"It's Raining Men," by Martha Wash. From the album *Get The Feeling.*

"I've Still Got My Health," by Bette Midler. From the album *Beaches.*

"Jenny Got a Big Ol' Butt (So I'm Leavin' You)" (unknown artist).

"Kansas City," from *Oklahoma!,* by Rodgers and Hammerstein.

"Keep That Fat," by Hank Ballard and the Midnighters, from the album *Naked in the Rain.*

"King Size Poppa," by Nelly Lutcher.

"Kiss of Life," by Peter Gabriel, from the album *Security.*

"Large Ladies with Cakes in the Oven," by Nurse with Wound.

"Let My Stomach Be Soft and Round," by Grit Lafkin.

"The Losing Game," by Cosy Sheridan. From the album *Quietly Led.*

"Magic Massive Woman," by Phrinn Pricket.

"Mama," by the Sugarcubes. From the album *Life's Too Good.*

"My Baby Loves Me," by Martina McBride. From the album *The Way That I Am.*

"My Very Own Frame," by Jan Nigro, from the album *Swingin' in the Key of L.*

"New Chub-ette," by the Crabs.

"No Rain," by Blind Melon. From the album *Blind Melon.*

"Ode to a Gym Teacher," by Meg Christian. From the albums *I Know You Know* and *Best of Meg Christian.*

"Plump," by Hole. From the album *Live Through This.*

"Roly Poly," by Joey Dee and the Starlighters.

"Roly Poly," by Bob Wills. From the album *Western Standard Time.* Also recorded later by Asleep at the Wheel.

"Sex," by Frank Zappa. From the album *The Man From Utopia.*

"Some Girls are Bigger than Others," by the Smiths. From the album *The Queen Is Dead* and *Best of the Smiths, Volume I.*

"A Song for the Roly Poly People," by Judy Small, from the album, *Ladies and Gem.*

"Them Heavy People," by Kate Bush, on the *Kick Inside* album.

"These Hips," by Girls in the Nose. From the album *Girls in the Nose.*

"These Thunder Thighs," by Uppity Jazz Women.

"This Heavy Heart," by Cynthia McQujillin, on the album *This Heavy Heart.* Also on the same album, "My Own Best Friend," "Diet-ribe," "Shifting Focus," "Guilt Trip," "Pound Foolish," "Shootout at the I'm Okay Corral," "Big Fat Momma and Her Big Fat Bike."

"Three Hundred Pounds of Heavenly Joy," by Howlin' Wolf. From the album *The Chess Box.*

"Ton of Love," by Devo. From the album *Freedom of Choice.*

"Two Ton Tessie from Tennessee," theme song of Tessie O'Shea.

"Unskinny Bop" (unknown artist).

"Whole Lot of Rosie," by AC/DC. From the albums *Live, If You Want It You've Got It,* and *Let There Be Rock.*

"You Can't Fool the Fat Man," by Randy Newman. From the album *Little Criminals.*

"You Shook Me All Night Long," by AC/DC, from the albums *Back in Black, Who Made Who,* and *Live.*

"You're the One for Me," by Morrissey. From the albums *World of Morrisey* and *Your Arsenal.*

EROTICA

2XL Video Magazine TV for the massives.

The Fat Fantasy Line "A line where fat women and their admirers can share their fantasies!" This is not a matchmaker line. It is strictly a fantasy line. You can place your own fantasy through a toll-free number or call the 900 number and listen to others' fantasies. The cost is approximately $1.50 a minute and you must be over eighteen to call.

➡ If any data listed in this chapter need to be corrected, please let me know. If you know of a service or product useful to people of size, please write to me about it. The information may be made available to readers through the newsletter "Size Wise Update!," the Size Wise web site, or through possible future revisions of this book.

PERSONAL GLIMPSE:
RICK

A divorced father of an adult daughter, Rick is also a painter, gifted singer, composer, and songwriter. He has struggled with the pressures society puts on fat people all of his life. At forty years of age, after every diet from fasting to Weight Watchers, the Grapefruit Diet to Dr. Atkins, Rick decided to go on the diet to end all diets. As added incentive, he decided to film his metamorphosis. The film that came out of his experience, *Fat Chance* (sometimes shown as *A Matter of Fat*), won a Peabody Award. It was originally intended to document the difference in the way society treated Rick as a fat man and then as a thin man. Instead of reaching a weight-loss goal, however, he accomplished something far more important . . . self-acceptance. The film is touching; the man is extraordinary.

I'm not afraid of emotions, but I always feel sort of guarded. It has a lot to do with how we are interpreted. If a normal-size person stands up for himself he is considered to be assertive; if a fat person does it, he is a bully. The same rules don't apply. My daughter could walk down the street eating an ice cream cone and, no problem. She's enjoying an ice cream cone. For a fat person to do the same thing is an act of courage.

If you are fat, people just don't equate you with positive things. That attitude is backed up by the media, the fashion industry, the weight-loss industry, and the medical community. There are assumptions . . . if you are fat you are stupid, a joke, gluttonous, and have some deep-rooted psychological problem. It is assumed you are hiding your sexuality, are not to be taken seriously. You are basically pretty much discounted and often taken advantage of. Someone even explained to me that in a past life I had starved to death and the imprinting of that life was still with me. As a result I was on some unconscious level making sure that never happened again.

People say, "It's not how you look on the outside, it's what you are on the inside." Well, that's nice, but what does that mean? Unfortunately, it is the person on the outside for many people.

A friend and I were to meet for coffee one day. On my way to the café some young jocks drove by. They threw a soda can and yelled insults at me. It just infuriated me. I jumped back into my car and was driving like a maniac after them. All of a sudden it hit me that I was endangering my life and the lives of other people. I calmed down, stopped my pursuit, and went to meet my friend. Normally I am pretty upbeat, but I was visibly shaken. She tried to console me. As we talked she reached over and was holding my hand, telling me, "You're a beautiful person inside. That is what counts." Suddenly she realized that other people could be interpreting that she could be my lover or girlfriend. She quickly let go of my hand and backed off, then began talking loudly about her boyfriend, making sure the people around us knew she wasn't my girlfriend.

When that kind of stuff happens . . . even when you hear people saying things that may be very genuine . . . I just feel so unsalvageable. That anything I get is really plastic. You kind of feel like the elephant man at times. You just want to put your fist in your mouth and say, "I am not an animal. I am not an animal."

All I knew was I was very very unhappy with who I was. I felt like an alien. Just based on my size I felt like a whole other species, not even in the running with other people. It affected me in every walk of my life. I would look at people in relationships and be amazed at what idiots can have relationships but just by being fat I wasn't even considered. I had just come to the end of my rope.

It was going to be a commonsense type of thing, this last diet. Eating healthy foods, about 1,200 calories a day, and being physically active. At the end of three months on this medically supervised program, exercising every day, and starving myself, I had lost thirty-five pounds and didn't feel any better about myself. I had thought I would. If anything, I was more depressed.

It's very bizarre that the medical community keeps pushing this treatment at us (dieting) when it has such a high failure rate. Once the procedure fails they don't blame the procedure, they blame the patient. That just goes to tell you how bizarre this whole thing is.

Even the medical terms are horrible . . . "obese" has a disease sound to it. Then you go to "gross obesity." Then to "morbid obesity." I always tell people that if I lose another fifty pounds I'm not going to be morbid anymore, I'm going to be gross.

When Leslie Lampert donned her fat suit and wrote her critically acclaimed article, "Fat Like Me," people were appalled at the treatment she received. She was believed. Why was she believed? Because Leslie Lampert was able to slip out of her fat suit, and what she had to say came out of a thin person. Yet when those same words come out of a fat person they are not believed. Some people's mentality allows them to think they have a license to validate or discount the oppression of others.

The whole area of men in the size-acceptance movement is highly underdeveloped. Two years ago, when I first started to get turned around, I was told by a few of the leaders at an AHELP conference that this was not a man's issue, that I was wasting my time doing it from a man's perspective. It was like they saw it not only as a woman's issue but as a feminist issue. I was not taken seriously . . . not by a few people, anyway. But I received a lot of encouragement and support from others there. I don't think the gender issue enters my mind because I come from a fat family. Pain is pain. I've been asked to lead the special interest group for men at the twenty-fifth anniversary NAAFA convention in Washington.

The original concept for the film was to show the difference between how I am treated as a fat person and how I would be treated as a thin person. I saw and felt some very significant prejudice.

We sort of stayed with the original concept, but no one knew where we were going. I didn't know so much what I wanted, but I knew what I didn't want. The traditional methods of getting thin had failed me. The medical community has always made me feel at fault. I didn't want to do something and have it taken to the medical community for validation or to be discredited.

I guess I did find myself through the whole process of making the film. There are so many things I had to come in touch with. My anger and hurt . . . the floodgates had been opened. You do in a way have to grieve your losses at what you have been dealt. It isn't pity or anything. Just putting it into a sort of perspective. The word *acceptance* sounds easy. It's not that simple. What do you do with the years?

I've had so many different responses to the film from people . . . from both fat people and people who aren't fat. It heightens the awareness of people who felt for a long time that whatever treatment they doled out to us was justified. I've gotten calls from people who say "You are my hero" and from people who were disappointed with the message. They saw acceptance as giving up, copping out.

The film seems to affect people who have been abused, no matter if the abuse was a result of being fat or whether it was some other form. It seems to trigger something in people. It gives hope to people.

I was so nervous at the premier of *Fat Chance*, but the response was overwhelming. People were so openly emotional. Weeping would not be an understatement. I had to leave the auditorium at one point because I couldn't keep it together. When the film ended there was a standing ovation and I was called up to the front. I couldn't even speak. If the film never played again that would have been enough for me.

Looking at some of the interviews I did during the promotion of the film, it is interesting to see to what degree I defended acceptance and how violently I was attacked by not only the media but the public. For instance, this guy called in saying, "I hate to interrupt your festival of niceties, but I abhor this man. I think everything he is saying is a pack of lies. He is a con artist.'' He ranted on and on, saying things I hadn't even said, making things up. He said he was so repulsed by me he couldn't even hear what I was saying. This man was so full of anger. Here is a person with all this venom and poison dripping off every word and he is asking, ''What about the health issues?'' Like he is concerned about my health. Later a woman phoned and said, ''Wow, that guy could have been my ex-husband.''

Without having moved to a strong position of acceptance I couldn't stand up and defend myself. There is no way I could be this strong. Before, all it took was a mild slap on the face and I would sit down. Now I slap back. It's got people baffled. You have to give your body and soul permission to be what they are. It's got to do with freedom.

Recently I have met someone special and we are working on a serious relationship. I feel worthy, not only of being loved but of loving someone. There are people starting to approach me, which wouldn't have happened years ago. I was sending out the wrong signals.

Interviewers have asked me, ''Are you really fat and happy now or are you just fat and angry?'' My response is that I am both. Why is that so unusual? If someone insults you, what are you supposed to feel? I've stopped giving people permission to beat me up.

Quote from *Fat Chance:* ''I've come from a form of imprisonment, and although I'm not really sure where I'm going, I feel that the chains are off. I'm walking with freedom.''

"Another Media Trojan Horse"

At the same time that we can't exorcise such long-standing inferiority complexes about our bodies, we see women trying to reclaim the fitness movement from Kellogg's, Diet Pepsi, Biotherm, and all the rest of the buttocks and thighs cartel. Women know, in their heads if not their hearts, that buns of steel are not about fitness; they are about pretending that some anorexic, unnatural, corporate-constructed ideal is really the norm. Buns of steel are designed to humiliate women and to make us complicit in our own degradation, and most women know this too. Silly as they may seem, buns of steel are worth being angry about because of the eating disorders they promote among young women and the general sexism they reinforce in society. So the next time some curled-up rump is forced into your field of vision, view it not with envy but with contempt. For it doesn't reflect hard work or entitlement so much as mindless narcissism, unproductive self-absorption, and the media's ongoing distortion of feminism to further their own misogynistic, profit-maximizing ends. Buns of steel are just another media Trojan horse, pretending to advance feminism but harboring antifeminist weaponry.

From Where the Girls Are: Growing Up Female with the Mass Media, *1994, by Susan J. Douglas.*

7

ALL THAT'S FIT TO PRINT

The number of publications that are size friendly seems to grow daily. I have found many wonderful books, newsletters, workbooks, brochures, magazines, and videos that you will enjoy.

It has been my experience that small, local bookstores are generally more interested in helping you locate books that are available through small presses or that are self-published. The larger chains may tell you that a book is unavailable. Don't give up. What they sometimes mean is that it is not cost-effective for them to take the time to order the book for you. Ordering directly from the publisher is possible but will most likely take extra time and will probably require that you pay shipping and handling charges. Some of the books listed are no longer in print, but they may be available from your local library or a used book store.

As many of us who write books for large-size people have discovered, publishers in general don't believe that a book will sell to that market unless it includes a weight-loss diet. As a result, many excellent, helpful books never see print. Those that do are often labors of love, published at the authors' expense and sold generally through mail order. When listing those books here, I have included the information needed to obtain a copy.

I have chosen not to include books on weight loss, eating disorders, diabetes, heart problems, and other medical topics; neither will you find listings about knitting, gardening, or dog breeding. Some big people have eating disorders; some of us own dogs. Neither necessarily has anything to do with size. You will, however, find several excellent books on improving your health, reclaiming your self-esteem, and developing a more active lifestyle.

I have noted a few books I found to be exceptional and heartily recommend.

You will find some publications that are definitely adult oriented, containing explicit sexual references and/or nudity. Those are noted with an "adult material" note.

NEWSLETTERS

Subscription information has been included except in the cases of some small press publications that prefer to be contacted directly for up-to-date pricing and availability.

AHELP Newsletter Biannual newsletter of the Association for Health Enrichment of Large People, a nondiet professionals group headed by Dr. Joe McVoy. Available to AHELP members or through AHELP's web page.

Abundantly Yours Monthly size-positive publication of the New Mexico Fat Acceptance Network. One-year subscription: $15.

Ample Information This monthly newsletter focuses mainly on information of interest to members of a support/social group in Portland, Oregon. There is, however, a lot of very good information available for everyone interested in size acceptance. Contact: Ample Opportunity. One-year subscription: $12.

The Ample Shopper Quarterly newsletter focusing exclusively on the large-size marketplace. This is a small newsletter but a great resource—*Consumer's Report* for large people. Easily worth the price. One-year subscription: $12. Sample issue: $3.

Big Events Monthly newsletter offering local support, activist, and social information. Call or write for a complimentary copy. Contact: NAAFA, Connecticut Chapter. One-year subscription: $15.

DB: The Freedom to Be Yourself British size-acceptance newsletter, published quarterly. Contact: Diet Breakers. One-year subscription: £10. Overseas; add £5.

Fat Admirers News (FAN) Bimonthly newsletter for people who admire large-size women. One year subscription: $10.

FaT GiRL: The Zine for Fat Dykes and the Women Who Want Them This lesbian 'zine began publication in the fall of 1994 with a sixty-two-page issue filled with comics, fiction, activism, and an unusual Dear Abby–type column . . .

"Hey, Fat Chick!" Definitely not for the faint of heart, *FaT GiRL* isn't shy about its opinions. (Be sure to request a copy of *FaT GiRL*'s resource list, available for $5.) Adult material. Published quarterly. One-year subscription: $20.

Fat News Homemade, feisty, quarterly size-acceptance newsletter with editorials, personal stories, word games, book reviews, and support. Also available on tape. Contact: Fat Women's Group. One-year subscription: £1.50 in England; £2 overseas.

Fat!So? Marilyn Wann, publisher. "For People Who Don't Apologize for Their Size." This bold, innovative, and straightforward entry to the size-acceptance movement will certainly grab your attention. Though small, it is filled to the brim with interesting photos (the very first issue was bright pink with a microscopic view of fat cells), articles, poetry, fiction, and quizzes. (Sample question: "When I see waiflike supermodel Kate Moss, I want to . . . a) Vomit three times a day to make myself just like her; b) Suggest a nutritional diet, because I am so concerned for her health; c) Congratulate her for doing such a lifelike impression of a stick figure; d) Give her a National Association to Advance Fat Acceptance brochure."

Do you remember paper dolls? *Fat!So?* has their own version . . . the Venus of Willendorf Paper Doll, complete with bikini, lingerie, and luau dress. Adult material. Published quarterly. One-year subscription: $12.

Food for Thought Quarterly newsletter. Book reviews and who's who and what's what in the size-acceptance movement. Largesse is an organization with its finger squarely on the pulse of the size-acceptance movement, and this newsletter reflects that. Highly recommended. Contact: Largesse, the Network for Size-Esteem. Subscription includes bimonthly copies of *Size Esteem*, a bulletin from Largesse, and periodic *Action Alerts*. Yearly subscription: $20 U.S., $24 Canada and Mexico, $31 international.

The Goddesses Quarterly newsletter of the social club of the same name in the New York City area. You don't have to be a member to receive the newsletter. Yearly subscription: $12.

Grace-Full Eating Quarterly, nondiet, size-acceptance newsletter. Contact Diet/Weight Liberation. A subscription is included when you make a tax-deductible contribution to the program of $25 or more. Special sliding scale rates are available for students, seniors, and low-income households.

HUGS Club News "Support for the decision to get off the diet roller coaster." An ongoing support network, information exchange, and feedback forum. Membership is not required to receive the newsletter. Contact: HUGS International, Inc. Published quarterly. One-year subscription: $16 Canada, $15 United States.

LFAN Newsletter Fat lesbian newsletter. Adult material. Activist, social, and support information. Contact: the Lesbian Fat Activist Network for subscription information.

Large as Life Newsletter Quarterly size-acceptance publication with fashion tips, an "ask-the-doctor" column, book reviews, recipes, and travel information. Yearly subscription: $10.

Large Encounters Newsletter of the social group of the same name in the New York/New Jersey area. Write or call for subscription information.

Living Large Kathleen Madigan's "interactive group newsletter requires participation (two pages of original material every other issue) to continue receiving copies." Published bimonthly. $1.25 an issue, plus postage.

Love Handles Singles publication for large people and their admirers. Send a self-addressed stamped envelope for subscription information.

The Marigold Size-positive newsletter for fat people and their families. Contact NAAFA, Families Sig, for subscription information.

NAAFA Newsletter Available only to members of NAAFA. Published quarterly.

Nothing in Moderation Small newsletter from the owner of a store by the same name in Oak Park, Illinois. This is mostly a sales circular, but there are also some interesting updates on size acceptance. Write for subscription information.

Nothing to Lose Bimonthly social, support, and activist information. Adult material. Contact the Fat Lesbian Action Brigade. One-year subscription: $10.

On a Positive Note Quarterly newsletter from a nondiet support group, Largely Positive, headed by Carol Johnson. Contact Largely Positive, Inc. One-year subscription: $12 (U.S.), $16 (foreign).

P.L.E.A.S.E. Newsletter Information on legislation and legal reform that pertains to fat people. The name stands for Promoting Legislation and Education About Self Esteem. Published quarterly by Lisa G. Berzins, Ph.D. Write or call for subscription information.

P.S. Style This bimonthly newsletter's mission is to "identify resources and provide counsel to help plus-size women look their best." This excellent resource gives you real help in dealing with all sorts of figures in all sizes. For up-to-date news on designers, the newest fashions, and the right look for you, check this one out. Fashions are modeled by plus-size women, generally sizes 14 to 16. One-year subscription: $30.

People At Large Monthly newsletter from a social-support network of the same name (or PAL). "Our goal is to strive towards an enriched quality of life, thereby ending social isolation." One-year subscription: $10 (Canada), $8 (U.S.), $15 (international).

Phat Phree! Free quarterly 'zine available only through E-mail or by accessing the web site. To subscribe, send E-mail with subject line "more info."

Roundup Quarterly newsletter with local support, activist, and social information. Contact NAAFA, Hudson Valley Chapter, for subscription information.

Sabrina's Food for Thought Art, updates on the diet industry, book reviews, health issues, recipes, and fiction (some of the fiction is a bit racy). Published monthly. One-year subscription: $10.

SAFFIR (Seattle Area Fat Feminists Inspiration and Rage) Newsletter Quarterly newsletter offering news of local events, activist, and support activities. Contact Seattle NOW Body Image Task Force for subscription information.

Seeds of Change Newsletter "Say No to Diets—Say Yes to Life." Size-acceptance newsletter published by an R.N., Jennifer Carney. Write for subscription information.

Size Wise Update! Published quarterly by Judy Sullivan. Revisions of material in this book, new information and resources, plus detailed looks at the people, organizations, companies, and publications we report on. One-year subscription: $24.

Southern California Size Acceptance Coalition Newsletter Size-positive infor-

mation. Published on a quarterly basis by the group of the same name. One-year subscription: $10.

Super Woman Quarterly newsletter for women over size 46+. Must be a member of NAAFA and the Super Sig to subscribe. Contact NAAFA, Super Sig. One-year subscription: $25 (U.S.), $35 (foreign).

WLSS SIG Newsletter Quarterly newsletter providing support to those who have had weight-loss surgery and information to those who are considering it. Contact NAAFA, Weight-Loss Surgery Survivors Sig. One-year subscription: $15.

Well-Rounded Club Monthly newsletter for the social club of the same name in Rhode Island, Connecticut, and Massachusetts area. Some personal ads. Call hotline to be added to the mailing list. No charge.

Well Rounded Woman Bimonthly newsletter of interest mostly to people in northern Ohio, with information on products, businesses, restaurants, and other resources of interest. Write for subscription information.

Women Unlimited Newsletter Size-acceptance news for women in New Zealand from the organization of the same name. Write for subscription information.

MAGAZINES

All of Me "Audio magazine for abundant women. Enlightening, entertaining, and empowering." $2 a minute. Average call, 5 minutes. Adult material. Available from Strauss Communications.

BBW (Big Beautiful Woman) *BBW* is the original fashion magazine for plus-size women. This magazine has done a lot for the large-size woman in the fifteen years it has been published and even includes fashions for supersize women. *BBW* seems to be evolving into something more than just a fashion magazine for big women since Janey Milstead took the helm as editor in chief. Now there are more articles covering health, discrimination, and lifestyle issues. One-year subscription: $10 (U.S.), $20 (foreign).

BBW Express "The magazine of personal classified ads for BBWs (Big Beautiful Women) and the men who love BBWs." Published by the people at *BBW* magazine. No 900 number; all ads have a code number. If someone interests you, you write to him or her via the code listed in the magazine. Subscription: approximately $20 for 12 issues.

Beautiful Girls German personals magazine. Subscription: approximately $10 (U.S.), 15 DM.

Belle Quarterly fashion/lifestyle magazine for African-American women of size. One-year subscription: $13.

Big Ad International personals for large gay men. *Big Ad* offers fiction, articles on pertinent issues, and personal ads, many with pictures. Each month four men are featured, complete with three pages of photos for each man. Published bimonthly. $6.95 per issue or $38 for a one-year subscription (which allows you to place one free fifty-word ad), $40 (Canada), $75 (international).

Body-Pride: Redefining Beauty This Canadian magazine is aimed at improving body image through personal stories, poetry, fiction, art, book and play reviews, news, information and resources, and input from readers. Write for subscription information.

Diet Direction Liz Manley, publisher. Size-acceptance magazine available in New Zealand. Write for subscription information.

Dimensions "The lifestyle magazine for men who prefer large, radiant women." Lots of personals ads with some photos. Adult material. Bimonthly. 6 issues for $24.

Hysteria Comics, photos, silliness, and feminism. 4 issues for $18; sample issue, $4.95.

Healthy Weight Journal "Research, News & Commentary Across the Weight Spectrum, formerly *Obesity & Health,* Journal of Research, News and Contemporary Issues." Francie M. Berg, editor and publisher. Excellent resource journal for keeping up with the latest medical research and issues. Also available through the Healthy Living Institute is a comprehensive report by Francie M. Berg, *The Health Risks of Weight Loss*. Both highly recommended. Published bimonthly. One-year subscription: $60; special student rate, $27.

HUES: Hear Us Emerging Sisters "It takes a lot more than a size-five figure and built-in tip-toes to be a woman." Aimed at young women, this magazine is upbeat, funny, and right on target regarding body image issues and self-esteem. Right now *HUES* is published twice a year, March and October, but hopes to go quarterly soon. Two-year subscription: $15.

Pretty Big "The quarterly Fashion & Lifestyle Magazine for women who are size 16+." Published in England. One-year subscription: £16 (overseas).

Radiance: The Magazine for Large Women Published quarterly. "Since 1984, *Radiance* has been a friend to more than 500,000 women worldwide, helping inspire them to live proud, full lives, with self-love and self-respect." This magazine has been around since 1984 and provides articles on fashion, travel, health, and self-esteem. You will also find fiction and poetry here, all aimed at celebrating women of all sizes of large. Also available in recorded subscriptions for blind or disabled readers. Rates are same as for print copies. One-year subscription: $20.

Rump Parliament Lee Martindale, publisher. Look to this publication for no-holds-barred reporting on the size-acceptance movement and all of the issues surrounding it. Lee Martindale has no problem whatsoever with blowing the whistle on discrimination. An excellent magazine, *Rump Parliament* is a must-have for anyone interested in staying on top of the issues. I especially enjoy the "Rump Roasts." Lee has a sharp eye for fat bigots and cuts them down to size with wit and incisiveness. This is not a bitter publication, though. It's chock-full of positive information, humor, and strokes for those moving in the right direction.

A one-year subscription is $24 for 6 issues ($28 in Canada and Mexico, $35 overseas [U.S. funds only, please]), published bimonthly. The "Seen on a Button" sayings sprinkled throughout this book, along with many others, can be purchased from *Rump Parliament* on buttons, note cards, mugs, and tankards.

Un Peu Plus [A Bit More], *C'est Bien!* French Canadian magazine along the lines of *BBW*. Bimonthly, written completely in French, *Un Peu Plus* looks to bring real fashion to its large-size readers.

Yes! The Positive Approach to Large Sizes Bimonthly British lifestyle magazine for large women, covering fashion, beauty, fiction, book reviews, and a shopping directory. Write or call for subscription information.

Yarnome Full Figure Woman "Plus size women now have a fresh, new resource on how to look good and feel great every other month." (Yarnome is the name of the daughter of the founders of this publication.) Keeping tabs on who's who in the large-size fashion industry, *Yarnome Full Figure Woman* is an am-bitious production. Look for issues that cover plus-size models and designers, mail-order fashions, holiday shopping, intimate apparel, and accessories. Published bimonthly. Two-year subscription: $9.95.

BOOKS

• Fiction •

The fat characters who leap off the pages of well-known fiction—Ignatius J. Reilly, Nero Wolfe, Hercule Poirot, Mr. Pickwick, Father Brown, Friar Tuck, Bertie Wooster's Aunt Dahlia, Falstaff, and Mycroft Holmes—populate our imaginations with colorful images. Finding a character who is fat and positively portrayed is no easy task, especially in more current literature. You might enjoy some of these titles.

The AfterLife Diet Written by Daniel Pinkwater (Random House, 1995). This comic novel is witty and definitely unique, following the adventures of a sleazy book editor, Milton, after he is murdered. Almost everyone in this book is "circumferentially challenged" and, unfortunately, gluttonous. If you overlook the stereotypes, this book is a riot and a lot of fun to read.

The Axeman's Jazz Written by Julie Smith (St. Martin's Press, 1991). The detective in this mystery, Skip Langdon, is not exactly fat (6' tall, maybe twenty pounds "overweight"), but she experiences many of the prejudices and self-doubts that all women who are larger than average have to deal with.

Blanche on the Lam Written by Barbara Neely (St. Martin's Press, 1992). Blanche is a woman of size who finds herself in a sticky situation. This won-derful character uses her brains, friends, humor, and intuition to outsmart those who would do her harm. You'll enjoy and identify with many of Blanche's thoughts as she rescues herself in this mystery. Highly recommended.

The Book of Moons Written by Rosemary Edghill (Forge Books, 1995). Lace, a secondary character in this book, was written without even a thought being given to her size beyond a brief description. Very positive character, great book.

The Bowl of Night Written by Rosemary Edghill (Forge Books, 1996). Ms. Edghill introduces yet another positive person of size in the character of Madjine.

The Changewinds Written by Jack L. Chalker (Ace Books, 1987). This author is reportedly very size-friendly. You might want to check out some of his other, more recent books. Out of print.

Circle of Friends Written by Maeve Binchy (Delacorte Press, 1995).

The Dead Room Written by Herbert Resnicow (Dodd Mead, 1989). Written by the author of the Gold series (see below), *The Dead Room* gives us another mystery that includes large, lusty characters. Out of print.

The Dieter Written by Susan Sussman (Pocket Books, 1989).

Fat, Fat Rosemarie Written by Lisa Passen (Henry Holt Press, 1991).

Fat Girl Dances with Rocks Written by Susan Stinson (Spinsters Ink, 1994). This novel is a coming of age story, a story of a fat girl ''coming into her own body—all the way to the edges of her skin.''

Fish Whistle: Commentaries, Uncommentaries, and Vulgar Excesses Written by Daniel Pinkwater (Addison-Wesley, 1989). Pinkwater also put out *The Best of Daniel Pinkwater: Everyday Life* (cassette). Commentaries on life as a fat man.

Flavor of the Month Written by Olivia Goldsmith (Pocket Books, 1993). Written by the author of *First Wives Club, Flavor of the Month* takes us behind the scenes of the television/movie industry where beauty has very narrow standards. Mary Jane is a talented actress stuck in character actress roles because she is overweight and unattractive. When the man she loves goes to Hollywood, leaving her behind in New York, Mary Jane undergoes a complete transformation through surgery. Success comes quickly once she is beautiful but happiness remains elusive.

Flesh Written by David Galef (Permanent Press, 1995). Set on a university campus in the South, this academic novel will catch you up in intriguing characters and Southern culture. Max Finster, newly arrived professor from New York, moves into the apartment next to English professor Don Shapiro. As their friendship grows, so does the size of Max's sexual conquests. Don treats us to a fascinating narrative as he obsesses over Max and develops an interest in larger women himself. Jarringly accurate in describing attitudes toward fat women, this book may offend some.

The Gold Series Written by Herbert Resnicow (St. Martin's Press, 1983–1988). Alexander Magnus Gold, 240 pounds, 5'6" tall, genius, powerlifter, much loved by family and friends. His wife, Norma, is ''a tall dark handsome woman. Dignified, like a duchess; a goddess come to earth. Make that a multigoddess. Mostly Athena the Wise. Obviously Juno from the neck down, as painted by Rubens, who understood what a real woman should look like.'' Out of print.

The Gold Solution (1983)

The Gold Deadline (1984)

The Gold Frame (1984)

The Gold Curse (1986)

Good Enough to Eat Written by Lesléa Newman, (Firebrand Books, 1986). Liza's life revolves around food and how to avoid it. She obsesses with calorie counting and numbers on the scale, makes lists of projected weight-loss goals, and plans her next fast while gulping down Oreos. As Liza battles with bulimia she also learns to deal with coming out as a lesbian. No matter what your sexual persuasion or food tendencies, you will almost surely identify with Liza on her journey toward self-acceptance. Graphic sexual scenes may not be for everyone, but this book is well worth picking up if you aren't offended by such.

From Liza's journal:

I will not eat Harvey's knish. I want to weigh 125 pounds by May 25th. I refuse to spend another summer being fat. I am going to fast for fifteen days on nothing but apple juice, coffee and Tab. After that I am going to eat 500 calories a day. If I don't weigh 125 by May 25th, I am going to kill myself. And that's all. I don't want to think about it anymore."

Jazz Funeral Written by Julie Smith (St. Martin's Press, 1993).

Larger Than Death Written by Lynn Murray (Orloff Press, 1997). Josephine Fuller introduces herself: "I've never weighed less than 200 pounds in my life—counting the chip on my shoulder." In this first book of what I hope is a series, Josephine investigates the murder of her best friend and sets herself up as possibly the next victim.

Lillian Written by Laura Platts (Sun-Shine Press Publications, 1994). An emotional story of overcoming prejudice.

Martha Moody Written by Susan Stinson (Spinsters Ink, 1995). This fantastical western is an old-fashioned love story detailing the lives of a fascinating group of women in the west of the 1800s.

. . . Martha is a magic woman, huge past the point where size can be considered anything less than a blessing of range to the human world. She doesn't have to consider it at all. When she walks through the streets of town, her clothes stream off her, transformed into feathers, wings, colored sheets, strips of cloth, petals that fly off in a burst. She has majesty.

Murder Can Kill Your Social Life Written by Selma Eichler (Signet/Penguin USA, 1994). She also wrote *Murder Can Ruin Your Looks* (1995) and *Murder Can Stunt Your Growth* (1996). If you love a good mystery with delightful characters and a wicked sense of humor, these books are for you. Desiree Shapiro is the private investigator and main character in each book. Shapiro is a middle-aged widow who describes herself as: "I'm five-foot-two with auburn hair (abetted somewhat by Egyptian henna) and blue eyes. Plus I've got dimples. Not—unfortunately—on my face. But on my elbows and hand and knees and a lot of places the world will never see."

New Orleans Mourning Written by Julie Smith (St. Martin's Press, 1990).

The Secret Garden Written by Frances Hodgson Burnett (Viking Kestrel, 1988). Mary is pleased to be "getting fatter every day"; her cousin Colin, after being thin and frail, happily gains weight and grows stronger. A very nice, feel-good book.

Significant Others by Armistead Maupin (Harper and Row, Publishers, 1987). Delightful comedy about marriage (straight, gay, and lesbian), good friends, and sexual relationships. Wren Douglas, "the World's Most Beautiful Fat Woman," finds herself at the end of a book tour with an interesting proposition, and things heat up in ways she never expected.

A glamorous star-filtered cover photograph seemed to confirm the claim. The woman was big, all right, but her face was the face of a goddess: full red lips, a perfect nose, enormous green eyes fairly brimming with kindness and invitation. Her raven hair framed it all perfectly, cascading across her shoulders toward a cleavage rivaling the San Andreas Fault.

What's Eating Gilbert Grape Written by Peter Hedges (Poseidon Press, 1991). Life for Gilbert Grape of Endora, Iowa, as it evolves around his sisters, retarded younger brother, and supersize mother. This book is funny, sweet, and full of humor. Gilbert's love/hate relationship with his mother is tender in its anger. I hesitated to include this book because the story is not really size-positive. But I do feel it is an insightful look at attitudes toward and interactions around supersize people—and "Mama" is presented in a realistic, loving manner.

• Romance •

Always There Written by Emily Frost (Adams Print, 1991). A self-published book with innovative packaging. The heroine is a large, self-confident woman of intelligence.

Just Desserts Written by Dixie Browning (Harlequin Silhouette Series, 1984). Out of print.

Love in the Pyramid Written by Abigail Sommers (Rubenesque Romances, 1995). The heroine of this story, a fat woman named Melissa, meets Matthew inside a pyramid and discovers love while helping to unravel a mystery.

That Look Written by Emily Frost (Adams Print, 1991). Big, beautiful heroine in a light-hearted, romantic tale.

• Nonfiction •

The Adventures of Stout Mama Written by Sibyl James (Women's Voices, 1994). A series of vignettes describing Stout Mama's take on life as a fat woman.

All Shapes and Sizes . . . Promoting Fitness and Self-Esteem in Your Overweight Child Written by Teresa Pittman and Dr. Miriam Kaufman (Harper Collins, 1994).

Am I Fat? Helping Young Children Accept Differences in Body Size Written by Joanne Ikeda, M.A., R.D., and Priscilla Naworski, M.S., C.H.E.S. (ETR Associates, 1992). This book should be required reading in Life 101. It's an excellent source that will guide parents and teachers who are in a position to help a child develop good self-esteem. It also teaches sensitivity to people who are critical of large children and their families. With chapters on body image, nutrition, and handling hurtful situations, the authors have created a "must-read" for everyone concerned with happy, healthy children. I especially appreciated the chapter dealing with people who tease and call names.

Eating a variety of healthy foods and engaging in regular physical activity benefits everyone, regardless of body size. When we help children learn to take care of their bodies, we promote their general health and well-being, as well as a positive body image.

Highly recommended.

American Beauty Written by Lois W. Banner (University of Chicago Press, 1983). The social history of feminine beauty perceptions in America.

Appearance Obsession: Learning to Love the Way You Look Written by Joni E. Johnston (Health Communications, Inc., 1994).

Beauty Bound Written by Rita Freedman (Lexington Books, 1986). Excellent book addressing the issues of body size, beauty pageants, and American standards of beauty. Out of print.

The Beauty Myth Written by Naomi Wolf (Anchor/Doubleday, 1992). Just who sets the standards of beauty in our society? Do you strive to look good for yourself or are you trying to fit into an unattainable ideal? Ms. Wolf lays it all out, including a fascinating look at the industries that tell us what is attractive and what isn't. Individual beauty is celebrated and some amazing truths are told.

Beauty Secrets: Women and the Politics of Appearance Written by Wendy Chapkis (Southend Press, 1986). Personal accounts and photos present looksism as it affects women on both political and private levels.

Being Fat Is Not a Sin Written by Shelley Bovey (Pandora Press, 1991). This feminist author takes a look at fat hatred from a British perspective. Not available in the United States.

Before and After: Living Fat in a Thin Society Written by Pattie Thomas. 1995. Self-published collection of essays and poems detailing the experiences of being a fat woman. Available from the author. $5.

Belly Songs: In Celebration of Women Written by Susan Stinson (Orogeny Press, 1993).

Beyond the Looking Glass: America's Beauty Culture Written by Kathrin Perutz (William Morrow and Co., 1970). Ms. Perutz seems to have a bit of a problem with fat people, but this book still offers an interesting look at the differences between what is expected of men versus women in looks. Out of print.

Big and Beautiful Written by Ruthanne Olds (Acropolis Books, 1982). Out of print.

The Big Beauty Book: Glamour for the Fuller-Figure Woman Written by Ann Harper (Holt, Rinehart, and Winston, 1983). Out of print.

Big Clothes For Big Men Written by Freda Rosenberg, updated regularly. Sources of outerwear, officewear, work clothes, casuals, shoes, underwear, and more. Available from author.

The Big Fat Lie or The Truth About Your Weight Written by William B. Fears, M.D. (Chariot Press, Inc., 1994). Well-

thought-out book by a doctor with a little more faith in dieting and the future of medications than I have, but a good source of information nonetheless.

Big Fat Lies: The Truth About Health and Weight Written by Glenn A. Gaesse, Ph.D. (Fawcett Columbine, 1996). This book does an exceptional job of pointing out how research regarding fat people and their health is skewed by the diet industry and what the evidence really shows. Dr. Gaesse believes it is certainly possible to be fat and fit, and his ideas for a healthier lifestyle are meant for people of all sizes.

Bigger Ideas from Colour Me Beautiful: Colour and Style Ideas for the Fuller Figure Written by Mary Spillane (Judi Piatkus Publishers, Ltd., 1994). This book was published in England and may be difficult to find here. Write directly to the publisher for a copy. Cost is £15.99.

Body Traps: Breaking the Bonds that Keep You from Feeling Good About Your Body Written by Judith Rodin, Ph.D. (William Morrow and Co., Inc., 1992). The shame, fitness, and food traps are exposed and explored, examining their social significance.

Bodylove: Learning to Like Our Looks and Ourselves Written by Rita Freedman (Harper and Row, 1990). An excellent book exploring how women see themselves, how society has skewed that view, and how to change negative perceptions to self-acceptance.

The Bodywise Woman From the Melpomene Institute (Prentice-Hall, 1990). An excellent resource for anyone beginning to be active again at all ages. The chapter on becoming active is especially good.

Breaking All the Rules Written by Nancy Roberts (Viking Press, 1987). With an emphasis on exercise for feeling better, not for weight loss, this book tells of one woman's struggle with self-acceptance. The chapters on clothing were especially good. Out of print.

> There has been so much nonsense written about what big women should and should not wear that I hardly know where to start. All of the so-called rules of "fat dressing" are based on the premise that we should be trying to make ourselves look slimmer. I am always infuriated when I read some article aimed at big women, or see in some catalogue for outsize clothes, descriptions of clothes that tell you how much thinner they make your arms look or how they flatter you by fitting loosely and covering up a "protruding tum."

Highly recommended.

Breaking the Diet Habit: The Natural Weight Alternative Written by C. Peter Herman and Janet Polivy (Basic Books, 1983). Out of print.

Consuming Passions: Feminist Approaches to Weight Preoccupation & Eating Disorders Edited by Carina Brown and Karin Jasper (Second Story Press, 1993). Personal stories and thoughts of twenty-two women on the path to empowerment, learning to relax about their eating habits and accepting their bodies.

Diet Breaking: Having It All Without Having to Diet Written by Mary Evans Young, founder of Diet Breakers (Hodder and Stoughton, 1989). Advice, practical guidance, and inspiration you need to end the guilt trip. Available through Diet Breakers in London.

Dieter's Dilemma Written by William Bennett, M.D., and Joel Gurin (Basic Books Press, 1982). A comprehensive discussion of the set-point theory and why dieting doesn't work. Out of print.

Dieting Makes You Fat Written by Geoffrey Cannon and Hetty Einzig (Simon and Schuster, 1983). Discussion of the perils of dieting followed by a sensible eating plan (aimed at weight loss to some extent, but more toward increased good health) and becoming active. Out of print.

Eating Our Hearts Out: Personal Accounts of Women's Relationship to Food Written by Lesléa Newman (Crossing Press, 1993). A collection of 103 stories and poems written by women about their skewed relationships with food. If you are a victim of an eating disorder, you are sure to find yourself in these pages. Sometimes it helps to know there are others who play the same games and have the same obsessions with food.

Our culture makes it nearly impossible for us as women to have a healthy, easy relationship with food. On one hand, we are supposed to be the nurturers of the world, perfecting recipes to delight our families, and, on the other hand, we are supposed to deprive ourselves of these delicious meals in order to look the way our society deems it best for us to look, which can be summed up in one four-letter word: thin.

Face Value: The Politics of Beauty Written by Robin Tolmach Lakoff and Raquel L. Scherr (Routledge and Kegan Paul, 1984). How the beauty ideal is created and how it affects women. Out of print.

Fat and Thin—A Natural History of Obesity Written by Ann Beller (Farrar, Strauss, 1977). An interesting compilation of early studies showing the wisdom of questioning dieting and society's attitude about size. Out of print.

Fat Can Be Beautiful Written by Marilyn Friedman and Abraham I. Friedman, M.D. (Berkeley Publishing Corporation, 1974). A book we should have all listened to way back when. Dr. Friedman talks of sensible eating (not dieting) to stabilize one's natural weight, size acceptance, health, and sexual activity as good exercise. (And we chose Jane Fonda over this?) Some dated information, but interesting reading. Out of print.

Fat Chance Written by Harry Gossett (Independent Hill Press, 1986). An ex-FBI agent gives us a humorous look at weigh-ins and yo-yo dieting.

FBI regulations were clear on the subject of overweight. It rendered you "Unfit for Duty"; it was an "Offense" punishable by oral reprimand the first time, up to a five-day suspension the second time and as much as a fifteen-day suspension the third time. . . . Regulations didn't say what they do to a four-time loser, but I knew that sooner or later I was going to find out.

Available from Amplestuff and NAAFA Bookservice.

Fat Is a Feminist Issue: A Self-Help Guide for Compulsive Eaters Written by Susie Orbach (Berkeley Publishing, 1978). This book addresses compulsive eating patterns through case histories.

Fat Is a Feminist Issue II Written by Susie Orbach (Berkeley Publishing, 1982). Help with ending food obsessions. Out of print.

Fat Is Not a Four-Letter Word Written by Charles Roy Schroeder, Ph.D. (Chronimed Publishing, 1992). A history of coming to terms with fatness—both the world's in general and Dr. Schroeder's--and an excellent, bold overview of the diet industry. Well researched and written.

Fat Girl: One Woman's Way Out Written by Irene O'Gaden (Harper San Francisco, 1994). This woman's way of dealing with her size was not exactly "size accepting," but her thoughts on food issues and relationships to food are interesting.

Fat Power: Whatever You Weigh Is Right Written by Llewellyn Louderback (Hawthorne Books, 1970). The bible of the fat liberation movement. A classic. "In short, it is this book's contention that the fat person's major problem is not his obesity but the view that society takes of it." Out of print.

Fat Underground—The Original Radical Fat Feminists Edited by Karen Stimson (Largesse Press, 1994). Sourcebook of the history of the fat feminist movement.

Fed Up! A Woman's Guide to Freedom from the Diet/Weight Prison Written by Terry Nicholetti Garrison with David Levitsky, Ph.D. (Carroll and Graf Publishers, Inc., 1993). From her workshops of the same name, Ms. Garrison helps women come to terms with their bodies—at any size.

It takes tremendous courage to contradict a cultural attitude that is as deeply ingrained as the fear of fat and the imperative to be thin. Getting fed up at the oppression of weight prejudice and restrictive dieting will help us find that courage.

Fed Up and Hungry: Women, Oppression and Food Edited by Marilyn Lawrence (P. Bedrick Books, 1987). Feminist articles on eating disorders and social forces that cause them. Out of print.

Feeding on Dreams: Why America's Diet Industry Doesn't Work—and What Will Work for You Written by Diane Epstein (Macmillan Press, 1994). Written by a woman who at one time worked for one of the diet clinics, this book gives us the real skinny on what goes on behind closed doors in the diet industry. Fascinating reading.

The customers of diet centers other than Nutri/System are, frequently, putting their health and weight in the hands of a high school graduate who has taken classes at the center and sat in on some sessions with customers. A great deal of the counselors' training will have covered selling the program, keeping a customer in the program, and selling the program's food. And the selling is based on emotional manipulation of frightened, desperate people.

The Female Body in Western Culture: Contemporary Perspectives Edited by Susan Rubin Suleiman (Harvard University Press, 1986). Scholars and critics discuss Western attitudes toward female beauty and their impact on culture and art.

Female Desires: How They Are Sought, Bought and Packaged Written by Rosalind Coward (Grove Press, Inc., 1985). How the media tells us who we are and what we need.

Fitness the Dynamic Gardening Way Written by Jeffrey Restuccio (Balance of Nature Publishing, 1992). Turning your love of gardening into a pleasurable way to add healthful exercise to your life.

For Her Own Good: 150 Years of the Experts' Advice to Women Written by Barbara Ehrenreich and Dierdre English (Anchor/Doubleday Books, 1978). A look at the history of medical attitudes and treatments of women. Out of print.

The Forbidden Body: Why Being Fat Is Not a Sin Written by Shelley Bovey (Harper, 1994). A British look at fat hatred in today's society. Very well researched.

The Four Conditions of Self-Esteem: A New Approach for Elementary and Middle Schools Written by R. Bean (ETR Associates, 1992). An excellent book covering many areas of self-esteem. Teaches adults to recognize problems; offers techniques for both one-on-one and group interactions, and activities designed to improve and maintain good self-esteem.

If children consistently receive messages that one or more of their characteristics are not liked or valued by their caretakers, they will believe these messages and absorb them as part of their sense of self. This becomes even more damaging if children are criticized or shamed for characteristics they have no control over, such as their size, color, coordination, dress or looks.

Full Lives: Women Who Have Freed Themselves from Food & Weight Obsession Written by Lindsey Hall (Gürze Press, 1995). Personal stories of women who have grappled with repeated attempts to be thin, finally arriving at the conclusion healthy is what counts.

Full Style: Style and Fashion for the Fuller Figure Written by Karen Jackson (self-published, 1993). This book actually falls somewhere between book and newsletter. Ms. Jackson, who used to sell clothing through her mail-order business, gives tips on finding and choosing clothing and accessories, working with a tailor or dressmaker, and makeup. Available from the author.

Getting in Touch with Your Inner Bitch Written by Elizabeth Hilts (Hysteria, 1994). Leading us away from "Toxic Niceness" into getting in touch with the part of ourselves that looks out for what is really best for us. This is not only about learning to take care of ourselves, but about accepting our right to be whatever we are. Put up with being harassed for being big? "I don't think so."

The Gifted Figure: Proportioning Exercises for Large Women Written by Ann Smith (Capra Press, 1984). Illustrated. Using large models and placing an emphasis on exercising for enjoyment and improved health, rather than weight loss, Ms. Smith presents graceful yoga/dance-style movements. Out of print.

Good Looks: The Full-Figured Woman's Guide to Beauty Written by Pat Swift (Doubleday, 1982). How to take care of yourself and look your best. The author is the head of a modeling agency for plus-size models. Out of print.

Goodbye Jumbo, Hello Cruel World Written by Louie Anderson (Viking Penguin/Louzel Productions, Inc., 1993). Humorous, sad, moving, and introspective. Louie Anderson, popular comedian and author of another book, *Dear Dad,* shares his ongoing battle to love himself as a man who is fat. While approaching self-acceptance, Louie reaches some basic truths about himself and the shared experience of being fat. You'll surely see yourself in many of his memories and observations.

The Great American Waistline Written by Chris Chase (Coward, McCann and Geoghegan, 1981). A fascinating look at America and its obsession with food, weight, and the diet industry. The chapters in part one ("Putting It On") include "*Gourmet* Magazine and the Beginnings of Sauces for the Lower Classes," "Fast Foods: From Oeufs à la Neige to Egg McMuffin," and a look at the size-acceptance movement in "The Other Side of Fatness: Big Is Beautiful." Part two ("Taking It Off") gives us an overview of the diet industry in "Diet Books: Hoping for a Winner, Would-be Losers Buy 'Em All," "Diet Gimmicks, Diet Gadgets, and Creams to Melt," and "Radical Solutions: Wiring Your Jaws, Bypassing Your Stomach, and Chomping Down All That Rice . . ." While not exactly pro–size acceptance, Chris Chase presents a very thorough and fascinating look at the world we live in. Out of print.

Great Shape: The First Fitness Guide for Large Women Written by Pat Lyons and Debby Burgard (Bull Publishing, 1990). An exercise guide for large women *by* large women. Enjoy movement again and feel better about yourself with your improved flexibility. This is not your typical exercise book full of skinny models and exercises that would tax Jane Fonda. Pat and Debby address all of the issues that surround becoming active again . . . from all of the excuses we use to avoid activity to finding the recreation you will love indulging in to tips on getting started. Very positive, fun, absolutely liberating.

> *There are people who will argue to the death that fat people cannot be healthy and fit, that the terms* fat *and* fit *are mutually exclusive. While experts will continue to disagree, even contradict one another on the actual health risks of fat, you need not wait for their consensus to become more fit and healthy regardless of your weight. Most important is to define what health means to you and reach for that goal.*

Highly recommended.

Handicapped in Walt Disney World: A Guide for Everyone Written by Peter Smith (Southpark Publishing Group, Inc., 1993). Don't go letting a label like "handicapped" put you off. This book is invaluable in describing exactly what to expect when visiting this theme park. Why wait until you have stood in line for forty-five minutes to find out the Haunted Mansion ride requires that you be able to fit through a narrow eighteen-inch doorway into the vehicle. The author takes you to each attraction in Disney World, including restaurants, shops, and parades. The descriptions are quite detailed, and you have a real good idea before even leaving home about what to expect.

Health Risks of Weight Loss   Edited by Francie M. Berg (*Healthy Weight Journal*, 1995). Considered to be an "outstanding book of the year" by the American Library Association, this book is filled with facts about dieting and health issues.

Healthy Pleasures   Written by Robert Ornstein and David Sobel (Addison Wesley, 1990). This wonderful book tells us it's okay to enjoy life. Good research and a big helping of common sense document the benefits of relaxing, not overdoing (food *or* dieting, sloth *or* exercise). "In short, the healthiest people seem to be pleasure-loving, pleasure-seeking, pleasure-creating individuals."

How to Get Your Kid to Eat... But Not Too Much   Written by Ellyn Satter (Bull Publications, 1987). Just as the title says, this book deals with creating healthy eating habits and environments for our children.

Even the fat child is entitled to regulate the amount of food he eats. You don't have to do that and you shouldn't try. Don't try to assume that responsibility even in sneaky ways, because your child will be on to you.

The Hungry Self: Women, Eating and Identity   Written by Kim Chernin (Harper Perennial, 1985). A look at eating disorders. Ms. Chernin's theory is that eating disorders are caused by an identity crisis today's women suffer from because of traditional women's roles in society.

The Invisible Woman: Confronting Weight Prejudice   Written by W. Charisse Goodman (Gürze Books, 1995). This very-well-researched and -presented book angrily confronts many of the issues that come with being larger-than-"average." Highly recommended.

Journeys to Self-Acceptance: Fat Women Speak   Written by Carol A. Wiley (Crossing Press, 1994). The stories of twenty-four women who have learned to love themselves as they are.

Just the Weigh You Are   Written by Eileen Wegeleben (self-published, 1986). Feel good about yourself, no matter what your size-of-large is. Available from Amplestuff.

Largely Positive: Self Esteem Comes in All Sizes   Written by Carol Johnson (Doubleday-Bantam, 1995).

Live Large! Ideas, Affirmations, and Actions for Sane Living in a Larger Body   Written by Cheri K. Erdman, Ed.D. (Harper San Francisco, 1997). A positive voice supporting you through your journey to size acceptance and helping you to change your mind to fit your body through thoughts and deeds.

Losing Weight Is Not for Everyone Written by Jan Troske (Star Books, 1991.)

Love Your Looks: How to Stop Criticizing and Start Appreciating Your Appearance Written by Carolyn Hillman (Simon and Schuster, 1996).

Making Peace with Food: Freeing Yourself from the Diet/Weight Obsession Written by Susan Kano (Amity Publishing, 1985).

Minding the Body: Women Writers on Body and Soul Written by Sally Tisdale, Hanan Al-Shaykh, and Jenefer Shute (Anchor Books, 1994). The experiences of finding peace with one's self-image from three very different perspectives.

Mirror, Mirror: The Importance of Looks in Everyday Life Written by Rita Freedman (Harper and Row, 1986). The value placed on looking good in America. Out of print.

Never Satisfied: A Cultural History of Diets, Fantasies and Fat Written by Hillel Schwartz (Free Press, Macmillan, Inc., 1990). Very thorough look at dieting, big business, and food in America. A must-read for anyone interested in the history of diets and dieting and of our culture's fatphobia.

Never Too Thin: A History of American Women's Obsession with Weight Loss (Why Women Are at War with their Bodies) Written by Roberta Pollack Seid, Ph.D. (Prentice Hall, 1989). Where

did this obsession with thinness in our society come from? Can we overcome it? Dr. Seid thinks we can and tells us how. Excellent book, highly recommended.

The New Our Bodies, Ourselves By the Boston Women's Health Collective (Simon and Schuster, 1992). Always an excellent source of information for women of any size, any age. Of particular interest is the chapter on women and exercise.

Nothing to Lose: A Woman's Guide to Sane Living in a Larger Body Written by Cheri K. Erdman, Ed.D. (Harper San Francisco, 1995). Dr. Erdman is one of the warmest, most empowering women in the size-acceptance movement today, and her book reflects this in every way. I especially appreciate the section on putting together and utilizing a support group. Highly recommended.

The Obsession: Reflection on the Tyranny of Slenderness Written by Kim Chernin (Harper/Collins, 1994). This book on eating disorders, women, and fat provides some interesting insights into the hatred of fat in our society.

One Size Does Not Fit All Written by Beverly Naidus (Aigis Publications, 1993). Beautiful original art.

One Size Fits All and Other Fables Written by Liz Curtis Higgs (Thomas Nelson Publishers, 1993). Every fat fable you ever heard (fat people are jolly; you can lose it if you really want to; you'll never get a man) is examined, turned inside out, then set right. Very humorous, very insightful book with a Christian slant. Available from the author.

> Too often, we postpone joy until we are, say, a size 10. I've been a size 10, and was no more joyful at that size than I am now as a size 22 Tinkerbell. "Thin" does not guarantee health, happiness or a husband. Today, and every day, you need to be assured that you are a woman of immeasurable worth and great beauty "as is," not "when."

Overcoming Fear of Fat: Fat Oppression in Psychotherapy Edited by Laura S. Brown and Esther Rothblum, Ph.D. (Harrington Park Press, 1989). A collection of articles by feminist therapists. Available from NAAFA Bookservice.

Plus Style: The Plus Size Guide to Looking Great Written by Suzan Nanfeldt (Plume Books, 1996). Humorous, down-to-earth instructions for improved self-esteem and increased confidence in selecting clothing, makeup, and hairstyles that best suit your personality and body. This book doesn't teach you how to look thinner . . . it does better than that. It teaches you how to look your best at any size.

Positively Different: Creating a Bias-Free Environment for Young Children Written by A. C. Matiella (ETR Associates, 1991). The message here is not only that we all have differences— race, religion, hair color, and body size—but that those differences are to be celebrated, not glossed over or hidden.

This is an idea whose time has certainly come.

> In our society, being different has been defined as something negative. We have actively promoted the "we are all the same" ideal—also referred to as the "colorblind approach." Without bad intentions, in an attempt to deal with the differences in a positive manner, we have denied differences and promoted the value of sameness.

Pound Foolish: The Tyranny of Thinness Written by Hillel Schwartz (Free Press, 1986). An examination of why society has developed its obsession with being thin. I loved his description of what life would be like in a fat society. Imagine guilt-free meals of real food, not vitamin supplements and powdered drinks. Children raised without the anxiety that causes bulimia and anorexia. A standard of beauty that doesn't accept weight as a condition. And this gem: "Fat women would not live in the future conditional, suspended between what they are and who they will be when they are finally thin."

A fascinating view, full of an incredible amount of information. (Did you know that Servia, Indiana, used to bill itself as "A Town of Fat People" and was just that?) Out of print.

Preventing Childhood Eating Problems: A Practical, Positive Approach to Raising Children Free of Food & Weight Conflicts Written by Jane R. Hirschmann and Lela Zaphiropoulos (Gürze Books, 1993). An insightful guide to teaching your children to let their bodies decide when enough is enough.

Real Women Don't Diet! Written by Ken Mayer (Bartleby Press, 1993). Anti-dieting book for women.

Resourceful Woman (Expanding Mind Books, 1994). Inspiration and resources for the large woman. Available from Expanding Mind Books.

Schoolgirls: Young Women, Self-Esteem, and the Confidence Gap Written by Peggy Orenstein in association with the American Association of University Women (Doubleday, 1994). An up-close inspection of the lives and influences on young girls in the 90s. Reading this book may well cause reconsideration of our own attitudes and subtle messages passed along to our daughters.

Self-Esteem Comes in All Sizes: How to Be Happy and Healthy at Your Natural Weight Written by Carol A. Johnson (Doubleday, 1995). Urging readers to go on a diet of self-esteem, Carol Johnson, founder of the support group Largely Positive, creates a book of inspiration and love: "It's no sin to be big. There's a lot worse things you could be—such as cruel, uncaring, or selfish."

Shadow on a Tightrope: Writings by Women on Fat Oppression Edited by Lisa Schoenfielder and Barb Wieser (Aunt Lute Books, 1983). This collection of articles, personal stories, and poems by fat women was the first to present fat liberation theory and its connection to radical feminism. Includes writings by NAAFAns and members of the original Fat Underground. Available from NAAFA Bookservice.

Short Rations: Confessions of a Cranky Calorie Counter Written by Joan Scobey (Holt, Rinehart, and Winston, 1980). Out of print.

Sizing Up: Fashion, Fitness, and Self-Esteem for Full-Figured Women Written by Sandy Summers Head (Simon and Schuster, 1989). Out of print.

Smiling at Yourself: Educating Young Children About Stress and Self-Esteem Written by A. N. Mendler (ETR Associates, 1990). A very upbeat book designed for caregivers of young children. Not just about being fat, this book talks about stress of all kinds, how it affects children, and how to help them deal with it.

> *It helps for kids to think about things I worry about that I can control and things I worry about that I can't control. Action can help the former while acceptance is necessary for the latter.*

SomeBODY to Love: A Guide to Loving the Body You Have Written by Lesléa Newman (Third Side Press, 1991). Writing exercises designed to help you focus on your body image and eating patterns. This is a book to be lingered over and worked through slowly. With no right or wrong answers, the exercises guide you to a better understanding of yourself and your relationship with food.

I believe that anorexia nervosa, bulimia, and compulsive overeating are all symptoms of a disease that has reached epidemic proportions among women in this country. That disease is called self-hate. No matter how old you are, no matter how much of a feminist you are, if you look in the mirror and respond with anything less than pure joy when you gaze at the reflection of your own unique gorgeous self—you've got it. The disease of self-hate. It's in all of us."

Style Is Not a Size—Looking and Feeling Great in the Body You Have Written by Hara Estroff Marano (Bantam Books, 1991). Practical clothing tips.

Such a Pretty Face: Being Fat in America Written by Marcia Millman (Berkeley Books, 1980). While the pictures in this book may seem dated, the attitudes expressed of and toward fat people certainly aren't. Out of print.

Surviving Exercise Written by Judy Alter (Houghton Mifflin Company, 1990). Excellent resource for anyone about to begin or add to an exercise program. Full of safe exercises for any body type.

Tailoring Your Tastes Written by Linda Omichinski, B.Sc. (F.Sc.), R.D., and Heather Wiebe Hildebrand, R.N., B.S.N. (HUGS International, 1995). Healthier eating without restrictive diets. Available from HUGS International.

Transforming Body Image: Learning to Love the Body You Have Written by Marcia Germaine Hutchinson, Ed.D. (Crossing Press, 1985). This workbook takes you through a series of mental exercises meant to help you improve your body image. Excellent book. A set of five audiocassettes has been recorded that was designed to be used only as a companion to the book. Available from Body-Mind Productions.

Trusting Ourselves: The Complete Guide to Emotional Well-Being for Women Written by Karen Johnson, M.D. (Atlantic Monthly Press, 1990).

The Untold Truth About Fatness Written by Dean Kimmell (Corbin House, 1988).

You Count, Calories Don't Written by Linda Omichinski, R.D. (Hyperion Press Ltd. of Canada, 1992). Develop some positive, healthy habits through this humorous, commonsense approach. Available from Amplestuff and HUGS International, Inc.

What You Can Change and What You Can't: The Complete Guide to Successful Self-Improvement Written by Martin E. P. Seligman (Knopf Books, 1994). Pretty much what the title implies, with an excellent chapter on weight.

When Women Stop Hating Their Bodies: Freeing Yourself from Food and Weight Obsession Written by Jane R. Hirschmann and Carol H. Munter (Fawcett Columbine, 1995). Addressing what they feel to be the single most pervasive reason women stay stuck in the diet/binge cycle, the authors of this book challenge women to accept their bodies, whatever their shape.

Where the Girls Are: Growing Up Female with the Mass Media Written by Susan J. Douglas (Times Books, 1994). Fascinating reading, presenting not only the negative influences but also the positive impact of the way women have been presented in the media. Curl up with this book when you are ready for a flood of memories.

> The TV grilling of Anita Hill made many of us shake our fists in rage; Special K ads make most of us hide our thighs in shame. On the one hand, on the other hand—that's not just me—that's what it means to be a woman in America."

Woman Here Within Written by Karen Bert (self-published, 1993). A volume of poetry and prose. Available from the author.

Womanspirit: A Guide to Women's Wisdom Written by Hallie Iglehart (Harper, 1983). Out of print.

A Woman's Conflict: The Special Relationship Between Women and Food Edited by Jane Rachel Kaplan (Prentice-Hall, 1989). An impressive collection of articles written by some of the major researchers of food and body size.

Women and Self-Esteem: Understanding and Improving the Way We Think and Feel About Ourselves Written by Linda Tschirhart Sanford and Mary Ellen Donovan (Viking-Penguin, 1984).

Wonderful book covering many areas of self-esteem for women.

Women En Large: Images of Fat Nudes Written by Laurie Tody Edison and Debbie Notkin (Books in Focus, 1994). The culmination of ten years of fat activism and five years of work specifically for this project, *Women En Large* presents forty-one black-and-white fine art photos of fat women. Sure to stir controversy and perhaps change the way you feel about beauty, fat women, and society.

Women Who Run with the Wolves: Myths and Stories of the Wild Woman Archetype Written by Clarissa Pinkola Estes (Ballantine Press, 1992). A wonderful, empowering book of stories, multicultural myths, and fairy tales used to help bring women back to an inner source of strength and peace.

> A woman cannot make the culture more aware by saying "Change." But she can change her own attitude toward herself, thereby causing devaluing projections to glance off. She does this by taking back her body. By not forsaking the joy of her natural body, by not purchasing the popular illusion that happiness is only bestowed on those of a certain configuration or age, by not waiting or holding back to do anything, and by taking back her real life, and living it full bore, all stops out. This dynamic self-acceptance and self-esteem are what begins to change attitudes in the culture."

Highly recommended.

BROCHURES, CALENDARS, PAPERS, DIRECTORIES, AND WORKBOOKS

"Ample Hygiene for Ample People"
Twenty-page booklet written by Nancy Summer with straight talk about cleanliness for large people. Ms. Summer addresses chafing, odor, irritations, and other concerns, and presents simple, easy-to-handle solutions. Excellent resource. $5.

Sources: Amplestuff

The Association for the Health Enrichment of Large People (AHELP) has produced the following tapes from its 1994 annual conference. The topic of the conference was "Freeing the Fat Child."

"Helping the Large Child and Adolescent: Setting a National Agenda," featuring Bonnie Brigman, Ph.D.; Ellyn Satter, M.S., R.D., M.S.S.W.; Joanne Ikeda, M.A., R.D.; Janet Polivy, Ph.D.; Cheri Erdman, Ed.D.; and Roxy Walker (2 tapes). $16.

"Kids Come in All Sizes: Interrupting Size Bias in a Sixth Grade Population," featuring Nancy Summer. $8.

"Large Children: A Reflection of Family," featuring Carol Johnson, M.A., and Shay Harris, M.S.W. $8.

"Parental Activism on Behalf of the Large Child," featuring Jody Savage, M.S. $8.

"Building Big Beautiful Self-Esteem"
Pamphlet by Stacy Alberts (1992).
Sources: Pen-A-Friend

"Building Blocks for Children's Body Image" Brochure produced by Body Image Task Force. Send a self-addressed stamped envelope or request by E-mail.
Sources: Body Image Task Force

Children and Weight: What's a Parent to Do? Tape and booklets by Joanne Ikeda, R.D., and Rita Mitchell, R.D. (ANR Publications).

Children and Weight: What's a Parent to Do? A twelve-minute videotape, available in Spanish and English. The tape is accompanied by the three booklets *If My Child Is Too Fat, What Should I Do About It?*, *Children and Weight: What's a Parent to Do?* and *Food Choices for Good Health.* $35.

Children and Weight: What's A Parent to Do? Booklet designed for low-literacy audiences; summarizes *If My Child Is Too Fat, What Should I Do About It?*

Food Choices for Good Health Eight-page leaflet. Lists familiar foods and how they fit into a healthy diet.

"Good News for Big Kids" A wonderful pamphlet that speaks directly to kids about body size, how to be liked, how to make friends, and how to appreciate all the really good things about themselves. Not at all preachy and very well done. Includes information about finding help, including the Youth Crisis Hotline (1-800-HIT-HOME) kids can use to find someone to talk with if they don't have a friend, teacher, relative, or other adult to turn to.

If My Child Is Too Fat, What Should I Do About It? Twenty-page booklet offering advice about encouraging sensible eating habits and an active lifestyle.

"Fat Feminist Herstory" Pamphlet by Karen Stimson (1994).

SOURCES: Largesse Presse

Fat Underground: The Original Radical Fat Feminists Compiled by Karen Stimson (1994). Archival sourcebook of writings, letters, news clippings, and other materials covering the legendary fat feminist collective from 1973 to 1976, with introductory essay.

SOURCES: Largesse Presse

Freda's Secrets Written by Freda Rosenberg, updated regularly. Guide to large women's fashions.

SOURCES: Freda Rosenberg

"Full Figured Woman's Guide to Happiness" Pamphlet by Stacy Alberts (1992).

SOURCES: Pen-A-Friend

"Full Figured Woman's Guide to Sexuality" Pamphlet by Stacy Alberts (1992).

SOURCES: Pen-A-Friend

International No Diet Coalition Directory of Resources Contact information and description of groups in the antidiet, size-acceptance movement. Available from the International No Diet Coalition. $13.

NAAFA Educational brochures for yourself, family, friends, and health care providers.

"Declaration of the Rights of Fat People in Health Care"
"Guidelines for Health Care Providers in Dealing with Fat Patients"
"Guidelines for Therapists Who Treat Fat Clients"
"Facts About Hypertension and the Fat Person"
"How to Weigh Your Supersize Patient"
"Dispelling Common Myths About Fat People"
"Size Discrimination Is a Civil Rights Issue"
"Size Discrimination: Its Link to Other 'isms' "
"Airline Travel Tips"

Prices: Less than twenty-five brochures, any combination: 25 cents each; twenty-five to one hundred brochures, any combination: 20 cents each; one hundred or more brochures, any combination: 10 cents each.

SOURCES: NAAFA Bookservice

"NAAFA Newsletter" Back issues, 1970 to 1992, in volumes of six issues each. $8 to $20. Also available in a combination offer, the entire set for approximately $70.

SOURCES: NAAFA Bookservice

NAAFA Workbook (1996). An introduction and orientation to the body of
writing, theory, and policy that has
evolved in NAAFA and the size-
acceptance movement. Includes chapters on health, fashion, employment,
self-esteem, fat admirers, and activism.
Approximate price: $11.

SOURCES: NAAFA Bookservice

Personal Hygiene for the Ample Person
Written by Nancy Summer, third edition.
This booklet covers special hygiene prob-
lems large people encounter. $5.

SOURCES:

Amplestuff, Ltd.

NAAFA Bookservice

"Plus-Size Fashion Model Calendar"
Includes shopping directory. $12.

SOURCES: XL Mystique

***Rethinking Obesity: An Alternative View
of Its Health Implications*** Written by
Paul Ernsberger and Paul Haskew
(Human Sciences Press, 1987). Rebuttal
to National Institutes of Health's pro-
nouncements on "killer obesity."

SOURCES: Amplestuff

Royal Resources Written by Jan Her-
rick, this work used to be *Help for Heft-
ies.* A resource guide of products and
services. $30.

SOURCES: Vendredi Enterprises

**"Sex Appeal Secrets for Full Figured La-
dies"** Pamphlet by Stacy Alberts (1991).

SOURCES: Pen-A-Friend

Size-Acceptance Packet A resource
packet for integrating size acceptance
into health-promotion programs. $7.50
(make check out to Regents of UC).

SOURCES: Cooperative Extension, Nutritional Sciences, UC/Berkeley

Size Diversity Empowerment Kit
A collection of articles, brochures, catalogs, and fliers for size-friendly products,
services, and events from Largesse, the
Network for Size Esteem. Many of these
items are from Body Image Task Force
(BITF) and are available through that
organization also. $18. Though content
is regularly updated, articles and brochures currently include:

"Are Diets Just a Consumer Scam?"
(magazine article)

"Big Bytes—Internet Resources for Fat
Folks" (Size Esteem bulletin)

"Building Blocks for Children's Body
Image" (BITF)

"Body Image Solutions" (BITF)

"Body Image Books" (BITF)

"Cancer and the 'Fat' Issue" (BITF)

"Confident, Beautiful Women: A
Healthy Self-Image Knows No Size"
(interview of Cheri Erdman, newspaper article)

"Coming Soon: Bottoms-up Jeans"
(magazine article)

"Discovery of Obesity Gene Brings
Worry, Hope, and Joy" (newspaper
article)

"Do-It-Yourself Self-Esteem Repair"
(from *Largely Positive*)

"Fourteen Ways to Better Health Right Now"

"Go Ahead—Do a Good Deed and Trash That Diet" (newspaper article)

"Heart Study Challenges Diet Theory" (newspaper article)

"International No Diet Day Conquers Our Fear of Fat" (newspaper article)

"Invocation for the Size Rights Movement"

"Largesse: The Network for Size Esteem" (brochure)

"Learning to Love Yourself in Spite of Your Weight" (newspaper article)

"Newfound Gene May Control Fat Storage" (newspaper article)

"Our Vision for the Next Ten Years" (magazine article by Miriam Berg)

"Queen-Size for a Day" (newspaper article)

"Raising Largely Positive Kids" (from *Largely Positive*)

"Reward Notice for Proof That Fat Is Unhealthy"

"Rockefeller Study Supports Theory That Body Has Fat-Maintenance System (newspaper article)

"Sizing Up Discrimination as Some Workers Find Laws, Attitudes Are Slow to Change" (newspaper article)

"Ten Tips For Professionals Working with Larger Clients" (from *Largely Positive*)

"Thinking Big" (magazine article about Karen and Richard Stimson)

"Want a Cookie, Maybe Two? No-Diet Day is Just for You" (newspaper article)

"WARNING: Dieting Has Been Shown . . ." (BITF poster)

"Weight Loss and Your Health" (BITF)

"Weight Loss Surgery" (magazine article)

"Woman Says Fat's Not Such a Big Deal" (interview of Lee Martindale, newspaper article)

"Women Say No to Dieting" (newspaper article)

"Celebrate International No Diet Day" (article)

"Waist Size Isn't About Self-Worth" Brochure by Joyce Rue-Potter. $5.

SOURCES: Abundantly Yours

AUDIOTAPES, FILMS, AND VIDEOS

A Matter of Fat
(see *Fat Chance,* below)

Body Trust: Undieting Your Way to Health and Happiness
By Dayle Hayes, M.S., R.D. (1993). $28.95.

Ms. Hayes, a registered dietitian and president of the Montana Dietetic Association, encourages three principles in this tape:

1. Feed Your Body (stop dieting, legalize all foods, listen to your

body's inner signals, and eat what you want when you want it).

2. Move Your Body (find safe, comfortable activities you love to participate in, then start slowly).

3. Learn to Love Your Body (throw away your scale, fill your closets with beautiful comfortable clothes, invest in yourself not the diet industry, and build an accepting support system).

She goes on to warn against "diets in disguise"—programs that are critical or judgmental; tell you how much, what, and when to eat; and override your body's natural signals.

Sources: Production West

Facets of NAAFA 1986 photo journal by NAAFA. Collection of NAAFA memories captured on film. Limited quantity. $4.

Sources: NAAFA Bookservice

The Famine Within Produced by Katherine Gilday. There are three versions of this video: a 55-minute classroom version, a 90-minute theatrical version, and a 118-minute unedited version. The 90-minute version is most commonly used. Institutional/educational use— $195, purchase; $75, rental. Home video—$40. Add $5 for shipping.

Sources: Direct Cinema Limited

Fat Chance By the National Film Board of Canada, featuring Rick Zakowich (1994). This film (also shown under the title *A Matter of Fat*), has been picked up by the Arts and Entertainment channel. Check local listings for times when it will be shown.

This is the true story of Rick Zakowich, an attractive, very talented man who has grown to despise his size and the life he feels trapped in because of the attitudes of others. *Fat Chance* takes us along on his journey from thinking, "I'm a fat man and I hate myself for it. I'm forty years old and weigh four hundred pounds and can't really remember the last time I was happy. I want to change and dieting is the only way I know how," to looking at himself in a whole new light. Rick begins the film on a diet, determined to become a thin man. Instead he discovers new values and attitudes and finds personal acceptance to be far more satisfying than chasing after unattainable goals set by society.

Fat Chance, in its original Peabody Award–winning form, is highly recommended. A chubby thumbs-up! Unfortunately, it has been changed by the National Film Board of Canada into a mere shadow of itself and a less than size-positive presentation. Before ordering it, be sure to ask which version you're getting. (See also the profile of Rick Zakowich on page 183.)

Sources: Bullfrog Films

Fat World Produced by Lorna Boschman. This 25-minute video offers a fat perspective of life from a fat woman.

Sources: Video In Studios

Foodfright Produced by Barbara Harrington, Gisele L'Italien, and Roger M. Sherman. Film adaptation of a popular stage review that explores society's preoccupation with thinness: "You diet till you die with food fright." Set in the Hungry Woman Cabaret, *Foodfright* is wildly funny at times, and equally as sad when it zeroes in on the pain inflicted by this obsession. Centering mainly on eating disorders, this film offers a lot of insight into the feelings we all deal with to some degree. Includes a wonderful song, "Fat Rap" ("I'm not size five and I'll never be, So take a good look and get used to me"). 28 minutes. Educational/institutional video—$150, purchase; $50, rental. Home use—$25. Shipping is an additional $5.

SOURCES: Direct Cinema Limited

Gracious Flab, Gracious Bone Produced by Evie Leder. This fifteen-minute tape offers a profile of writer Susan Stinsom and her work. This tape has received some excellent reviews and is well worth checking out. $12.

SOURCES: Call (413) 586-9012

HUGS Affirmation Tapes Set of three audiotapes addressing lifestyle patterns and skills, positive language, assertiveness, and size acceptance. $50 (Canadian), $40 (American).

SOURCES: HUGS International, Inc.

In Search of Fullness: Women, Eating Disorders & Body Image Produced by Maya Webb. Personal profiles of several women dealing with eating disorders. Excellent discussion starter for your own group. 60 minutes. $25.

SOURCES: Body Image Task Force

Improve Body Image—Develop Self Empowerment By Sharon Anne Delconte, M.S.W., M.P.A., A.C.S.W., clinical social worker, clinical director, and workshop presenter. Positive visualizations for positive life changes.

SOURCES: New Resources

Just Liz By Liz Curtis Higgs, author of *One Size Fits All and Other Fables*. A certified speaking professional and entertainer, Ms. Higgs appears at many NAAFA gatherings, encouraging women to enjoy their lives and be comfortable with themselves at any size. 52 minutes. $20 plus shipping.

SOURCES: Liz Curtis Higgs

Killing Us for Our Own Good: Dieting & Medical Misinformation Produced by GynoCentrics. Medical facts, fat realities, and a serious stomping of the diet industry. Excellent tape. 120 minutes. Video, $30; audio, $17.

SOURCES:
Body Image Task Force
GynoCentrics

The Losing Game An interesting overview of body image and size-acceptance issues. $25.

SOURCES: Allbritton TV Productions

No Apologies Size-positive film by Wry Crips. 30 minutes.

SOURCES: Wry Crips

Nothing to Lose By FAT LIP Readers Theatre. This video is a sampling of the kind of work done by this group of innovative, talented women. The message: "Here we are. Deal with us. We are not going to hate ourselves if we get bigger and we're not going to like ourselves more if we get smaller. We like ourselves now. We are not going to put our lives on hold one minute longer." 30 minutes, VHS. Approximate cost, $33.

SOURCES:

FAT LIP Readers Theatre

Collage Video

Nothing to Lose—Women's Body Image Through Time This educational tape examines the history of body images. 30 minutes. $70.

SOURCES: College of DuPage, Office of Educational Telecommunications

Slim Hopes—Advertising and the Obsession with Thinness By Jean Killborn. An excellent, thorough look at how advertisers help to create our negative body images and then use them to sell their products to us. 30 minutes. Colleges—$250, nonprofit groups—$215, individuals—$75.

SOURCES: Media Education Foundation

Throwing Our Weight Around Produced by Sandy Dwyer. Discussions among fat women on the issues many of us have faced, from job discrimination to popular media. 60 minutes. $33.

SOURCES: Roundabout Productions

Warning: The Media May Be Hazardous to Your Health Produced by Janai Lane. Not so much about size acceptance as it is about how women are portrayed in, and used by, media. 60 minutes, VHS. $45.

SOURCES: Media Watch

ARTISTS AND THEIR ART

Being Yourself This beautiful 18" × 24" color pencil drawing shows four beautiful little girls practicing ballet. The artist, Sue Shanahan, depicts each as different in her own way; all are accepted and happy. $17.

SOURCES: Amplestuff

Fernando Botero Contemporary South American artist whose works feature very round and pear-shaped men and women. Works in a variety of media: drawings, paintings, and monumental sculpture.

Paul Delacroix Studios Historical/mythological-styled works on canvas. Prints of Mr. Delacroix's own work are seen often in size-positive publications, including *Rump Parliament*. Special commissions and portraits are also available.

D. C. Dixon D. C. Dixon's art celebrates the large woman with beauty and energy. Contact her for a catalog ($2, refundable with purchase) of her work on T-shirts, greeting cards, and gift items.

Lucian Freud Etchings and paintings that often include models of "wonderfully buoyant bulk." Especially provocative and powerful are works that include Leigh Bowery, a designer and performance artist.

R. C. Gorman Painter who specializes in scenes of the American Southwest and whose works often include large women.

Barbara Lavalee Alaskan artist who specializes in beautiful, colorful prints and paintings, often of Eskimo women, depicting merry, playful scenes of bountiful women, children, and cats. If you're in Alaska, her work can be seen everywhere on greeting cards, mugs, aprons, and other items, and can be purchased through a catalog.

Susan Mason Artist whose drawings grace T-shirts from design firm Myles Ahead and A Well-Rounded Woman.

B. Neil Osbourn Creator of *New Perspective Images, Big Beauty and Big Beauty II,* collections of photographs that celebrate round, soft bodies. 5" by 7" copies, $8; 11" by 14" copies, $15; 16" by 20" posters, $30; and 20" by 30" posters, $35.

SOURCES: New Perspective Images

Peter Rubino Painter and sculptor whose favorite subject is the Rubenesque female. Mr. Rubino presented a statue, *Abundant Beauty,* to Bill Fabrey, founder of NAAFA, on the occasion of NAAFA's tenth anniversary.

SOURCES: Bountiful Productions

Star River Productions Sculpture, musical instruments, books, and jewelry by artist Nancy Blair.

Tip Toe Arts Chrissa O'Brien's work is just plain fun. Her fat ladies are sassy, playful, and confident as they cavort on the beach, swing on the trapeze, and sun by the pool. You can find these drawings for framing or, in some instances, on T-shirts. Contact Tip Toe Arts for more information.

Yuri Vann Art Collections of pencil etchings include *Art of Yuri Vann,* $10; *Scraps,* $15; *Artistic Fusion,* $15; *YV Revised,* $15; and *The Dark Side,* $20. (Prices approximate.)

Zoftig Nudes by Rhonda Grossman Pencil etchings, limited-edition prints, portraits, boudoir sketches, computer drawings, block prints, and commissioned work.

BUTTONS AND MUGS

Largesse, the Network for Size Esteem Buttons offering a choice of several sayings in a variety of background colors. $1.50 each plus postage.

National Association to Advance Fat Acceptance (NAAFA) Buttons with the NAAFA logo, "Celebrate INDD May 6," "Large & In Charge," "Don't Weigh

Your Self-Esteem," and a no-diets logo on buttons. $2 each.

Rump Parliament The "Seen on a Button" sayings throughout this book came from *RP*'s button list and are available, along with many others, reproduced on buttons. $2 each. Mugs and tankards are also available. $20–$24.

NOTE CARDS

A Well-Rounded Note Full-figured females drawn by Susan Mason, printed on white card stock with black ink. Each card is 4" by 5" and comes in a set of 5. $11.

Sources: Largesse, the Network for Size Esteem

Cards of Class Cards written to put insensitive people in their place. $15 for 6 cards.

Sources: C.D.C.

DJ's Positive Images Four fat-positive designs on the fronts of 5" by 7" cards, blank on the inside, accompanied by lavender envelopes. $1.75 for single cards; $6.50 for 4; $12 for 8 (2 of each design); $18.00 for 12 (3 of each design).

Deborah C. Dixon Christmas, Hanukkah, and general note cards featuring beautiful, size-positive art. Each box contains 12 cards, 3 different images. $15.

F'Attitude Cards, prints, and gifts that depict the beauty of fat women.

Goddess Greetings "Celebrating Women of Size." Greeting cards with attractive images of large women. The insides of the cards are blank and there are thought-provoking messages on the back. "Know that: A new Fashion Role Model is starring on the runway. We are women who are not afraid of what we weigh, and want to show the world 'women of size' are here to stay." $2 each.

Largesse, the Network for Size Esteem Amazon card in black with red background on a 5" by 7" white card. $2.50 plus postage.

Rump Parliament Note cards with size-positive greetings. $1.50 each.

POSTERS

The Belly Project This poster depicts bellies of all sizes and shapes, aimed at expressing a universality of bodies as they really are, not as they are depicted in advertisements and other media. Originally begun as a project in response to antiabortion demonstrations, the Belly Project has major exhibits all over the country. $13.

Kari Ann Owen Ms. Owen has designed and produced two size-acceptance posters. One is an outcry over the Patricia Mullen incident in Chicago (see chapter "Fat: The Last Safe Prejudice for more information on Patricia); the other protests "National Rib Check Day" (you're supposed to check to see if your dog is overweight by feeling his ribs). Contact Ms. Owen for further information. $30.

COMICS, EROTICA, FAT ADMIRERS (FAS), AND WEIGHT-GAIN PUBLICATIONS

Amazon Women Videos Three videos featuring very tall, very large women. Adult material. $50 each.

SOURCES: Wig, Inc.

American Bear Bimonthly magazine featuring fiction, personals, articles, and photos. Subscription: $38 (U.S.), $46 (Canada/Mexico), $65 outside North America.

SOURCES: Amabear Publishing, Inc.

Belly Busters Newsletter for feeders and feedees. Pro-weight-gain personals, ads, and erotica. Adult material. Subscription is $35 for 4 issues. Free ad placement with subscription.

SOURCES: Caldera Company

Big and Beautiful Pictures and amateur videos of big and beautiful ladies. Adult material. Write for pricing information.

SOURCES: *Big and Beautiful*

Big and Fat This British magazine, designed for FAs, lacks a certain subtlety. The logo reads: "If you like women so large that they should be carrying license plates, then you're going to think you've died and gone to heaven!" Adult material. Write for pricing information.

SOURCES: Big Magazines, Ltd.

Bountiful Productions Supersize ladies in lingerie. Adult videos and photos. Write or call for free catalog. $35 for 10 photos.

Brie Fan Club (BFC) "The Perfect Pear Shape." Adult material. For more information, send $1 plus SASE.

Buf A men's magazine featuring fat women and "dedicated to the principle that large women are attractive, delightful, and loaded with sex appeal." Adult material. $24 for 6 issues.

SOURCES: Buf Publications

Bodacious Babes, Christine and Carla, Love's Savage Cupcake, and Roman Toga Party. "These films are a glorification of fat women and their admirers." Erotic and sensual situations. Each 60 minutes in length. Adult material. $35 each.

SOURCES: Films by Raphael, Inc.

Bulk Male, the Magazine for Large Men A magazine for gay men, *Bulk Male* contains photos with full frontal nudity and stories of sexual acts. Plenty of personals from all over the world, issue articles, information on events, and fiction. Adult material. Published bimonthly. $36 for 6 issues, $54 in Canada and Mexico, $66 international.

Divine Delights Quarterly adult newsletter. Adult material. $20 year, $6 single copy.
SOURCES: Double D Productions

Fat Admirers News Articles, stories, and pictures in newsletter form for admirers of large-size women. One-year subscription: $10.
SOURCES: I. Y. Murphy

Fat Kat Comics These comics (#1 and #2) are available for downloading through your computer. After signing on, search the files for uploads by "geepster." There are plans to add more.
SOURCES: Available only through America Online

Heavy Duty This gay men's magazine's goal is "to fulfill the visual representation of sexually attractive large framed men . . . who appreciate tasteful erotica . . . to be a forum for the large man to be proud of his sexuality . . . to offer a variety of nude, gorgeous, large framed men . . . for your viewing pleasure, admiration and fantasies." Steamy erotic fiction, big man articles, information on all the latest happenings, personal ads, and color layouts. Quarterly.

One-year subscription: $30; Canadian, $35; international, $45.

Largesse (Not affiliated with Largesse, the Network for Size Esteem.) Collection of erotica by fat women about fat women and the men who love them. Adult material. $11 per issue, $30 for 4 issues.
SOURCES: Paradigm Press

Life in the Fat Lane CD-ROM collection of images of fat women. $15.
SOURCES: BR News

Melody Z-cup woman featured in color videos. $50 each.
SOURCES: Phaeton Classic Products

Oinquirer A weight-gain tabloid. Adult material. Write for pricing information.
SOURCES: Rick Suseoff

Paulette Photo sets of 10 images in lingerie or bathing suit. Write for pricing information.

Pearshaped Babes 60-minute videotapes, rated R. Adult material. $40.
SOURCES: Wild Bill Video

Plumpers and Big Women Magazine of erotic pictures and fantasies for men who love big women. Adult material. $18, United States; $24, foreign.
SOURCES: Dugent Publishing

Porkers & Gainers Gazette Newsletter for gainers and encourgers. Fat fantasy stories, jokes, and personals. Write for subscription information.

Sources: Meyers Jacobsen

Round House By Victor Gates (self-published, 1993). Fat-positive fiction in comic book form. $1 per copy.

Sources: Victor Gates

Wide Angle Videos of women who have appeared in the pages of *Dimensions* magazine. Currently available: Heather and Brie. Adult material. $40 per video.

Sources: *Dimensions* magazine

Wilson Barbers Quarterly Adult newsletter featuring fat admirer fiction and weight-gain fantasies. Adult material. $20 yearly.

Sources: Oakhaus

XXXLNT, the Newsletter for Weight Gain This newsletter offers personal ads for gainers and encouragers along with social events and news relevant to its readers. Oh, yeah . . . and lots of recipes you won't find in any of the Weight Watchers' cookbooks. Adult material. $15 for 4 editions. Make checks payable to Ollie Lee Taylor.

Sources: XXXLNT

➡ If any data listed in this chapter need to be corrected, please let me know. If you know of a service or product useful to people of size, please write to me about it. The information may be made available to readers through the newsletter "Size Wise Update!," the Size Wise web site, or through possible future revisions of this book.

PERSONAL GLIMPSE:
WILLIAM J. FABREY

Bill is an electrical engineer, entrepreneur, feminist, human rights activist, writer, husband, and father. Though his size is only slightly larger than "average," Bill has been at the forefront of the battle against discrimination against fat people. In 1969 he brought together a group of nine individuals who laid the groundwork for the formation of the National Association to Advance Fat Acceptance (NAAFA) and was active in that organization's leadership until 1990. He continues his size-acceptance work today as a director of the Council on Size & Weight Discrimination. His column, "Big News," is a regular feature of *Radiance* magazine; he also co-edits the "Ample Shopper" newsletter. Bill has always wanted to do something to contribute to the betterment of society; he can be proud of his achievements in the size-acceptance movement.

When I started NAAFA, I discovered a tremendous amount of apathy, even among fat people themselves. The truth is, I had trouble finding leadership for the organization among people who were actually fat. They were trained not to make waves or draw attention to themselves. Fat people accepted society's harsh judgment of them. This was the old "blaming the victim" kind of thing. The overwhelming majority grew up thinking there was something wrong with them. Most people I approached said things like, "Why would anyone want to form an organization to fight for acceptance? Shouldn't we be trying to lose weight?" This attitude is still common among fat people, but there are many "points of light" in the darkness.

If you have been told all your life that something is wrong with you and you don't deserve to have the better things in life, that you aren't going to find a mate or sex partner, and that you might as well not try to look good until you lose weight, for some people it can be almost like questioning the existence of God to say, "Well, maybe I'm okay." It's like telling people that all the energy they put into trying to be thin was a waste. Not just a waste, but maybe actually harmful. Some people have some real trouble facing that, while others blossom when they are exposed to this concept.

There are some parallels between the struggle of fat people and the struggle faced by other oppressed groups, such as black people or women, but also differences. When a black person is rejected for being black, for example, it is not done in the belief that it is his fault for being black. A black kid can go home to his family and not be rejected there, because he is the same as they are; a fat kid goes home to his family and, more often than not, is also rejected or teased by his family. Fat people are often perceived as having chosen their own body size (by their eating styles), so it is seen as being their "fault." That is the perception, though I think that response has diminished somewhat with recent medical findings, especially the genetic link to obesity.

The long-standing myths held by the medical profession, felt to be partly responsible for discrimination against fat people, are beginning to crumble. The Council on Size & Weight Discrimination was formed in 1990 to address very specific issues. One of the most exciting things we are doing is to try to make sure all of the major medical obesity conferences have at least one bona-fide fat person attending and acting as an advocate. We are at the point where we have convinced professionals to invite an advocate to these conferences, undoubtedly to present an appearance of fairness and, in some cases, to hear what we have to say. At many of these conferences there are one or more researchers who stand up and say exactly what we have been saying, although they are still in the minority. The council also does media monitoring, some projects involving the ADA (Americans with Disabilities Act), and educational programs—particularly with preteens. We also partly fund (and help run) the International No-Diet Coalition, a group consisting of more than forty organizations and publications and many individuals. The council is open to all sorts of projects and will accept proposals from outside the group.

I still follow very closely what happens in the movement and report on it in my column in *Radiance*. The size-acceptance movement has been a major life effort on my part. I have expended a large chunk of energy over the years, but I've gotten back perhaps even more than I put into it. The payoff has come in various and diverse ways: meeting new friends, my wife, and compatriots; and the good feeling and excitement from having touched many people's lives in a positive way.

"A Vision of Peace"

When I envision a peaceful world,
I see a giant, round table
and people of all colors, ages and sizes
holding hands and chanting their thanks
for all the abundance of this Earth.
And I smell the aromas of all the wonderful, special holiday foods
each person has lovingly prepared to share with us.
And I see us sitting down together and taking what we want.
No one is watching to see how much or what we put on our plates.
We're all satisfied because we know there is enough for everyone.
I hear many conversations among the people as we pass the platters.
And then, when we all have received as much as we want, our talking slows.
All our energies are focused on savoring the tastes and textures
of the friendship and food which nourishes our bodies and our souls.

PEACE is the sharing of the enjoyment of food and culture.
PEACE is knowing that the world can provide food for all if we choose to make it so.
PEACE is celebrating the diversity of all humanity.
PEACE is sharing what is life-affirming to all.
PEACE is sampling from all of the world's rituals and cultures.
PEACE is integrating what is unfamiliar and discordant into a rich harmony.
PEACE is possible when we at the table partake fully in the feast of life.

Segment of a FAT LIP Readers Theatre script by Nancy Thomas.

8

FAT: THE LAST
SAFE PREJUDICE?

In May 1993 a staff member at *Ladies' Home Journal* created a bit of a stir by telling the story of a week she spent as a fat person. Leslie Lampert wore a "fat suit" specially designed to make her look as if she weighed about 250 pounds. She wanted to sample life as an "overweight" person. As she put it, "For one heart-breaking, exhausting week, I lived as an obese woman—and endured, every day, the kind of openly contemptuous behavior most people never have to suffer." What did she find?

Ms. Lampert experienced firsthand an intolerance for "honorable, oversize citizens" and an indulgence of "ill-mannered, indecent individuals who are slim." As she put it, "Our society not only hates fat people, it feels entitled to participate in a prejudice that at many levels parallels racism and religious bigotry."

Her husband of twelve years expressed repulsion for the fat version of his wife; her children asked her not to pick them up at school. Her family was embarrassed with her new look, but they also were concerned about people saying things that would hurt her feelings.

In her five days of being fat, Ms. Lampert was laughed at by a taxi driver, mocked by two teenage boys while driving home one night, suffered dirty looks and comments from people everywhere she went, and had difficulty fitting into some spaces.

While dining out with her at a very chic restaurant in New York, a male friend was asked by complete strangers why he was "out with that fat pig."

None of this is a surprise to anyone who has had to deal with the attitudes of a fatphobic culture daily. (How sweet it would be to be able to remove our own "fat suits" whenever we had gathered enough information or grew tired of the reactions.) The fat individual who has managed to grow up strong, self-confident, and blessed with good self-esteem is an amazing person indeed.

Despite the general attitude that we live in a civilized society, prejudice of all sorts is still all too common. Size discrimination is not aimed just at fat people. Short men and tall women are laughed at and suffer from prejudice as early as elementary school—as soon as a size difference becomes apparent. Racial bigotry, while not socially acceptable or politically correct in most circles, seems always to remain with us; the incidence of hate crimes directed at people of color is on the rise. Gay men and lesbian women, Mexicans . . . anyone who differs from the "norm" can be a target. Religious and ethnic prejudice breed wars. Discrimination of all types still exists, but no prejudice is so generally socially acceptable as fat prejudice.

According to a study reported recently by the Associated Press, women who are "overweight" during early adulthood are 20 percent less likely to get married, have much lower household incomes ($6,710 a year), have a 10 percent greater chance of living in poverty, and will acquire less schooling than other women. "Overweight" men fare better, being 11 percent less likely to get married, and with an average family income that is merely $2,876 lower a year than other men.

> *Years ago, I was looking for a job and applied for a receptionist position. I was dressed in a really nice dress and heels. I was looking really good. At the interview this man looked me over and told me, "I can't have you greeting people." Like I would knosh on them or something!*
>
> —CHRIS

I suggest that the researchers keep digging. This is just a small part of the experience of being a large person. They should go back to early childhood if they want to get the full picture. Just about any fat child over the age of six can tell stories of being treated badly—and not just by playmates and peers. Teachers call on the fat child to participate less often than other children, allow ridicule of fat children in their classrooms and on playgrounds, and sometimes even join in with the teasing. Discrimination and prejudice touch every part of a fat person's existence, from birth right through to that visit from the grim reaper.

In May 1996, a thirty-one-year-old fat woman in Chicago, Patricia Mullen, passed away. Her body was found by her children when they returned home from school. Policemen responding to the call for help allegedly removed Ms. Mullen's nude body from the bathroom and left it lying, uncovered, on the living room floor for several hours. The crowd gathering outside, including many children, could see her body through the window. According to witnesses, the officers made crude comments about her size, even jiggling the fat on her body with a boot and joking with some kids peering in the window. They played video games, listened to music, and even helped themselves to food from Ms. Mullen's kitchen while waiting for the coroner. When the coroner's van arrived, Ms. Mullen's body was allegedly dragged by the ankles out of the house and was dropped at least once. This woman who had had to fight discrimination and humiliating treatment while alive was afforded no dignity even in death. A formal complaint has been filed by Ms. Mullen's family, and this incident is under investigation by the Chicago Police Department's Internal Office of Professional Standards.

Who else do these officers mock when they are helpless or, as in this case, dead? Is this acceptable behavior? Can the people we depend on for assistance be allowed to treat us this way? Absolutely not!

IT'S NOT A JOKE ... IT'S DISCRIMINATION

Scenario: You're out on a date with the person who sets your heart afire. Dinner was perfect, the conversation witty, and romance is in the air. You're looking forward to watching a movie together, hands entwined, popcorn shared, legs touching. Unfortunately, once you are squeezed into one of the tiny seats in the theater, the circulation in your lower limbs is cut off so severely you wouldn't feel love rubbings from Godzilla. By the time you leave the theater your hips and thighs are bruised and the mood is ruined. Thank goodness that ordeal is over with. All you want now is a long soak in a bubble bath to soothe your tender body.

Scenario: Flipping through the channels after a hard day at work, you put your feet up, pull a comforter over yourself, and snuggle in for an evening of reading and watching television. Pausing at the Fox channel, you smile as Peg Bundy and her kids exchange quips about Al. He comes in complaining of his day at work. "A fat lady clip-clops into the shoe store today . . . " he begins. Okay, so what did you expect from *Married with Children?* This is not exactly a politically correct, sensitive show.

Changing to NBC, you are pleased to see that *Seinfeld* is about to begin. Ahh, much better. This is a hip, clever show with characters who are smart and aware. You watch as Elaine rediscovers a boyfriend she had dropped because he had gained weight. Depressed at their breakup, he had stopped eating. Now he is thin again, and she is wildly attracted to him. All is good until, in his happiness to have her back, the boyfriend starts eating and gaining weight. End of romance. Elaine just can't stomach a fat boyfriend. End of *Seinfeld.* Time for a break.

After a shower and a couple of phone calls, you decide to try one more time. Switching the television back on, you turn to CBS and chuckle over David Letterman's opening monologue. Wait a second . . . a big man in the audience has been singled out by Dave and the camera. After making comments about the man's size, Mr.

Letterman gives him a gift . . . a Thighmaster. The audience boos his gesture but your enjoyment of the show has seriously declined.

Many people would say, "It's just a joke! Lighten up!" But it is this kind of joking that further ingrains the stereotypes and condones the mistreatment of fat people. Insert a similar African-American or Jewish jab in the place of a fat joke and the same routine becomes a bit shocking . . . and something you won't hear coming from the lips of Dave (or even Al Bundy). No network seems to be immune.

Scenario: Scouring the help-wanted section of the newspaper, you spot it . . . the perfect job. It's as if this position was tailored just for you. You have the training, experience, and excellent references. Mr. Phatphobia, the boss, talks with you over the telephone when you call to inquire about an interview. He is enthusiastic and practically promises you the job as you state your qualifications. You are exactly what he had in mind when he placed the ad. Why, you are the answer to his prayers! "Please, hurry right down!" he says. "Let's get this formalized!"

From his enthusiasm, you can picture him putting your name on the office door before you even fill out the Social Security information. As you drive to the interview you can't help but smile with delight. At last the long search is over! Your fears of becoming homeless are not going to be realized.

Mr. Phatphobia's enthusiasm turns to stuttering bewilderment, however, when he turns to greet you as you step into his office. "There has been a mistake," he mumbles as he shuffles papers around on his desk, not even looking you in the eye. "What I mean to say," he blurts out, "is that the position has already been filled." You know what has really happened. It isn't the first time.

Discrimination against people of size is common. Consider these instances:

Joseph Gimello, 5'8", 270 pounds, was working for a car rental agency in New Jersey when he was fired because of his appearance. Mr. Gimello had an excellent work record, having received commendations, letters praising his job performance, and bonuses. However, when the regional manager and the vice president of operations met him, they allegedly told Mr. Gimello's supervisor that Gimello was not promotable . . . that "if this fat slob" were put in a position to hire other people, he would hire fat, sloppy people.

Mr. Gimello had to apply for food stamps, sell off assets, and borrow money from relatives to support his family. In a hearing, the director of the Division on Civil Rights ruled that obesity is a handicap, making it unlawful to fire someone based solely on weight unless that person is physically unable to do the job.

Mr. Gimello was awarded $10,000 plus six years' back pay. It would be normal in such cases for a job to be reinstated, but Mr. Gimello was already working for another car-rental agency and had not requested reinstatement.

Toni Cassista, a forty-four-year-old, 305-pound woman, was denied employment in a natural foods supermarket because of her size. Ms. Cassita stood up for herself and took the company, Community Foods of Santa Cruz, to court. She lost the first round but vowed to fight on. In making his ruling, California Supreme Court Justice Armand Arabian stated that antibias laws apply only to people who are fat because of an underlying medical condition and stated that protection isn't owed to a person who "eats twenty-four hours a day and becomes three hundred and five pounds." Judge Arabian, fortunately, has since retired.

New Zealand's Prime Minister Bolger drew the ire of women the world over by referring to the plump Victorian premier, Joan Kirner, with this remark: "You know what they say. The show's never over until the fat lady sings. I think it was her we heard warming up in the wings this week." Even members of his own party were appalled at what was considered to be an insensitive and sexist attitude. Alison Roxburgh, president of the National Council of Women in New Zealand, said, "All women are a little tired of having their performances judged by their shapes, when men are never judged by their shapes."

Jerald James works as a scorekeeper at tennis tournaments around the country. While working the U.S. Open in 1989 he was told his "image was so overwhelming, it was distracting," and he was let go. At 325 pounds, Mr. James continues to work, but not at the bigger tournaments, where, he says, "There's no gray hair, glasses, overweight. It's not a secret. They just don't want to talk about it."

Bruce A. Tanberg was staying at a motel when he suffered a back injury. In pursuing a lawsuit against the motel, Mr. Tanberg was ordered by a judge to lose weight to decrease pain and avoid risking more serious complications. According to the *National Law Journal*, when he failed to do so, the supreme court of Iowa ruled that his failure to "make a reasonable attempt to lose weight can be considered fault."

County workers in Key West, Florida, were admonished to lose weight by one commissioner, Earl Cheal. The unenlightened Mr. Cheal complained that extra weight gives a "fat and lazy" impression of government.

A surgical nurse, Lieutenant Commander Valerie Saad, has been with the U.S. Navy Reserves for fifteen years. Despite an exemplary record and a special commendation from former President Reagan for helping care for him after his cancer surgery, the navy has decided she "weighs too much" and they want to relieve her of duty. This comes one year and two months short of Lieutenant Commander Saad's retirement. She is suing the navy on the grounds of discrimination against women.

According to the American Airlines manual for flight attendants, "A firm, trim silhouette, free of bulges, rolls, or paunches, is necessary for an alert, efficient image." After more than two hundred flight attendants were let go, members of the Association of Professional Flight Attendants rebelled, claiming the weight limitations were discriminatory on the basis of age and sex, and sued American. (The women fired for being "overweight" were generally a size 10.) Though unable to completely abolish the standard height/weight charts, the attendants were able to bring about an adjustment in the top weights allowed . . . an increase of twenty-five pounds for women in their mid-fifties.

American Airlines was the last airline in the United States with such strict weight rules. Most airlines have changed their limitations to vary with age; Continental and Northwest airlines have dropped weight rules completely.

Bonnie Cook, thirty-three years old, fought back when she was denied a job as an attendant at a state facility for the mentally ill. Despite having passed a physical exam, having a nurse state that there was nothing limiting her ability to do everything the job required, and a spotless record when working in the same position for seven years previously, the agency refused to hire her. Their contention was that Ms. Cook's weight compromised her ability to help with patients in emergency situations and increased the chances of workers' compensation claims.

Ms. Cook took her battle all the way to the first U.S. Circuit Court of Appeals, where extreme overweight was declared to be a disability covered under federal antidiscrimination law. This ruling applies only to states under the jurisdiction of this court, but is significant for all of us in that it provides precedent for any future cases.

Judge Ernest Torres ordered Ms. Cook reinstated in her job with retroactive seniority. A jury awarded her $100,000 in damages. In arguing their side, the Rhode Island Department of Mental Health, Retardation and Hospitals had claimed that obesity is voluntary, making federal antidiscrimination laws void. The three-judge appeals panel replied to that point by stating that the law "indisputably applies to numerous conditions that may be caused or exacerbated by voluntary conduct, such as alcoholism, AIDS, diabetes, cancer resulting from cigarette smoking, heart disease resulting from excess of various types, and the like."

Judge Torres wrote: "In a society that all too often confuses 'slim' with 'beautiful' or 'good,' morbid obesity can present formidable barriers to employment. Where, as here, the barriers transgress federal law, those who erect and seek to preserve them must suffer the consequences."

This ruling apparently struck a nerve in Margaret Carlson. In the December 6, 1993, issue of *Time*, she ranted against people who would dare to demand legal protections against fat discrimination. Stating "Only the government could think of obesity as a new entitlement," she pointed out the already "bursting-at-the-seams body politic" and worried about handicapped parking spaces being given to undeserving fat people. In one breath admitting that the attainment of a tolerant society is a worthy goal, her next words call for a limit to public sympathy.

She concludes with a paragraph that begins, "There should be a way to recognize that something is too bad without saying it can be fixed. To do otherwise is to fail to protect the truly vulnerable, the truly prejudged, the truly disadvantaged."

This article is, in itself, worthy of little note except as an example of the kind of attitude that creates and allows bigotry against fat people to be such a socially acceptable stance. What is seen by Ms. Carlson as an intrusion on her overtaxed sensibilities is a serious issue with millions of people. The assumption that being fat is a personal choice leads size bigots to feel they have every right to negate the feelings, needs, and rights of people who are large.

Letters to the editor following the printing of this essay drew out the bigots in fine form . . . a woman complaining of having to sit next to a "stocky" person on an airplane and suggesting that "overeaters" purchase two seats (perhaps that would be possible if job discrimination didn't limit the incomes of fat people) a man expressing fear of being "trampled as a horde of new 'victims' who have overindulged in designer-label diet foods rush directly to the federal courthouse," and a clever fellow suggesting a possible lawsuit against Ben & Jerry's for his ten-pound "overweight" physique.

What can you do? Maybe a lot.

Many of us have been involved in campaigns to save endangered species, end nuclear proliferation, outlaw line dancing, and any of a hundred other issues of importance. We write letters of protest when nuclear power plants are built and refuse to buy fur coats when our concern for baby seals kicks in. Is it any less important to stand up for ourselves?

•
Judge me by my work, not by my waistline.
•

There are many ways to express your feelings and to get satisfaction. The path you take depends on the circumstances, your goals in any situation, and your own personal methods of being assertive.

You don't have to walk a protest line or even get involved in legislative issues. I love dolphins, but you aren't going to see me out in a little Greenpeace boat putting myself between sea mammals and angry fishing crews. I will, however, send a check to someone who is so motivated so he or she can do what I can't. Everyone can contribute in some way. If you encounter or hear of discrimination and want to do something about it, consider these possibilities:

- Phone calls and letters can be very effective in many situations. Businessmen and politicians pay attention to public opinion.

- Write to newspapers, television stations, and magazines. A well-placed article or letter to the editor can help raise the public consciousness.

- Speak out! If you are comfortable about public speaking, step forward. Let your voice be added to that of others who are demanding change.

- Organize. Get a group of like-minded individuals together and plan some changes.
- Don't forget . . . when you find someone handling things in a way you approve, say so.
- Support the people, organizations, and publications you feel are working to end size discrimination.
- Stay informed. Subscribe to magazines such as *Radiance* and *Rump Parliament*. Order information about the size-acceptance movement from Largesse, the *Network for Size Esteem.* (See Resources section for additional information on how to contact these organizations.)

In 1995, at a convention in San Marcos, the Texas State chapter of the National Organization for Women passed a resolution condemning size discrimination. It reads:

> *Whereas weight and size discrimination adversely affects the lives and livelihoods of millions of Americans, especially women,*
> *Whereas every day thousands of highly qualified candidates are refused employment, promotions, benefits, and opportunities for advancement, with weight and size often being used to circumvent other illegal discriminations,*
> *Whereas anorexia, bulimia and other eating disorder syndromes are endemic in America and are appearing in ever-younger people, especially girls,*
> *Therefore, be it resolved that Texas NOW proceed to add "weight and size" to its statement of purpose in Article II, section A of the Texas NOW by-laws,*
> *"And that Texas NOW support efforts to promote fat acceptance and support legislation in Texas against size and weight discrimination, to reflect and expand upon the National Board resolution of 1990.*

Lee Martindale, editor of *Rump Parliament* and longtime size-rights activist, spoke to the convention and was instrumental in the inclusion of this important resolution.

In some ways, we are each in this alone. We must have the strength within ourselves to deal with the intolerance on a day-to-day basis. Much of it is subtle . . . the barely concealed look of disgust from a stranger, the "You have such a pretty face! Have you ever thought about dieting?" comments, and the overheard remarks about the way you look. Those things can be devastating in their own way. They happen so often and chip away at our self-esteem. But we can find strength in supportive family and friends and in each other.

The network of intelligent, informed, and outspoken

people who fight size prejudice is growing. There are many wonderful people publishing newsletters, books, and magazines; forming support groups; and demanding protection from the courts and legislators. The time of passively accepting boorish behavior and repressive attitudes is past.

LEE MARTINDALE

Lee is the editor and publisher of *Rump Parliament*, an activist magazine for the size-acceptance movement. Feisty and full of self-confidence, she keeps tabs on what is happening and informs her readers with no holds barred.

I have been fat all of my life. My early history is probably a dead ringer for most people's. My mother put me on my first diet when I was eight or nine. Our family doctor put me on amphetamines when I was sixteen. From the time I was in college until I was thirty I went on a diet every six months. Like most people I didn't stay on it, of course. I figure I probably lost roughly a thousand pounds in my first thirty years. Depending on whose rubber ruler you use, I'd estimate I am somewhere between 235 and 250. Which for my height puts me somewhere between 100 and 125 pounds "overweight." My question is, "Over who's weight?" Ten years ago I decided dieting was a form of suicide. My body is happy with how it feels. If I'm going over a comfortable limit it will let me know.

It wasn't the weight that made me diet. It was society. Society kept giving me these messages that I wasn't worth anything unless I fit a certain artificial standard. When I was a teenager, in the mid- to late-60s, "Twiggy" was the preferable body style. Whoever is turning the crank on this universe decided to build me like a woman. Not a twelve-year-old boy. I never heard messages that your ideal weight is whatever you weigh without starving yourself. So I fell into the same trap that everybody else did. Which was, I had to look a certain way (thin) to look beautiful.

Somewhere between age thirty and thirty-three I took a good long look in the mirror and decided this body was just fine the way it was and that I would probably kill myself with all this yo-yo dieting. I had discovered, toward the end of some of the nondieting periods (about the time I started to think, "I guess I had better go on another diet again"), that I was starting to feel better eating balanced meals. Then I started thinking, "When I'm on a diet I don't feel well." Common sense and being in tune with my own body were finally getting me through all of the negative programming. It wasn't a case of strength, it was a case of survival. This was about the time I discovered the National Association to Advance Fat Acceptance (NAAFA). I was married, but I was getting divorced. I had been married for six years to a gentleman who was also becoming involved in NAAFA and coming out as a fat admirer. The negative message from him was that I wasn't fat enough. The outcome of all this was the mind-set that the only person who has any right to tell me what I should weigh is me.

I feel better now than I ever have in my life. I'm stronger and I'm healthier. Two years ago I was hit with a viral inflammation of the lining of my spinal cord that left me pretty much the better part of a paraplegic. I use a wheelchair and have about 10 percent mobility in my legs. The neurologist who finally diagnosed the thing told me that if I had been less fit I would have ended up a quad instead of a paraplegic. I consider that a real good reason to have a big, healthy body.

I am not currently a member of NAAFA, nor was I terribly active when I first discovered it. It seemed to be primarily a social outlet. More men was the last thing I needed. Being more of a full-fledged activist, I felt my energies would be better served elsewhere. When I came down with the viral infection I had to rethink my job situation, so I started my own company. I do size-positive buttons, coffee mugs, and note cards with selected slogans. I also publish and edit Rump Parliament.

Rump Parliament *is by and for people working to change the way society treats fat people. It's a forum for discussing all of the many forms of activism and for getting news of things that are happening or are about to happen within the size-acceptance movement. There are features, interviews with interesting people within the size-acceptance community, news items, letters to the editor, size-positive fiction, and discussion sections with questions involving a wide range of problems and situations. But we primarily concentrate on activism. I do some of the writing myself, but most of our articles come from the readers.*

Our readers range from longtime veteran activists to folks who are just getting into the movement and maybe aren't real sure what activism is but want to hear a little more about it. Not everybody in the size-acceptance movement is an activist. There is no other publication totally concentrating on activism except Rump Parliament. Radiance *magazine is a wonderful publication for issues of self-esteem. And again, they delve into activism a bit. I don't believe anyone, at least that I am aware of, is concentrating on it except us.*

Self-esteem needs to be stressed within the size-acceptance community. I recognize that there are men out there who prefer large women. Their preferences are no different from the guy who prefers to date blondes. But I don't want to be the object of someone's affection strictly based on how much room I take up. There is no difference between someone telling me "You're gorgeous because you are fat" and "You're not gorgeous because you are fat." Body size is a lousy reason to get involved with someone. The problem with dating some FAs [fat admirers] is that they are the kid in the candy store and you're the next chocolate bar.

I am picky. Real picky. Always have been. I am fearful, tremendously fearful, that we are not teaching people to "like yourself enough to be picky." That's one of the stereotypes I got hit with all of my life. "What do you mean, you don't want to go to bed with me? Who else is going to be interested?" We get the same stereotypes from different ends in the same breath. We're either sexless or promiscuous. My usual reaction to this is to look at them, sort of to cock an eyebrow and say "What? Excuse me? I like myself too much to be promiscuous."

Before my current husband and I ever talked about intimacy, I hauled him off to my doctor for a blood test. And he went willingly, which shows that I have good taste. There are too many large people and their admirers who think we are immune to AIDS and behave accordingly. One of these days it's going to catch up with us. You would not believe what I get hit with when I say things like that. I have been accused of trying to deny fat people the right to be sexual because I am saying "Be careful."

I cannot tell you how many times I've heard both men and women, mostly women because of our society, say, "Well, when I lose X number of pounds I'm going to . . ." followed by "get a new wardrobe," "get a makeover," "get a better job," "find the love of my life," and so on. The list is endless. It's a direct result of the brainwashing done by the diet industry and the segment of the medical profession that is making most of its bucks from diet products. That is probably the saddest thing I've ever heard; it's also the thing that makes me the angriest. There is no reason, none at all, to put your life on hold until you fit somebody else's idea of what is acceptable. I know far too many people who have done incredible things, things they have always wanted to do, when they decide, "I'm not going to wait, I'm going to do it now." As far as I am concerned, the only limitation is in your own mind. For people who decide, "I'm okay, whatever my size," there are enormous opportunities and enormous joy in living. The only roadblock for most of them has been that "I've got to wait to be thin" attitude. Nobody has to wait.

INTERNATIONAL NO DIET DAY

Diet Breakers of England called for the first National No Diet Day on May 5, 1992. A group of women and children gathered in Hyde Park for a picnic celebrating healthy living and self-acceptance and "drawing attention to the perils and futility of dieting." Just one year later, people in nine countries, including the United States and Canada, had joined in. Paul Harvey made mention of International No Diet Day on his radio spot, stating, "Only in this so-called civilized country do people starve themselves on purpose."

Watch publications like *Radiance* and *Rump Parliament* for information on future International No Diet Days. Plan a wonderful picnic of healthy, delicious, satisfying foods; gather up friends and family; and head for the park. Use this day to concentrate on all of the wonderful things about yourself and your life.

The official symbol of International No Diet Day is a light blue ribbon worn on your lapel.

- Founder and Great Britain Coordinator: Mary Evans Young, Director, Diet-Breakers UK
- Canadian Coordinator: Linda Omichinsky, HUGS International Inc.
- United States Coordinator: Lee Martindale, *Rump Parliament* Magazine
- NAAFA Coordinator: Sharon McDonald
- Networking Coordinators: Karen and Richard Stimson, Co-Directors, Largesse, the Network for Size Esteem

• International No Diet Day Materials •

May 5th Coalition Maintains a list of organizations, businesses, politicians, and professionals who endorse International No Diet Day. The coalition works to spread the word and generate support.

"No Diets" T-shirts Available in white or black with design in black, white, and red. Shirt sizes 2X to 11X, your choice of sleeve length. $28.
SOURCES: NAAFA Feminist Caucus

"No Diets" buttons $3.
SOURCES: NAAFA Feminist Caucus

International No Diet Coalition Resource Directory: Available through Amplestuff or Willendorf Press. $20 plus $2.50 shipping and handling.

"Women of Substance/Women of Power" T-shirt Available on white, lilac, or fuchsia background. Sizes 2X to 11X. $28.
SOURCES: NAAFA Feminist Caucus

At the first NAAFA convention I went to I experienced fat shock, if you can call it that. I had to face my own prejudice upon seeing a 500-pound woman in a bikini. I had to look at my internalized oppression and my shock that I wouldn't go out of the house in shorts and here was a 500-pound woman in a bikini. At the same time I met all of these wonderful women and could see the beauty in them.

I thought I was attractive in spite of my body. Now I had to learn a new concept of beauty. I had to learn the other positive aspects of fat. To be able to hug another fat person and see how warm and cushy that was. How nice it felt. Why not review and reconceptualize all these stereotypes?

Even using the word fat involves a process of desensitizing or being around people who use the term. That word becomes more of an alternate view of the world. It's a very different world. I've noticed, for instance, that walking down a hallway fat women don't look at other fat women. They divert their eyes. When I staff tables at NAAFA events, it's usually thin people who come over. Fat people tend to avoid the table. Like "That's not me." Fat people tend to avoid being friends with a fat person because it's multiplied . . . two fat people together become a larger target. At NAAFA events people go out to dinner as a group. In a sense it is becoming a target but in another sense there is added strength . . . a strength in numbers.

—LAURA

HEALTHY WEIGHT WEEK

Scheduled for the third week in January, Healthy Weight Week is an annual event organized by Frances Berg of *Healthy Weight Journal*. Healthy Weight Week promotes changing our nation's January focus to healthy lifestyles and away from the dieting-and-bingeing cycle that typically begins the New Year.

Tuesday is "Rid the World of Fad Diets and Gimmicks Day," when the Slim Chance Awards are presented for the worst weight-loss products of the year. Thursday is "Women's Healthy Weight Day," honoring size diversity in women, and is a protest against the media's overemphasis on thinness.

Size acceptance and eating disorders groups all over the country are invited to join to confirm that beauty, health, and strength come in all sizes. For more information, contact Ms. Berg at *Healthy Weight Journal*.

WHY WEIGHT BODY IMAGE AND
EATING DISORDERS AWARENESS WEEK

Sponsored by the Size Acceptance Network and the Eastern Community Health Service, this New Zealand–based body image and eating disorders awareness activity is generally held in early September. Health professionals, organizations, and volunteers work together to increase the general community's awareness of body size, weight, and appearance issues. If you would like to participate, offer ideas for activities, or receive a kit, contact Linda Crutchett.

LEGISLATION

It isn't as if politicians are unaware of the problems of their larger constituents. Legislators are no thinner than the general population. In the early 1900s William Taft was president while tipping the scales at about 350 pounds. President Clinton is chided in the press about his shape (though I personally think he has an adorable body) and his enjoyment of fast foods. I could run through a long list of people on Capitol Hill who are big, popular, and powerful. It is interesting to note that they go through the same yo-yo diet problems as the rest of us and feel the same pressures to conform to a thin image.

A few areas of the country offer some legal protections. Michigan accords the "opportunity to obtain employment, housing and other real estate, and the full and equal utilization of public accommodations, public service and educational facilities without discrimination because of religion, race, color, national origin, age, sex, height, weight or marital status. . . ." This is known as the Elliot-Larsen Civil Rights Act and was enacted in 1977.

In 1992 the city of Santa Cruz, California, amended it's prohibition against discrimination bill to include "the right and opportunity of all persons to be free from all forms of arbitrary discrimination, including discrimination based on age, race, color, creed, religion, national origin, ancestry, disability, marital status, sex, gender, sexual orientation, height, weight or physical characteristic." This is a significant piece of legislation that should be used as a model at state and federal levels.

In 1993, New York State Assemblyman Daniel Feldman proposed that "weight" and "height" be added to "age, race, creed, color, national origin, sex and marital status" as categories protected from discrimination in housing, employment, and education under the New York Civil Rights Law. This would make New York the second state that provides protection for its fat, short, and tall people. Similar legislation has been considered in other states, such as Maryland, but as yet Michigan is the only one with laws on the book.

Washington, D.C., and Alameda County, California, both offer some legal protections to large-size people.

Thanks to the efforts of Dr. Lisa Berzins of PLEASE (Promoting Legislation and Education About Self-Esteem), the New England chapter of NAAFA, and other dedicated activists, the state of Connecticut passed House Bill 5621, the "Diet Program Disclosures Bill," in 1996. This bill requires companies to provide real data on real customers to potential customers. It is hoped that other states will consider similar legislation.

In a perfect world, activism and legislation would be unnecessary. People would be treated fairly and with respect in all situations. Access to public areas and services would be available, and seating would take into account all body types. Health care would be equitably distributed. Discrimination would not exist. No one is asking for special treatment, only the same rights and privileges available to others.

Legislation cannot change attitudes. It can't make anyone like you and it can't make people understand. Behavior, however, can be legislated. Laws offer recourse if you are discriminated against. In a court of law, the judge needs legislation on which to base decisions. He interprets; he does not establish. The time for establishing protection against discrimination through legislation is now.

Outside of our own personal, day-to-day lives, the most effective method of calculating discrimination is to cause the enactment of legislation on the state or federal level. You don't have to be a politician to draft a bill and have it presented. You can do it yourself or with a group of like-minded friends. Of course, it's easier to get results with a large number of people.

In drafting your bill, look to other bills of a similar nature that have been passed. Then begin by stating your intent in simple language. Make your points clearly and in short sentences. This brief (one- or two-page) document will set the guidelines for the legislation you hope to see come out of it.

- Contact groups and organizations in your state composed of large-size members (is there a local NAAFA chapter?) to find support for your bill.

- Locate grass roots organizations and talk with them about the nature of your state's legislators. Determine which ones will be the most receptive to your bill, then choose the most likely candidate. Approach that person.

- Your bill will need to be presented to a committee. Study your state government committees and decide which would be the best to introduce your legislation. The legislator you have chosen to introduce the bill doesn't need to be on the committee you have chosen.

- Once your bill is introduced, work to inform every committee member about its importance. At this point the more people you have involved in support the better. Get them involved.

- Keep the media informed of what you are doing. Newspaper articles and television coverage can be invaluable in achieving success.

•Where to Write•

Share experiences and express your concerns regarding the diet industry and your support of strong regulation with:

- Representative Ron Wyden (D-Oregon), who headed a congressional subcommittee investigating diet industry marketing practices and coaxed the Federal Trade Commission (FTC) to investigate diet industry claims

- the Federal Trade Commission
- the Secretary of Health and Human Services
- the Food and Drug Administration

Keep your representatives, senators, and the president aware of your concerns regarding legislation to protect the rights of fat people. Write, phone, or fax them regularly and keep tabs on their moves in this direction. Be sure to let them know what you think of their actions—both negative and positive. Your input really counts. (If you aren't sure who your senators and congressmen are, call the local newspapers. They probably know.)

Write to your senators, representatives, and the president in care of the following addresses:

Senators: United States Senate, Washington, D.C. 20510

For your senator's email address, visit www.senate.gov/senate/members.html.

Representatives: United States House of Representatives, Washington, D.C. 20515

EMAIL HOUSEHELP@HR.HOUSE, GOV FOR YOUR CONGRESSMAN'S EMAIL ADDRESS.

President: The White House, 1600 Pennsylvania Avenue, Washington, D.C. 20500

email: president@whitehouse.gov or vice.president@whitehouse.gov

ACTIVISM ON A MORE PERSONAL LEVEL

I don't mean to brag, but . . .

Although we seldom dine out, my fourteen-year-old daughter, Elizabeth, and I decided to have dinner at a restaurant one evening. After I squeezed my wide hips into a rather smallish but sturdy wooden chair with arms, we studied the menu while admiring a gorgeous sunset over the Pacific Ocean.

We had just given our orders to the waiter when I heard an elderly woman at the table next to us say, "Look at that fat woman! What is she doing in here stuffing her face?" I turned to look at the source of this rudeness. She was looking down at her plate, busily cutting her food. Her husband glanced at me, then went back to his dinner. A moment passed, then another comment. "She's disgusting. She barely fits in that chair." The woman continued her one-sided conversation, barely pausing to chew her food.

Elizabeth and I had a brief discussion about how unkind, bigoted, and rude people can be. I just wanted to ignore the woman. We had come out for a nice evening and meal. Also, the tables were quite close together and I didn't want to subject other people to additional unpleasantness. And, quite frankly, sometimes I just don't have the heart for a confrontation.

My daughter, however, was angry. Rising from her seat, she walked over to the woman and calmly but firmly said, "What you said about my mother was very rude. I think you owe her an apology." No response. The husband said something about his wife not meaning to speak so loudly. Elizabeth replied, "What she said was rude and hateful, no matter how loudly it was said." The woman mumbled an "I'm sorry," more to her plate of food than to either of us. Elizabeth returned to her seat. She had confronted the bigoted woman who thought nothing of insulting a fat person. Something tells me she taught the woman a lesson.

I am always proud of Elizabeth . . . for many reasons. At that particular moment I was doubly so.

In the end I believe it is these individual refusals to accept boorish behaviors and attitudes that will end discrimination and bigotry aimed at fat people. African Americans had to demand respect. Women had to demand respect. Gay people had to demand respect. Now we, as fat individuals, have to do the same.

ACTIVIST PUBLICATIONS

Rump Parliament

Lee Martindale, publisher. Look to this publication for no-holds-barred reporting on the size-acceptance movement and all of the issues surrounding it. Lee Martindale has no problem whatsoever with blowing the whistle on discrimination. An excellent magazine, *Rump Parliament* is a must-have for anyone interested in staying on top of the issues. I especially enjoy the "Rump Roasts." Lee has a sharp eye for fat bigots and cuts them down to size with wit and incisiveness. This is not a bitter publication, though. It's chock-full of positive information, humor, and strokes for those moving in the right direction.

A one-year subscription is $24 for 6 issues ($28 in Canada and Mexico, $35 overseas [U.S. funds only, please], published bimonthly. The "Seen on a Button" sayings sprinkled throughout this book, along with many others, can be purchased from *Rump Parliament* on buttons, note cards, mugs, and tankards.

ACTIVIST INFORMATION AND SUPPORT GROUPS

Many of these groups work on a national and international level to promote size acceptance.

• California •

Body Image Task Force (BITF)

Dawn Atkins, contact. " . . . dedicated to promoting the concept of positive body image for all people." Body Image

Task Force works to educate the public about looksism and fatphobia. They are particularly interested in working with young people to help stop prejudices taught early in life and are active in presenting films, lectures, discussions, workshops, performances, art shows, school presentations, protests, rallies, and marches in Santa Cruz. An excellent resource for information on all areas of size acceptance.

Southern California Fat Acceptance Coalition (SCFAC)

Suzanne Szames, acting president. Activist/social organization based in San Diego.

Women of Width (WOW)

Joyce Wermont, contact. WOW meets twice a month in Menlo Park for discussion of issues pertaining to being fat. Activities (creative writing workshops, activism, and so on) are planned on alternate meetings. Open to women of any sexual persuasion or size.

Let It All Hang Out (LIAHO)

Marilyn Kalman, contact. This fat lesbian group sponsors dances and other fund-raisers in the Oakland, California, area for a float in the Lesbian/Gay/Bisexual Freedom Day Parade held yearly in San Francisco.

National Association to Advance Fat Acceptance (NAAFA)

NAAFA, based in Sacramento and claiming a membership of three thousand, is struggling with an identity crisis, internal upheaval, and chapter resignations. As board members attempt to define NAAFA's role in the size-acceptance community, local chapters are moving forward on both the activism and social fronts. Special Interest Groups (SIGs) include Bigman's Sig, Couples, Diabetic, Feminist Caucus, Lavender (for lesbians, gays, and bisexuals), Leadership, Lesbian Fat Activist Network, Mental Health Professionals, Military, Parents and Caregivers of Fat Children, Singles, Sleep Apnea, Super (for women over size 48), Teen/Youth, and Young Adult.

Phat Chat

Discussion/activist group formed by Marilyn Wann, editor of the newsletter "Fat!So?" Meetings held the first of each month in the San Francisco Bay Area.

• Connecticut •

Largesse, the Network for Size Esteem

Karen and Richard Stimson, codirectors. An excellent size-esteem information and resource network located in New Haven and coordinated by Karen and Richard Stimson. Contact Largesse for information on just about any aspect of the size rights movement, both nationally and internationally. Largesse offers a wonderful Size Diversity Empowerment Kit (see chapter 7, "All That's Fit to Print," for more information) and a variety of books, T-shirts, bulletins, International No Diet Day materials and information, and a newsletter entitled "Food for Thought."

Promoting Legislation and Education About Self-Esteem (PLEASE)
Dr. Lisa Berzins is the director of this activist organization in West Hartford.

Especially noteworthy is their part in getting Connecticut's "Diet Program Disclosures Bill" passed.

• Georgia •

Association for Full Figured Women of Atlanta
Monthly networking functions.

• Michigan •

The Venus Group
Size-acceptance group for women in the Ann Arbor area.

• Minnesota •

Sisters Are Fighting Fat Oppression! (SAFFO)
Size woman-positive lesbian/bi/trans- gendered support group in the Minneapolis/Saint Paul area. Films, discussions, and lectures.

• New Jersey •

Fat Lesbian Action Brigade (FLAB)
Activist group in Princeton formed to gain acceptance for fat lesbians within the world at large and to address size-acceptance issues.

• New Mexico •

International Fat Acceptance Network (IFAN)
Mark Mitcham, contact. This cooperative of rebellious ex-NAAFA chapters in Albuquerque is intent on promoting communication, access, and organization between all existing and fledgling size rights and size-acceptance groups.

New Mexico Fat Acceptance Network (NMFAN)
Karen S. Smith, chairperson. Based in Albuquerque, this former NAAFA chap- ter has become a strong support group, watchdog, information center, and activist organization. Publishes a monthly newsletter.

Weight Loss Surgery Survivors Sig
Karen S. Smith, coordinator. "The purpose of this sig [special interest group] is to offer support to those who have had weight-loss surgery, and provide information to those who are considering it." Based in Albuquerque. Yearly dues: $15 (includes subscription to the WLSS Sig Newsletter, published quarterly).

• New York •

Council on Size and Weight Discrimination

William J. Fabrey; Lynn McAfee; Nancy Summer; Miriam Berg; Neil Dachis, Esq.; Paul M. Dachis; and Carrie Hemenway, founders. The Council on Size and Weight Discrimination, located in Mount Marion, was formed to address very specific issues. One of the most exciting things it is doing is trying to make sure all of the major medical obesity conferences have at least one bona-fide fat person attending and acting as an advocate. It is at the point where it has convinced professionals to invite an advocate to these obesity conferences, both to "look good" and sometimes to actually listen. All of those who have done these conferences have gotten the impression that some people there are polite to them and pay lip service. Others thank them honestly for their input and for attending. And now at all of these conferences there are one or two professionals who will stand up and say exactly what the members are saying. The Council also does media monitoring, ADA watching, and educational programs—particularly with preteens. It is open to all sorts of projects.

Diet/Weight Liberation

This project of the Center for Religion, Ethics, and Social Policy at Cornell University in Ithaca publishes a quarterly newsletter, "Grace-full Eating," and sponsors local events with size-acceptance messages. One of the most notable achievements brought about by Diet/Weight Liberation was the proclamation of Size Acceptance Month in September 1993 by Ben Nichols, the mayor of Ithaca.

Fat Is a Lesbian Issue

A fat-positive, antidiet discussion group in Manhattan that helps women learn to accept their bodies at any size. Monthly meetings discuss food, clothing, health care, sex, exercise, self-esteem, and other issues that impact the lives of fat lesbians and bi women.

Fed Up

Organization aimed at activism on a national and international level. Occasional social events for fund-raising purposes in the Ithaca area.

Lesbian Fat Activists Network (LFAN)

A special interest group (sig) of NAAFA for size-friendly lesbians across the country from their base in Woodstock. Membership includes monthly newsletter.

Substantial Women

Linda Baker Abrahamsen, contact. Support group in Mid-Hudson Valley area.

• North Carolina •

Abundantly Yours

Joyce Rue-Potter, founder. Support for people of all sizes of large, located in Fletcher. Send self-addressed, stamped envelope for information.

•Oregon•

Ample Opportunity
Nonprofit, dedicated to the health and happiness of fat women. Support for people of all sizes and a good source for medical information. Ample Opportunity "works to assure accessibility to a high quality of life for fat women and to create a social environment more accepting of all body sizes" in Portland. Membership is $35 a year. Newsletter only, $12 yearly.

Lesbians of Size (LesbOS)
Political/social organization in the Portland area formed for the empowerment of fat lesbians.

•Texas•

Innerworks/Food for Thought
Melissa Popp, contact. Body image support group in Grand Prairie.

Texas Size Acceptance Coalition
Newly formed activist group in Houston. They are organizing events and working with legislators to make some real impact for size rights.

•Washington•

Seattle Area Fat Feminist Inspiration & Rage (SAFFIR)
Martha Koester, contact. This support, discussion, and action group meets on the first Saturday of every month in Seattle. "As women, we all face pressure to meet the thin/young/temporarily-abled/white/heterosexual packaged 'ideal.' Women of all sizes are welcome; it helps if you can say 'fat.' We are Seattle NOW's Body Image Task Force."

Sisters of Size
Weekly support group meetings and monthly pool parties in a safe environment for fat lesbians (generally over 200 pounds) in the Seattle area. Monthly newsletter: $5 a year.

•Washington, D.C.•

National Organization for Women (NOW)
NOW is a national organization based in Washington, D.C., with a task force working against the diet industry. NOW's by-laws include an anti-size-discrimination clause.

•Wisconsin•

Largely Positive
Carol Johnson, founder. Support group in Glendale promoting size acceptance. Publishes a quarterly newsletter and offers workshops and special events. Largely Positive also offers a manual on forming support groups. Send self-addressed, stamped envelope for further information.

• Canada •

The Brotherhood of Girth

Ottawa, Ontario–based men's group dedicated to improving the lives of fat people everywhere. Although it's not a gay men's group, gays are welcome to participate. Social and political activities, information databases, and charity events benefiting various causes.

HERSIZE

Women's group in Toronto, Ontario, fo-cused on educating people about size discrimination. Publishes a quarterly newsletter. Membership is $25 a year. Resource guide of health information, $5.

People At Large (PAL)

Support network "to promote size ac-ceptance, self-esteem and social integra-tion" in Etobicoke, Ontario.

• England •

Diet Breakers

Mary Evans, founder. Ms. Evans is a Gestalt therapist and management con-sultant whose specialty is developing self-esteem and confidence in women and working to enhance their careers. Ms. Evans has also served as Agony Aunt (the British version of our Dear Abby).

Diet Breakers, located in London, is a quickly growing organization dedicated to "fighting the tyranny of thinness and the diet industry." This looks like a group to keep an eye on. Already they have made news around the world through their National No Diet Day and received more than five thousand letters during their first year of operation.

Fat Women's Group

Charlotte Cooper, founder. Formed in 1988, this women's support group meets the first Wednesday of every month, from seven to nine P.M. in Lon-don. All fat women are welcome to at-tend. The mood is positive, the support is eagerly given, and fat bodies of every shape and size are celebrated. The Fat Women's Group publishes a bimonthly newsletter, "Fat News."

• France •

Allegro Fortissimo

Paris-based organization with weekly support meetings and its own line of large-size clothing.

• Germany •

Dicke e.V.

Kassel-based organization whose goals are "to promote a positive body image for all people, establish equal rights for fat people, fight size discrimination, pro-vide help for everyday life for fat people, improve contact among fat people, and improve cooperation of fat people and organizations on a European and inter-national level."

• The Netherlands •

Bond van Formaat (Society of Size)
Size activism group in the Netherlands.

Newsletter (in Dutch) and many fat-acceptance activities.

• New Zealand •

Women Unlimited
Celia James, contact. Aiming to promote size acceptance, lobby government and promote education in the community, this organization is based in Wellington South.

Size Up Wise Up
Cathy Baker, managing director. National support group in Christchurch that pressures for changing public and clothing industry perception of women's sizes.

• Russia •

Moscow Overweight People's Club
Marya Slobodskaya, contact. Support organization in providing psychological, medical, social, and other assistance to its members while working to fight discrimination.

If you don't find a support group here that fills your needs, consider starting your own. The book *Nothing to Lose* by Cheri Erdman (Harper: San Francisco, 1995), has an excellent chapter that should get you started.

LEGAL RESOURCES

• California •

Maureen J. Arrigo-Ward
San Diego law professor who has written articles on weight discrimination.

• Pennsylvania •

Yvonne G. Bach
Philadelphia attorney experienced in handling cases involving weight-loss surgery.

Edith Benay
Strong background in weight discrimination cases in the San Francisco Bay Area.

Tony Cassista
Santa Cruz size rights advocate who has

become quite knowledgeable about size discrimination through her own lawsuit.

Carol Cullum
Handles size discrimination cases in the San Francisco Bay Area.

Barbara Lawless
Handles size discrimination cases in the San Francisco Bay Area.

Robert Z. Lazo
San Francisco attorney who is very knowledgeable about size discrimination laws.

• Connecticut •

Kenneth I. Friedman
Handles size discrimination cases in the Manchester area.

• Georgia •

James Goodman
Handles size discrimination cases in the Atlanta area.

• Illinois •

Employment Discrimination Project
Sends people on job interviews to test for discrimination in the Chicago area. Contact LeeAnn Lodder (project manager), Teresa Matthews (project associate), or Anna Marrs (project associate).

Marilyn H. Marchetti
Handles size discrimination cases in the Chicago area.

• Michigan •

James J. Parks
This Bloomfield attorney handled the first size harassment case under Michigan's Elliott-Larsen Civil Rights Act and continues to litigate size discrimination cases.

• Rhode Island •

Lynette Labinger
Providence attorney who set legal precedent for the inclusion of fat people in the American Disabilities Act in the case of *Cook* vs. *the State of Rhode Island*.

• Washington, D.C. •

Equal Employment Opportunity Library
Provides information of a technical and advisory nature regarding employment discrimination. Also investigates charges of discrimination.

James Loots
Handles size discrimination cases.

Karin Stackpole
Is experienced in size discrimination cases.

Project Legislation 2000
Lee Martindale is coordinating efforts to add size and weight to civil rights legislation in every state and at the federal level by the year 2000.

Contact Largesse, the Network for Size Esteem, for a legal kit that includes up-to-date information on legislation, attorneys, and legal decisions directly impacting size rights. Largesse has two excellent papers available: "Size Rights: The Disability Debate," by Karen W. Stimson, and "Nine Frequent Objections to Size Rights Legislation and the Arguments Against Them," by Lee Martindale. $1 each.

SPEAKERS, WORKSHOPS, ACTIVIST ENTERTAINERS, AND PRESENTATIONS

Abundia

Cheri Erdman, Ed.D. in counseling

Susan T. Ross, B.S. in nutrition, M.S.W, Ed.D. in adult continuing education

Barbara Spaulding, M.S.W.

Sally Strosahl, M.A. in clinical psychology

These women offer continuing education for professionals interested in the nondieting, size-acceptance philosophy and workshops or presentations for groups. Dr. Erdman is the author of *Nothing to Lose: A Guide to Sane Living in a Larger Body* and its sequel, *Live Large! Ideas, Affirmations, and Actions for Sane Living in a Larger Body*.

Abundia sponsors summer weekend retreats for women of size. Contact Barbara Spaulding if you are interested in attending one of these supportive events.

For those of you in the Chicago area, Dr. Erdman also offers a college course through the Instructional Alternatives at the College of DuPage. The class, "Nothing to Lose," is aimed at increasing self-esteem for the larger woman and is sometimes presented in conjunction with a fitness activity class. The fitness activity class is led by Barbara Spaulding. Call the college for more information about the course.

Charlotte Cooper

Ms. Cooper is a member of the Fat Women's Group in London, England. Her master's degree dissertation, "The Fear of Fat: An Investigation into the Politics of Size Acceptance," was the natural continuation of her years of fat activism. She has produced a video, *Growing Up Fat, 1983–1990,* has a book in the works, and is working to put together a business in size awareness training. Ms. Cooper is available to speak at conferences and women's groups about fat issues and rights.

Seattle NOW Body Image Task Force

This segment of Seattle NOW is an excellent source of information for forming size-positive protests and demonstrations.

YOU*NIQUE

Kaca Henley. Self-acceptance and self-esteem seminars for large women. Ms. Henley is based in Toronto, Ontario.

➡ If any data listed in this chapter need to be corrected, please let me know. If you know of a service or product useful to people of size, please write to me about it. The information may be made available to readers through the newsletter "Size Wise Update!," the "Size Wise" web site, or through possible future revisions of this book.

PERSONAL GLIMPSE:
LESLIE

With a graduate degree in criminal justice and psychology, and an M.B.A. in personal administration, Leslie is a busy attorney, wife, and mother.

I have been fat all of my life. I was called names and teased a lot about being fat and for not being the same as everybody else. I have a distinct impression of the boys in my fifth and sixth grade class calling me Voracious, which was the name of one of the elephants on one of the kids' shows. That wounded me deeply. You go through all the junior high and high school trauma knowing that you're smart, knowing that you are witty, charming, and intelligent, and not being able to get a date because you're not cutsey and you're not a size 6. It seems people go out with girls who are as dumb as dirt, but they are cute. Those girls would get dates and I wouldn't. It was frustrating.

My family is not large, though my older brother was heavy when he was growing up and suffered the same kind of torments as I did. He lost eighty or ninety pounds when he went in the navy and has kept it off for ten or fifteen years now. Periodically my mother would try to get me to diet and help me lose weight. My dad would, too. But only because they saw that I was miserable. And only because they saw the pain I was going through. They were trying to help me like myself and to be happy and well-adjusted. They weren't embarrassed of me or anything like that. I had a very happy childhood as far as my family is concerned. I was very loved, very wanted. It's only been in my adult years that I have been what they call "morbidly obese." As a child I was maybe twenty or thirty pounds over my ideal weight. In high school I was a size 16 instead of a 10. In college maybe I was a size 18. Then 20, 22 . . . just getting bigger and bigger.

I never really felt any size discrimination until the interview process in law school. To compensate for my physical "defect," and I think many fat women do this, I had developed other areas. Many fat women have wonderful personalities or they are very very smart. Because I was very very smart I was always able to find a job. Particularly as an administrative assistant or as a secretary . . . something where somebody would depend on me to run things. I was very good at what I did. But in law school everybody is like you from an intelligence standpoint, which evens out the playing field. So, I think they make the decisions based on other criteria. With women it is, I think, based on looks. I can't tell you how many times after graduation I found out that girls in my class who I considered to be pretty stupid had five or six job offers. I couldn't even get one. If it had just been me, I would have said that the problem was just me. But I had several large friends who didn't get jobs either. It's very sad. I really felt it for the first time.

I have always been self-assured. I think it's a function of my family. I'm the youngest. I'm the only daughter. I have two older brothers, so I was always pushed to do "manly" things. My father was an engineer for General Motors. He always pushed me to take math and sciences. He wanted me to be an engineer just like him. I was pushed to interact in a man's world. I didn't develop these female stereotypical mind-sets. My mother has always been pretty forceful, too. She was never subservient to my father. They worked more as a team. And so I never was raised with the idea that a woman was to be docile and tame. That worked to my advantage when I was growing up. When there was a boy I liked, I would call him. Why not? I always rebelled against those strictures that society places on women. A lot has to do with how my parents raised me. It was always "You're smart, you're bright, you are a wonderful person. You go and you get what you want and what you deserve." They pushed all of us to do that. All three of us kids are that way. Whenever I was upset or hurt, my dad was the only one who could comfort me. I would be on my bed sobbing and he would come in and put his arms around me and stroke my hair and say, "You know, one of these days you're going to meet a man who likes a woman who has some meat on her bones." And he was right. I did. It took a long time, but I finally did. Robert just doesn't have a problem with my weight at all. He just loves me to death. If I want to lose weight, that's fine. If I don't want to lose weight, that's fine. He doesn't really care.

If you don't feel good about yourself, you should get some help. You're going to lead your life cowering all the time if you don't. You're a good person inside and to heck with what everybody else says. Don't let them run your life and control your life just because you are fat. I get very angry when I see women like that. And men are like that too sometimes. I have male friends who are large. They are either very docile because society has beat them down so badly or overly aggressive to counteract.

I used to think, "When I'm twenty pounds thinner, I'll buy this skirt." Now I just go ahead and do what I want, buy what I want now. You'll be waiting your whole life if you think like that.

"The Feeling Never Went Away"

A few hours into the flight I flashed on my first memory of being fat.

I was in kindergarten, and the teacher was showing the class a new toy someone had donated. It was a white milk truck that could be ridden around the room. All of us kids stood in line, waiting our turn to drive it around the room. We didn't have any toys like that at my house. It looked like fun. I was so excited to take it for a spin I could hardly wait.

Then my turn came. But as I swung my leg over the seat, a little girl screamed, "Hey, you can't go on the truck! You're too fat! You'll break it!"

Several of the other kids laughed. Already my weight was generating laughs. I could have charged at the door. My kindergarten class could have been the only one in school with a two-snack minimum.

However, I didn't know what to do when people laughed at me then. I looked around for help. But none was offered. The teacher was occupied with something else and she didn't hear. So I did the only thing I could. I got off the truck, relinquished my turn, and, with my head bowed and tears in check, slunk humiliated back into the corner.

I was wounded, scarred for life, though I didn't know it yet.

But I had also realized for the first time that I was different from everybody else. I was fat.

The feeling never went away, and neither did the weight.

From Goodbye Jumbo, Hello Cruel World *by Louie Anderson.*

OUR BIG BEAUTIFUL KIDS

9

It is estimated that there are over 7.5 million kids in the United States who are 20 percent above "ideal" weight. That is approximately one in five of our children, an increase by 54 percent over the last twenty years. Presumed causes for this increased incidence of "overweight" children vary from expert to expert and from week to week. Genetics is certainly a factor, but only one. Decreasing involvement in physical activity, poor eating habits, and various psychological factors all play a part to one degree or another. The jury is also still out on what health problems are a direct result of a child's being larger than "ideal."

Even children who aren't fat are scared to death of being so. A recent study of over three thousand children between the ages of ten and thirteen concluded that over half the girls and one fourth of the boys thought they were fat. One third of these children had dieted to lose weight, and almost 5 percent reported vomiting to lose weight. The figures for high school students are even more alarming. Another study found two thirds of high school girls dieting, many of them using diet pills, laxatives, diuretics, and fasting to lose weight.

An American Association of University Women (AAUW) study released in 1991 documented the drop in self-esteem as our daughters enter their teens, especially children of white or Hispanic families. During elementary school, 60 percent of the girls reported being happy with themselves just as they were; by high school there was a dramatic reversal, with more than 60 percent finding fault with their bodies. African-American girls apparently have a much better body image; 58 percent report being quite happy with their bodies. Boys also did much better, dropping only from 67 percent to 46 percent who were satisfied with their bodies. Interestingly enough, in listing things they like about themselves, boys listed talents; girls judged themselves on physical appearance. Our kids aren't born with this obsession to be thin . . . it's our gift to them, taught through words, actions, and media representations.

To be quite honest, what concerns me most are the debilitating self-esteem issues brought on by the outrageous treatment of fat children by their peers, teachers, caregivers, doctors, coaches, and families. (Yes, families.)

> *I come from a family of physicians, very antifat. One of my strongest memories is when I was about 12 years old. My dad was treating me for a cold and I had to take my shirt off. He was totally, visibly disgusted. He called me a fat ugly toad, dragged my mom into the room, and said, "Jesus, will you look at this? He has stretch marks. He's disgusting!" I'll never forget that.*
>
> *My parents still are very unhappy I am fat. It bothers them to have a fat son.*
>
> —RANDY

So much of what we think and feel about ourselves is based on what we were taught as children. Children who are raised in an environment of total love and acceptance are better able to handle the often harsh treatment they receive outside the home; children who are not have a very difficult time of it . . . at any size. The most important thing we, as parents, can do for our big kids is to love and accept them completely.

My son, Michael, was born big. Weighing almost twelve pounds, he entered the world already the size of a two-month-old baby. He loved to sleep . . . in fact, he slept most of his first nine months away. As he grew up he stayed on the large side. He had a good appetite, but didn't consume any more (or any different) food than other kids.

He began to be excluded from games and play groups during first grade. Already shy, Michael withdrew more as the children either ignored him or openly refused to play with him. On the playground kids would sometimes run away when he would try to join in their play. Sometimes they would gather around him in a circle and call him names. When asked what he did when that happened he once said to me, "I close my eyes and just smile real big. Like this." He displayed a huge, forced smile, tears welling up in his beautiful brown eyes.

Not All Good Things Come In Small Packages

When he approached his teachers and playground supervisors with a request that they do something to stop these situations, their responses were twofold.

First, they explained that children are "like that"; when Michael learned to stand up to them, they would search for another victim. When I suggested that children should not be "like that" and should be taught kindness, respect, and acceptance of all types of people, these experts on childhood behavior acted as if my suggestion was an interesting but impossible expectation.

I asked the vice principal, "If a black child were being teased, called names, and ostracized by white children because of his color, would that behavior be allowed to continue?" Her reaction was immediate and indignant.

"Of course not!" she replied, highly offended at the suggestion that she might be so bigoted.

"Then why do you tolerate those same behaviors when directed at a child because of his size?" She didn't get it. Most people don't . . . yet.

The second part of the "solution" was to bring Michael into special groups of kids (other "outcasts") in the counselor's offices to learn socialization, as if he were the problem. It seemed to me that the children who were teasing him should have been brought into socialization groups to be taught that bigotry and meanness are unacceptable. This suggestion fell on closed, "expert" minds.

This is not to say there were never any sympathetic people available. There have been some wonderful teachers and counselors in Michael's schools, and they are to be commended for the kindnesses they have shown to him and to the countless other children who have been helped by them and others like them. But they are the exceptions.

School personnel can make such an overwhelming difference in a child's life. Teaching all children simple respect, manners, and acceptance, and refusing to tolerate any type of cruel behavior seem so basic.

Michael is a wonderful person . . . extremely bright, loving, witty, very kind, and a lot of fun to be with. He knows his family thinks he is terrific, is very proud of him, believes him to be as cute as can be, and loves him deeply. No matter what his size.

I grew up feeling very loved and wanted in my family. Then I started school. It was at that point I started to experience some social rejection.

School for me was difficult. I was a fat kid and was also considered ethnic. We were Ukrainian, and there was still some of the discrimination directed toward immigrants, especially Ukrainian people. Along with the continual teasing there was a particular period of time that really stands out. During recess kids would come up and spit on me and call me names. It became this sort of spectacle. You know, spit on the fat kid and get him to chase you. But once this kid from my room spit in my face and as he turned to run he lost his footing, tripping on the gravelly playground. I was able to catch him and, being very angry, punch him in the nose. Of course, then he looked like the victim, with skinned knees and a bleeding nose. The teacher's response was that I had to write on the blackboard "Sticks and stones will break your bones and names will never hurt you."

I remember sort of breaking down again and saying, "But he was spitting on me and calling me names." I thought she would understand. Instead I then had to write "Tattletale tit, your tongue is going to split, every little puppydog will have a little bit." I had to write this in front of the class. Every time I wrote the word tit *the class would laugh because I had a fat chest that made it look like I had breasts. It was just a very humiliating experience. And then I was strapped. I don't advocate punching people, but he never spit on me again.*

—Rick

I'm adopted. The adoption agency told my parents that my natural mother was a fat woman and therefore I needed to be monitored very closely so I didn't turn out to be a fat child. I was cursed from the get-go, so to speak.

My parents took this advice seriously. My first diet began when I was three years old. I have memories of dieting . . . of being hungry all the time. Sometimes doctors would prescribe diet pills (amphetamines). Looking back at photos of myself I can see that I was a chunky kid, but I wasn't huge. Nothing that running around and exercise wouldn't have taken care of in a few years. I think that the dieting only made it worse.

In kindergarten I was made to eat different foods than what the rest of the children in my class ate. My parents made arrangements that I was to have salad at lunch and was not to be given any cookies at snack time. I was singled out from the very beginning. It's so painful to think back on this.

In the fifth grade I was taken for a whole series of tests at the University of Arizona so they could finally figure out what was "wrong" with me. But the doctors concluded there was nothing physically wrong—I was just fat and my parents should teach me to eat correctly. I was so disappointed that there wasn't a cause or a cure for my body size. I would have to continue to live with the thought that I was a bad girl. There were a lot of shame issues involved.

I had had problems with bulimia and anorexia when I was in junior high school. It took me till I was about twenty-one to really get off the diet roller coaster. I finally said, "I'm not doing this anymore, it's stupid."

—Janine

ELLYN SATTER, M.S., R.D., M.S.S.W.

Ellyn Satter is a registered dietitian, a holder of the Diplomate in Clinical Social Work, a therapist at the Family Therapy Center in Madison, Wisconsin, and the author of *How to Get Your Kid to Eat . . . But Not Too Much* and *Child of Mine: Feeding with Love and Good Sense*.

Ellyn offers excellent advice in her books for helping your child to grow up happy and healthy. She says, "I am absolutely opposed to putting children on diets. In my view, no person has the right to impose starvation on another, even if that other person is your child." Instead she recommends teaching healthy eating habits, providing plenty of healthy foods with a variety of fat contents, treating your fat child as you would any other child when making food decisions, providing plenty of opportunities for exercise, and valuing your child and your child's body. She adds:

> *While size acceptance is extremely important, we have to make sure that we are attending to influences that are making children heavier than they naturally would be. Most of the determinations of the body and the degree of fatness or thinness that a child will show has to do with his genetic inheritance. However, there are environmental factors that have an impact on children's weight as well.*
>
> *A 14-year longitudinal study [Shapiro, et al.] I mention in my book,* How to Get Your Kid to Eat . . . But Not Too Much, *showed that feeding problems between parent and child seem to be connected with fatness in later life. It's a very logical association. The association that doesn't follow quite as logically is when the feeding problem relates to the child's finickiness, or the child's refusal to take the bottle or other food. These other kinds of struggles around eating apparently also disrupt the child's ability to be effective in managing their eating and can compromise their ability to regulate their eating and body weight.*
>
> *A study done at Duke University indicated that children who are fed in a restrained fashion tend to be fatter. The research looked at eight-year-old boys and girls. The boys liked certain things and put limits on what they would accept, but parents didn't see that as being problematic. Parents tended to cater to their likes and dislikes and didn't mind catering. They saw the behavior as being appropriate for a boy. On the other hand, the girls, who were very similar in their behavior, were perceived as being obstreperous, troublesome, and problematic. Parents accepted and condoned the same behavior in boys that they condemned in girls.*
>
> *For the most part, when I work with feeding problems I see parents trying to control what they shouldn't and failing to control what they should. Parents should maintain a division of responsibility for feeding. The parent needs to be responsible for what, when, and where; the child for how much and whether.*
>
> *Oftentimes I find parents don't keep control over the menu and the timing of meals but will scold the child for snacking. It's terribly confusing to the child. The parent is failing to do what they should, and they are interfering*

with the child's prerogative of how much they eat. It's not good parenting, let alone good feeding.

The trend in our society is away from family meals, from taking feeding ourselves seriously. So many people try not to eat nowadays, try to lose weight, to avoid fatty foods, red meat, etc. There is so much avoidance going on with food that we no longer have the rituals around food. We no longer make feeding ourselves a priority. That's not good for children.

When I speak to groups of dietitians they are so happy and relieved to hear what I have to say. They say, "You know, that's what I've been thinking but haven't quite been able to put in words yet." They work with people and know darn well that their patients adhere to their 1,200-calorie diets and still can't lose weight. They know what kind of pain people have when they can't. Dietitians feel immobilized by the whole enterprise and are looking for another way of dealing with this whole weight issue.

When your child comes in crying and says someone has been teasing them, it's awfully hard not to say, "Let's just get you slimmed down and this won't happen." In the long run those tactics do more harm than good. Children take away a powerful message that they are not all right the way they are. If children think they are going to be restricted or deprived of food, they become preoccupied with food and tend to overeat when they get a chance.

You should evaluate carefully the kinds of limits you set on your fat child's eating. Make sure that what you are doing is what you would do with any child. For instance, you might cringe when your child goes back at the potluck dinner for their fifth brownie and say, "Now, that's enough. You go and get something that's a little more healthy." That's something you would say to any child. The reason for it is nutritional well-being.

It's important to raise children so that when they grow up they will maintain a body that is right for them. The way you do that is by feeding them in a way that is really positive. If a child is growing in a consistent fashion, even if he is large, he is doing fine. If a child starts to diverge from a normal growth curve and puts on a lot of weight, a parent needs to consider what is going on. It takes a lot to disrupt that normal growth pattern; parents need to realize that a child who is gaining an unusual amount of weight is struggling in some way. Parents need to figure out what is going on. They definitely should not put the child on a diet. That is a simplistic solution that rarely works. Dieting simply accentuates the negative in what could already be a pretty negative situation."

* * *

I was put on my first formal diet at the age of seven. I was given a bowl of Wheaties with skim milk and no sugar while the rest of the family had normal foods. When my mom would finally give in and let me have a cookie, I had to tell her how many were left in the box before I took one so I couldn't sneak *another one. I was on diet pills at the age of eight. By the age of nine I was having trouble sleeping because of the diet pills, so they started giving me librium. When I was about ten or twelve there was a story in a magazine about a woman who almost died from diet pills. I flushed mine down the toilet. My mother tried to reassure me that the doctor would never give me anything that wasn't perfectly safe for me. I didn't believe that even then.*

I remember sneaking food and hiding it under my pillow. I had become a compulsive eater; I think I was groomed to be one through the denial. They took food away from me and made it a big issue. If I had been allowed to have a cookie without having to fight for it, maybe it would have been all right to have just one instead of having to have the whole box and get sick over them.

I would lose weight, then gain weight. In the seventh grade I went to Weight Watchers. My homeroom teacher had gone and lost sixty-six pounds. He took me aside and had a "talk" with me. He told me if I didn't lose the weight now I was going to have a terrible life, people would make fun of me, I wouldn't have a boyfriend, and I would never get married. I was twelve years old. Give me a break. I didn't even have my first period yet.

I know why I got fat. The more I was told no, the more food became a compulsive, obsessive center of my life. Everything began to revolve around food and the denial of it. I used to think that when I grew up I was going to have bags and bags of Cheez Doodles in the cabinets. My mother would buy them for my brother but I wasn't allowed to have them. If a bag was being passed around on one of those rare occasions when we had snack food just for the sake of it, my mother would watch me carefully and say, "Haven't you had enough already?" or "You just had a big dinner. You don't need that," when my brother had eaten the same dinner.

I learned very early to hate my own body.

—SUSAN MASON

DIET CAMP?

My only experience with sleepover camps as a kid involved troops of little girls excited about the prospect of sticky-gooey marshmallows, sort-of melted chocolate bars, and broken graham crackers plastered together for dessert. "Exercise" was finding little frogs to put inside Mrs. Brockleman's sleeping bag, and the only work on self-esteem involved getting up enough nerve to enter the witch's cave (in later years we discovered it was just the handyman's storage shed).

Today there are camps for kids of almost every interest. Summer can be spent computing, horseback riding, playing tennis, scuba diving, learning what it's like to be an astronaut, or being involved in dozens of other pursuits. Then there are diet camps. These run the gamut from expensive resort area playgrounds to the stereotypical cabins in the woods. Most diet camps cost $60 to $85 a day (many health insurance programs cover these costs), with a promised weight loss of three to five pounds a week. Camp La Jolla in California, for example, charges $4,595 for seven weeks, serves a diet of 1,000 to 1,200 calories a day, and guarantees weight loss. Camp Camelot, with locations on college campuses in Pennsylvania, California, and Massachusetts, offers seven weeks for $4,750, a diet of 1,200 calories for girls, 1,500 for boys, and says in its brochures, "lose 20–45 pounds in seven weeks."

Activities tend to be varied—from kickball to swimming, weight training to dance—and kids are sometimes allowed to choose which they prefer to participate in. Some camps, however, are strict about exercise and are very regimental from the moment kids arrive until they go home. Many of the camps offer trips to local zoos, beaches, and other attractions as diversions.

The literature and videos provided by many of the camps are slick and professionally done. Kids are shown having a great time splashing in beautiful swimming pools and riding bikes . . . always smiling . . . and the counselors look friendly; the meals are represented as filling. The entire experience of attending these camps is endorsed as one of the high points of life.

In going over the materials sent from each camp, it suddenly struck me that what they are really selling in the brochures is acceptance. Almost every picture in these packets of information shows the kids surrounded by others and involved in group activities. Not only are smiles abundant, but hugs and friendships are waiting. Pretty heavy stuff for children who are often ignored or picked on by their peers and teachers. This is a serious hard sell—and extremely enticing. I did speak with one woman, Sharon, who loved her experience at a weight-loss camp. She said it was the first time she had ever excelled at sports and really fit in. And she did lose forty pounds.

So what is wrong with this picture?

A diet is a diet; 1,000 to 1,200 calories a day is a weight-loss diet. Diets don't work for adults and they don't work for children. Sharon eventually regained her lost weight and today is a supersize woman. Weight lost on diets is regained by 95 percent of all dieters. This is true if you are dieting with NutriSystem, in a hospital, or in a camp. My eleven-year-old son, Michael, watched the tape from Camp Camelot with me, then said, "I notice they are careful not to say anything about whether anyone keeps the weight off." (Michael's mother isn't raising any dumb kids.)

Children especially should not be on weight-loss diets. Their bodies are still developing, and they may not get all the nutrients they need while on a reducing diet. And what kind of message is being given to children sent to diet camps? "This is what is wrong with you. We're sending you to get fixed."

Ellyn Satter, when asked how she felt about weight-loss camps for children, said, "I think diet camps are a really bad idea. It would be much better to have a camp for children who are physically challenged, as many larger children are, to help them learn to use their bodies well, to work for achievement and acceptance rather than to change their size and shape.''

You are doing your child no favor whatsoever by starting him or her on a course of yo-yo dieting or communicating (either verbally or by your actions) that losing weight will make him or her better. Consider, instead, finding ways to give your child a healthy lifestyle complete with good nutrition, fun activities, and healthy attitudes. If you are really gung-ho on sending your kid to camp, how about space camp . . . or horse camp . . .

If you are still dead set on a weight-loss camp, research the choices carefully. Talk to parents and children who have attended the camps and find one with a comfortable atmosphere for your child. The ideal situation would be a camp that:

- Teaches good nutrition but doesn't limit servings, and offers many of your child's favorites.
- Stresses self-acceptance while teaching good health habits.
- Provides lots of fun activities geared to all levels of ability.
- Doesn't ever pressure a child for weight-loss "success."

I didn't encounter any camps of this sort in researching this book. At best they talk the talk but don't walk the walk. The very nature of the beast—a weight-loss camp—makes it very difficult for any of them to teach size acceptance honestly. To keep those sizable checks rolling in they have to produce weight loss. Never mind the fact that the loss is usually temporary—that can be ignored or worked on next summer. After all, the basis for any successful business is the repeat customer. Just ask Jenny Craig.

The American Camping Association investigates and certifies camps of all sorts. Contact them for a complete list of accredited facilities.

If you locate a camp with a truly good attitude about size acceptance please let me know about it. I'll share your experiences with readers in future editions of this book or in newsletters.

My parents never gave up. When I was twelve they sent me to a diet camp in upstate New York. I begged to come home but was told I had to stick it out. We had a skinny counselor who didn't know anything about what it was like to be fat. She paraded around in a bikini and told us we had to work hard so we could look like that. I guess it was supposed to be an incentive, but it was very intimidating to us. She talked about going into town on her day off and having a decent meal.

This camp was built in what used to be a country club. Our dorms were old country club chalets, but in horrible condition. They built bunk beds for fat girls in these cabins. I can't tell you how many times those beds collapsed!

After four weeks (I was supposed to stay for eight weeks) the camp director called my parents and told them to come pick me up. I had all twenty-four girls in my cabin on strike, refusing to go to activities. I didn't know I had been expelled. My mother called me and said she had decided to come get me. I was so happy, and thanked her profusely. I was packed and ready right away but they didn't come get me until the next day. I hated that place!

All through that weekend after they picked me up, they kept track of everything I put in my mouth. Even if it was just my finger to bite my fingernail. I couldn't think of anything else but being alone on Monday while they were at work so I could have anything I wanted to eat.

—Susan Mason

JOANNE P. IKEDA, M.A., R.D.

Joanne Ikeda is a nutrition education specialist with Cooperative Extension, Department of Nutritional Sciences, at the University of California at Berkeley.

In 1983, as a member of the Ad Hoc Interdisciplinary Committee on Children and Weight, Joanne helped to write and publish a position paper called *Children and Weight, a Changing Perspective*. This paper became the basis of an in-service training program for health professionals that included dietitians, nutritionists, nurses, physicians, and school personnel such as guidance counselors and physical education, science, and home economics teachers. The program tried to help them see what they could do to make an impact on the problem of pediatric obesity. This in-service training program has reached over ten thousand professionals nationwide.

Joanne speaks extensively at workshops and conferences and works diligently to improve the lives of all our big children.

Genetics plays a strong role in setting a person's size range. There is a huge continuum for human weight. What genetics probably does is set high and low limits. That means someone who is 5'8" and large-boned does not have the genetic potential to weigh ninety pounds; no matter what they did, they probably could never achieve that. It would take incredibly dramatic measures, and they wouldn't be able to maintain that weight even if they got there. Where we fall within our genetic range is determined environmentally. I don't know, for myself, whether that range is from 125 to 175 pounds or 135 to 165. It isn't as if genetics says you are going to be 152 pounds and you are going to be that no matter what you do. You have the potential to be a range of weights, but nobody knows at this point the breadth of the range.

We often think it's bad that genetics plays such a strong role in determining weight and body shape because that places them beyond our control. In reality there is a lot of interaction between genetics and environment. What we are trying to do, as dietitians and nutritionists, is to help people fall at the lower end of their range, because that tends to be a healthier weight for them.

If a child needs to be at a healthier weight, I consider weight stabilization and letting a child grow into his or her weight the best strategy. I don't advocate weight loss for children because there has been research to show that restricting calorie intake during periods of growth can stunt growth in height, even in children who are overweight. On the other hand, growth in height can take care of a child's weight problem. What I usually tell parents is, if a child can stay at the same weight for a few months, height growth may very well take care of the problem.

What I focus on are healthy eating and activity habits. If the child does not grow into his or her weight through an increase in height, I tell a parent not to worry. It may very well be that this child is meant to be a larger size. The most important thing is to help the child have healthy habits. Have them adopt a healthy lifestyle. That includes proper eating. I don't advocate a strict diet of carrots and broccoli. I believe in a balanced diet that has room for things like soft drinks, ice cream, and candy on occasion. I eat those things on occasion myself, and I expect large people to be able to eat and enjoy them. I don't believe in any off-limits kinds of foods.

People often call me at Halloween asking if a fat child should be allowed to go trick-or-treating. My response is "You must be kidding!" Why would anyone even ask such a question? What is going on here? The next question then is "Should the child be allowed to eat the candy?" Sure! In fact, if the kid wants to overdose on the candy, let him. Every child goes through that overdosing.

I recommend bringing home a limited amount of foods that you feel are tempting your child. For instance, once every week I go to the supermarket. I buy a six-pack of soft drinks. There are four people in the family. Usually before my husband and I even get one my two daughters have had the whole six-pack. But I figure, "That's it. They've had their three soft drinks for the week." That's not an unreasonable amount when you figure most kids are drinking two or three a day. There is a limited amount available, they can drink three cans at a time as far as I am concerned, but then there isn't any more until the next week's shopping trip.

I don't believe in applying external controls except for reasons of fairness—for example, everyone getting their share of an apple pie. I never tell someone what is enough for them or what should satisfy their hunger. It is only the individuals themselves who can hear the hunger cues, who can know when those have been satisfied. If you start doing that externally, the kid starts to distrust his or her body and thinks, "My body doesn't tell me when I'm hungry" or "My body doesn't tell me when it's full. I need somebody else to do that for me." That's ridiculous. Who is going to be there twenty-four hours a day the rest of their life policing their eating? They will start sneaking, beg-

ging, and stealing food. Whenever you start to restrict a child's food intake you get all of that backlash. I think most pediatricians don't think that through when they give dieting advice to parents.

People need to start listening to those hunger cues and satiety cues, and if they end up being large then they need to accept that. But it doesn't mean giving up on yourself and thinking you can't be a healthy person. It is not a choice between being thin, happy, and attractive and being a fat slob. The choices are being large, attractive, and happy or being large, unattractive, and unhappy. Most people who like themselves choose the former.

Some families seem to feel that making fat children feel badly about themselves helps. But it doesn't. If it did help, all fat people would have been thin a long time ago. The truth of the matter is, making people feel badly makes them feel helpless and hopeless. It makes them feel out of control, discouraged, and pessimistic. That is not helping the situation at all. In fact, it's aggravating and contributing to it.

Harassment because of body size and shape is appalling to me. I've gone to high schools where the boys will stand around and make comments on the size and shape of every girl who passes by. That is harassment and should not be allowed. What kind of values are you teaching children when you allow that sort of behavior?

Sit down and listen to your children and what they have to say. Don't deny their experiences. Don't say things like "Oh, those kids really like you. You just think they don't like you." Hear what the child is going through and try to help the child cope with these situations, particularly the teasing aspect. Large children are teased, sometimes unmercifully, by other children. The old idea of turning the other cheek and ignoring teasing often doesn't work because it turns the child into a victim.

Teach children to stand up for themselves, to think of things to say when they are teased, to come off being assertive and strong. A parent might try role-playing with their kids, where the parent is the nasty kid and the child responds with some verbal assertiveness. Kids feel good about handling themselves that way, and the other children are thrown off because they are stunned and surprised. Usually they will lay off because they are not getting the victim result that they want.

PRACTICAL TIPS FOR PROMOTING INCREASED PHYSICAL ACTIVITY

Parents:

- *Have a television budget. Say something like "You've got two hours of TV-watching time and you can spend that 120 minutes any way you want. But it's just like money. When you run out of it, it's gone and you don't get any more." Two hours a day, maximum, is the amount I recommend. After all, if children are spending more time in front of the TV set, when are they getting their schoolwork done? When are they getting some physical activity?*

- *Turn on the radio and get the kids to start dancing. Large kids often feel uncomfortable with their bodies. One of the things we can do is make them feel more comfortable. Large people can dance and have rhythm and have a lot of fun moving their bodies.*

- *Purchase toys that promote physical activity. Buy things like punch balls, paper airplanes, sidewalk chalk for drawing hopscotch boards, balloons you can keep bouncing in the air, roller skates, a jump rope or ten-inch rubber ball.*

- *Plan family activities. Take a hike, go to a park, fly a kite, or go to the mall and walk around. Get out and do things together that promote physical activity.*

- *Don't make your kid do any of these things as a punishment. Give them the list and let them choose something. Physical activity should not be viewed as something that is a punishment imposed upon you because you are fat.*

Health care providers:

- *Keep lists of parks, playgrounds, and free swimming pools available in your area. I keep information from the Parks and Recreation Department available, such as classes, summer programs, etc.*

- *My feeling is that focusing on a healthy lifestyle is going to reduce the chronic disease risk that we are concerned about. Even if the kid does grow up to be a large adult, if he or she has a healthy lifestyle, they are at lower risk of chronic disease than the person who doesn't.*

All This And Brains Too!

In August 1996 a twelve-year-old boy, Samuel John Graham, of Fort Lauderdale, Florida, hung himself from a tree in his back yard. Samuel, 5'4" tall and 174 pounds, had been "overweight" for years and had been tormented and teased so badly he had talked of killing himself. According to detectives investigating his death, Samuel was terrified of facing the teasing again when school began the next day.

A couple of years earlier an elementary student facing similar treatment at the hands of his peers stood in his classroom and shot and killed himself in front of the very kids who had persecuted him.

These are extreme reactions, but they illustrate the pain and suffering children endure.

Teasing, ostracism, bullying, and harassment of children who are different in any way should never be allowed to happen. The excuse "Kids can be cruel" should absolutely never be accepted. Kids learn their behaviors and attitudes from adults. It is outrageous that this type of behavior is allowed to continue.

Love your big, beautiful children unconditionally. Let them know they are loved and that you are proud of them. We know how cruel people can be to adults; kids suffer even more and carry the scars with them throughout their lives. Stand up for them; insist they be treated with respect. Tell them that you love them in every way you know how and be there to help them wherever you can. Help them to be healthier, self-confident, and happy. Everything else will fall into place.

© PAWS

Who doesn't know and love Garfield? With his cuddly charm, round little body, and sharp wit, he has been a staple of our daily comic strip enjoyment for years. His books line my son's shelf, my daughter has a stuffed version of him on her bed, and I . . . well, I read the books and (don't tell a soul) sneak a hug with the Garfield doll on occasion. Garfield has no problem at all letting people know he's just perfect the way he is, thank you. Garfield was kind enough to find time between a nap and harassing Odie to visit with Michael.

MICHAEL: Hey, Garfield . . . you're pretty cool. Were you as smart and cute as a kid . . . uh . . . I mean, as a kitten?

GARFIELD: You have to ask? Beauty and brains like these don't just happen. It's all in the genes.

MICHAEL: I like to ride my bicycle and jump around on my trampoline. Running is pretty fun too, but I'm not all that fast. Do you play soccer or anything like that?

GARFIELD: Please! I'm more of the spectator type. On the other hand, you should see me run when an ice cream truck goes by! I'm also against this exercise thing—my favorite exercise is a brisk nap.

MICHAEL: My cousin, Ryan, is my best friend. He's really smart, like me. We do lots of stuff together, like play on the computer. Is Odie your best friend?

GARFIELD: Actually, it's my mirror. Then Odie. He's brainless as a brick, but you gotta love 'im.

MICHAEL: What is your favorite thing besides napping?

GARFIELD: Hmm—well, I never met a lasagna I didn't like. And I love TV—*Bowling for Donuts* is my favorite. And abusing the mailman—why should dogs have all the fun?
   I like birds—preferably on wheat toast with a little mustard. I also love parties and Pooky (my teddy bear).

MICHAEL: Speaking of lasagna, it seems like Jon always wants to put you on a diet. Does that mean he'd love you more if you were thin?

GARFIELD: No, it just means his grocery bill wouldn't be the size of the national debt. Are you kidding? When it comes to humans—they don't make 'em any better than Jon.

MICHAEL: Sometimes at school kids call me names like ''Chubs.'' Does that ever happen to you?

GARFIELD: Chubs? That's kind! I've been called ''Blimp,'' ''Beached whale,'' ''Comatose hippo,'' and ''Overstuffed sofa'' . . . you name it. If it's a body-slam, I've heard it. I prefer to think of myself as ''dinner-friendly,'' ''experiencing cell abundance,'' ''up-sized petite,'' and ''Santa-waisted.''

   I think I'm in perfect shape. In fact, I wouldn't change a whisker. Listen, kiddo, it's not survival of the fittest. It's survival of the fattest!

MICHAEL: My mom says I'm really cute, but moms are supposed to think that. Sometimes I don't feel so cute. Do you ever feel that way?

GARFIELD: When I look in the mirror, I see someone handsome, lovable, and intelligent. Oh, oops—that was you! But enough about you—back to me. I'm the perfect shape for my weight. That's all I know!

MICHAEL: You're pretty cool, Garfield! Wanna come over and play sometime?

GARFIELD: Oh, I don't know. You got a mailman?

CLOTHING

Grand Kids Custom-made clothing, including formalwear, for big kids.

J.C. Penney Big Kids Penney's is doing a better job of providing big kids with stylish clothing. The Girls Plus sizes are for kids up to 66" tall and run to size 18½ (37" bust, 32" waist, and 41" hips); Husky is for boys up to 70" tall and goes to size 22 (40" chest, 33" waist, and 41" "seat" [this must be what boys have instead of hips]), with a Shorter Husky for kids up to 62" tall (38" chest, 32" waist, and 39" seat). Big, adorable kids are modeling these clothes.

J.C. Penney Class Favorites Casual through dressy school clothing for boys and girls from average sizes through "Extended Student." Boys' Husky runs from size 8 (44" tall, 28" chest, 26" waist, and 28" seat) through size 20 (68" tall, 38" chest, 32" waist, and 39" seat). Boys' Extended Student goes to size 36 (70" tall, 41" chest, 36" waist, and 42" hips). Girls' Plus sizes run from size 10½ (54" tall, 30" bust, 27" waist, 32" hips) to Juniors size 13 (67" tall, 38" bust, 30" waist, 41" hips). The catalog features big kids as models.

J.C. Penney Scouts Boy Scout and Girl Scout uniforms in up to 32" waist belts for girls, up to size 22½ for clothing; 46" waist for boys' belts, to size 36 Husky for clothing.

Johnni's Treasures Halloween costumes for kids of all sizes. These are custom-made, so plan ahead.

Lands' End Warm, cozy pajamas, robes, sleepers, and coats in sizes small to XL (33" chest for girls, 36" chest for boys).

SIZE-POSITIVE PUBLICATIONS FOR AND ABOUT KIDS

•Magazines and Newsletters•

New Moon: The Magazine for Girls and Their Dreams This magazine for eight- to fourteen-year-old girls received the Parent's Choice Foundation 1995 Gold Award. The editorial board, consisting of twenty girls aged eight to fourteen, was named for the Center for Women's Policy Studies' 1995 Wise Woman Award. Dealing with issues of importance to young girls, including self-esteem and body image, *New Moon* offers fiction, poetry, and a variety of features. "*New Moon* challenges stereotypes by accepting girls as they are, listening to them, and honoring their diverse experience and dreams." Published bimonthly. One-year subscription: $25 (U.S.), $35 (Canada), $37 (all other countries).

New Moon Network: For Adults Who Care About Girls From the adults at

New Moon, a bimonthly magazine for professionals who work with, and parents of, young girls. An excellent resource for ideas in raising girls with a healthy body image and self-esteem. One-year subscription: $25 (U.S.), $35, (Canada), $37 (all other countries).

Real Girls Susan Brooks, publisher. An alternative to teen magazines, this homegrown quarterly deals with body image and weight consciousness and features realistic articles and poetry on friendships, earning money, and family dynamics. One-year subscription: $12.

•Books, Fiction•

It's difficult to find fat characters presented in a positive light in children's literature. Of course, there is always Santa and the Mrs. (They belong in nonfiction, though, right?) Check these titles out and share them with the kids.

Are You Too Fat, Ginny? Written by Karin Jasper (Is Five Press, 1988). Teaching positive attitudes about their bodies to young girls, this book addresses adolescent dieting and size acceptance. Boy, will this book ever take you back to childhood and those first diets! But in this circumstance, Ginny is luckier than we were. A school counselor explains the dangers of dieting to Ginny and her mother, and Ginny learns about self acceptance. Available from NAAFA Bookservice.

Belinda's Bouquet Written by Lesléa Newman and Michael Willhoite (Alyson Publications, 1991). Belinda decides to diet and lose weight but later realizes she is great just the way she is. Give this book to the large child in your life and donate a copy to your school library's juvenile section. *Belinda's Bouquet* offers a lot of understanding that is sorely needed. I was temporarily confused by the two mothers of one of Belinda's friends, but my kids didn't bat an eye. (Give me a break . . . I've never claimed to be quick.)

Fat Chance Written by Lesléa Newman (G. P. Putnam's Sons, 1994). This young adult novel received the Parent's Choice Foundation 1994 Story Book Honor. Thirteen-year-old Judi's diary shows us her deepest dreams and fears. She yearns to be like Nancy—pencil-thin and glamorous. She begins a binge-and-purge attempt at weight loss but realizes that there is more to life than numbers on a scale when Nancy ends up in the hospital from her attempts at dieting. Witty, emotional, fun to read, insightful, and entertaining.

Fat Girl Dances with Rocks Written by Susan Stinson (Spinsters Ink, 1994). Char is seventeen years old and coming into her own body—"all the way to the edges of her skin." Her best friend, Felice, collects rocks and deals with her mother; Char counts calories and diets with her mother. The book covers a summer of working at a nursing home, fake IDs, geology, friendships, and coming out.

I Like Me Written by Nancy Carlson (Puffin Books, 1991). Published in England but available through your local bookstore, this delightful book is perfect for reading aloud to your youngest kids. An adorable little pig feels really good about herself, from her hobbies (drawing and riding her bike) to ". . . my curly tail, my round tummy, and my tiny little feet."

Sharing Susan Written by Eve Bunting (Harper Collins, 1991). Susan and another baby were mixed up at birth and now her biological parents want to share in her life. Susan's "new" mother is described as fat and very attractive. Susan tells a friend that being fat isn't a bad thing. A subtle message overall, but well done.

The World of Christopher Robin Written by A. A. Milne (1958). Look for the charming poem "Teddy Bear" for Pooh's thoughts about being short, fat, and still quite adorable.

•Nonfiction for Parents and Caregivers•

All Shapes and Sizes . . . Promoting Fitness and Self-Esteem in Your Overweight Child Written by Teresa Pittman and Dr. Miriam Kaufman (Harper Collins, 1994).

Am I Fat? Helping Young Children Accept Differences in Body Size Written by Joanne Ikeda, M.A., R.D., and Priscilla Naworski, M.S., C.H.E.S. (ETR Associates, 1992). This book should be required reading in Life 101. It's an excellent source that will guide parents and teachers who are in a position to help a child develop good self-esteem. It also teaches sensitivity to people who are critical of large children and their families. With chapters on body image, nutrition, and handling hurtful situations, the authors have created a "must-read" for everyone concerned with happy, healthy children. I especially appreciated the chapter dealing with people who tease and call names.

Eating a variety of healthy foods and engaging in regular physical activity benefits everyone, regardless of body size. When we help children learn to take care of their bodies, we promote their general health and well-being, as well as a positive body image.

Highly recommended.

The Four Conditions of Self-Esteem: A New Approach for Elementary and Middle Schools Written by R. Bean (ETR Associates, 1992). An excellent book covering many areas of self-esteem. Teaches adults to recognize problems and offers techniques for both one-on-one and group interactions and activities designed to improve and maintain good self-esteem.

If children consistently receive messages that one or more of their characteristics are not liked or valued by their caretakers, they will believe these messages, and absorb them as part of their sense of self.

This becomes even more damaging if children are criticized or shamed for characteristics they have no control over, such as their size, color, coordination, dress or looks.

How to Get Your Kid to Eat . . . But Not Too Much Written by Ellyn Satter (Bull Publications, 1987). Just as the title says, this book deals with creating healthy eating habits and environments for our children.

Even the fat child is entitled to regulate the amount of food he eats. You don't have to do that and you shouldn't try. Don't try to assume that responsibility even in sneaky ways, because your child will be on to you.

Positively Different: Creating a Bias-Free Environment for Young Children Written by A. C. Matiella (ETR Associates, 1991). The message here is not only that we all have differences—race, religion, hair color, and body size—but that those differences are to be celebrated, not glossed over or hidden. This is an idea whose time has certainly come.

In our society, being different has been defined as something negative. We have actively promoted the "we are all the same" ideal—also referred to as the "colorblind approach." Without bad intentions, in an attempt to deal with the differences in a positive manner, we have denied differences and promoted the value of sameness.

Preventing Childhood Eating Problems: A Practical, Positive Approach to Raising Children Free of Food and Weight Conflicts Written by Jane R. Hirschmann and Lela Zaphiropoulos (Gürze Books, 1993). An insightful guide to teaching your children to let their bodies decide when enough is enough.

Schoolgirls: Young Women, Self-Esteem and the Confidence Gap Written by Peggy Orenstein (Doubleday, 1994). An up-close inspection of the lives and influences on young girls in the 90s. Reading this book may well cause reconsideration of our own attitudes and subtle messages passed along to our daughters.

Smiling at Yourself: Educating Young Children About Stress and Self-Esteem Written by A. N. Mendler (ETR Associates, 1990). A very upbeat book designed for caregivers of young children. Not just about being fat, this book talks about stress of all kinds, how it affects children, and how to help them deal with it.

It helps for kids to think about things I worry about that I can control and things I worry about that I can't control. Action can help the former while acceptance is necessary for the latter.

ADDITIONAL MATERIALS

AHELP (Association for the Health Enrichment of Large People) has produced the following tapes from its 1994 Annual Conference. The topic of the conference was "Freeing the Fat Child."

"Helping the Large Child and Adolescent: Setting a National Agenda," featuring Bonnie Brigman, Ph.D.; Ellyn Satter, M.S., R.D., M.S.S.W.; Joanne Ikeda, M.A., R.D.; Janet Polivy, Ph.D.; Cheri Erdman, Ed.D.; and Roxy Walker (2 tapes). $16.

"Kids Come in All Sizes: Interrupting Size Bias in a Sixth Grade Population," featuring Nancy Summer. $8.

"Large Children: A Reflection of Family," featuring Carol Johnson, M.A.; and Shay Harris, M.S.W. $8.

"Parental Activism on Behalf of the Large Child," featuring Jody Savage, M.S. $8.

Contact the Educational Equality Specialist at the Maryland State Department of Education for information about a diversity training program for educators. This program is meant to make teachers more aware of and sensitive to size issues.

"Building Blocks for Children's Body Image" Brochure produced by Body Image Task Force. Send a self-addressed stamped envelope or request by E-mail.
Sources: Body Image Task Force

Children and Weight: What's a Parent To Do? Tape and booklets by Joanne Ikeda, R.D., and Rita Mitchell, R.D. (ANR Publications).

Children and Weight: What's a Parent To Do? A twelve-minute videotape, available in Spanish and English. The tape is accompanied by the three booklets *If My Child Is Too Fat, What Should I Do About It?*, *Children and Weight: What's a Parent to Do?*, and *Food Choices for Good Health*. $35.

Children and Weight: What's a Parent To Do? Booklet designed for low-literacy audiences, summarizes *If My Child Is Too Fat, What Should I Do About It?*

"Food Choices for Good Health" Eight-page leaflet lists familiar foods and how they fit into a healthy diet.

"Good News for Big Kids" A wonderful pamphlet that speaks directly to kids about body size, how to be liked, how to make friends, and how to appreciate all the really good things about themselves. Not at all preachy and very well done. Includes information about finding help, including the Youth Crisis Hotline (1-800-HIT-HOME) kids can use to find someone to talk with if they don't have a friend, teacher, relative, or other adult to turn to.

If My Child Is Too Fat, What Should I Do About It? Twenty-page booklet offering advice about encouraging sensible eating habits and an active lifestyle.

Teens and Diets: No Weigh! A program developed by Linda Omichinski, B.Sc. (F.Sc.), R.D., and HUGS, International, Inc. Working with a facilitator and a kit that includes books, a fitness video, an audio affirmation tape set, a journal, and a lifestyle program, teens form groups to work their way to improved health and self-esteem. A newsletter, "HUGS Club News," is sent to each participant. Teens learn to take responsibility for their own appetite and tastes, critically evaluate media messages, use criteria other than scales to measure their health, and have a healthier body image. A facilitator kit costs approximately $600 with a $50 annual membership fee. Each teen participant purchases a basic material package for $30.

➤ If any data listed in this chapter need to be corrected, please let me know. If you know of a service or product useful to people of size, please write to me about it. The information may be made available to readers through the newsletter "Size Wise Update!," the "Size Wise" web site, or through possible future revisions of this book.

RESOURCES LIST

1-800-Pro-Team
3000 S.W. 42nd Avenue
Palm City, FL 34990
(800) 776-8326

2XL Video Magazine
311 Bellevue Avenue East, Suite B
Seattle, WA 98102
E-mail: editor2xl@aol.com

A & E Apparel
2636 Walnut Hill Lane, #100
Dallas, TX 75229
(800) 541-7057

**AHELP (Association for Health
Enrichment of Large People)**
P.O. Drawer C
Radford, VA 24143
(540) 951-3527
(800) 368-3468, ext. 501
E-mail: ahelp@nrv.net
http://www.nrv.net/~ahelp/

AHT Designs
15709 Ancient Oak Drive
Darnestown, MD 20878
(301) 670-1041

ANR Publications
University of California
6701 San Pablo Avenue
Oakland, CA 94608-1239
(510) 642-2431

A Personal Touch
1411 Broadway
New York, NY 10018
(212) 398-1987

Abigail Starr
Logan Square
1 Village Row
New Hope, PA 18938
(215) 862-2066

Ableware
Maddak, Inc.
Pequannock, NJ 07440-1993
(201) 628-7600

Above & Beyond
P.O. Box 666
Stockton, MO 65785
(417) 276-6255

Abundance
3870 24th Street
San Francisco, CA 94114
(415) 550-8811

**Abundance: Full Lives for Large
    Women**
18 Pine Crest Road
Newton Center, MA 02159

Abundantly Yours
P.O. Box 907
Fletcher, NC 28732

Abundia
P.O. Box 252
Downers Grove, IL 60515
(630) 897-9796

Adams Print
P.O. Box 571
Kouts, IN 46347

AdaptAbility
P.O. Box 515
Colchester, CT 06415-0515
(800) 288-9941

Adaptations with Attitude
Designers Unlimited
P.O. Box 523
Canoga Park, CA 91305
(800) 990-3033

Adini En Plus
725 Branch Avenue
Providence, RI 02904
(800) 556-2443

Adirondack Designs
350 Cypress Street
Fort Bragg, CA 95437
(800) 222-0343

Affiliated Big Men's Clubs, Inc.
584 Castro Street, Suite 139F
San Francisco, CA 94114
http://www.skepsis.com/.gblo/g_and_m/
    index.html

Aigis Publications
1449 West Littleton Boulevard, #200
Littleton, CO 80120
(303) 730-6232

Air Physics
2701 East Camelback Road, Suite 440
Phoenix, AZ 85016
(602) 553-0001
(800) 553-0353

Alfred Angelo
(800) 528-3589
(215) 659-8700

Alice's Undercover World
23820 Crenshaw Boulevard
Torrance, CA 90505
(310) 326-6775

AliMed
297 High Street
Dedham, MA 02026-9135
(800) 225-2610

All Texas T's
(800) 367-2600

Allbritton TV Productions
3007 Tilden Street, NW
Washington, DC 20008

Allegro Fortissimo
26, Rue de la Vega
75012 Paris, France
Phone: 011-3345-405-52-00

Amabear Publishing, Inc.
P.O. Box 7083
Louisville, KY 40257
(502) 894-8573

The Amazon Arena
(614) 353-7620 (modem)

Amazon Designs
1473 Old Airport Road
Paris, AR 72855
(501) 963-6548
(800) 315-8332

Ambassador Value Showcase
Palo Verde at 34th Street
P.O. Box 28807
Tucson, AZ 85726-8807
(602) 747-5000

American Camping Association
5000 State Road 67
North Martinsville, IN 46151-7902
(317) 342-8456

America Online (AOL)
(800) 827-6364 customer service

American View
340 Poplar Street
Hanover, PA 17331
(717) 663-3389
(800) 854-2795

American Wilderness Experience
P.O. Box 1486
Boulder, CO 80306
(800) 444-0099

America's Shirt Catalog
(800) 259-7283
http://a1.com/shirt/bigtall.html

America's T-Shirt Catalog
(800) 259-7283
http://a1.com/shirt/genius.html

Amigros France
12, 2 Avenue Chaperon Vert, 9
4250 Gentilly France

Amish Country Collection
RD 5, Sunset Valley Road
New Castle, PA 16105
(412) 458-4811

Amity Associates
11 Holiday Drive
Wayland, MA 01778
(508) 358-9611

Diane Amos
(see Amy Glin or Stars, the Agency)

Ample Awakenings
(215) 602-2064
(609) 877-9116

Ample Opportunity
P.O. Box 40621
Portland, OR 97240-0621
(503) 245-1524

The Ample Shopper
Department BG2, P.O. Box 116
Bearsville, NY 12409

Amplestuff, Ltd.
Department BG2, P.O. Box 116
Bearsville, NY 12409
(914) 679-3316
E-mail: amplestuff@aol.com

Amtrak
1-800-USA-RAIL

Ana's Accoutremonts
834 Pinetree Street
Slidell, LA 70458-4514
(504) 641-7501

Andrew Barry Associates
565 Potter Road
Framingham, MA 01701
(508) 877-3131

Ange D' Amour
(800) 288-3888

Anne Terrie Designs
129-G Derby Boulevard
Harrison, OH 45030
(800) 774-6898

Anthony Richards
6864 Engle Road
P.O. Box 94549
Cleveland, OH 44130
(216) 826-3008

Apples & Pears, Inc.
20488 S.W. Inglis Drive
Aloha, OR 97007
(503) 649-4601
(800) 475-5166

Appleseeds
(see Just Right!)

Arctic Sheepskin Outlet
I-94 and County Road T
Hammond, WI 54015
(800) 657-4656

Aria
1017 West Washington, Suite 2A
Chicago, IL 60607
(312) 248-9400

Armand's
219 Elm Street
Reading, PA 19696
(610) 370-2799

Mary Armstrong
8048 Creed Court
Indianapolis, IN 46268
(317) 876-7222

Maureen Arrigo-Ward
California Western School of Law
225 Cedar Street
San Diego, CA 92101
(619) 525-1430
E-mail: marrigo@cwsl.edu

Art-Wear
P.O. Box 691
New Cumberland, PA 17070
(800) 543-0431

Arthur M. Rein
32 New York Avenue
Freeport, NY 11520
(516) 379-6421

Association for Full Figured Women of Atlanta
(404) 243-6862

Association for the Health Enrichment of Large People
(see AHELP)

Association for Full Figured Women of Atlanta
(see also Lynell's World of Difference Production Company)
(404) 243-6862

Astárte: Woman by Design
24520 Hawthorne Boulevard
Torrance, CA 90505
(310) 373-0638
(800) 789-6626

At Large
4201 Neshaminy Boulevard, Suite 231
Bensalem, PA 19020
(215) 552-8534

Attitudes and Lace
(800) 519-5568
E-mail: lorilee@cris.com
http://shops.net/shops/showcase/

August Max Woman
P.O. Box 20919
Los Angeles, CA 90006
(213) 252-0412
(800) 778-7709

Aussie Connection
825 N.E. Broadway
Portland, OR 97232
(503) 284-2228
(800) 950-2668

Avenues Unlimited, Inc.
1199-K Avenida Acaso
Camarillo, CA 93012
(800) 598-9739

Avia Shoes
(503) 520-1500
(800) 345-2842

B. A. Mason
1251 First Avenue
Chippewa Falls, WI 54774
(800) 422-1000

BBW (Big Beautiful Woman)
P.O. Box 458
Mount Morris, IL 61054
(800) 707-5592 (subscriptions)
or
LFP, Inc. (*BBW* offices)
9171 Wilshire Boulevard, Suite 300
Beverly Hills, CA 90210

BBW Express
P.O. Box 458
Mount Morris, IL 61054
(800) 453-7277 (credit card orders only)

BBW Pantyhose
Call for nearest store
(800) 554-2522

B. R. Anderson Enterprises
5308 Chateau Place
Minneapolis, MN 55417

BR News
3208 Guadelupe
Austin, TX 78705
(512) 454-9110

BABES!
Point Hueneme, CA
(805) 986-9777

Baby Becoming
P.O. Box 7238
Cumberland, RI 02864
(401) 658-0688
E-mail: babybecoming@igc.apc.org

Yvonne G. Bach
2 Penn Center Plaza, #1204
15th and JFK Boulevard
Philadelphia, PA 19102
(215) 496-9900

Back to Basics Soft-Wear
P.O. Box 432
Bahama, NC 27503-0432
(919) 477-5669

Balance of Nature Publishing
Box 637
Cordova, TN 38088

Barb's Abundant Jewels
2000 North Racine
Chicago, IL 60614

Barbara Stone Designs
1800 Shasta Street, Suite B
Redding, CA 96001
(916) 246-1927
(800) 393-9214

Barely Nothings
897 Oak Park Boulevard, Suite 163
Pismo Beach, CA 93449-3293
(805) 489-5592
(800) 422-7359

Bart's WaterSports
Highway 13, P.O. Box 294
North Webster, IN 46555
(800) 348-5016

Bartleby Press
11141 Georgia Avenue
Silver Spring, MD 20902
(800) 448-1076

Bartley Collection
3 Airpark Drive
Easton, MD 21601
(301) 820-7722
(800) 227-8539

Basic Comfort, Inc.
445 Lincoln Street
Denver, CO 80203
(800) 456-8687

Bass Pro Shops
1935 South Campbell
Springfield, MO 65807
(417) 887-1915

Basta Sole
4901 East 12th Street
Oakland, CA 94601
(510) 436-6788

Beautiful Babes
6705 North Seneca
Portland, OR 97203
(503) 286-1119

Beautiful Girls
P.O. Box 1137
W-7737 Bad Durrheim
Germany

Beauty Trends
(a Revlon company)
P.O. Box 9323
Hialeah, FL 33014-9323
(800) 777-7772

Bellamy Manufacturing
222 North 11th Street
Clarksville, TN 37040
(615) 645-8249

Belle **Magazine**
475 Park Avenue South
New York, NY 10016
(212) 689-7933
(800) 877-5549

The Belly Project
R.R. 1, Box 2273
Morrill, ME 04952
(207) 342-5703

Edith Benay
(415) 621-4449

Bench Manufacturing Company
P.O. Box 158
Concord, MA 01742
(508) 371-3080

Bencone Casuals
The Comfort Corner
P.O. Box 649
Nashua, NH 03061
(603) 598-4785
(800) 735-4994

Bencone Professional Uniforms
121 Carver Avenue
Westwood, NJ 07675
also
P.O. Box 251
Winston-Salem, NC 27101-0251
(800) 521-5030
(800) 631-4602 (orders)

Bentley's
2122 Shattuck Avenue
Berkeley, CA 94704
(415) 843-7595

Berlin Glove Co.
(see MidWestern Sport Togs)

Karen Bert
12830 Burbank Boulevard, #205
Valley Village, CA 91607

Betsy & Company
P.O. Box 1911
Philadelphia, PA 19105-1911
(800) 772-3879

Bianchi
(800) 669-2346

Big Ad Productions
P.O. Box 14725
San Francisco, CA 94114
or
592 Castro Street, Suite A
San Francisco, CA 94114
(specify *Big Ad* subscription department or
    Heavy Duty subscription department)
(415) 626-6350
(800) 783-2441 (*Big Ad*)
(800) 672-3287 (*Heavy Duty*)
E-mail: BigAdMag@aol.com
http://mediapub.com/bigad

Big Ad Personals Line
(900) 484-2441

Big, Bad & Beautiful
19225 Ventura Boulevard
Tarzana, CA 91356
(818) 345-3593
(800) 347-3593

Big and Beautiful
P.O. Box 1304
Weatherford, TX 76086

Big, Beautiful Images
(310) 428-3772

Big But Beautiful
P.O. Box 1222
Media, PA 19063
(215) 565-3914
(215) 565-1717

Big & Bold
P.O. Box 10
Pine City, NY 14871
(607) 733-0068
(717) 537-6024

Big, Bold & Beautiful
1263 Bay Street
Toronto, Ontario
Canada M5R 2C1
(416) 923-4673
(800) 668-4673

Big Day at the Beach
P.O. Box 271
Bryn Mawr, CA 92318
(909) 653-1654

The Big Difference
P.O. Box 66656
Los Angeles, CA 90066-6656
(310) 398-5113
http://www.rotunda.com/Big_Diff/
    home.html

The Big Difference Talking Personals
(800) 752-5179 (place ad)
(900) 988-4237 (retrieve messages)

Big Dreams
P.O. Box 2195
Saint Petersburg, FL 33731
(813) 824-7720

Big Guys
Locust Grove Plaza
1692 Clements Bridge Road
Deptford, NJ 08096
(609) 696-9055
(800) 848-8255

Big in Pictures
109 Wareham Road
Corfe Mullen, Wimbourne
Dorset BH21 3JZ New Zealand
Phone: 01860 356149

Big Magazines Ltd.
P.O. Box 381, 4 Selsdon Way
London E14 9GL
United Kingdom

Big Men/Stout Men's Shop
59 Temple Place/2nd floor
501 Washington Street
Boston, MA 02111
(617) 542-5397
(617) 542-7610
(800) 458-5650

The Big Picture
(805) 765-7512 (modem)
(805) 765-6494

Big Sensations
(617) 893-1985

Big Stitches by Jan
2423 Douglas Street
San Pablo, CA 94806
(phone not listed by request)

Big Stuff Dances
Emeryville, CA
(805) 874-4702
E-mail: aleashka@aol.com
http://www.wine.com/obaby/bigstuff.html

Bizon
2000 Glen Echo Road, Suite 207
Nashville, TN 37215
Attn: Dominique
(615) 298-4420

Nancy Blair
(see Star River Productions, Inc.)

Blair Shoppe
220 Hickory Street
Warren, PA 16366
(800) 458-6057 (customer service)
(800) 458-2000

Kelly Bliss
(see Work It Out, Inc.)

Bob Abrams Photography
(213) 651-4107

Body Image Task Force
P.O. Box 934
Santa Cruz, CA 95061-0934
(408) 457-4838
E-mail: datkins@blue.weeg.uiowa.edu

Body-Mind Productions
88 West Goulding Street
Sherborn, MA 01770

Body-Pride: Redefining Beauty
78 Pleasant Boulevard, Box #1015
Toronto, Ontario
Canada M4T 1K2

Body Trust
2110 Overland Avenue, Suite 120
Billings, MT 59102
(800) 321-9499

Body Webs
4418 Cypress Mill Road
Kissimmee, FL 34746
(407) 870-2701

Bond van Formaat
p/a Voorde 5
P.O. Box 216
5500 TG Veldhoven
The Netherlands
+31 40 254 05 64 (Dutch language only)
E-mail: elly@win.tue.nl (group member
   who speaks fluent English)

Books in Focus
P.O. Box 77005
San Francisco, CA 94107
(800) 463-6285

Born Free Motorcoach, Inc.
Highway 169 North, P.O. Box 39
Humboldt, IA 50548
(515) 332-3755
(800) 247-1835

Bosom Buddies
P.O. Box 6138
Kingston, NY 12401
(914) 338-2038

Botero
347 Nashua Mall, Suite 288
Nashua, NH 03063
(603) 883-5546
(800) 362-5167

Bountiful Productions
(used to be More Is OK)
18-53 College Point Boulevard, Suite 14
Flushing, NY 11356
(401) 761-6598

Brass Beds Direct
P.O. Box 78370
Los Angeles, CA 90016
(213) 737-6865
(800) 242-1330

Breckenridge Outdoor Education Center
P.O. Box 697
Breckenridge, CO 80424
(303) 453-6422

Brega
3512 Sunset Boulevard, #103
Los Angeles, CA 90026

Sue Brett
P.O. Box 8301
Indianapolis, IN 46283-8301
(800) 784-8001

Bridal Originals
(312) 467-6140
(800) 876-4696

Brooks
(206) 488-3131
(800) 227-6657

Brookstone Hard-to-Find Tools
5 Vose Farm Road
Peterborough, NH 03460-0803
(800) 926-7000

The Brotherhood of Girth
2210 C Bank Street, Suite 104
Ottawa, Ontario
Canada K1V 1J5
E-mail: ian_maclatchie@ccigate.acdi-
    cida.gc.ca
http://home.sprynet.com/sprynet/imac

Brownstone Woman
P.O. Box 3356
Salisbury, MD 21802
(800) 221-2468

Brie Fan Club (BFC)
P.O. Box 1202
Waltham, MA 02254-1202

Bruce Medical Supply
411 Waverly Oaks Road
P.O. Box 9166
Waltham, MA 02254
(800) 225-8446

Buf Publications, Inc.
63 Grand Avenue
River Edge, NJ 07661

Bulk Male
P.O. Box 300352
Denver, CO 80203
(303) 784-5823

Bull Publishing
P.O. Box 208
Palo Alto, CA 94302
(415) 322-2855

Bullfrog Films
P.O. Box 149
Oley, PA 19547
(800) 543-3764

Burda
GLP International
P.O. Box 9868
Englewood, NJ 07631-1123
(212) 736-7455

Burke Mobility Products
1800 Merriam Lane
Kansas City, KS 66106
(913) 772-5658
(913) 722-2614 (fax)
(800) 255-4147

The Bust Stop
8270 East 71st Street
Tulsa, OK 74133
(800) 858-3887

Butcher Block & More Furniture
1600 South Clinton Street
Chicago, IL 60616

By Ro! Designs
567 West 5th Street, Suite 1
San Pedro, CA 90731
(310) 221-0509

C.D.C.
4326 S.E. Woodstock Boulevard,
   Suite 233
Portland, OR 97206

C. Flaherty
634 North Glenoaks, Suite 4
Burbank, CA 91502

Cabela's
812 13th Street
Sidney, NE 69160
(800) 237-8888
(800) 237-4444

Cahall's Brown Duck Catalog
P.O. Box 450
Mount Orab, OH 45154
(800) 445-9675

Caldera Company
P.O. Box 1892
South San Francisco, CA 91083

California Rainbow Tie Dye
E-mail: jholland@mcn.org
http://www.catalog.com/giftshop/tiedye/
   td.htm

Campmor
Order Department
Box 700-E
Saddle River, NJ 07458-0700
(800) 525-4784 (product information)
(800) 226-7667 (orders only)

Cameo Coutures, Inc.
(see Colesce Couture)

Can-Do Products
27 East Mall
Plainview, NY 11803
(800) 537-2118

Canterbury Designs, Inc.
P.O. Box 5730
Sherman Oaks, CA 91413
(213) 937-7111

Carlson Publishing
P.O. Box 888
Los Alamitos, CA 90720

Carmi Couture
(212) 921-7658

Carole Little
102 East King Boulevard
Los Angeles, CA 90011
(800) 816-7951

Carol's Creative Corner
(800) 695-4005
E-mail: carolscorner@delphi.com

Carolina Made
400 Indian Trail Road
Indian Trail, NC 28079
(800) 222-1409

Casablanca
6255 Barfield Road, Suite 165
Atlanta, GA 30328
(404) 705-9494

Toni L. Cassista
P.O. Box 2968
Santa Cruz, CA 95063
E-mail: TLC1248@aol.com

Castles Direct
P.O. Box 202724
Houston, TX 78720-2724
(800) 424-1008

Casual Male Big & Tall
http://www.thinkbig.com/

Cathy O
2101 West Alice Avenue
Phoenix, AZ 85021
(800) 878-2086

Celtic Costumes
1777 Woodlawn, #G-18
Upland, CA 91786
(909) 981-7248

Centerville BBS
(214) 275-4454 (modem)

Chadwick's of Boston
One Chadwick Place
P.O. Box 1600
Brockton, MA 02403-1600
(508) 583-6600
(800) 525-6650

Champagne & Lace Boutique
1850 Union Street, #1
San Francisco, CA 94123
(415) 776-6900

Chefwear, U.S.A.
833 North Orleans, fourth floor
Chicago, IL 60610-3049
(312) 654-2200
(800) 568-2433 (orders)

Cheney
2445 South Calhoun Road
P.O. Box 51188
New Berlin, WI 53151-0188
(800) 508-1222

Cherokee Designs by Judy
401 South Lee Street
Fort Gibson, OK 74434

Chic Full-Figure Fashion
(312) 868-3884
(800) 347-8453
E-mail: chichexpo@suba.com

Chief Postal Inspector
U.S. Postal Service
Room 3100
475 L'Enfant Plaza SW
Washington, DC 20260-6444
(800) 654-8896

Chilbert's & Company
408 Mill Street
Lock Drawer #151
Coraopolis, PA 15108-1608
(412) 264-3700
(800) 289-2889

Chock
74 Orchard Street
New York, NY 10002
(212) 473-1929
(800) 222-0020

Christos, Inc.
575 8th Avenue
New York, NY 10018
(212) 714-2496

Chub Club
P.O. Box 11
St. Louis, MO 63006
(314) 758-7534 (Jeanie)
(314) 394-3890 (Barb)

Chubby Companions
21 Ulundi Street
Radcliffe, Greater Manchester
M26 3AN England
Phone: 0161 724 0791

Chubby Connections
P.O. Box 1110
Levittown, PA 19058
(215) 949-0370

Clark's
(800) 425-2757

Classic Country Chairs
3365 West 201st Street
Farmington, MN 55024
(612) 460-6184

Clothz Biz
7250 Auburn Boulevard, #R-150
Citrus Heights, CA 95610

Clotilde
2 Sew Smart Way B8031
Stevens Point, WI 54481-8031
(715) 341-2824
(800) 772-2891

Club 14 Plus
12228 Venice Boulevard, Suite 172
Los Angeles, CA 90066
(213) 954-0346

CME Medical Equipment
1130 Donamy Glen
Scotch Plains, NJ 07076
(201) 561-0696

The Coca-Cola Catalog
2515 East 43rd Street
P.O. Box 182264
Chattanooga, TN 37422
(800) 872-6531

Colesce Couture
9004 Ambassador Row
Dallas, TX 75247
(214) 631-4860

Collage Video
5390 Main Street N.E.
Minneapolis, MN 55421
(800) 433-6769

Color Me Big
P.O. Box 9773
San Bernardino, CA 92427
(909) 887-8969

Colorado Coyote
1366 South Elm Street
Denver, CO 80222
(303) 758-5399

College of DuPage
22nd and Lambert Road
Glen Ellyn, IL 60137
(630) 942-2356

Comfort Corner
Box 649
Nashua, NH 03061
(800) 735-4994

Comfort House
189 Frelinghuysen Avenue
Newark, NJ 07114-1595
(800) 359-7701

Comfortably Yours
2515 East 43rd Street
P.O. Box 182216
Chattanooga, TN 37422-7216
(800) 521-0097

Company of Women
102 Main Street
P.O. Box 742
Nyack, NY 10960-0742
or
P.O. Box 2526
Kearneysville, WV 25430
(800) 937-1193

The Competition Group
390 Fifth Avenue
New York, NY 10018
(212) 268-9707

CompuServe (CIS)
(800) 848-8990 (customer service)
(800) 848-8199 (new customers,
   software and information)

Concepts in Comfort
9 Circus Time Road
South Portland, ME 04106
(207) 775-4312

The Consumer Advocate
U.S. Postal Service
Washington, DC 20260-2200
(202) 268-2284

ConvaQuip Industries
P.O. Box 3417
Abilene, TX 79604
(800) 637-8436

Charlotte Cooper
8 Hanley Court
Hanley Road
London N4 3QB England

Cooperative Extension, Nutritional Sciences
Morgan Hall, Room 9
University of California
Berkeley, CA 94720-3104
(510) 642-2790

Cornucopia
At the Appleworks
P.O. Box 01451
Harvard, MA 01451
(617) 772-0023

Cotton Threads Clothing
Route 2, Box 90
Hallettsville, TX 77964
(409) 562-2153

Council of Better Business Bureaus
(703) 276-0100

Council on Size and Weight Discrimination
P.O. Box 305
Mt. Marion, NY 21045
(914) 679-1209

Country Bed Shop
Richardson Road, RR 1, Box 65
Ashby, MA 01431
(508) 386-7550

Country Store
5925 Country Lane
P.O. Box 990
Greendale, WI 53129-0990
(800) 558-1013

Coward Shoes
Palo Verde at 34th
P.O. Box 27800
Tucson, AZ 85726-7800
(602) 748-8600
(800) 362-8410

COY
24843 Del Prado, Suite 249
Dana Point, CA 92629
(714) 496-7042

Craftmatic Comfort Manufacturing
2500 Interplex Drive
Trevose, PA 19047
(800) 458-4170

Creative Health Products
5148 Saddle Ridge Road
Plymouth, MI 48170
(313) 996-5900
(800) 742-4478

Creative Square Dancer
Route 9-D, Box 423
Hughsonville, NY 12537
(914) 297-8504

Crossing Press
P.O. Box 1048
Freedom, CA 95019
(800) 777-1048

Crossroads Country Store
Route 1, Box 201
Edgemoor, SC 29712
(803) 328-8076

Cruise World Representatives
11656 Lake Willis Drive
Orlando, FL 32821
(407) 239-4061
(407) 239-4232 (fax)
(800) 874-3220

Carol Cullum
290 Nevada Street
San Francisco, CA 94110
(415) 863-5300

Cunningham, Escott, Dipene (CED)
10635 Santa Monica Boulevard,
   Suite 135
Los Angeles, CA 90025
(310) 475-7573

Custom Coat Co.
(see Midwestern Sport Togs)

Cyberbaby
(860) 749-1696
E-mail: hm25@tiac.net
http://www.tiac.net/users/hm25/bra.html

Cynthia Rae—For Well Rounded
   Women
4617 Excelsior Boulevard
Minneapolis, MN 55416
(612) 929-7593
(800) 929-7593

D D & E Designs
P.O. Box 32877
Palm Beach Gardens, FL 33420

DJ's Positive Images
8110 214th Place S.W.
Edmonds, WA 98026
(206) 774-3732

DJ's Plus Sizes
4931 South Orange Avenue
Orlando, FL 32806

D & M Enterprises
P.O. Box 290630
Brooklyn, NY 11229-0011
(718) 998-0546

D. P. Moves
P.O. Box 5201
San Jose, CA 95150-5201
(408) 241-1510

Dallas Fashion
34 West 37th Street
New York, NY 10018
(212) 967-9744

Damart
3 Front Street
Rollinsford, NY 03805
(800) 258-7300

Dan Wilson & Company
P.O. Box 566
Fuquay-Varina, NC 27526
(919) 552-4945

Danskin Plus
350 Fifth Avenue
New York, NY 10018
(800) 283-2675

Daphne
473 Amsterdam Avenue
New York, NY 10024
(212) 877-5073
or
6399 Wilshire Boulevard
Los Angeles, CA 90048
(213) 653-5585

David & Lee Model Agency
70 West Hubbard, Suite 200
Chicago, IL 60610
Attn: Karen Marshall
(312) 661-0500

Decent Exposures
P.O. Box 27206
Seattle, WA 98125-1606
(206) 364-4540
(800) 505-4949 (request brochure)

Defender Industries
P.O. Box 820, 255 Main Street
New Rochelle, NY 10801-0820
(914) 632-2318

The Dehner Company, Inc.
3614 Martha Street
Omaha, NE 68105
(402) 342-7788

Delphi
(800) 695-4005 (customer service)

Desert Rain Mercantile Company
4705 Sanders Road
Tucson, AZ 85743
(800) 771-9771

Designs by Elba Manfredi
34 Lutz Drive
Valley Stream, NY 11580
(516) 561-7187

Designers Unlimited
(see Adaptations with Attitude)

Designs by Norvell
P.O. Box 37
Alexandria, TN 37012
(615) 529-2831

Deva Lifewear
P.O. Box 5AJS
Westhope, ND 58793-0266
(800) 222-8024, ext. 5AJS

Diamond Collection
(212) 302-0210

Dicke e.V.
P.O. Box 410 105
34063 Kassel, Germany
Phone: 0561/39018
E-mail: mrp@prian.Physik.Uni-
    Dortmund.DE
http://prian.physik.uni-dortmund.de/
    ~mrp/dicke

Diet Breakers
18 Durham Terrace
London, England W2 5PB
Phone: 071 221 8479
or
Diet Breakers UK
Church Cottage
Barford St. Michael
Banbury, Oxon OX15 OUA England
    Phone: 0869-37070

Diet/Weight Liberation
CRESP
Anabel Taylor Hall
Cornell University
Ithaca, NY 14853
(607) 257-0563

Dimensions (organization)
Box 7256
Canton, OH 44705
(216) 649-9809

Dimensions **(magazine)**
P.O. Box 640
Folsom, CA 95763

Dimensions **Personals**
(900) 420-5575

Dimensions Plus Models
P.O. Box 141078
Cleveland, OH 44114
(330) 649-9809
(800) 663-3503

The Dinner Group
P.O. Box 92994
Long Beach, CA 90809-2994
(310) 830-0810

Dion-Jones, Ltd.
3226 South Aberdeen
Chicago, IL 60608
(312) 927-1113

Direct Cinema Limited
P.O. Box 10003
Santa Monica, CA 90410-9003
(310) 396-4774

Direct Marketing Association
(mail-order action line)
1101 17th Street NW, Suite 705
Washington, DC 20036
(202) 347-1222

The Disney Catalog
One Disney Drive
P.O. Box 29144
Shawnee Mission, KS 66201-9144
(800) 247-8996

Distant Caravans
P.O. Box 5254
Reno, NV 89513
(702) 746-0416

Distinctions
8650 Genessee Avenue, Suite 200
San Diego, CA 92122
(619) 550-1775
(800) 467-6363

D. C. Dixon
P.O. Box 60106
Santa Barbara, CA 93160
(phone not listed by request)

Double D Productions
P.O. Box 12393
Augusta, GA 30914-2393.

Double XX Riders
3256 West Country Road 72
Fort Collins, CO 80524

Drysdales, Inc.
1555 North 107th East Avenue
Tulsa, OK 74116
(617) 982-8681
(800) 608-9800

Dugent Publishing
Subscription Department
2600 Douglas Road, Suite 600
Coral Gables, FL 33134
(305) 443-2370

Dunn's Inc.
1 Madison Avenue
Grand Junction, TN 38039-0449
Special sizes and customer service
(800) 367-2940
(800) 223-8667

Dvora Dreams
P.O. Box 9287
Anaheim, CA 92812
(714) 520-3232

E Style
(by Spiegel and *Ebony* magazine)
Suite A
P.O. Box 182556
Columbus, OH 43218-2556
(800) 237-8953

E. T. Moore Company
3100 North Hopkins Road
Richmond, VA 23224
(804) 231-1823

ETR Associates
(800) 321-4407

Easy Spirit
(800) 327-9242

Eddie Bauer
P.O. Box 3700
Seattle, WA 98124-3700
(800) 426-6253
(800) 645-7467

Dean Edell, M.D. (medical journalist)
900 Front Street
San Francisco, CA 941
(415) 954-7276

Eden
(818) 441-8715

18th Century Woodworks
Gordon Clidence
272 James Trail
West Kingston, RI 02892
(401) 539-2558

Electronic Erotica BBS
(313) 854-1428 (modem)

Electropedic Products
907 Hollywood Way
Burbank, CA 91505
(800) 662-4548

Elegance at Large
3200 Adams Avenue, Suite 105
San Diego, CA 92116
(619) 284-0900

Elianna
7758 Via Rosa Maria
Burbank, CA 91504
(212) 622-8868

Elite Model Management
212 West Superior
Chicago, IL 60610
(312) 943-3226
or
181 14th Street
Atlanta, GA 30309
(404) 872-7444

Elk River Enterprises
P.O. Box 7701
Monroe, OK 73153

Emerging Visions Enterprises (EVE)
P.O. Box 5516
New York, NY 10185-5516
(800) 759-7747

Employment Discrimination Project
Legal Assistance Foundation of Chicago
343 South Dearborn
Chicago, IL 60604
(312) 431-2270

Encore
(Nordstrom)
1501 Fifth Avenue
Seattle, WA 98101-1603
(800) 695-8000

Enchanted Collection, Ltd.
P.O. Box 235
1031 South Main Street
Kalispell, MT 59901
(800) 408-0087
E-mail: enchant@netrix.net
http://www.netrix.net/enchantweb/
    Welcome.html

Enlargements
4430 West Oakton Street
Skokie, IL 60076
(847) 673-2550

Enrichments
P.O. Box 579
Hinsdale, IL 60521
(800) 323-5547

Entrance
P.O. Box 11627
Marina Del Ray, CA 90295
(213) 749-8369
(800) 800-2394

**Equal Employment Opportunity
    Library**
2401 East Street NW, Room 242
Washington, DC 20507
(204) 634-6990

Ernest Thompson Furniture
2618 Coors SW
Albuquerque, NM 87105
(505) 873-4652

Essence
P.O. Box 62
Hanover, PA 17333-0062
(717) 633-3347
(800) 882-8055

Essence by Esther
(714) 961-8884

Estar Fashions
5765 Arapahoe Road, Suite B
Boulder, CO 80303-1361
(303) 433-7732
(800) 967-8953

Ethnic Attitudes
210 College Square Shopping Center
Newark, DE 19713
(302) 368-8886

Ethnicity
25 Sweetbrier Road
East Granby, CT 06026
(800) 741-2376

Etonic
(800) 334-0008

Eve of Milady
(212) 302-0050

Exclusive Appeal
4809 Avenue N, Suite 306
Brooklyn, NY 11234
(718) 604-9297

Exotica International
(803) 245-5440

Expanding Mind Books
P.O. Box 9044
San Bernardino, CA 02427
(909) 887-9415

Extra!
P.O. Box 57194
Sherman Oaks, CA 91413

Extra Dimensions
P.O. Box 21025
Raleigh, NC 27619
(919) 831-8616

Extra Emphasis
P.O. Box 1725
Tahoe City, CA 96145
(800) 539-0030

F'Attitude Productions
P.O. Box 5362
Concord, CA 94524

Fabulous Fakes
(Donna Salyers' Fabulous Furs)
700 Madison Avenue
Covington, KY 41011-2412
(606) 291-3300
(800) 848-4650

Fairbanks Scales
(816) 842-5300

Fairy Godmother at Large
133 South Murphy Avenue
Sunnyvale, CA 94086
(408) 737-7684

Far & Wide Source Guide
P.O. Box 1284
Wiarton, Ontario
Canada N0H 2T0
(800) 820-7403

Fashion Fit Pattern Service
http://www.finhost.fi/fashion/fashion.htm

Fashion Galaxy
P.O. Box 26
Hanover, PA 17333-0228
(717) 633-3343

Fashion Touches
P.O. Box 804
Bridgeport, CT 06601
(203) 333-7738

Fat Admirers News (FAN)
c/o I. Y. Murphy
P.O. Box 14822
Chicago, IL 60614-8222

Fat Chance Theatre
418 Marston Avenue
Madison, WI 53703

Fat Fantasy Line
(800) 934-7082
(900) 835-0260

Fat and Fit Group Health Action
1 Pink Lane
Newcastle-Upon-Tyne, England NE1
SDW

FaT GiRL
2215-R Market Street, #193
San Francisco, CA 94114
E-mail: airborne@sirius.com
http://www.fatgirl.factory.net

Fat and Happy Club
P.O. Box 99
Somerset, MA 02726

Fat and Terrific (FAT)
1080 San Miguel Road, #119
Concord, CA 94518-1341
E-mail: avery@ccnet.com
http://www.ccnet.com/~avery/place.html

Fat Is a Lesbian Issue
Lesbian and Gay Community Services
  Center
208 West 13th Street
New York, NY 10011-7702
E-mail: sestone@princeton.edu

FAT LIP Readers Theatre
P.O. Box 29963
Oakland, CA 94604
(510) 841-3438
E-mail: carolguy@netcom.com

Fat Lesbian Action Brigade (FLAB)
255-C King Street
Princeton, NJ 08540
(609) 924-9321 (Gail)
amy@interport.net

Fat Women's Group
Wesley House, Wild Ct.
London WC2B 5AU England

Fat!So?
P.O. Box 423464
San Francisco, CA 94142
(800) 643-2876
Email: marilyn@fatso.com
http://www.fatso.com/

The Fatimas
Contact: Rhonda Wood
(310) 693-1844

Fed Up
E-mail: getfedup@aol.com

Federal Trade Commission
Division of Enforcement
6th and Pennsylvania NW
Washington, DC 20580
(202) 326-3768

Femme Fancy
217 South Ellsworth
San Mateo, CA 94401
(415) 340-8392

Films by Raphael, Inc.
245 8th Avenue, Suite 138
New York, NY 10011

Fine and Fancy Lingerie Co.
2325 Third Street, #346
San Francisco, CA 94107
(415) 861-4576

Fingerhut
11 McLeland Road
St. Cloud, MN 56395

Fink
(212) 921-5683

Firebrand Books
141 The Commons
Ithaca, NY 14850
(607) 272-0000

Fit for a Queen
(see Lane Bryant and Roaman's)

Fit for Two
(call for information)
(707) 829-1360

Fit to Be Tried
4754 East Grant
Tucson, AZ 85712
(520) 881-6449
(800) 669-6409

Food and Drug Administration
5600 Fishers Lane
Rockville, MD 20857

Food and Nutrition Program
P.O. Box 356, Carlton
Victoria 3053 Australia
Phone: 03 660
E-mail: rosey@deakin.edu.au

Fontaine Agency
9255 Sunset Boulevard, Suite 727
Los Angeles, CA 90069
Attn: Carri
(213) 969-8398

For Play
540 North Santa Cruz Avenue, Suite 187
Los Gatos, CA 95030
(800) 464-8300

For You
(from Spiegel)
P.O. Box 6105
Rapid City, SD 57709-6105
(800) 345-4500

Ford 12+/Big Beauties
344 East 59th Street
Today's Woman Division
New York, NY
(212) 753-6500
or
957 North Cole Avenue
Los Angeles, CA 90038
(213) 462-7274

The Forgotten Woman
34-24 Hunters Point Avenue
Long Island City, NY 11101
(800) 839-1424

Franklin Custom Furniture
193 East Main Street
Franklin, NC 28734
(704) 369-7881

Frankly Carmen
1442 North Mandalay Road
Salt Lake City, UT 84116
(801) 531-8280
E-mail: franklycarmen@sisna.com

Frederick Shirt Co.
140 West Main Street
Fleetwood, PA 19522
(800) 247-1417

Frederick's of Hollywood
P.O. Box 229
Hollywood, CA 90078
(800) 323-9525

Kenneth I. Friedman
Beck and Eldergill
447 Center Street
Manchester, CT 06040
(203) 646-5606

Friedman's Shoes
209 Mitchell Street
Atlanta, GA 30303
(404) 524-1311
(800) 886-3668

From Here to Maternity
(purchasing information)
(702) 733-6667

Full Bloom
185 South Pearl
Denver, CO 80209
(303) 733-6264

Full Figure Design Company
490 South Stone Mountain-Lithonia
    Road, #59
Stone Mountain, GA 30088
(770) 413-9520
E-mail: fulfig@mindspring.com

Full Figure Woman's Lingerie
http://www.w2.com/docs2/a3/iasa.html

Full Fitness by Jazel
P.O. Box 40531
Philadelphia, PA 19106
(215) 386-5085

Full of Life
131 Halstead Avenue, Suite 232
Mamaroneck, NY 10543
(212) 388-8189

Furniture Makers Guild
1150 Tryon Avenue
P.O. Box 2081
High Point, NC 27261
(919) 884-4524

G & L Clothing
901 Locust
Des Moines, IA 50309
(800) 222-7027

GLP International
P.O. Box 9868
Englewood, NJ 07631-1123
(212) 736-7455
(201) 871-1010

Galina
(212) 564-1020

Gander Mountain, Inc.
Box 248, Highway W
Wilmot, WI 53192
(414) 862-2331
(800) 426-3371
(800) 558-9410 (orders)

Victor Gates
552 Lancelot Drive
North Salt Lake, UT 84054-2230

Gendron, Inc.
P.O. Box 197
Archbold, OH 43502
(800) 537-2531

GEnie
(800) 638-9636

Gilda Marx
(800) 825-2639

Ginza Collection
(800) 654-7375

Girth & Mirth Clubs
(see Affiliated Big Men's Clubs)

Gitano
(check local department stores)

GlamourPuss
662 West Huntington Drive, Suite 339
Monrovia, CA 91016
(818) 357-7277

Amy Glin
3153 Hollyridge Drive
Hollywood, CA 90068
(213) 467-7944

Global Business Furniture
National Order Processing Center
22 Harbor Park Drive, Department 9417
Port Washington, NY 11050
(800) 472-0101

Glori-Us
(614) 444-7001

Gloria Vanderbilt
(check local department stores)

Goddess Greetings
20583 Painter Street, #D
Bend, OR 97701
(503) 389-6200
(800) 344-7338

Goddesses
P.O. Box 1008, JAF Station
New York, NY 10116
(718) 456-9119 (Nancy)
(718) 386-1076 (Joey)

Good Vibrations
RR #2, Box 317
Englishtown Road
Old Bridge, NJ 08857
(908) 251-5959

James Goodman
Persons with Disabilities Law Center
56 17th Avenue, NE
Atlanta, GA 30309
(404) 892-4200

Gotcha Covered
(formerly Blue Sky Designs)
P.O. Box 40443
Downey, CA 90239
(800) 767-1011

Grand Form Enterprises, Ltd.
P.O. Box 87000
North Vancouver, British Columbia
Canada V7L 4P6

Grand Kids Clothing
B. J. McCabe
Box 674, RR #1
Stroud, Ontario
Canada L0L 2M0
(705) 431-2933

The Grande Connection
(900) 776-1155

Great Changes Boutique
12516 Riverside Drive
North Hollywood, CA 91607
(818) 769-4626

Great Discoveries
150 Middlefield Court, Suite F
Brentwood, CA 94513
(800) 622-0192

Great Fit Patterns
2229 Northeast Burnside, Suite 305
Gresham, OR 97030
(503) 665-3125

Great Goddess Collection
(see Star River Productions, Inc.)

The Greater Salt Lake Clothing Co.
1955 East 4800 South
Salt Lake City, UT 84117
(801) 273-8700

Greater Woman
19269 Ellison Circle
Omaha, NE 68134
(800) 689-6626

Greater Woman Model Search
10360 Ellison Circle
Omaha, NE 68134

The Green Pepper
3918 West First Avenue
Eugene, OR 97402
(503) 345-6665
(800) 767-5684

G.U.I.D.E.
University of Pennsylvania, Box 745 HUP
Philadelphia, PA 19104-4283
(215) 573-3525

Gürze Books
P.O. Box 2238
Carlsbad, CA 92018
(800) 756-7533

GynoCentric
P.O. Box 861
Iowa City, IA 52244-0861

Gypsy Moon
1780 Massachusetts Avenue
Cambridge, MA 02140
(617) 876-7095 (customer service)
(800) 955-Gypsy

Hanes Fitting Pretty
(800) 522-0889

Hanes/L'eggs/Bali/Playtex
P.O. Box 748
Rural Hall, NC 27098
(800) 300-2600

Hangouts
1328 Pearl Street Mall
Boulder, CO 80302
(303) 442-2533
(800) 426-4688

Hanover House
P.O. Box 2
Hanover, PA 17333-0002
(717) 633-3377

Harriet Carter
Department 15
North Wales, PA 19455
(215) 361-5151

Harriet's Tailoring
P.O. Box 1363
Winchester, VA 22604
(703) 667-2541

Healthy Weight Journal
Healthy Living Institute
Route 2, Box 905
Hettinger, ND 58639
(701) 567-2646

Heart Inc. Tuxedos
(408) 462-4115

Heart's Delight
1011 Boren Avenue, #178
Seattle, WA 98104
(206) 329-4761

Heidi's Pages and Petticoats
810 El Caminito
Livermore, CA 94550

Heinz Gift Shop
P.O. Box 18714
San Antonio, TX 78218
(210) 657-9421

Helen Wells Agency
11711 North Meridian Street, #640
Carmel, IN 46032
(317) 843-5363

Hep Cat
P.O. Box 40223
Nashville, TN 37204
(615) 298-2980

Hepp Industries, Inc.
687 Kildare Crescent
Seaford, NY 11783
(516) 735-0032

HERSIZE
517 College Street, Suite 410
Toronto, Ontario
Canada M6G 4A2
(416) 656-5570

Hersey Custom Shoe Co.
RFD #3, Box 7390
Farmington, ME 04938
(207) 778-3103

Hidalgo
45 La Buena Vista
Wimberly, TX 78676-3657
(512) 847-5571

Liz Curtis Higgs
P.O. Box 43577
Louisville, KY 40253-0577
(800) 762-6565
E-mail: lizhiggs@aol.com

High Places
P.O. Box 620155
Littleton, CO 80162
(303) 973-3412

Hinsdale Furriers
33 East First Street
Hinsdale, IL 60521
(708) 323-1840

Hodder and Stoughton, mail order
Bookpoint
39 Milton Park
Abingdon, Oxon OX14 4TD
Phone: 0235 831700

Holy Cow, Inc.
P.O. Box 906
Middlebury, VT 05753
(802) 388-6737
(800) 543-2697

Homestead Furniture
114 Commerce Drive
Hesston, KS 67062
(316) 327-2711

The Horse's Mouth
131 South Orange Street
Escondido, CA 92025
(619) 737-9509

Hot Off the Tour
(209) 368-1211
(800) 991-1211

Hovis Jeans/Hoveland Manufacturing
3204 Reesy Road, Box 1717
Cody, WY 82414
(307) 587-5233
(800) 383-4684

Dan Howard
(800) 468-6700 (for nearest location)

Hue Q
(check local department stores)

HUES (Hear Us Emerging Sisters), Inc.
P.O. Box 7778
Ann Arbor, MI 48107-8226
(313) 971-0023
(313) 971-0450 (fax)
(800) 483-7482 (subscriptions)
http://www.lifeplay.net/magazines/hues/
   hues.html

HUGS International, Inc.
Box 102A, RR#3
Portage la Prairie, Manitoba
Canada R1N 3A3
(800) 565-4847
E-mail: lomichin@portage.net

Hunt Galleries, Inc.
2920 Highway 127 North
P.O. Box 2324
Hickory, NC 28603
(704) 324-9934
(800) 248-3876

Hy Fishman Furs
305 Seventh Avenue
New York, NY 10001
(212) 627-4920

Hysteria, the Women's Humor
   Magazine
Box 8581 Brewster Station
Bridgeport, CT 06605
(203) 333-9399

I. Spiewak
505 Eighth Avenue
New York, NY 10018
(212) 695-1620
(800) 223-6850

I.Y.M.
P.O. Box 148222
Chicago, IL 60614-8222

Ilissa
(212) 967-5222

Imperial Wear
48 West 48th Street
New York, NY 10036
(212) 719-2590
(800) 344-6132

Impression Bridal
10850 Wilcrest
Houston, TX 77099
(713) 530-6695
(800) BRIDAL-1

In Grand Form Enterprises
#5-1272 Emery Place
North Vancouver, British Columbia
Canada

Inclinator Co.
2200 Paxton Street
P.O. Box 1557
Harrisburg, PA 17105-1557
(717) 234-0941

Independent Living Aids, Inc.
(see Can-Do Products)

Innerworks/Food for Thought
2321 East Avenue H, #2103
Grand Prairie, TX 75050
(214) 606-1160

International Male
741 "F" Street
P.O. Box 129027
San Diego, CA 92112-9027
(619) 544-9939
(800) 293-9333

Intimate Appeal
Arizona Mail Order Company, Inc.
Palo Verde at 34th
P.O. Box 27800
Tucson, AZ 85726-7800
(520) 747-5000

Intimate Attitudes
3240 East 26th Street
Vernon, CA 90023
(213) 261-0265
(800) 421-9359

Intimate Encounters
540 North Santa Cruz, #187
Los Gatos, CA 95030
(800) 464-8300

Invenco
P.O. Box 3480
Lynchburg, VA 24503
(804) 845-2529
(800) 440-9588

It's a Revolution
1870 North Vermont Avenue,
    Department 530
Los Angeles, CA 90027
(213) 661-1431

It's a Secret Plus
P.O. Box 5001
Englewood, CO 80155-5001
(303) 220-9311
(800) 390-3528

The J
Western Division
507 East 10th
Spokane, WA 99202
(509) 624-4795

J. Jill Ltd.
P.O. Box 3006, Winterbrook Way
Meredith, NH 03253
(800) 642-9989

J. Lumarel Corporation
801 South University Drive, #C-110
Plantation, FL 33324
(800) 606-1816

J.C. Penney
Big and Extra Tall Men, Big Kids,
    Workwear, For Your Special Needs, It's
    Totally for Kids, Bridal Collection,
    Fashion Influences, Uniforms and
    Scrubs, Women's Sizes 16W and Up,
    Uniforms, Especially for Talls, Simply
    for Sports, Scouts, Class Favorites
(800) 222-6161

J.D. Products
P.O. Box 5442
Indian Rocks, FL 34635

J W Ramàge
P.O. Box 442
Lafayette, CA 94549-0442
(800) 715-7587

JWO
(415) 621-0555

Meyers Jacobsen
671 South Riverside Drive, #4
Palm Springs, CA 92264

Jalon Enterprises
P.O. Box 751014
Forest Hills Station, NY 11375
or
500 Seventh Avenue
New York, NY 10018
(212) 398-0855
(800) 316-2877
http://www.jalon.com

Jamin' Leathers
(518) 581-9668
E-mail: jamin@leathercat.com
http://www.leathercat.com

JaneEtte, Inc.
P.O. Box 26458
Tucson, AZ 85726
(602) 746-9474

Jasco Uniform Company
P.O. Box 677
Northbrook, IL 60065-0677
(800) 222-4445

Jasmine
(708) 519-7778

Jenny Gapp (JG:2)
P.O. Box 6545
Long Beach, CA 90806-6545
(310) 492-9100

Jessica McClintock Inc.
1400 Sixteenth Street
San Francisco, CA 94103

Jim Hjelm
(212) 764-6960

Joan Bartram Designs
27 Marsh Street
Newport, RI 02840
(401) 847-2519

Johansen Brothers Shoe Co., Inc.
1915 West Main
Corning, AR 72422-2499
(800) 624-9079

John Sun Silks
3935 East Broadway, Suite 271
Long Beach, CA 90803

Johnni's Treasures
762 Elochoman Valley
Cathlamet, WA 98612
(360) 795-3946

Jozell Fashions Plus
Department R., P.O. Box 218
3470 McClure Bridge Road
Duluth, GA 30136

Judi Piatkus Publishers Ltd.
5 Windmill Street
London, England W1P 1HF

Julen Furs
(703) 525-0510

Julianna's
5192 Bell Avenue
Cincinnati, OH 45242
(513) 891-4970

Junonia
The Minnesota Building, Suite 216
46 East 4th Street
Saint Paul, MN 55101
(612) 224-9497
(800) 671-0175 (customer service)
(800) 586-6642

Jus-Lin Belts
4757 West Park, #106-410
Plano, TX 75093
(phone not listed by request)

Just Big Sportswear
4700 Rozzelles Ferry Road
Charlotte, NC 28216
(704) 391-3000

Just My Size
P.O. Box 748
Rural Hall, NC 27098
(800) 522-9567

Just Right!
(Appleseeds)
30 Tozer Road
P.O. Box 1020
Beverly, MA 01915-0720
(800) 767-6666

Just·4·U Jewelry
Geri Fosseen, owner
P.O. Box 35
Radcliffe, Iowa 50230
(800) 298-4867

K-Log, Inc.
P.O. Box 5
Zion, IL 60099-0005
(800) 872-6611

K. S. Jackson
1622 North Cheyenne
Tulsa, OK 74106
(918) 592-4023

Kaiser-Permanente
1950 Franklin, 17th floor
Oakland, CA 94612
(415) 987-3107
(415) 259-4546

Karl's Woodworking Mill
1104 State Street
Norton, KS 67654
(800) 342-7793

Katarzyna Zaremba
Krotex-Poland
UL Poznanska 7 M 9
00-680 Warszawa Poland
Phone: (48-2) 628 39 03

Keltic Kate's Tams
615 John Muir Drive, #519
San Francisco, CA 94132
(415) 239-7619

Kenneth D. Lynch and Sons, Inc.
Wilton, CT 06897
(203) 762-8363

Key Industries
(800) 835-0365 (purchasing information)

Kim Dawson Agency
P.O. Box 585060
Dallas, TX 75258
(214) 638-2414

The King Size Co.
P.O. Box 8385
Indianapolis, IN 46283-8385
(800) 846-1600
(800) 682-8095 (TDD)
(800) 682-8109 (fax)

Kishu's East-West Fashions
Kowloon, Hong Kong
E-mail: suits@netcom.com

Klein Design, Inc.
99 Sadler Street
Gloucester, MA 01930
(508) 281-5276

Kohler Company
Kohler, WI 53044
(800) 456-4537

Krüh Knits
P.O. Box 1587
Avon, CT 06001
(800) 248-5647

Kwik-Sew
3000 Washington Avenue N
North Minneapolis, MN 55422
(800) 328-3953

LA Designs
P.O. Box 6405, Department B
Woodland Hills, CA 91365

L B W by L. Bates
1900 Walker Avenue
Monrovia, CA 91016
(213) 627-7554
(800) 305-1330

L'eggs Just My Size
P.O. Box 6000
Rural Hall, NC 27098
(800) 522-0889

L. L. Bean
Freeport, ME 04033-0001
(800) 221-4221
(800) 545-0090 (TDD)

La Costa Spa
(800) 522-6782

Lynette Labinger
Roney and Labinger
344 Wickenden Street
Providence, RI 02903
(401) 421-9794

Lady Grace Stores, Inc.
P.O. Box 128
61 Exchange Street
Malden, MA 02148
(617) 322-1721
(800) 922-0504

Lands' End, Inc.
1 Lands' End Lane
Dodgeville, WI 53595
(800) 356-4444
(608) 935-6170 (international)
(800) 541-3459 (hearing impaired)

Lane Bryant
Customer Service
P.O. Box 8320
Indianapolis, IN 46283-8320
(213) 613-9500 (corporate office)
(800) 477-7070
(800) 456-7161 (hearing impaired)

Langlitz Leathers, Inc.
2443 Southeast Division
Portland, OR 97202
(503) 235-0959

Large Encounters
P.O. Box 364
Island Park, NY 11558
(718) 322-0700

Large Encounters Newsletter and Chat Line
(900) 226-0344

Large and Lovely Bridal Center
381 Sunrise Highway
Lynbrook, NY 11563
(516) 599-7100

Large As Life
P.O. Box 573
Great Barrington, MA 01230

Large Lovely Lady
P.O. Box 4385
Chatsworth, CA 91313
(818) 709-0950

Largely Positive
P.O. Box 17223
Glendale, WI 53217
(414) 224-0404

Largesse, the Network for Size Esteem
P.O. Box 9404
New Haven, CT 06534-0404
(203) 787-1624
E-mail: 75773.717@compuserve.com
http://www.fatgirl.com/largesse/

Largesse Presse
P.O. Box 9404
New Haven, CT 06534-0404
(203) 787-1624

Laughing Sisters
4514 Manitou Way
San Diego, CA 92117
(619) 272-1976

Barbara Lavalee
(800) 764-2787

Barbara Lawless
San Francisco, CA
(415) 391-7555

Robert Z. Lazo
San Francisco, CA 94114
(415) 864-1900

Le Grande Weekend
38 Westbury Lodge Close
Pinner, Middlesex
HA5 3FG England

Lebow Brothers Clothing for Men and Boys
178 Linden Street
Diehl's Plaza
Wellesley, MA 02181
(617) 431-7194
(800) 814-2229
http:/www.tiac.net/users/lebow/

Lefty LaRue Productions
4013B Valleyview Road
Austin, TX 78704
(512) 462-1683

The Lerner Woman
P.O. Box 7211
Indianapolis, IN 46207-0211
(800) 288-7704

Lesbian Fat Activists Network (LFAN)
P.O. Box 635
Woodstock, NY 12498
E-mail: 76473.2141@compuserve.com
or
ltisoncik@mhv.net

Lesbians of Size (LesbOS)
(503) 233-1816

Let It All Hang Out (LIAHO)
P.O. Box 27206
Oakland, CA 94602
(510) 658-3300

Levenger
420 Commerce Drive
Delray Beach, FL 33445-4696
(800) 544-0880

Lili
(818) 282-4326
(800) 258-7944

Lillian Lavergne Designs
7401 Lunar Drive
Austin, TX 78745-6480
(800) 416-0063

Lillian Vernon
Virginia Beach, VA 23479-0002
(914) 633-6300

Limited Editions
P.O. Box 20
Farmington, CT 06034
(203) 677-9225

The Lingerie Wearhouse
6836 Engle Road
P.O. Box 94543
Cleveland, OH 44101-4543
(800) 800-0100

Lisa Victoria Beds
17106 South Crater Road
Petersburg, VA 23805
(804) 862-1491

Livin' Large
(800) 527-4075
E-mail: djvision@aol.com

Livin' and Lovin' Large
P.O. Box 8295
Fort Wayne, IN 46898-8295
(219) 424-5519
E-mail: donnapol2@aol.com

Living Epistles
P.O. Box 77
Klamath Falls, OR 97601
(800) 874-4790

Living Large Newsletter
160 South Bolingbrook Drive, #159
Bolingbrook, IL 60440

Livingsoft
P.O. Box 970
Janesville, CA 96114-0970
(916) 253-2700
(214) 528-1527
(800) 626-1262

Lonely Mountain Forge
2803 Faringdon Drive
Tallahassee, FL 32303
(904) 562-8723

Look
166 Geary Street, Suite 1400
San Francisco, CA 94108
(415) 781-2822

James Loots
Barrymore and Loots
815 Connecticut Avenue N.W., Suite 125
Washington, DC 20006
(202) 466-4950

Lori-Alexandre
7999, Boul. Les Galeries D'Anjou
Anjou, Quebec
Canada H1M-1W6
(514) 355-8500
(800) 648-4735

Lorrini Shoes Inc.
1420 Stanley Street
Montreal, Quebec
Canada H3A 1P8
(514) 842-5925

Love Handles
P.O. Box 41—DIM
Camas Valley, OR 97416
(900) 329-2629

Loving You Large Dateline
(800) 289-5196 (to place an ad)
(900) 726-9004

Luskey's
101 North Houston Street
Fort Worth, TX 76102
(800) 752-7081

Lynell's World of Difference Production Company
(see also Association for Full Figured Women of Atlanta)
(404) 243-6862

Lyon-Shaw
1538 Jake Alexander Boulevard
Salisbury, NC 28144
(704) 636-8270

M. Coleman
634 North Glenoaks, Box 4
Burbank, CA 91502

MPU, Inc.
P.O. Box 694703
Miami, FL 33269
(800) 269-3081

Mack and Rodel Cabinet Makers
Leighton Road
Pownal, ME 04069
(207) 688-4483

Madame X Lingerie
3023 North Clark Street, Suite 271 B
Chicago, IL 60657

Magnolia Lingerie
1498M Reistertown Road, #357
Baltimore, MD 21208
(410) 358-0120

Mail Preference Service
P.O. Box 9008
Farmingdale, NY 11735-9008

MailHawk Manufacturing Co.
P.O. Box 445
Warm Springs, GA 31830
(404) 655-3849

Majestic Mountain Art Jewelry
Department B1294, Box 701994
West Valley, UT 84170-1994

Make It Big
111 Moray Place
Dunedin, New Zealand
Phone: (03) 474-0888
E-mail: jane.hinkley
  @stonebow.otago.ac.nz

Making It Big
P.O. Box 203
501 Aaron Street
Cotati, CA 94928
(707) 795-1995
E-mail: gwenn@sonic.net
http://www.sonic.net/~gwenn/

Liz Manley
17 Rimutaka Place
Titirangi, Auckland, New Zealand
Phone: 09 817 7381

Manny's Baseball Land
3000 S.W. 42nd Avenue
Palm City, FL 34990
(407) 221-7100

Mansour's Men's Wear
27 Church Street
Amherst, Nova Scotia
Canada B4H 3A7
(902) 667-8577
(800) 929-3992
E-mail: nstn4704@fox.nstn.ca
http://fox.nstn.ca/~nstn4704/

Mar-Chelle
(800) 872-5347

Marilyn H. Marchetti
Oppenheimer, Wolff, and Donnelly
2 Prudential Plaza
180 North Stetson Avenue
Chicago, IL 60601
(312) 616-5838

Marcus and Wiesen
27-01 Queens Plaza North
Long Island City, NY 11101
(718) 361-9025

Marietta Hosiery
484 Lake Park Avenue, #408
Oakland, CA 94610

Marketplace: Handwork of India
1455 Ashland Avenue
Evanston, IL 60201-4001
(800) 726-8905

Marlene's Craft and Design
12788 Via Del Carmel
Santa Maria, CA 93456
(805) 937-6415

Lee Martindale
P.O. Box 181716
Dallas, TX 75218
(phone not listed by request)

Maryland State Department of Education
Office of Equity Assurance and Complaince
200 West Baltimore Street
Baltimore, MD 21201
 Attn: Educational Equality Specialist
(410) 767-0431

Maryland Square
1350 Williams Street
Chippewa Falls, WI 54729-1500
(800) 727-3895

Mary's
(713) 933-9678

Susan Mason
c/o Largesse, the Network for Size Esteem
74 Woolsey Street
New Haven, CT 06513-3719
(203) 787-1624
E-mail: leiba@eskimo.com
http://www.eskimo.com/~leiba/

Masseys
601 Twelfth Street
Lynchburg, VA 24506-0088
(800) 462-7739

Matchmaker
(713) 480-4466 (modem)

Maternity Club
(call for nearest location)
(215) 425-6606

Mature Wisdom
Hanover, PA 17333-0028
(800) 638-6366

Mary Maxim
2001 Holland Avenue
P.O. Box 5019
Port Huron, MI 48061-5019
(800) 962-9504

May 5th Coalition
P.O. Box 305
Mt. Marion, NY 12456
(914) 679-1209

McB's
715 Market Street
San Francisco, CA 94103
(415) 546-9444

Liz McGee
P.O. Box 1997
Dallas, TX 75221
(214) 553-1750

Media Education Foundation
26 Center Street
Northampton, MA 01060
(413) 586-4170

Media Watch
P.O. Box 618
Santa Cruz, CA 95061-0618
(408) 423-6355

Mellinger's Inc.
2310 West South Range Road
North Lima, OH 44452-9731
(216) 549-9861
(800) 321-7444

Melpomene Institute
1010 University Avenue
Saint Paul, MN 55104
(612) 642-1951

Merlyn Custom Costuming
6646 East Lovers Lane, #506
Dallas, TX 75214
(214) 739-1265

Michelle Pommier
1 Baltimore Plaza, Suite 360
Atlanta, GA 30308
(404) 815-5888
or
81 Washington Avenue
Miami Beach, FL 33139

Michelle's
6802 Ingram
San Antonio, TX 78238
(210) 521-8337

Midwest XXXtras
(816) 483-5498
(816) 765-9823
E-mail: victoria@sky.net

MidWestern Sport Togs
227 North Washington
Berlin, WI 54923
(414) 361-5050

Miles Kimball
41 West Eighth Avenue
Oshkosh, WI 54906
(414) 231-3800

Missouri Mail Order, Inc.
P.O. Box 28681
Saint Louis, MO 63146-1181

Mitchell Management
323 Geary Street, Suite 302
San Francisco, CA 94102
(415) 395-9291

Mitzi Baker Footwear
8306 Wilshire Boulevard, Suite 943
Beverly Hills, CA 90211
(213) 655-2743

Mixables
(800) 541-7057

Model Mugging
1251 10th Street
Monterey, CA 93940
(408) 646-5425

Mon Cherie
(609) 530-1900

Monaco Coach Corporation
325 East First Street
Junction City, OR 97448
(800) 634-0855

Moonlight Design, Inc.
P.O. Box 1129
Wheeling, IL 60090
(708) 540-0402

More to Hug
(800) 850-8525
http://www.vcnet.com/moretohug/

More 2 Luv
9302 Valley View Avenue
Whittier, CA 90602
(310) 693-1844

Mori Lee
(212) 947-3490

Mormax Company
1455 Cromwell Avenue
Bronx, NY 10452
(718) 293-0800

Moscow Overweight People's Club
House 13/Apartment 28
Shmitovsky, Proyezd
Moscow 123100
Russia
Phone: 095-256-56-28

Thomas Moser, Cabinetmakers
415 Cumberland Avenue
Portland, ME 04101
(207) 774-3791

Mour to Dri
P.O. Box 2162
San Bernardino, CA 92402
(909) 885-8460

Movers and Shakers
(707) 643-4733

I. Y. Murphy
Box 148222
Chicago, IL 60614-8222
E-mail: hawke4@aol.com

My Mother's Star
(618) 656-9221

Myles Ahead
6652 Northwest 57th Street
Tamarac, FL 33321
(305) 724-0500

NAAFA (National Association to Advance Fat Acceptance)
National Office
P.O. Box 188620
Sacramento, CA 95818
(916) 443-0303
E-mail: NAAFA@world.std.com
http://naafa.org

NAAFA Connecticut Chapter
c/o Juanita Sanford
15 Todd Drive
Milford, CT 06460
(203) 878-7127

NAAFA Date Talking Personals
(900) 454-4884

NAAFA Families Sig
c/o Jody Savage, Coordinator
P.O. Box 11351
Oakland, CA 94611

NAAFA Feminist Caucus
c/o Lynn Meletiche
2065 First Avenue, Suite 19-D
New York, NY 10029

NAAFA Hudson Valley Chapter
c/o Marcella Laramee
P.O. Box 220
Hartsdale, NY 10530
(916) 576-5471

NAAFA New England Chapter
(617) 937-7033
E-mail: vwzd53b@prodigy.com
http://pages.prodigy.com/MA/necnaafa/
    necnaafa.html

NAAFA Super Sig
c/o Sherry Collins-Eckert
P.O. Box 25083
Lemay, MO 63125-0083

**NAAFA Weight Loss Surgery
    Survivors Sig**
P.O. Box 7441
Albuquerque, NM 87194-7441
(505) 247-4359
E-mail: KssNewMex@aol.com

Nadina Plus
1124 Lonsdale Avenue, #1176
Vancouver, British Columbia
V7M 3J5 Canada
(604) 985-2356

Nakazawa
132 Thompson Street
New York, NY 10012
(212) 505-7768

Nancy's Notions
P.O. Box 683
Beaver Dam, WI 53916
(414) 885-9175
(800) 833-0690

National
400 National Boulevard
Lexington, NC 27294
(704) 249-0211

**National Association to Advance Fat
    Acceptance**
(see NAAFA)

National Business Furniture
Atlanta, GA
(404) 351-1948
(800) 438-4324 (for nearest store)
(800) 558-1010

National Film Board of Canada
P.O. Box 6100
Station Centre-Ville
Montreal, Quebec
H3C 3H5 Canada
(204) 983-7996

National Fraud Information Center
(800) 876-7060

**National Insurance Consumers
    Organization**
121 North Payne Street
Alexandria, VA 22314
(703) 549-8050

**National Organization for Women
    (NOW)**
1000 16th Street NW
Washington, DC 20036
(202) 331-0066

Naturally Yours
P.O. Box 86481
Portland, OR 97286
(503) 777-1027

Mara Lindsey Nesbitt
P.O. Box 19141
Portland, OR 97219
(503) 244-1114
E-mail: anpn96a@prodigy.com

Network Publications
(same as ETR Associates)
P.O. Box 1830
Santa Cruz, CA 95061-1830
(408) 438-4060
(800) 321-4407

**Neuropedic Development Group
  (medical)**
(717) 506-1323

New Balance
(617) 783-4000
(800) 253-7463

**New Mexico Fat Acceptance Network
  (NMFAN)**
P.O. Box 432
Albuquerque, NM 87102
(505) 873-9095
E-mail: markm@unm.edu
http://www.unm.edu/~markm/nm-
  fan.html

New Moon and New Moon Network
P.O. Box 3587
Duluth, MN 55803
(218) 728-5507

New Look from Sharon J
(800) 998-1985

New Perspective Images
P.O. Box 135
Avon, CT 06001
(203) 693-2816

New Resources
7266 Buckley Road
North Syracuse, NY 13212
(315) 458-0919

Newark Dressmaker Supply
6473 Ruch Road
P.O. Box 20730
Lehigh Valley, PA 18002-0730
(215) 837-7500
(800) 736-6783

Newport News
Avon Lane
Hampton, VA 23630-1267
(804) 827-9000
(800) 688-2830

Next Management
622 North Robertson Boulevard
West Hollywood, CA 90069
(310) 358-0100

Nicole Summers
P.O. Box 3003
Winterbrook Way
Meredith, NH 03253
(800) 642-6786
(603) 279-6229 (fax)

Nightlines Plus
(see J W Ramàge)

Nike
(503) 671-3939

Nightlines Plus
P.O. Box 442
Lafayette, CA 94549-0442
(510) 284-7528
(800) 715-7587

Nordstrom
(see Encore)

Northern Sun Merchandising
2916 East Lake Street
Minneapolis, MN 55406-2065
(800) 258-8579

Northstyle
P.O. Box 1360
Minocqua, WI 54548
(715) 356-9800 (from Canada)
(800) 336-5666

Northwest Traders
5055 West Jackson Road
Enon, OH 45323-9725
(513) 767-9244
(800) 458-8227

Not So Subtle Tees, Inc.
P.O. Box 410
Lincolndale, NY 10540
(914) 248-5769 (customer service)

Nothing in Moderation
801 Lake Street
Oak Park, IL 60301-1301
(630) 386-9750

NurseMates Professional's Choice
P.O. Box 649
Nashua, NH 03026
(800) 735-4994

Nurses Station
P.O. Box 398
Centerbrook, CT 06409-0398
(800) 227-1927

Oakhaus
910 West Division
Normal, IL 61761

Obelisk Modeling and Talent Agency
P.O. Box 6089
Elko, NV 89802
(702) 753-2426

The Offner Team
7815 Quebrada Circle
Carlsbad, CA 92009
(619) 943-9374
(800) 655-6668

Oh! Such Style
13823 Cypress Hollow, #403
San Antonio, TX 78232-5416
(210) 490-4895

Oh! Susanna
206 Culver Street
Chattanooga, TN 37415
(423) 874-0792

Old Pueblo Traders
Palo Verde at 34th
P.O. Box 27800
Tucson, AZ 85726-7800
(602) 747-5000

Olde Mill House Shoppe
105 Strasburg Pike
Lancaster, PA 17602
(717) 299-0678

Ole Fashion Things
402 Southwest Evangeline
Lafayette, LA 70501
(318) 234-7963

One Bad Bear
P.O. Box 31755
Seattle, WA 98103
(206) 547-9708
http://www.onebadbear.com

oooO Baby Baby Productions
P.O. Box 4546
Vallejo, CA 94591
(707) 643-4733
E-mail: ldysrches@aol.com
http://www.wine.com/obaby

Orchid Leaf Productions
P.O. Box 72
Flint, MI 48501

Original Jo's
8766 Wicklow Lane
Dublin, CA 94568-1149
(800) 352-9156

Orogeny Press
P.O. Box 433
Northampton, MA 01061

B. Neil Osbourn
P.O. Box 135
Avon, CT 06001
(203) 693-2816

Other Times Productions
361 60th Street, Department R
Oakland, CA 94618

Kari Ann Owen
P.O. Box 1424
El Cerrito, CA 94530-1424
(510) 215-7062
E-mail: penomee@value.net

PF 147
824 South Los Angeles, Suite, #409
Los Angeles, CA 90014
(213) 488-1046

PFI Fashions
1986 Highway B
Genoa City, WI 53128
(800) 251-2112

Pamper Me Services
P.O. Box 3374
Beverly Hills, CA 90212-0374
(213) 755-7005

Pandora Press
15-17 Broadwick Street
London W1N1FP England

Pango Pango Swimwear
1905 East Atlantic Boulevard
Pompano Beach, FL 33060-6562
(305) 786-0255

Paradigm
P.O. Box 4021-B
Los Angeles, CA 90051

Paradigm Press
1550 California Street, Suite #113
San Francisco, CA 94109

Park's Fantasyland Costume Co.
24715 Sunnymead Boulevard
Moreno Valley, CA 92553
(909) 247-5006

James J. Parks
Gabrian and Parks, P.C.
2525 Telegraph, Suite 303
Bloomfield, MI 48302
(810) 334-6464

Deb Parks-Satterfield
343½ 17th Avenue
Seattle, WA 98122-5706
(206) 323-5171

Parsinen Design
1011 Boren Avenue, Suite 178
Seattle, WA 98104
(206) 329-4761
(800) 422-5808

Past Patterns
P.O. Box 7587
Grand Rapids, MI 49502-1014
(616) 245-9456

Pastille
P.O. Box 650503
Dallas, TX 75265
(800) 727-3900

Paul Delacroix Studios
P.O. Box 1418
Cedar Hill, TX 75106-1418

Paulette
P.O. Box 293017
Sacramento, CA 95829

Paul's Waka Waka BBS
(206) 783-7979 (modem)

Peaches
P.O. Box 268
Cedarhurst, NY 11516
(800) 732-2403

Peacock Clothes
558-B South Murphy Avenue
Sunnyvale, CA 94086
(408) 730-0941

Pen-A-Friend
P.O. Box 874
Point Pleasant, NJ 08742

Pendleton
Portland Pendleton Shop
900 Southwest 5th Avenue
Portland, OR 97204
(503) 242-0037
(800) 241-9665
(800) 362-9665 (East)
(800) 368-9665 (mid-states)
(800) 358-9665 (West)

Peggy Lutz for Lutes Design
6784 Depot Street
Sebastopol, CA 95473
(707) 824-1634

People at Large (PAL)
600 The East Mall
P.O. Box 11522
Etobicoke, Ontario
Canada M9B 4B0

People of Size Social Club
P.O. Box 9002
Dallas, TX 75209
(903) 629-7177

Perfect Comfort
(see Marcus and Wiesen)

Personality Plus
P.O. Box 239
Pearl River, NY 10965
(914) 620-1959

Phaeton Classic Products
805 Central, #151
Bedford, TX 76022

Phat Phree!
E-mail: oscar@netasx.com
http://www.netaxs.com/~oscar

Philips Medical Systems
(800) 526-4963

Sharon Philips
(800) 477-1733

Phoenix Big and Tall
805 Branch Drive
Alpharetta, GA 30201
(404) 751-8640
(800) 251-8067

Planet Big Girl
P.O. Box 4110
London SE15 4LR England
Phone: 01 716 390 914

Playtex
(call for nearest store or catalog)
(800) 537-9955

Plump Partners Dating Agency
8 Sealand Avenue
Holywell
Clwyd CH8 7BU England
Phone: 01 352 715 909

Plus Models Management Ltd.
49 West 37th Street, 18th floor
New York, NY 10018
Attn: Pat Swift
(212) 997-1785

Plus Publications
Box 265, Suite 200
Scotland, CT 06264
(203) 456-0646
(800) 793-0666

Plus Woman
60 Laurel Haven
Fairview, NC 28730
(704) 628-3562
(800) 628-5525
E-mail: pluswoman2@aol.com

**Poestenkill Hiking Staff
Manufacturing Company**
Plank Road
P.O. Box 300
Poestenkill, NY 12140
(518) 279-3011

Poley's Big and Tall
E-mail: poleyk@rcinet.com
http://porthos.itribe.net/shops/
Poleys_Big_and_Tall_Clothing/

Portland Health Institute
(503) 222-2773

Potbelly Cycling Association
45 Munson Road
Pleasantville, NY 10570
E-mail: wb2vvs@execnet.com

Preferred Living
Clermont County Airport
Batavia, OH 45103-9747
(800) 543-8633

Prescription Sportswear
9892 Vicksburg Drive
Huntington Beach, CA 92646
(800) 557-4478
E-mail: rx@ix.netcom.com
http://www.gsn.com

Pretty Big magazine
One the Dale
Wirksworth, Matlock
Derbyshire, London DE4 4EJ
01629 824949

The Primary Layer
P.O. Box 6697
Portland, OR 97228
(800) 282-8206

Prodigy
(800) 776-3449 (customer service)

Production West
2110 Overland Avenue, Suite 120
Billings, MT 59102
(406) 656-9417
(800) 321-9499

Promoting Legislation and Education
   About Self Esteem (PLEASE)
c/o Dr. Lisa Berzins
91 South Main Street
West Hartford, CT 06107
(860) 521-2515

Provocative Lady
P.O. Box 367
Sterling Heights, MI 48311
(800) 952-8012

Pudgy Love
P.O. Box 10671
Burbank, CA 91510-0671
(818) 566-3667

Putnam Ladders
32 Howard Street
New York, NY 10013
(212) 226-5147

Quartermaster
P.O. Box 829
Long Beach, CA 90801-0829
(800) 444-8643

Queen of Hearts, Inc.
19 Merrick Avenue
Merrick, NY 11566
(516) 377-1357

Queentex
111 Chabanel Street West
Montreal, Quebec
Canada H2N 1C8
(800) 367-1929

Quinn's Shirt Shop
Route 12, P.O. Box 131
North Grosnenordale, CT 06255
(508) 943-7183

R J's Apparel
(704) 527-9767

Radiance: the Magazine for Large
   Women
P.O. Box 30246
Oakland, CA 94604-9937
(510) 482-0680
E-mail: radmag2@aol.com

Radiance Tours
P.O. Box 30246
Oakland, CA 94604
(510) 482-0680
(800) 933-7327
E-mail: radmag2@aol.com
          cruisexpert@aol.com

Rainbow Tees
E-mail: rainbowt@usa.pipeline.com
http://www.xmission.com/~gastown/
  rainbow/

Rainy County Knitwear
P.O. Box 7852
Everett, WA 98201-0852
(206) 653-7189

Real Girl **Magazine**
1154 Washington Avenue
Albany, CA 94706
(510) 528-9453

Reebok
(800) 382-3823

Regalia
Palo Verde at 34th
P.O. Box 27800
Tucson, AZ 85726-7800
(602) 747-5000 (orders)
(602) 748-8600

Renaissance Dancewear
5625 State Farm Drive, Suite 13
Rohnert Park, CA 94928
(707) 585-9262

Repp Ltd./Big and Tall
1492 Bluegrass Lakes Parkway
Alpharetta, GA 30201
(800) 690-7377

The Richman Cotton Company
2631 Piner Road
Santa Rosa, CA 95401
(707) 575-8924
(800) 992-8924

The Right Touch
Department D-205
95-60 Queens Boulevard
Rego Park, NY 11374
(718) 899-5743

River Bend Chair Company
P.O. Box 856
West Chester, OH 45069
(513) 554-490

Roaman's
P.O. Box 46283
Indianapolis, IN 46283-8301
(800) 274-7240

Robin Barr Enterprises
8306 Wilshire Boulevard, #614
Beverly Hills, CA 90211
(310) 358-7351

Rockport
(617) 485-2090
(800) 343-9255

Rocky Mountain Clothing
8500 Zuni Street
Denver, CO 80221
(800) 688-4449

Rocky Mountain Connection
141 East Elkhorn Avenue
P.O. Box 2800
Estes Park, CO 80517
(800) 679-3600

RogersWear
P.O. Box 191577
Los Angeles, CA 90019
(213) 734-3664

The Romance Line
(900) 226-1140
(800) 289-5435 (to place ads)

Romantic Interludes
P.O. Box 206
Jenks, OK 74037
(918) 299-9700

Romantic Notions
P.O. Box 6783-X
Bryan, TX 77805-6783

Roselyn
347 14th Street
Oakland, CA 94612
(510) 444-7472

Freda Rosenberg
P.O. Box 27465, Department F
Philadelphia, PA 19118

Ross-Simons Company
Providence, RI 02920-4476
(800) 556-7376

The Rotunda
(510) 658-4423 (modem)

Roundabout Productions
c/o BAFL
P.O. Box 1836
Jamaica Plains, MA 02130

Rubenesque/Full Figured Dances
Fort Lauderdale, FL
(954) 832-2501
(407) 276-7467

Rubenesque Romances
P.O. Box 534
Tarrytown, NY 10591-0534
(800) 211-1660
http://www.bookport.com/htbin/
    publishers/rubenesque/pubrow

Rump Parliament
P.O. Box 181716
Dallas, TX 75218
E-mail: lmartin@airmail.net
http://www.airmail.net/~lmartin/

S. Johnson
30141 Antelope, #D228
Menifee, CA 992584

Sisters Are Fighting Fat Oppression!
   (SAFFO)
c/o University of Minnesota YMCA
244 Coffman Union
300 Washington Avenue S.E.
Minneapolis, MN 55455
(612) 625-0607

S.E.S. Patterns
P.O. Box 610935
San Jose, CA 95161

S G D Merchandising
625 Madison Avenue
New York, NY 10022
(800) 772-1234

SMLA Modeling Agency
8660 Melrose Avenue, #225
Los Angeles, CA 90046
(213) 782-8999

S W's Full Figure Designs
490 Stone Mountain, Lithonia #59
Stone Mountain, GA 30088
(404) 469-6139

Sabrina's Food for Thought
P.O. Box 46404
Philadelphia, PA 19160-6401

Saks Fifth Avenue
611 Fifth Avenue
New York, NY 10022
(800) 345-3454
(800) 347-9177

Sally's Place
P.O. Box 1397
Sausalito, CA 94966
(415) 898-5683
(800) 877-2559

San-Martin Bridals
3353 Verdugo Road
Los Angeles, CA 90065
(213) 257-5333

Sandi Kent
612A Venice Boulevard
Venice, CA 90291
(310) 574-3164
(800) 466-5368

**Sandra Williams' Full Figure
   Designs**
(800) 276-2041

Sandy's Wearable Art
6293 River Road
Flushing, MI 48433
(810) 732-5303

Juanita Sanford
The Travel Shoppe
15 Todd Drive
Milford, CT 06460
(203) 878-7127

Sankofa
c/o It's a Revolution
1870 North Vermont Avenue, #530
Los Angeles, CA 90027
(213) 661-1431

Sarah's Bare Necessities
1909 Salpio Street
Concord, CA 94518
(510) 680-8445

Saucony
(800) 728-2669

Jody Savage
P.O. Box 11351
Oakland, CA 94611
E-mail: jody_savage@cc.chiron.com

Sawtooth Valley Woodcrafts
4600 Ginzel
Boise, ID 83703
(208) 342-5265

Says Who?
3903 Piedmont Avenue
Oakland, CA 94611
(510) 547-5181

Scantihose/Limited Editions
P.O. Box 20
Farmington, CT 06034
(203) 677-9225

Scarlett Crane
P.O. Box 1931
Sausalito, CA 94966
(415) 332-5266

Scotch House
187 Post Street
San Francisco, CA 94108
(415) 391-1264

Sears Big and Tall
P.O. Box 9115
Hingham, MA 02043
(800) 679-5656

Sears Home Healthcare
20 Presidential Drive
Roselle, IL 60172
(800) 326-1750

Sears Size 14 and Up
P.O. Box 8361
Indianapolis, IN 46283-8361
(800) 944-1973

Seattle Area Fat Feminist Inspiration and Rage (SAFFIR)
4649 Sunnyside Avenue N, #222
Seattle, WA 98103
(206) 632-8547
E-mail: eridani@scn.org

Seattle NOW Body Image Task Force
4649 Sunnyside Avenue N, #222
Seattle, WA 98103
(206) 632-8547
E-mail: eridani@scn.org

Secret Pleasures
1800 South Robertson Boulevard, Suite 69
Los Angeles, CA 90035
(800) 822-6969

Sears catalogs
(800) 366-3000

Secretary of Health and Human Services
200 Independence Avenue SW
Washington, DC 20201

Seeds of Change Newsletter
c/o Jennifer Carney, R.N.
2865 South Colorado Boulevard, Suite 200
Denver, CO 80222

Sensations
(617) 893-1985

Serengeti
P.O. Box 3349
Serengeti Park
Chelmsford, MA 01824-0933
(800) 426-2852

Sexy Fat Boys
8360 Northwest South River Drive
Miami, FL 33166
(305) 623-7970
http://www.netrunner.net/~fatboys

Sharon J's
1960 Del Amo Boulevard
Torrance, CA 90501
(800) 998-1985

Sheer Mahogany
3870 Crenshaw Boulevard, #781
Los Angeles, CA 90008

Shepler's Western Wear
P.O. Box 7702
Wichita, KS 67277-7702
(800) 833-7007
(800) 835-4004

Shirley's Square Dance Shoppe
(see Creative Square Dancer)

Shoe Express
P.O. Box 31537
Lafayette, LA 70593-1537
(318) 235-5191

Short Sizes, Inc.
5385 Warrensville Center Road
Cleveland, OH 44137
(216) 475-2515

Sign of the Unicorn
P.O. Box 77370
San Francisco, CA 94107
(415) 826-8262
E-mail: ltedison@igc.apc.org

Signals
WGBH Educational Foundation
P.O. Box 64428
Saint Paul, MN 55164-0428
(800) 669-9696

Silhouettes
5 Avery Road
Roanoke, VA 24012
(800) 704-3322

Sisters of Size
(206) 789-1267
(206) 937-5286

Sit and Be Fit
P.O. Box 8033
Spokane, WA 99203-0033
(509) 448-9438

Sizable Difference
4114 East Fairmount, #3
Tucson, AZ 85712
(800) 936-4936

Size Acceptance Network
Eastern Community Health Service
Box 5, 5 Darley Road
Paradise, South Australia 5075
Phone: (08) 207 8933

Size Up Wise Up
P.O. Box 539
Christchurch, New Zealand
Phone: (03) 365-1578

Size Wise Update and Web Site
c/o Judy Sullivan
1054 Los Osos Valley Road
Los Osos, CA 93402
E-mail: jsulliva@slonet.org
       judy@SizeWise.com
http://www.SizeWise.com

Skin Diver Wetsuits
1632 South 250th Street
Kent, WA 98032
(206) 878-1613

Smith & Nephew
One Quality Drive
P.O. Box 1005
Germantown, WI 53022-8205
(800) 558-8633

The Snack Bar
(203) 888-3981 (modem)

Snake & Snake Productions
Route 3, Box 165
Durham, NC 27713
(919) 544-2028

Society of Size
(see Bond van Formaat)

Sodhoppers
(800) 763-6777

Soft Sensations
3870 La Sierra Avenue, #352
Riverside, CA 92505

Solomon and Associates
4757 West Park, #106
Suite 410
Plano, TX 75093
(214) 985-0074

Southeast Super Singles
P.O. Box 14635
Atlanta, GA 30324
(404) 871-8838

Southern California Size Acceptance Coalition (SCSAC)
P.O. Box 500293
San Diego, CA 92150-0293
(619) 496-3317 (hotline)
E-mail: scsac@aol.com
http://alumni.caltech.edu/~hanshorn/
    coalition/

Southpark Publishing Group, Inc.
4041 West Wheatland Road,
    Suite 156-359
Dallas, TX 75237-999
(214) 296-5657

Barbara Spaulding, M.S.W.
(630) 942-2356

Special Delivery Plus
P.O. Box 1418
Duluth, GA 30136

Specialty Models
1170 Broadway, Suite 902
New York, NY 10001
(212) 889-4680

Specialty Photography by Laurice
65 Manchester
San Francisco, CA 94110
(415) 648-2675

Spiegel catalogs
P.O. Box 182555
Columbus, OH 43218
(800) 345-4500

Spinsters Ink
32 East First Street, #330
Duluth, MN 55802-2002
(218) 727-3222

Karin Stackpole
Barrymore and Loots
815 Connecticut Avenue NW, Suite 125
Washington, DC 20006
(202) 466-4950

The Stallari Armory
c/o Jeffrey L. Williams
13355 Southwest Rita Drive
Beaverton, OR 97005
(503) 646-0445

Star River Productions, Inc.
P.O. Box 7754
North Brunswick, NJ 08902
(908) 247-9875

Stars, the Agency
777 Davis Street
San Francisco, CA 94111
(415) 421-6272

Stars Casting
1301 20th Street NW, Suite 102
Washington, DC 20036
(202) 429-9494

Stop Dieting, Inc.
37 Parkwood Avenue
Toronto, Ontario
Canada M4V 2W9
(416) 968-3942

Stout Men's Shop
59 Temple Place
Boston, MA 02111
(617) 542-5397

Strauss Communications
(408) 625-1910
(900) 420-3713

Stretch & Sew
Valley River Drive
Eugene, OR 97401
(503) 686-9263

Styleplus
1201 North Dearborn Parkway, Suite 134
Chicago, IL 60610
(800) 347-8453
http://www.webcom.com/~cfffnews/
    styleplus.html

Substantial Women
RR 2, Box 562
Kerhonkson, NY 12446
(914) 626-2257

Joe Sugar
(800) 367-8427

SuitAbility
848 South Myrtle Avenue, #5
Monrovia, CA 91016-3455
(818) 303-5730

Suits Me Swimwear
2377 Deltona Boulevard
Spring Hill, FL 34606
(904) 666-1485

Judy Sullivan
1054 Los Osos Valley Road
Los Osos, CA 93402
E-mail: jsulliva@slonet.org
        judy@SizeWise.com
http://www.SizeWise.com

Sungold Enterprises
P.O. Box 190
Oceanside, NY 11572
(800) 645-2254

Support Plus
99 West Street
Box 500
Medfield, MA 02052-0500
(800) 229-2910

Rick Suseoff
2336 Market Street, #103
San Francisco, CA 94114

Suzanne Henri, Inc.
P.O. Box 2399
Appomattox, VA 24522
(800) 634-2590

Suzanne's
108 West Oak
Chicago, IL 60610
(312) 943-8315

Sweet Cheeks Designs
P.O. Box 7767
Redlands, CA 92375
(909) 792-0454

Sweet Dreams Intimates, Inc.
81 Route 111
Smithtown, NY 11787
(516) 366-0565

Sweeter Measures
819 Front Street
P.O. Box 340
Gibbon, NE 68840-034C
(308) 468-5156

Sweetheart
(212) 868-7536

Swings 'n Things
527 Fourth Avenue
San Diego, CA 92101
(619) 544-0088
(800) 533-5177

T.C. Originals, Inc.
P.O. Box 447
La Puente, CA 91747
(818) 336-6688

T-Cole Designs
113 Daniel Street Extension
Hamlet, NC 28345

T.H.E.
3070 M Street NW
Washington, DC 20007
(202) 342-0933

TR Sports
(614) 444-7001 (purchasing information)

Tafford
P.O. Box 1006, 104 Park Drive
Montgomeryville, PA 18936
(215) 643-9666
(800) 283-0065

Telephone Preference Service
P.O. Box 9014
Farmingdale, NY 11735-9014

Tennessee Tub, Inc.
207 Donelson Park, Suite 201
Nashville, TN 37214
(615) 391-3828

Texas Size Acceptance Coalition
5935 High Star
Houston, TX 77081
(713) 666-5484 (Marie)
(409) 753-3451 (Terry)

Think Big!
4110 Butler Pike, Suite A-101
Plymouth Meeting, PA 19462
(800) 487-4244

This End Up
P.O. Box 2020
Richmond, VA 23216-2020
(800) 627-5161

Thomas Cook and King Size Co.
(617) 871-4100
(800) 846-1600

Pattie Thomas
P.O. Box 8507
Clearwater, FL 34620-8507
E-mail: dylancat@grove.ufl.edu

Three West Casting
3000 Chestnut Avenue, Suite 1407
Baltimore, MD 21211
(410) 366-7727

Tilley Endurables
300 Langner Road
Buffalo, NY 14224-9962
(716) 822-3052
(800) 363-8737

Tip Toe Arts
Chrissa O'Brien
1801 Lyndon Road
San Diego, CA 92103
(619) 294-4226

The Tog Shop
Lester Square
Americus, GA 31710
(800) 342-6789

Tops
P.O. Box 533
London SW6 2RQ England

Trafalgar Square Publishing
North Pomfret, VT 05053

Tropical Adventure
P.O. Box 6262
Burbank, CA 91510-6282
(800) 362-2682

Two Lipps Company
11684 Ventura Boulevard, #950
Studio City, CA 91604
(800) 874-3732

U.S. Plus Pageants
614 Portland, Suite 99
Saint Paul, MN 55102
(612) 292-0082

Ulla Popken
5 Hampston Garth
Lutherville, MD 21093
(410) 339-7864 (fax)
(800) 245-8552
or store at
Towson Town Center
825 Dulaney Valley Road
Towson, MD 21204
(410) 494-8108

Un Peu Plus, C'est Bien! (A Bit More)
CP 501
Boucherville, Quebec
Canada J4B 6Y2

Uncle Sam Umbrella Shop
161 West 57th Street
New York, NY 10019
(212) 582-1976

Undergear
741 F Street
P.O. Box 129027
San Diego, CA 92112-9027
(717) 633-3322
(800) 854-2795

Uniform Connections
P.O. Box 1104
Winston-Salem, NC 27102-1104
(800) 326-3261

Uniquity Plus
3360 E. Street
Eureka, CA 95503
(707) 441-1887

Unique Patterns Design Limited
(800) 543-4739

Unlikely Publications
P.O. Box 8542
Berkeley, CA 94707
(510) 843-6559

Unlimited Concepts
8371 La Palma Avenue, Suite #323
Buena Park, CA 90620
(714) 521-6222
(714) 522-5864

Upscale Sweats
P.O. Box 170665
San Francisco, CA 94117

USA Mom's
(call for nearest store)
(800) 872-6667

Vagabond Imports
391 School Road
Novato, CA 94945
(415) 897-1916
(800) 854-1470

Vanson Leathers
213 Turnpike Street
Stoughton, MA 02072-3719
(617) 344-5444

Vendredi Enterprises
P.O. Box 41
Carnas Valley, OR 97416-0041

The Venus Group
Ann Arbor, MI
(313) 482-5011

Vermont Country Store
P.O. Box 3000
Manchester Center, VT 05255-1108
(802) 362-4647
(802) 362-2400

The Very Thing!
(see also Nicole Summers)
P.O. Box 3003
Winterbrook Way
Meredith, NH 03253-3005
(800) 642-0001

Vibrant Handknits USA
Historic Savage Mill
8600 Foundry Street
Savage, MD 20763
(800) 765-KNIT

Video in Studios
(604) 872-8337

Vitality Leader's Kit
Health Services and Promotion
Health and Welfare Canada
Jeanne Mance Building, 4th floor
Ottawa, Ontario
K1A 1B4 Canada

Votta's Wearable Art
P.O. Box 243
Wilmington, IL 60481
(815) 476-2980

WalkUSA
6310 Nancy Ridge Drive, #101
San Diego, CA 92121
(800) 445-2209

Walpole Woodworkers
767 East Street
Walpole, MA 02081
(508) 668-2800
(800) 343-6948

Warner Vision
(818) 769-4626

Wearguard
P.O. Box 9105
Hingham, MA 02043-9105
(800) 388-3300

Wedding Web
http://www.weddingweb.com/

Weight Release Services
45 Munson Road
Pleasantville, NY 10570-1829
(914) 747-1527

The Well-Rounded Club
Diane Ilic, Founder
Cranston, RI
(401) 831-3400 (hotline)

Well Rounded Woman
P.O. Box 25
Perrysburg, OH 60657

Wendy Dale
P.O. Box 123
Newton Centre, MA 02159
(617) 244-1820

West One Video
1995 Bailey Hill Road
Eugene, OR 97405
(503) 683-2236
(800) 999-4952

What on Earth
2451 Enterprise East Parkway
Twinsburg, OH 44087
(216) 425-4600
(216) 963-6555

Wheelchairs of Kansas
P.O. Box 320
Ellis, KS 67637
(800) 537-6454
(800) 337-2447 (fax)

Wild Bill Video
2261 Market Street, Suite #310
San Francisco, CA 94114-1693

While You Wait
(call during mornings)
(800) 554-2522

Wide Angle Video Pictorials
(see *Dimensions*)

Wide Appeal Social Club
(703) 978-0221
E-mail: wideappeal@aol.com
        nrpx66a@prodigy.com
http://www.erols.com/acer75/wide.htm

Wide World of Mar-Lou
157 V Arcade
Cleveland, OH 44114
(216) 861-0730

WIG, Inc.
P.O. Box 2082
Huntington Beach, CA 92647-2082

Wilderness Inquiry
Mr. Tracy Fredin, Outreach Director
1313 Fifth Street, S.E., Box 84
Minneapolis, MN 55414-1546
(612) 379-3858
(800) 728-0719

Wilhelmina
300 Park Avenue South
New York, NY 10010
(212) 473-4884

Willendorf Press
P.O. Box 407
Bearsville, NY 12409

William James Roth Furniture
P.O. Box 355
Yarmouth, MA 02675
(508) 362-9235

Willow Moon Designs
P.O. Box 271
Route 2, Box 131-G
Elkins, AR 72727
(501) 643-3658

Mary Wilson
E-mail: mary.wilson
   @exchange.exchange.com

Windwalker Moccasins
P.O. Box 1838, Dept RH
Snowflake, AZ 85937

Wireless
Minnesota Public Radio
P.O. Box 64422
Saint Paul, MN 55164-0422
(800) 669-9999

Woman Catalog
60 Laurel Haven
Fairview, NC 28730

Womanswork
P.O. Box 543
York, ME 03909-0543
(207) 363-0804
(207) 363-0805
(800) 639-2709
E-mail: wmnsgloves@aol.com

Women at Large Systems, Inc.
1020 South 48th Street
Yakima, WA 98908
(509) 965-0115
(800) 477-2348

Women of Size
754 South Bryant Street
Denver, CO 80219
(303) 937-9648
P.O. Box 531
Morrison, CO 80465-9998
(800) 808-9883

Women of Width (WOW)
Two Sisters Bookstore
605 Cambridge Street
Menlo Park, CA 94025
(415) 965-8416
E-mail: jwermont@netcom.com

Women Unlimited
P.O. Box 16143
Wellington South, New Zealand
Phone: (04) 380-8066
E-mail: celia.james@vuw.ac.nz
        peterm@central.co.nz

Women's Voices
Columbia, MD
(410) 715-3993
(800) 871-3991

Wonderbed Manufacturing Company
P.O. Box 1551
Roswell, GA 30077
(800) 631-1746

Woodmont Eyewear
7707 North University Drive, Suite 203B
Fort Lauderdale, FL 33321
(305) 726-7707

Sasha Woods
E-mail: sasha@cs.cmu.edu

Work It Out, Inc.
(Kelly Bliss)
1594 Springhill Drive
Aston, PA 19014
(610) 459-5011

Worldesigns, Incorporated
P.O. Box 355
New York, NY 10024

WorldWide Outfitters
117 Benedict Street
Waterbury, CT 06722-1940
(203) 574-4090
(800) 243-3570

Write Weight
c/o South Tyneside Voluntary Project
Victoria Hall
119 Fowler Street
Tyne and Wear NE 33 1NU England

Ron Wyden
Subcommittee on Regulation
House Committee on Small Business
U.S. House of Representatives
Washington, DC 20515

Wry Crips
P.O. Box 21474
Oakland, CA 94620

Wyoming River Raiders
601 Southeast Wyoming Boulevard
Casper, WY 82609
(800) 247-6068

XL Connection
P.O. Box 20511
Rochester, NY 14602

XL Mystique
9903 Santa Monica Boulevard, #583
Beverly Hills, CA 90212
(310) 822-6447

XL's, Incorporated
P.O. Box 52394
Durham, NC 27717-2394
(919) 383-3009
(800) 772-0272

Xtras
4230 North Oakland Avenue, #210
Milwaukee, WI 53211
(414) 332-2631
(800) 647-8908

XXXLNT
P.O. Box 016686
Miami, FL 33101-6686

Yarnome Full Figure Woman
P.O. Box 578463
Chicago, IL 60657

Yellow Creek Originals
2901 Yellow Creek Road
Dickson, TN 37055
(615) 763-6147

Yes! **(magazine)**
Yes! Publishing Ltd.
90 Banner Street
London ECIY 8JU England
Phone: 071 608 3668
            081 677 6080 (subscriptions)

YOU•NIQUE
620 Jarvis Street, Suite 1023
Toronto, Ontario
M4Y 2R8 Canada
(416) 964-0292
(800) 663-9102 (toll-free in Canada)
E-mail: kaca.henley@ablelink.org

Yuri Vann Art
P.O. Box 15212
Lansing, MI 48901

Zala Design
P.O. Box 80018
Minneapolis, MN 55408
(612) 871-4809

Zen Home Stitchery
2693 Riverside Drive
Costa Mesa, CA 92627
(714) 631-5389

Zenobie F. Creations
4880 Janne Mance
Montreal, Quebec
H2V 4J7 Canada
(514) 273-9342

Zoftig Nudes by Rhonda Grossman
216 4th Street
Sausalito, CA 94965

Appendix A

The Diet Industry

(Don't Try This at Home)

The truth is that there is very little scientific data available about the long-term successes and/or failures of diet programs. However, there is no shortage of unsubstantiated claims from people and companies eager to lighten our wallets, if not our bodies. These claims are, to put it mildly, not full truths.

A quick check of the most recent copy of *Books in Print* shows 137 books listed under the key words *weight loss*. That's a lot of books trying to sell us the same tired concept in slightly different wrappers. Whether fruit, salads, chicken, or possum (the other white meat) is being stressed, it's still the same low-calorie diet that has failed us before.

Richard Simmons is pushing his latest incarnation of Deal-A-Meal ("even those of you who already have the original Deal-A-Meal owe it to yourself to purchase the new version") on the television shopping network. Infomercials featuring a wildly enthusiastic, buzz-cut, boot camp kind of woman used to leap off the screen to convince us we too can be like her. (Is this something we want?)

There are tapes we can fall asleep to while listening to the pounding surf, a hidden weight-loss message repeating in our ears throughout the night. We can check ourselves into in-hospital treatment programs to be starved and studied like rats. Churches offer wellness programs that emphasize weight loss. There are even computer programs designed to help us obsess electronically about calories and grams of fat.

Are you ready to give "anal leakage," stomach cramping, and loose stools a try? Those are just some of the rather distasteful side effects of products made with Procter and Gamble's fat substitute, Olestra. Can this be a good thing?

We can learn biofeedback, have staples put in our ears or stomachs, or be hypnotized. Before you try any of these treatments, ask questions! Research both the positive and negative aspects of any program or pill and make an informed decision. Don't take the word of the person who stands to make a profit. The bottom line is this—does the treatment offer safe, effective, sustained weight loss in a high percentage of its users? If not, move on.

DIET PILLS (JUST SAY NO!)

A National Institutes of Health panel on the treatment of obesity found drug therapy to be disappointing, with weight loss generally not sustained. Whatever benefits you may gain from diet pills are usually lost as soon as you stop taking them, and the possible side effects are numerous and, sometimes, deadly. Amphetamines, which must be prescribed by a medical doctor, can be addictive. Thyroid derivatives are unapproved for weight loss.

Most diet pills are appetite suppressants. While generally safe, they don't do much. Possible side effects include headaches, irritability, high blood pressure, seizures, nausea, sleeping disorders, and a general feeling of uneasiness.

The Food and Drug Administration, after reviewing approximately one hundred over-the-counter diet pill ingredients, found only two to be possibly effective. These two drugs are phenylpropanolamine (ppa) and benzocaine.

Phenylpropanolamine is supposed to trick your brain into thinking you are full. However, one study found that 86 percent of women who used pills containing ppa found it to have little or no effect as an appetite suppressant.

Benzocaine is a topical anesthetic that numbs your taste buds. You'll find it in items like Ayds candy.

Prozac (fluoxetine) and Zoloft (sertraline), antidepressants known to suppress appetite, are being studied for use in weight loss.

Pondimin (fenfluramine), a drug that increases the brain levels of serotonin, a neurotransmitter, produces a feeling of fullness, but its effectiveness is short-term. Researchers are working on developing a more potent form.

The FDA recently approved the long-term use of dexfenfluramine, a close relative to fenfluramine. Dexfenfluramine may cause up to 10 percent of total body weight loss when used in conjunction with a low-calorie diet. Potential side effects include primary pulmonary hypertension (PPH), a fatal heart/lung disease, and permanent brain damage. In parts of Europe, where this drug and its close cousins have been in use for years, these drugs have been severely restricted following a number of dexfenfluramine-related deaths.

Researchers are also looking into fat blockers (designed to retard fat absorption), a brain protein that ends the appetite for fat, pleasure blockers (designed to make food taste nasty), and a variety of drugs that speed up metabolism.

So far, as with all other weight-loss products, nothing works in the long term and there are many potential risks. Be cautious and ask a lot of questions if you consider taking these medications.

DIET CENTERS

Eight million Americans sign up with structured weight-loss programs yearly. We spend $2 billion a year on prepackaged, premeasured foods, counseling, meetings, and weigh-ins. These companies promise a lot. What are we getting for our money? I know I'm still fat with a much smaller checking account and Jenny Craig has some beautiful homes and can give her husband a multimillion-dollar racehorse for his birthday.

In 1992, after a two-year investigation into diet center advertising and marketing, the Federal Trade Commission determined:

- There is no evidence that any weight-loss product or service has long-term effectiveness.
- That companies exaggerate the ease and effectiveness of their services/products.
- That unsubstantiated claims are made in advertising and marketing and that pricing is deceptive.
- That consumer testimonials and program comparisons are misleading and that health risks aren't explained to potential customers.

Nutri-System, Physicians Weight Loss Centers, Healthy Concepts (was Diet Center), Health Management Resources (HMR Fasting Program), and several other weight loss companies signed agreements with the FTC to clean up their advertising practices. Two holdouts, Jenny Craig and Weight Watchers, claimed their programs are different and vowed to fight this out in court. Data meant to substantiate advertising claims and supplied by all of these companies have been called "scientifically inadequate" by the National Institutes of Health. The FTC investigation and ruling have sent the diet industry scrambling to obtain research that will support its claims about success rates. (Good luck.)

One interesting side effect of the FTC ruling, combined with the National Institutes of Health decision that dieting doesn't work, has been the change in advertising. The word *diet* has been dropped like a hot potato. Beautiful, charming, thin models dance in romantic settings, having finally achieved the bodies they have always wanted (seemingly promising the kind of sex life previously accomplished only through purchasing the right car or drinking the right beer). We are treated to a perfectly coiffed and poised Jenny Craig leaning into the picture purring and assuring us that it's our inner selves she is interested in. Does this mean Jenny wants to be our best friend now? Will she invite us to drop 'round the mansion for pajama parties? Can we take rides on her horses? I don't think so. I suspect (and I may be wrong about this) that she still just wants our money.

Now, there is nothing wrong with wanting money. But if someone wants *my* money in the future, I expect something in return that doesn't harm me, isn't an outright lie, and actually does what it promises.

All of the diet pushers we are used to (Jenny Craig, Richard Simmons, Weight Watchers, and others) are still with us, along with a new crop of thin faces. Some are dressed in white coats, using their medical licenses to assure us that their diets are medically sound. They strut, scoff at "diets," tell their own moving stories of weight loss (sometimes achieved with the help of plastic surgery, which isn't mentioned), and promote their own plans. They offer supplements, exercise regimens, and motivational tapes.

Infomercials are incredibly well done and come into our homes with low-calorie diets in new costumes. Don't you be fooled. A low-calorie "program" is still a low-calorie diet. Not a single one of these people can show us any proof that what he or she is selling has provided a significant number of people with a safe way of losing a substantial amount of weight and keeping it off for at least five years. They can all present honest, sincere, attractive people who have lost weight on their programs . . . after all, most programs can offer an honest 3 percent success rate. I want to see 100 percent of the people who have used their programs . . . five years after they began the program. If 80 percent of them aren't still at their goal weight, we have nothing to talk about. Heck, I'd even settle for 60 percent. Or 50 percent. You can bet your life that if someone ever achieves this level of success, he will be screaming it to the world and trotting out real proof. Every one of these weight-loss companies knows the statistics as well as we do. What galls me is that they have no problem taking our money and endangering our health for the sake of their own bank accounts.

In Connecticut the Diet Program Disclosures Bill went into effect in October 1996. This piece of legislation, House Bill 5621, demands truth in advertising from weight-loss companies. From now on claims will have to be backed up by data on actual customers. It's a start.

Some people just aren't ready to give up the hope that the next diet is going to be the one that does the trick for them. There is a lot of pressure to lose weight, and everyone has to make personal decisions regarding weight-loss attempts. If you just have to try again, do yourself a favor and choose your path carefully. Evaluate any weight-loss program or plan. Ignore the glitzy commercials you see on television and become an informed consumer! Before you hand over any cash, ask the following questions. If the company can't give you satisfactory answers, preferably in the form of peer-reviewed published studies, reconsider your participation very carefully.

- What is the exact cost of the program? (Advertised specials are often just a small portion of the actual price.)
- How is the amount of weight you need to lose determined? Insurance height/weight charts? Your own individual best weight based on family and personal history? The program "counselor's" perceived ideal?
- What percentage of people who begin the program actually see it through to the end?
- What percentage of people accomplish their weight goals and then maintain that loss for periods of two, three, and five years?
- What are the possible negative side effects of the program . . . both physical and psychological? How often are these encountered during this diet?
- Just what are you getting for your money? Are all of your meals prepackaged? Will you need to purchase any other food or supplements? Will you receive counseling? Is behavior modification an important part of the program? What about maintenance? Is exercise stressed?
- What kind of counseling is offered? What training does the counselor have?
- Is there a doctor supervising the program? If so, what is his training? How often is he on the premises? Will you be seeing him? How often? Exactly what is he monitoring?
- How important is the maintenance phase of the program?

As a consumer you are entitled to the answers to these questions and any others you might have before you begin a program. You also are entitled to a period of time after signing up (generally three days) to reconsider your decision to join a weight-loss program. This time varies from state to state. Check with your state attorney general, consumer affairs office, or Better Business Bureau to find out the specific regulations in your area. Don't be shy about changing your mind if you feel you have made a mistake in joining. Be sure and demand your money back if you do.

Here is a rundown on the six biggest centers:

Jenny Craig Weight Loss Centers
Headquarters: 445 Marine View Drive, Suite 300, Del Mar, CA 92014; (619) 259-7000. Established: 1983. Approximate cost: $300 to join; an average of an additional $60 a week for packaged food. Calories per day: 1,000 for women, 1,200 for men. Number of centers: 694 centers in the United States, Australia, New Zealand, Puerto Rico, and Mexico, and growing. Staff: Receives forty-eight hours of company training plus monthly continuing education classes. Controlling interest in Jenny Craig, Inc. is still held by Sid and Jenny Craig, with New York Life being the largest stockholder. Revenues for 1992 were approximately $461 million, but sales in the final quarter of 1993 dropped 22 percent while profits

plunged 84 percent. Approximately a third of the Jenny Craig centers are franchises.

After buying a program, you are introduced to a "counselor." (These "counselors" are actually salesclerks with little training for anything other than encouraging your continued participation in the program.) Once a week the "counselor" chats with you briefly, weighs you, scans your weekly food diary, processes an order for the next week's food, and encourages you to "stick with it." A weekly group meeting, called a "Lifestyle Class," is also available to discuss nutrition, dealing with special situations, and so forth. Nutritional supplements are pushed . . . er, made available.

Diet Workshop Headquarters: 10 Brookline Place West, Suite 107, Brookline, MA 02146; (617) 893-1007. Established: 1964. Approximate cost: (four-week program) $70 for group; $135 for one-on-one. Calories per day: 1,100. Number of centers: thirty franchises throughout East Coast, Midwest, and Florida. Staff: Former customers trained by company.

A variety of programs is available, based on a diet of food "units." Diet Workshop is similar in many ways to Weight Watchers. Packaged foods and supplements are available, but you are encouraged to use grocery store foods.

Healthy Concepts (formerly Diet Center, Inc.) Main office: 921 Penn Avenue, 9th floor, Pittsburgh, PA 15222; (412) 338-8700. Established: 1970. Approximate cost: $40 a week. Approximate

calories per day: 1,000 for women, 1,250 for men. Number of centers: 2,300 in the United States, Canada, Australia, and England. Staff: Former customers (usually) who have been through the Healthy Concepts training program.

This program consists of weekly weigh-ins and measurements, one-on-one "counseling," printed diet programs, and nutritional supplements. What I remember most about Diet Center is apples. The offices are apple-spice scented (at least the two I tried were), and the diet menu encourages you to eat lots of apples.

Nutri-System, Inc. Headquarters: 3901 Commerce Avenue, Suite 925, Willow Grove, PA 19090; (800) 321-8446. Established: 1971. Approximate cost: $600 to lose thirty pounds; an average of $65 a week for packaged foods. Calories per day: 1,000 to 1,500, depending on needs. Number of centers: 1,825 in the United States, Canada, Australia, and the United Kingdom. Staff: Trained at a three-month program at Nutri-System University.

Essentially the same program as Jenny Craig offers with a reported 750,000 customers and an estimated $232 million in annual sales. Nutri-System filed for bankruptcy in 1993, but after financial restructuring was soon reopened.

Physicians Weight Loss Centers Headquarters: 395 Springside Drive, Akron, OH 44443; (330) 666-7952. Established: 1979. Approximate cost: $200 for weight-loss phase. Calories per day:

1,000 to 1,500. Number of centers: 97, in Midwest and the South. Staff: Physician monitors programs and customers to some extent (very loosely). "Counselors" are generally graduates of the program.

Weight Watchers International Headquarters: Jericho Atrium, 500 North Broadway, Jericho, NY 11753; (800) 651-6000. Established: 1963. Owned by the H. J. Heinz food company. Approximate cost: $30 to join, $10 a week. Calories per day: 1,000 to 1,200. Number of groups: Undetermined; available in fifty-two countries. Staff: (Group leaders) successful customers who have completed a three-month training program.

Annual sales average either $750 million or $1.3 billion, depending on the source. Over 42 million people have enrolled in Weight Watchers since it was formed. Participants attend weekly meetings held at various locations around a city . . . church basements seem common. Diet plans are given out, weekly food diaries are kept, and each meeting begins with semiprivate weighins. Members are encouraged to purchase a variety of official Weight Watchers products . . . food scales, water bottles, and other items, and prepackaged foods are available both at the meetings and in grocery stores. These foods are the true moneymakers for the parent company.

LIQUID DIETS (DRINK YOUR POUNDS AWAY?)

Over 20 million Americans a year will spend $1 billion on liquid diets—both physician/clinic-supervised fasts (like Optifast) and over-the-counter modified fasts that recommend that a "sensible meal" be eaten in conjunction with shakes (Slim Fast and others). It's easy to see the appeal of such a simplified method of counting calories. Like the diet center programs where you purchase all of your food ready to microwave in premeasured, precooked portions, the decision making is already done for you.

What is even easier to see is why doctors and hospitals would be so eager to "help" us with these programs. In selling their product to the medical community, Medifast promises doctors an income of $62,000 a year for each fifteen patients on the program. (A twenty-six-week Optifast program will generally cost you between $2,500 and $3,000; $425 of that goes to pay for the powder.)

An estimated 50 percent of the people who sign up for these liquid fasts drop out before completing the program. An article in the October 1993 issue of the *Archives of Family Medicine* reports on a study of these very-low-calorie (800 calories a day) liquid diets. Two and a half years after ending their diets, two thirds of the users had regained their lost weight. The study further concludes that there are several side effects, including brittle nails, temporary hair loss, gout, gallstones, and heart disease.

People are quickly becoming disillusioned with these products. Sales of liquid diet meals peaked in March 1991; just a year later purchases were down 44 percent to $73.3 million in a thirteen-week period ending in September 1992. It would be interesting to know how many cartons of these powder mixes are lurking in the backs of peoples' kitchen cabinets.

SURGERIES AND OTHER INVASIVE PROCEDURES

In the thirty-plus years surgeons have been performing weight-loss surgeries, they have come up with some pretty inventive procedures. None are any more effective than dieting—and the risks are tremendous.

The first form of weight-loss surgery was the intestinal bypass. Good weight loss was reported, but the complications were so horrendous and widespread that this procedure is almost never used now. A section of the small intestine was closed off or removed, thereby limiting absorption of calories. It has been estimated that over 150,000 people have had this surgery. Of those, 74,000 have developed life-threatening complications, including liver malfunctions and recurring kidney stones. Other possible complications include cirrhosis of the liver, arthritis, and malnutrition.

An estimated 300,000 people have undergone one of the varieties of gastric bypass (stomach stapling, arevertical banded gastroplasty, Rouxen-Y, and others). This surgery, in whatever form, basically seeks to limit the amount of food that can be consumed at any one time . . . usually just a few bites . . . by sectioning off a part of the stomach. Reports on the success of this surgery vary considerably. The most extensive, following up on 6,000 cases, found that more than 50 percent of the patients lost less than 15 percent of their beginning weight. Another study showed that 75 percent of the patients regained all lost weight within three years. Possible complications include severe malnutrition, vitamin deficiencies (B_{12}, folate, and iron), stomach cancer, pernicious anemia, ulcers, immune deficiency, lung collapse, infections at site of surgery, osteoporosis, liver and gallbladder diseases, irregular heartbeat, and kidney and urinary infections.

Bilopancreatic bypass involves gastric restriction and diversion of bile and pancreatic secretions. Not much information is available on this procedure. A higher frequency of metabolic complications has been reported than with other weight-loss surgeries.

The insertion of a gastric balloon into a patient's stomach is a less intrusive measure that has been used on more than 20,000 people in this country. A cylindrical plastic balloon is passed down the throat into the stomach, inflated, and left to float freely. Again, reports on effectiveness vary. One study claims a 97 percent success rate, with patients losing an average of seventy-six pounds in ten months. Another study reported no significant difference in weight loss between patients with and without a balloon. Possible complications included stomach ulcers, partial gastric obstruction, spontaneous deflation of the balloon, and movement of deflated balloons into the intestines, causing blockage. This procedure is no longer used in the United States.

Dentists can also get into the act with jaw wiring. This procedure uses dental wires to hold the patient's teeth together, allowing only a straw for nutritional intake. This sounds simple enough and may work short-term for some patients. But once the wires are removed, lost weight is generally regained. People can also be pretty inventive making shakes. I have talked with people who have actually gained weight on chocolate shakes and puréed meatloaf. One of the most worrisome complications of this procedure is choking, and the wires can't be cut quickly enough if a person suddenly begins to vomit. Other possible complications include tooth position shifts, tooth decay (from inability to brush and floss effectively), and the danger of inhaling substances into the lungs.

Liposuction isn't really a weight-loss surgery, but many think of it as a way to get rid of "unsightly" fat. This is now the most common cosmetic surgery performed: hundreds of thousands have been done at a cost of $3,000 or more each. Performed for purely cosmetic reasons, liposuction involves the removal of small amounts of fat from "misshapen" areas of the body. Fat cells are literally sucked with a pump through a metal straw inserted beneath the skin. If done in a clinic, only four pounds of fat may be removed. Up to seven pounds can be removed in a hospital, though a blood transfusion is almost always necessary with the removal of more than four pounds. No more than seven pounds can be removed because of the strong possibility that the patient will go into shock. Any surgeon can become certified to perform liposuction after attending a two-day training course. Possible complications include permanent discoloration of the skin, bruising, dents, swelling and numbness in treated areas, blood clots, infections, and shock.

Weight loss is a more than $40 billion a year industry. We haven't even touched on all of the products advertised to "remove unwanted inches" through use of sweatsuits, body wraps, liniments, vibrating and roller machines, magic belts, high-fiber cookies, or psychiatric counseling. One city, Durham, North Carolina, rakes in $100 million a year from dieters who flock to its residential weight-loss centers. Here you can spend $2,000 a month for the rice diet (Elvis tried this one—before he died, not after), $4,200 for the first month of a behavior modification program, or $1,500 a month for a "Diet with Dignity."

In November 1993, at a conference of obesity researchers in Milwaukee, news of a cream that possibly reduces the size of women's thighs was presented. (Please be aware . . . presenting an idea at a medical conference doesn't make it fact any more than burning someone at the stake for witchcraft makes that person a witch.) The discovery was announced by the man who owns half the patent rights and stands to make a ton of money from this product. The cream's active ingredient is aminophylline, a chemically modified form of theophylline; both are prescription asthma treatments. In a very preliminary study of twenty-four women, the circumference of thighs was reduced approximately one half to one and a half inches over five weeks.

The developers hope to market the cream as a cosmetic rather than as a drug to avoid the years of testing required by the FDA. Pardon me for being skeptical, but this reminds me of so many other products in the past that have been proven to be ineffective in anything but making a lot of money for the P. T. Barnums of our time. At best, this is a potential alternative to liposuction, providing no health benefits and producing temporary, minimal weight loss. Keep an open mind . . . and a closed wallet . . . until conclusive studies have been made.

It comes down to this. Not one single product or service has been proven to deliver safe, effective, long-term weight loss to even a fourth of its users. If anyone has proof that this statement is not true, please send all of the relative documentation to me. I'll see to it the appropriate members of the scientific and medical communities have a chance to evaluate your evidence, and we skeptics will sing the appropriate praises.

Appendix B

Internet Size Acceptance

There is a wealth of information on the Internet and through mailing lists. I have made every attempt to give current addresses and site information. Visit the Size Wise site for current links and update information.

WORLD WIDE WEB

With millions of web sites already in existence and hundreds being added daily, there are bound to be many more on-line resources for people of size in the future. Most web sites offer links to other related sites, so be sure to check them out. You can also search for other size-acceptance-related web sites by using keywords at any of the search engines (www.lycos.com, www.yahoo.com, and others).

GENERAL INFORMATION

BHealthy Gym (Health and exercise in a size-accepting atmosphere)
  http://www.tera.virtual-pc.com/bhealthy/public_html/

Big Folks
  http://www.csun.edu/~hbjou033/BF.html

Dave's Fat Page (Collection of links to other size acceptance pages, catalogs, and usenet newsgroups)
  http://www.execpc.com/~allwardt/fat/fat.html

The Fabulous Miss Piggy Page (All that is Miss Piggy)
http://www-leland.stanford.edu/~rosesage/piggy.html

The Fat Person's Home Page (Thoughts about using the word "fat")
http://www.concentric.net/~joeobrin

The Fatty Zone
http://www.webcom.com/~jmikem

Fine Arts Museum of San Francisco (Use keyword "fat" to access over a hundred pieces portraying large people)
http://www.thinker.org

Jellyroll's Home Page (A woman's thoughts on being fat)
http://www.geocities.com/Heartland/2833/

Largesse, the Network for Size Esteem (The source of information on all aspects of size acceptance)
http://www.fatgirl.com/largesse/

Lauri Mann's Sizism Page (The barbarian guide to diet and exercise, information on fat children)
http://www.city-net.com/~/mann/women/resources/sizism.html

Lazarus
http://inforamp.net/~lazarus

Susan Mason (Artist and comedienne—a little bit of Susan)
http://www.eskimo.com/~lieba

Muskie's Bike Trip (A chubby man's bicycling adventures)
http://www.geocities.com/westhollywood/1123/biketrip.html

Acceptance Page (Excellent site offering current information on media, public attitudes, and feelings about being fat)
http://www.enteract.com/~hijinx/fat

Planet Fatdom
http://www.swschool.com/planet/planet.htm

Services for Bears (Excellent site for large gay men, with lots of links to resources)
http://www.skepsis.com/.gblo/bears/index.htm1

Size Wise (Updated information on all segments of this book)
http://www.SizeWise.com

Stefanie's Home Page (General thoughts from a proud woman of size)
http://www.bayarea.net/~stef

Charles VanDyke's Home Page (Activism, size acceptance, and life in general from the chairman of the board of NAAFA)
http://home.earthlink.net/~cvandyke

CLOTHING

America's Shirt Catalog (Men's shirts to neck 22, sleeve 38)
http://a1.com/shirt/bigtall.html

America's T-shirt Catalog (T-shirts with a variety of designs to size 2X)
http://a1.com/shirt/genius.html

Attitudes and Lace (Lingerie in sizes to 3X)
http://shops.net./shops/showcase

Big Ass Sportswear (T-shirts, sweats, tank tops, pants and shorts in sizes 2X to 10X)
http://www.naafa.org/ads/big_ass/

Big Times Internet Emporium (A selection of shops and services in Great Britain catering to larger ladies)
http://www.emporium.co.uk/bigtimes/

California Rainbow Tie Dye (T-shirts to size 3X)
http://www.catalog.com/giftshop/tiedye/td.htm

Casual Male Big & Tall (Catalog by the same name on-line, clothing to size 6X and 4XLT)
http://www.thinkbig.com/

Chic Full-Figure Fashion (Full-figure fashion news)
http://www.webcom.com/~cfffnews

Cyberbaby (Maternity shop for large women)
http://www.tiac.net/users/hm25/bra.html

Fashion Fit Pattern Service (Custom fit patterns)
http://www.finhost.fi/fashion/fashion.htm

Full Figure Woman's Lingerie (Lingerie to size 3X)
http://www.w2.com/docs2/a3/iasa.html

Grand Style (Virtual club for size 14+ women)
http://www.grandstyle.com

Jalon Enterprises (Leather fashions in sizes up to 5X)
http://www.jalon.com

Jamin' Leathers (Leather fashions up to size 2X)
http://www.leathercat.com

Lands' End (Classic casual styles in sizes up to 2X)
http://www.landsend.com

Lane Bryant (The catalog store on-line)
http://www.wfnnb.limited.net/lcs1.html

Lebow Brothers Clothing for Men and Boys (Regular, short, long, extra short and to size 52)
http://www.tiac.net/users/lebow

Making It Big (Women's natural fiber clothing for large and supersize women)
http://www.bigwomen.com

More To Hug (Fashions for women size 16 up to 10X)
http://www.vcnet.com/moretohug/

Plus Size Industry News (Fashion trends and news)
http://www.cfffnews.com/cfffnews/industry.html

Prescription Sportswear (T-shirts with hunting/fishing designs in sizes up to 6X)
http://www.gsn.com/sportswr.htm

Rainbow Tees (Tie-dye T-shirts and sweatshirts to size 6X)
http://www.xmission.com/~gastown/rainbow/

Sexy Fat Boys
http://www.netrunner.net/~fatboys

Stage Clothes, USA (Sexy lingerie in sizes up to 2X)
http://www.w2.com/docs2/a3/iasa.html

There is often an overlap between activism and socialization. You'll most likely find a little of both on sites in these next two lists.

ACTIVISM ONLINE

Dicke e.v. (German language only)
http://prian.physik.uni-dortmund.de/~mrp/dicke

The Electronic Activist (Excellent database of government and media contacts local and national)
http://www.berkshire.net/~ifas/activist/

International Fat Acceptance Network—New Mexico
http://www.unm.edu/~markm/nm-fan.html

National Association to Advance Fat Acceptance (NAAFA)
(See Social Organizations)

New Mexico Fat Acceptance Network
http://www.unm.edu/~markm/nm-fan.html

Rump Parliament (Current, aggressive, straightforward fat activism at its best)
http://web2.airmail.net/~lmartin/

SOCIAL ORGANIZATIONS

Affiliated Big Men's Clubs (Gay men's social club)
http://www.skepsis.com/.gblo/g_and_m/index.htm1

Ample Awakenings
http://www.voicenet.com/~oscar/ample.html

BBW (Dedicated to the big beautiful women of the world and the men that admire them. Gifts and lots of links to similar sites.)
http://wwwl.aksi.net/~bumpers/bbw.html

BBW Flirts Gallery
http://www.ccsi.com/~jmj/gallery

BBW Oasis Message Board
http://www.nebula.net/~ceh/oasis/wwwboard/oasis.html

BBW/FA Ring (Links to BBW/FA related sites)
http://www.geocities.com/Paris/4356/

Big Difference (Updates on Big Difference events and talking personals)
http://www.rotunda.com/Big_Diff/home.html

Big Girl's Homepage (Volumptous women and the men who love, respect, and admire them; lots of great links)
http://astro.ocis.temple.edu/~adonis1a/bbw.html

Big Stuff Dances (Current information on Big Stuff dances)
http://www.wine.com/obaby/bigstuff.html

The Brotherhood of Girth (Men's fat activism and social group)
http://home.sprynet.com/sprynet/imac

Bumpers BBW Homepage (Link to web pages dedicated to big beautiful women and fat admirers)
http://www.momi.com/

Chubby and Chaser Link (Gay men's club)
http://users.aol.com/bellylink/

Club BBW
http://www.largeluv.com

FA Homepage (For men who love big, beautiful women)
http://www.cybercity.hko.net/washington/ozzy/

Fat and Terrific (FAT)
http://www.ccnet.com/~avery/

Nancy Gold's Home Page (Personal page with some interesting thoughts on being fat)
http://reality.sgi.com/employees/nancyg/

International Fatty Festival—Italy
http://www.cibernet.it/cicciona/english.htm

International No Diet Day (Latest information on upcoming information and the history of INDD)
http://www.fatgirl.com/fatgirl/largesse/indd/

Living Large and Loving It (Bimonthly video magazine dedicated to fat acceptance)
http://www.io.com/user/joeobrin/LLLI.html

National Association to Advance Fat Acceptance (NAAFA):
  Michigan
      http://www.ic.net/~karle/naafa/naafa.html
  National
      http://naafa.org/
  New England
      http://www.pages.prodigy.com/MA/necnaffa/necnaffa.html
  Philadelphia
      http://naafa.org/chapters/philadelphia.html
  South Jersey
      http://www.voicenet.com/~oscar/about.html

One Bad Bear
      http://www.onebadbear.com

oooO Baby Baby Productions (Current information for activities and social events in the San Francisco Bay area)
http://www.wine.com/obaby

SeXy KiTTn's Big Beautiful Women (IRC chat information and lots of great links)
http://www.techline.com/~kitefvr/bbw.htm

Southern California Size Acceptance Coaliton
http://alumni.caltech.edu/~hanshorn/coalition/

Wide Appeal Social Club (Calendar of events)
http://www.erols.com/acer75/wide.htm

MEDICAL

Adipose 101 (Excellent, well-researched, detailed health and fatness paper)
http://www.omen.com

Association of Health Enrichment for Large People Page—AHELP (Professional association updates)
http://www.nrv.net/~ahelp/

Federal Drug Administration (Good source for information on diet medications awaiting approval)
htt;//www.fda.gov

Medical Sciences Bulletin—Focus on Obesity
http://pharminfo.com/pubs/msb/obesity.html

National Insitutes of Health (Studies and position papers regarding weight)
http://www.nih.gov/

PUBLICATIONS AND ARTICLES OF INTEREST

Allen's Big Beautiful World (BBW Fiction)
www.eden.com/~crusader.html

The AR-MEN (Comic)
http://www.eden.com/~crusader/armen144.html

Big Beautiful Woman (BBW) magazine
http://www.bbwonline.com

Big Ad Magazine (Gay Men's Personals)
http://mediapub.com/bigad

Big Girls Night Out (Comic)
http://www.display.co.uk/starr/fat.html

Dimensions magazine (Articles and photos of interest to FA's)
http://pencomputing.com/dim

FaT GiRl (Great 'zine)
http://www.fatgirl.com/fatgirl/

FaT GiRl comics
http://www.fatgirl.com/fatgirl/comics.html

Fat!So? (In-you-face, humorous and informative 'zine)
http://www.fatso.com/

HUES (Hear Us Emerging Sisters magazine information)
http://www.lifeplay.net/magazines/hues/hues.html

Phat Phree! E-Zine
http://www.netaxs.com/~oscar/phat.html

Plumpers and Big Women (Site related to magazine of same name)
http://www.dugent.com/pbw/index.htm

Rubenesque Romances (Order fiction featuring big, beautiful women)
   http://www.borkport.com/htbin/publishers/rubenesque/pubrow Saber

Comics Online (Action comic with large characters)
   http://www.spaceship.com/~cannibal/saber1.html

Time *magazine—article "Fat Times"*
   http://pathfinder.com/@@of@/vtdjgqweaqj@j/time/magazine/
   domestic/1995/950116/950116.cover.html

Time *magazine—Plus-Size Models Calendar*
   http://www.images/covers/xlmystique.html

Utne Reader Fat Lib Sites review
   http://www.utne.com/archive/lens06/bms/6bmsqnbig.html

Women En Large (Excellent, artistic collection of photographs of large nude women)
   http://www.igc.apc.org/BooksinFocus/

FREQUENTLY ASKED QUESTIONS (FAQS)

Maintained by Stefanie Jones (stef@bayarea.net), these FAQ's are an excellent source of information. Access them through the world wide web at http://www.cis.ohio-state.edu/hypertext/faq/usenet/fat-accep tance;faq/ or http://www.cs.ruu.nl/wais/html/na-dir/fat-acceptance-faq/. They are also posted bi-weekly in the alt.support.big-folks and soc.support/fat-acceptance newsgroups. FAQ titles include:

fat-acceptance-faq/clothing/us

fat-acceptance-faq/clothing/canada

fat-acceptance-faq/physical

fat-acceptance-faq/resources/
   publications fat-acceptance-faq/size-
   acceptance

fat-acceptance-faq/resources/other

alt.support.big-folks-faq

fat-acceptance-faq/clothing/uk-europe
   fat-acceptance-faq/fitness

fat-acceptance-faq/health

fat-acceptance-faq/research

USENET NEWS GROUPS

Usenet news groups are topic-specific but unmoderated. Anyone can join, and it takes an act of God (or a sysop) to get rid of any user who may be particularly abusive. As a result the atmosphere is generally very size accepting but occasionally combative. These groups are generally gold mines of information and support. Some of these discuss dieting, the majority do not. Join them through your server's usenet function. Current size-specific usenet news groups include:

alt.personals.big-folks	alt.sex.super-size
alt.personals.fat	alt.sex.weight-gain
alt.sigma2.height	alt.support.big-folks
alt.sex.fat	alt.support.obesity
alt.sex.fetish.fa	alt.support.tall
alt.sex.fetish.fat	soc.support.fat-acceptance

MAILING LISTS

Joining a mailing list gives you access to discussions on a specific topic with a bit more privacy than open forums and news groups. These are generally moderated, and troublemakers are ejected from the list.

Bears Send E-mail to: bears-request @spdcc.com

Big Moms Send E-mail to: big_moms _list-request@butler.hpl.hp.com In body of letter, type: subscribe <your E-mail address>

Fat and Fit Send E-mail to: listserv @unc.edu In body of letter, type: subscribe Fatand- Fit <your E-mail address>

Fat Lesbians Send E-mail to: fatdykes- request@apocalypse.org In body of letter, type: subscribe <your E-mail address>

Fatdykes Send E-mail to: fatdykes- request@apocalypse.org

In body of letter type: subscribe <your E-mail address>

NAAFA, members only Send E-mail to: majordomo@world.std.com In body of letter, type: subscribe naafa- members

NAAFA, open to nonmembers Send E- mail to: majordomo@world.std.com In body of letter, type: subscribe fat- acceptance

Fat Sex Send E-mail to: lists @rotunda. com In body of letter, type: subscribe fat_sex <your E-mail address>

Super Size Send E-mail to: bioaw124 @emory.edu Put SS in subject line. Nothing required in body of letter.

FORUMS

The Ample Living Forum on Compu-Serve (key word: ample)
This forum was established by Deidre Links in 1996 and discusses all aspects of being a larger person, including diet-ing. There are files to download, live chats (sometimes with guest speakers), and lively discussions through public posts.

LIVE CHAT AREAS

Most of the major on-line services like CompuServe and America Online offer live chat . . . at around $3 per hour. These costs vary with the service and change often. Talking with people on-line can be addictive, and the cost for your chat time varies considerably, so be sure to keep an eye on your tab.

Many computer users are switching to local servers with IRC (Internet relay chat) access and flat rates. For instance, the server I use offers twenty-four-hour-a-day unlimited access for just $13 a month. The phone number I dial to access the server is local, so there are no long-distance charges either. Once into a chat area, look for channels like big-folks, big-friends, bbwflirts, big&sexy, bearcave, and bbw and join in the fun.

Appendix C

For Further Reading:
Annotated Bibliography for P. Ernsberger, Ph.D.

Ernsberger, P., and Haskew, P.: News about obesity. *New England Journal of Medicine* 315:130–131, 1986. This letter noted that obesity is less likely to be associated with risk factors when it is genetic, so it may not be dangerous to be naturally fat. Reply by Theodore VanItallie, M.D., of Columbia University and Presbyterian–St. Luke's in New York City.

Ernsberger, P.: Does obesity kill? No. *Physicians Weekly* 3 (37):1 (10/6/86). Debate with Theodore VanItallie, M.D.

Ernsberger, P.: Body weight and longevity. *Journal of the American Medical Association* 257:1895–1896, 1987. Discusses the hazards of underweight.

Ernsberger, P.: Complications of the surgical treatment of obesity. *American Journal of Psychiatry* 144:833–834, 1987. Reviews complications of vertical banded gastroplasty. Reply by Albert Stunkard, M.D.

Ernsberger, P.: NIH consensus conference on obesity: by whom and for what? *Journal of Nutrition* 117:1164–1165, 1987. Summarizes the case against the NIH consensus panel report, establishing its bias in reviewing data on obesity and health. Reply by Jules Hirsch, M.D., of Rockefeller University.

Ernsberger, P., and Haskew, P.: Health implications of obesity: an alternative view. *Journal of Obesity and Weight Regulation* 6:55–137, 1987. (Published separately as a book titled *Rethinking Obesity: An Alternative View of Its Health Implications* [New York: Human Sciences Press, 1988]. Monograph reviews the evidence linking obesity and disease, and concludes that the ill effects of obesity have been exaggerated, potential health benefits have been overlooked, and that much of the ill health in obese persons is caused by adverse consequences

357

of treatment, either directly through hazardous weight-loss methods or indirectly through the yo-yo syndrome.

Ernsberger, P., and Nelson, D. O.: Refeeding hypertension in dietary obesity. *American Journal of Physiology* 254:R47–R55, 1988. Shows that losing and regaining weight can raise blood pressure, cause cardiovascular abnormalities, and increase the efficiency of fat storage. Animals placed on periodic low-calorie calories became obese without overeating relative to normal controls who never dieted.

Ernsberger, P., and Nelson, D. O.: The effects of fasting and refeeding on blood pressure are determined by nutritional state, not by body weight change. *American Journal of Hypertension* 1:153S–157S, 1988. Shows by a metaanalysis of human studies plus animal data that the blood pressure fall during dieting is a response to starvation rather than a result of weight loss. In other words, the fall in blood pressure during weight loss is due to the diet, not to the loss of body fat.

Ernsberger, P.: Obesity is hazardous to your health: negative. In *Debates in Medicine,* vol. 2, edited by H. V. Barnes (New York: Yearbook Medical Publishers, 1989), pp. 113–123. (*Debates in Medicine* 2:113–123, 1989). Debate with Ethan Allen Sims regarding whether or not obesity is a health hazard.

Ernsberger, P.: Rebuttal: negative. In Barnes, ed. *Debates in Medicine,* pp. 129–135. (*Debates in Medicine* 2:129–135, 1989). Rebuttal of Ethan Allen Sims.

Ernsberger, P.: Surgery risks outweigh its benefits. *Obesity & Health,* March/April 1991, pp.24–25. Argues against weight-loss surgery by presenting hazards and by showing that so-called "morbid obesity" decreases median life expectancy by no more than six years. Therefore, dangerous weight loss treatments, even if completely successful in the long term, are not justified.

Koletsky, R. J., and Ernsberger, P.: Obese SHR (Koletsky rat): a model for the interactions between hypertension and obesity. In *Genetic Hypertension,* edited by J. Sassard (London: John Libby Ltd., 1992), pp. 373–375. (*Colloque INSERM* 218:373–375, 1992). Findings on genetically obese rats. Shows that genetic obesity per se actually lowers blood pressure.

Ernsberger, P., Koletsky, R. J., Collins, L. A., and Douglas, J. G.: Autoradiographic visualization of renal angiotensin II receptors in obese SHR with glomerulopathy. *Hypertension* 21:1039–1045, 1993. Suggests that drugs that block the hormone angiotensin may be particularly effective in treating obese hypertension and protecting the kidney against diabetic and hypertensive damage.

Ernsberger, P., and Koletsky, R. J.: Weight cycling and mortality: support from animal studies. *Journal of the American Medical Association* 269:1116, 1993. Capsule review of animal studies showing that the yo-yo syndrome has harmful effects and how they support studies in humans.

Ernsberger, P., Koletsky, R. J., Baskin, J. Z., and Foley, M.: Refeeding hypertension in obese SHR. *Hypertension* 24:699–705, 1994. Further evidence for harmful effects of cycles of losing and regaining weight. Weight cycling in genetically obese animals causes even larger rises in blood pressure than seen previous in paper #7, enlargement of the heart, and increased stress hormones.

Ernsberger, P., and Koletsky, R. J.: Weight cycling. *Journal of the American Medical Association* 273:998–999, 1995. The NIH Task Force on the Prevention and Treatment of Obesity review on weight cycling is criticized and a conflict of interest is pointed out in the placement of six weight-loss clinic directors on an eight-person panel to review the hazards of weight cycling.

Koletsky, R. J., Boccia, J., and Ernsberger, P.: Acceleration of renal disease in obese SHR by exacerbation of hypertension. *Clinical and Experimental Pharmacology and Physiology* Animals who have periodically lost weight on Optifast are actually heavier and fatter than animals who never lost weight. Even though they were fatter, the rats that yo-yo'd ate precisely the same number of calories as their brothers and sisters that never dieted. The extra fat was deposited mainly in the abdominal area. Blood pressure rose more than twenty points during the regain of lost weight and stayed high for the whole five-month study. They showed enlargement of the heart and showed signs of excess adrenaline and noradrenaline in their bloodstreams.

RECENT PUBLISHED ABSTRACTS

Koletsky, R. J., Ernsberger, P., Baskin J. Z., and Foley, M.: Weight cycling in obese SHR exacerbates obesity and hypertension. *FASEB Journal* 6:A1674, 1992. Shows that cycles of weight loss and regain can increase weight and fat deposits in the abdomen.

Ernsberger, P., Koletsky, R. J., and Collins, L. A.: Lethal consequences of a high-salt diet in obese SHR. *Hypertension* 24:376, 1994. Shows that genetically obese animals with high blood pressure are very sensitive to increased dietary salt.

Koletsky, R. J., Collins, L. A., Bedol, D., and Ernsberger, P.: Obese SHR as a model of human Syndrome X. *FASEB Journal* 9:A187, 1995. Further studies of genetically obese rats.

Koletsky, R. J., Bedol, D., Farrell, C. J., Friedman, J.E., Collins, L. A., and Ernsberger, P.: Impact of sympathoinhibition with an imidazoline receptor agonist in obese hypertension. *FASEB Journal* 10:A632, 1996. Shows that treating obese and hypertensive animals with the appropriate blood pressure–lowering drug can improve not only blood pressure but many other factors such as triglycerides and blood sugar.

Ernsberger, P., Kilani, A., and Koletsky, R. J.: Regulation of kidney I1-imidazoline and 2-adrenergic receptors by genetic hypertension and obesity and by weight cycling. *FASEB Journal* 10:A691, 1996. Further evidence that cycles of weight loss and regain increase levels of stress hormones.

Paul Ernsberger, Ph.D., is a respected obesity researcher as well as Associate Professor of Medicine, Pharmacology and Neuroscience at Case Western Reserve School of Medicine, 10900 Euclid Ave., Cleveland, OH 44106-4982 E-mail: pre@po.cwru.edu; fax: (216) 368-4752.

Bibliography

"Americans with Disabilities Act of 1990—Interpretation and Construction," U.S. Chamber of Commerce, 1991.

Alexander, Anne. "The Best Shape of Your Life," *The Walking Magazine,* January/February 1994.

Anderson, Jack, and Binstein, Michael. " 'Medical Mafia' Makes $80 Billion Killing," *Washington Post,* February 17, 1993.

Angier, Natalie. "Why So Many Are Prejudiced Against the Obese," *New York Times,* November 22, 1992.

Bacon, Donald C. "An Environment That Everyone Can Use," *Nation's Business,* vol. 77 no. 5 (May 1989), p. 6(2).

Beck, Melinda; Springer, Karen; Beachy, Lucile; Hager, Mary; and Buckley, Linda. "Lifestyle/The Losing Formula" (cover story), *Newsweek,* April 30, 1990.

Bennett, William, M.D. "Indictment of Dieting—III," speech delivered at 1982 NAAFA Convention in Columbus, Ohio, NAAFA Press Kit.

Benson, Tracy E. "Poor Design Is Truly a Pain; Companies Can Stem the Flow of Workers' Comp Claims by Updating Office Furniture," *Industry Week,* vol. 239 (July 19, 1990), p. 60 (2).

Berg, Frances M. "Children and Teens in Weight Crisis," *Healthy Weight Journal* 1995.

———"Harmful Weight Loss Practices Are Widespread Among Adolescents," *Obesity & Health,* July/August 1992, pp. 69–72.

Berland, Theodore, and the editors of *Consumer Guide. Rating the Diets* (Skokie, Ill.: New American Library, 1979).

Bird, Laura. "Slim-Fast's Diet for Town Could Be Risky," *Wall Street Journal,* September 10, 1992.

Bishop, Jerry E. "Cut Your Blood Pressure by Changing Armbands," *Wall Street Journal,* September 12, 1990.

Blodgett, Bonnie. "Don't Be Conned by the Diet Racket," *Glamour Magazine,* January 1991, p. 136(7).

Brody, Jane E. "Research Lifts Blame from Many of the Obese," *New York Times,* March 24, 1987.

———. "Personal Health: Fighting Fat Without Being a Slave to Diet," *New York Times,* November 25, 1992.

Brody, Liz. "Scale Scams," *Shape,* March 1992.

———. "Are We Losing Our Girls?" *Shape,* November 1995.

Brown, Roxanne. "Full-figured Women Fight Back: Resistance Grown to Society's Demand for Slim Bodies," *Ebony,* March 1990, p. 27.

Brubach, Holly. "Fat Pride (fashions for overweight women)," *The Atlantic,* November 1987, p. 111(3).

Canning, H., and Mayer, J., "Obesity: An Influence on High School Performance?" *American Journal of Clinical Nutrition* 20:352–354, 1967.

———. "Obesity—Its Possible Effect on College Acceptance," *New England Journal of Medicine* 275:1172–1174, 1966.

Carlson, Margaret. "And Now, Obesity Rights," via America Online, *Time* magazine, December 6, 1993, p. 96.

Carter, Kathy Barrett. "Obese Worker Upheld on Biased Firing Based on Appearance Alone," Newark *Star-Ledger,* April 21, 1989.

Christensen, Deborah. "At 520 Pounds, Dieter Is Less Than Half His Old Self," *Los Angeles Times,* September 9, 1988, home ed. section 1, pt: 1, p. 2.

"Commercial Breakout," *The Economist,* October 31, 1992, p. 68(1).

Cooper, Claire. "State High Court Extends Partial Shield to Obese People," *Sacramento Bee,* September 3, 1993.

Corrigan, Patricia. "Weight & the Workplace," *Big Beautiful Woman,* August 1993, p. 43(2).

Costanzo, P. R., and Woody, E. Z. "Domain-specific Parenting Styles and Their Impact on the Child's Development of Particular Deviance: The Example of Obesity Proneness," *Journal of Social and Clinical Psychology* 3:425–445, 1985.

Crandall, Christian S. "Prejudice Against Fat People: Ideology and Self-Interest," *Journal of Personality and Social Psychology* 66(5):882–894, 1994.

Daufin, E. K. "Hold the Slurs—Fat Is Not a Four-Letter Word," *Los Angeles Times,* March 4, 1990.

Davis, Dan. "Fat Phobia & Children: Myth & Reality," *Radiance,* Fall 1987, pp. 29–31.

Deveny, Kathleen. "Marketing & Media/Advertising: "Nutri/System Is Struggling to Get TV Networks to Clear Its New Ads," *Wall Street Journal,* April 12, 1990.

————. "Marketplace/Marketing: Slim-Fast Maker Beefs Up Ads to Rebuff Rivals in Swelling Diet-Powder Market," *Wall Street Journal,* October 18, 1990.

————. "Marketplace/Marketscan: Blame It on Dashed Hopes (and Oprah): Disillusioned Dieters Shun Liquid Meals," *Wall Street Journal,* October 13, 1992.

"Dick Gregory Sees 'Crisis of Obesity,' Asks U.S. Help," *Los Angeles Times,* June 23, 1988, section 1, pt. 1, p. 15.

Dietz, W. H., and Gortmaker, S. L. "Do We Fatten Our Children at the Television Set? Obesity and Television Viewing in Children and Adolescents," *Pediatrics* 75:807–812, 1985.

Dolan, Carrie. "Getting Remodeled: Fat-Cutting Surgery Gains Wide Popularity But Can Be Dangerous," *Wall Street Journal,* June 26, 1987.

Dorfman, John R. "Heard on the Street, Jenny Craig Might Be on a 'Yo-Yo Diet," *Wall Street Journal,* May 27, 1992.

Ebron, Angela. "Why Whoopie Doesn't Worry About Her Weight," *Family Circle,* September 20, 1994.

Eller, Daryn, and Levin, Susanna. "Finally the Truth About Fitness," *Essence,* June 1993.

Enteen, Robert, Ph.D. *Health Insurance: How to Get It, Keep It, or Improve What You've Got* (Paragon House, 1992).

Epstein, Diane, and Thompson, Kathleen. *Feeding on Dreams: Why America's Diet Industry Doesn't Work—& What Will Work for You* (New York: Macmillan, 1994).

Ernsberger, P. "Surgery Risks Outweigh Its Benefits," *Obesity and Health,* March/April 1991, pp. 24–25.

Ernsberger, P., and Koletsky, R. J. "Weight Cycling and Mortality: Support from Animal Studies," *Journal of the American Medical Association* 269:116, 1993.

Farhi, Paul. "Government Weighs the Claims of Diets: FTC Boosts Scrutiny of Centers, Products," *Washington Post,* May 31, 1992.

"Fat in America: A Three-Part Series," *New York Times,* November 22–24, 1992. Angier, Natalie; "Why So Many Are Prejudiced Against the Obese." Brody, Jane E.; "For Most Trying to Lose Weight, Dieting Only Makes Things Worse." Kolata, Gina; "The Burdens of Being Overweight: Mistreatment and Misconceptions." Rosenthal, Elisabeth; "Commercial Diets Lack Proof of Their Long-Term Success."

"Fat Control Proteins Isolated," the Associated Press via CompuServe Readers News Service, October 19, 1993.

Federal Drug Administration transcript, open public hearings on dexfenfluramine, November 16, 1995.

Fletcher, Anne M. "Inside America's Hottest Diet Programs," part 5—Overeaters Anonymous, *Prevention*, May 1990, p. 46 (11).

Forsbert, Chuck. "Adiposity 101," 1995, 230 pages. Available from www.omen.com; INTERNET.

Fraser, Laura. "Should You Treat Obesity?" *Hippocrates*, women's health, May 1993, p. 24(3).

Freedman, Rita. "Life at Large (Being Comfortable with Being Large)," *Family Media, Inc.*, 1989.

"Frozen Light Entrees," *Consumer Reports*, January 1993, p. 27 (5).

Garn, Stanley M. "How Fat and Smarts Connect (a Study of Socioeconomic Status and Weight)," January–February 1990, p. 12 (1).

Garner, David M., and Woolely, Susan C. "Confronting the Failure of Behavioral and Dietary Treatments for Obesity," *Clinical Psychology Review* 11:729–780, 1991.

"Gastric Balloons to Treat Obesity," *Postgraduate Medicine*, vol. 83, no. 6, May 1, 1988.

Gerding, Andrea L., and Weinstein, Lawrence. "Taste Ratings of Obese People, and Taste Preferences Based on Geographical Location," *Bulletin of the Psychonomic Society*, November 1992, pp. 509–510.

Gil, Eliana. "The Inner World of the Fat Child: Challenge for a Child Abuse Counselor," *Radiance*, Fall 1987.

Gill, Mark Stuart. "Losing It in Fat City," *Los Angeles Times Magazine*, June 2, 1991.

Gillis, Jack. *The Car Book* (New York: HarperCollins, 1996).

Gleick, Elizabeth; Maier, Ann; and Harmes, Joseph. "How Thin Is Too Thin," *People Weekly*, September 20, 1993.

Gortmaker, Steven L., et al. "Social and Economic Consequences of Overweight in Adolescence and Young Adulthood," *New England Journal of Medicine*, 329 (14):1008–1012, 1993.

Gruzen, Tara. "Treatment of Obese Woman's Corpse Blasted," *Chicago Tribune* Metro Chicago Section, May 12, 1996.

"A Guide to Weight Loss Surgery," compiled from "Surgery for Morbid Obesity," *Postgraduate Medicine*, May 1, 1988.

Haddock, Vicki. "Job Prospects Cooled After Face-to-Face Test" and "Weight Bias Ruling Stirs Fight for Law," *San Francisco Sunday Examiner and Chronicle*, September 5, 1993.

"Hall of Shame: Kill All the Lawyers: And Don't Get Fat," *Insight Magazine*, June 17, 1991.

Hemenway, Carrie. "Children and Size Issues: Someday They'll Believe Me," *Radiance*, Fall 1987.

Higbie, Andrea. "Fat Women Say It's Not a Dirty Word," *New York Times*, Living Section, April 1, 1987.

Hirschman, Carolyn. "Casket Companies Ensure That Deceased Go Out in Style," *Business First—Columbus,* May 6, 1991, p. 16(2).

"Getting Slim" *U.S. News & World Report,* May 14, 1990, pp. 56–65.

James, Lorca. "Fat or Not: A Teenager Reports," *Radiance,* Fall 1987, pp. 9, 40.

"Jenny Craig, Inc.," *San Diego Business Journal,* October 12, 1992, p. 27(1).

"Kids Fear Fat Gain," *Obesity and Health,* March/April 1993, p. 31.

Klesges, R. C.; Mallott, J. M.; Boschee, P. F.; and Weber, J. M. "The Effects of Parental Influences on Children's Food Intake, Physical Activity, and Relative Weight," *International Journal of Eating Disorders* 5:335–346 (1986).

Laliberte, Richard. "Big Fat Lies," *Men's Health,* January–February 1993, p. 80(3).

Lampbert, Leslie. "Fat Like Me," *Ladies' Home Journal,* May 1993.

Larkin, J. C., and Pines, H. A., "No Fat Persons Need Apply: Experimental Studies of the Overweight Stereotype and Hiring Preference," *Sociology of Work and Occupations* 6:312–327, 1979.

Lee, I-Min, and Paffenbarger, Ralph S., Jr. "Change in Body Weight and Longevity," *Journal of the American Medical Association,* October 21, 1992, p. 2045(5).

"Liposuction: Quick Fix for Fat Pads, but No Substitute for Diet, Exercise," *Environmental Nutrition,* September 1987.

Lissner, Lauren; Odell, Patricia M.; D'Agostino, Ralph B.; Stokes, Joseph III; Kreger, Bernard E.; Belanger, Albert J.; and Brownell, Kelly D. "Variability of Body Weight and Health Outcomes in the Framingham Population," *New England Journal of Medicine,* June 27, 1991, p. 1839(6).

"Long-term Problems with Weight-Loss Programs," *Consumers' Research Magazine,* July 1992, p. 22(4).

Maddox, G. L., and Liederman, V. "Overweight as a Social Disability with Medical Implications," *Journal of Medical Education* 44, 1969, pp. 214–20.

Maiman, Lois, et al. "Attitudes Toward Obesity and the Obese Among Professionals," *Journal of the American Dietetic Association* 74, 1979, pp. 331–336.

Martindale, Lee. "Outrage in Chicago: The Death & Desecration of Patricia Mullen," *Rump Parliament,* July–August 1996.

McLean, R. A., and Moon, M. "Health, Obesity and Earnings," *American Journal of Public Health* 70, 1980, pp. 1006–1009.

Mehren, Elizabeth. "Is Nurse Fighting Textbook Case of Discrimination?" *Los Angeles Times,* December 18, 1990.

Moylan, Martin J. "Weight-loss Centers Hardly Starving," *Minneapolis–St. Paul City Business,* February 18, 1991, p. 11(2).

Bibliography 365

Murray, Christopher. "In Search of the Perfect Chair," *Home Office Computing*, August 1991, p. 39(3).

National Institutes of Health. Consensus statement on treatment of obesity, 1991.

Nelson-Horchler, Joani. "The Magic of Herman Miller," *Industry Week*, February 18, 1991, p. 11(4).

"NIH Consensus Statement Covers Treatment of Obesity," *American Family Physician*, July 1991, p. 305(2).

Noble, Barbara Presley. "Crash Is Out, Moderation Is In, and Diet Companies Feel the Pinch," *New York Times*, November 24, 1991.

"Overblown Fear of Flab (Vital Statistics: News You Can Use)," *U.S. News & World Report*, February 19, 1990, p. 70(1).

"Overweight People Unlucky in Love, Money," Associated Press, *San Luis Obispo County (California) Telegram-Tribune*, September 30, 1993.

Palmer, Jay. "Fat and Getting Fatter: Hey, Fatso!" (cover story), *Barron's*, July 1, 1996, p. 25(3).

Papazian, Ruth. "Never Say Diet?" *FDA Consumer*, October 1991, p. 8(5).

Perry, Pat. "Richard Simmons' New Year's Revolution," *Saturday Evening Post*, January–February 1989, p. 58(3).

"Prevalence of Overweight—Behavioral Risk Factor Surveillance System, 1987," Morbidity and Mortality Weekly Report, *Journal of the American Medical Association*, July 28, 1989, p. 471(2).

"Prevalence of Overweight for Hispanics—United States, 1982–1984" *Journal of the American Medical Association*, February 2, 1990, p. 631(2).

Price, Caroline. "Top Boxes," *Michigan Business*, September 1990, p. 42(2).

"Prime-Time Distortions: TV Portrayals of Women," *U.S. News & World Report*, November 26, 1990, p. 18(1).

Quincy, Matthew. *Diet Right! The Consumer's Guide to Diet & Weight Loss Programs* (Berkeley, Calif.: Conari Press, 1991).

"Report on Discrimination Due to Physical Size," National Education Association position paper, October 7, 1994.

Rothblum, Esther D., et al. "The Relationship Between Obesity, Employment, Discrimination, and Employment-Related Victimization," *Journal of Vocational Behavior* 37:251–266, 1990.

"The Seat Squeeze Aloft," *Consumer Reports Travel Letter*, September 1991, p. 99(3).

"Seven Fast Firm-ups for Bigger Bodies (Exercise for Overweight Women)," *Redbook*, August 1989, p. 92(4).

"She Challenged Television's Beauty Myth," *People Weekly*, March 7, 1994, p. 177(1).

Silberner, Joanne. "War of the Diets," *U.S. News & World Report*, February 3, 1992, p. 55(7).

Slater, Leslie Dickstein. "Built for Comfort," *Travel Weekly,* November 21, 1988, p. 36(2).

Rapson, Bevan. "PM Sets Off Chorus of Outrage," *New Zealand Herald,* August 10, 1992.

"Report of Weight Loss Surgery" (Bellerose, N.Y.: NAAFA, 1986).

Rovner, Sandy. "Yo-Yo Dieting: Worse Than Being Overweight," *Washington Post,* December 13, 1988.

Rubel, Jean. "When Children Hate Their Bodies: How Parents Can Help," *Radiance,* Fall 1987.

Rubin, Rita. "Losers Weepers; Why Most Diets Fail," American Health Special Report: Lose Weight and Keep It Off! *American Health: Fitness of Body and Mind,* July–August 1991, p. 46(3).

"Running Shoes," *Consumer Reports,* May 1992.

Satter, Ellyn, M.S., M.S.S.W., R.D. "Childhood Obesity Demands New Approaches," *Obesity and Health,* May/June 1991.

Seligmann, Jean; Springen, Karen; and bureau reports. "Lifestyles: The New Generation of Diet Pills," *Newsweek,* April 30, 1990.

Shapiro, L. R.; Crawford, P. B.; Clark, M. J.; Pearson, D. J.; Raz, J.; and Huenemann, R. L. "Obesity Prognosis: A Longitudinal Study of Children from the Age of 6 Months to 9 Years," *American Journal of Public Health* 74:968–972, 1984.

"Scaling Back" (Jenny Craig), "The Top 50 Women Business Owners, *Working Woman,* May 1994, p. 42(1).

Sherman, Rorie. "Diet Industry Faces Regimen of Legal Fights," *National Law Journal,* October 21, 1991, pp. 3, 35.

Silberner, Joanne. "War of the Diets," *U.S. News & World Report,* February 3, 1992, p. 55(7).

"Sofabeds," *Consumer Reports,* November 1992.

Tilke, Brenda. "Getting a Much Better Fit," *Advance for Occupational Therapists,* January 9, 1991.

Trebbe, Ann. "Sir Mix-a-Lot's Rap the Butt of Controversy," *USA Today,* July 21, 1992.

Tucker, Larry A., and Bagwell, Marilyn. "Television Viewing and Obesity in Adult Females," *American Journal of Public Health,* July 1991, pp. 908–911.

"Upholstered Furniture," *Consumer Reports,* January 1989, via CompuServe Online Services.

Valelriano, Lourdes Lee. "Diet Programs Hope Broader Services Fatten Profits, Industry Focus," *Wall Street Journal,* August 5, 1993.

Viedman, Christiane. "Obesity," *World Health Organization,* July–August 1991, p. 8(1).

"Vital Statistics: News You Can Use: Overblown Fear of Flab," *U.S. News & World Report,* February 19, 1990, p. 70(1).

Wadden, Thomas A.; VanItallie, Theodore B.; and Blackburn, George L. "Responsible and Irresponsible Use of Very-Low-Calorie Diets in the Treatment of Obesity," *Journal of the American Medical Association,* January 5, 1990, p. 83(3).

"Walking Shoes," *Consumer Reports,* February 1990.

"Walter Hudson: Was Once World's Heaviest Man," *Los Angeles Times,* December 25, 1991, home ed., pt. a. p. 46.

"Weight Restrictions . . ." *Wall Street Journal,* March 13, 1991.

Winfrey, Oprah. "Wind Beneath My Wings," *Essence,* June 1989, p. 44(5).

Wolfman, Ira. "Special Report: Health Fraud 1990," *New Choices,* December 1990.

Wooley, O. Wayne. "Indictment of Dieting—II," speech delivered at NAAFA's Tenth Anniversary Celebration, September 2, 1979, NAAFA Press Kit.

Wooley, Susan C., Ph.D. "Indictment of Dieting—I," speech delivered at NAAFA's Tenth Anniversary Celebration, September 2, 1979, NAAFA Press Kit.

"The Year of the Winners," *People Weekly,* January 10, 1994, p. 36(5).

Permissions

Excerpt from *Where the Girls Are: Growing Up Female With the Mass Media* by Susan J. Douglas, copyright © 1994 by Susan J. Douglas, reprinted with the permission of Times Books, a Division of Random House, Inc.

Excerpts from *Goodbye Jumbo, Hello Cruel World* by Louie Anderson, copyright © 1993 by Louie Anderson, reprinted with permission of Louzell Productions, Inc. and Penguin USA.

Excerpt from Mary Armstrong's comedy act, copyright 1992, reproduced with permission of author.

Conversation with Philip Charles Barragan, Jr., copyright 1997, reprinted by permission of author.

Conversation with Frances Berg, M.S., copyright 1997, reprinted by permission of author.

Conversation with Ruby Blickenstorfer, copyright 1997, reprinted by permission of author.

Excerpt from FAT LIP Readers Theatre script by Laura J. Bock, copyright 1992, reprinted with author's permission.

Conversation with Annette Bunnell, copyright 1997, reprinted by permission of author.

Conversation with "Buttercup," copyright 1997, reprinted by permission of author.

Conversation with Dee Davey, copyright 1997, reprinted by permission of author.

Conversation with Dean Edell, M.D., copyright 1997, reprinted by permission of author.

Conversation with Laura Elijiak, copyright 1997, reprinted by permission of author.

Conversation with William J. Fabrey, copyright 1997, reprinted by permission of author.

Conversation with Pam Hollowich, copyright, 1997, reprinted by permission of author.

Index

Hanes Fitting Pretty, 302
Hanes/L'Eggs/Bali/Playtex, 85, 302
Hangouts, 302
Hanover House, 302
Harriet Carter, 65, 303
Harriet's Tailoring, 92, 303
HBO Network, 174
Health care, 34–36, 39–41
    medical aids, 47–50
    on-line resources concerning, 352–53
    tips, 32
Health care professionals, 10–12
    continuing education for, 45–46
    open letter to, 41–44
    uniforms, 50–51
Health Risks of Weight Loss (Berg), 194, 206
Health and Welfare, 6
Healthy Concepts, 342
Healthy Pleasures (Sobel), 206
Healthy Weight Journal, 42, 46, 193–94, 303
Healthy Weight Week, 239
Heart Inc. Tuxedos, 303
Heart's Delight, 65, 303
Heavy Duty, 222
Heidi Marsh, 92
Heidi's Pages and Petticoats, 303
Heinz Gift Shop, 85, 303
Helen Wells Agency, 107, 303
Hep Cat, 77, 303
Hepp Industries, Inc., 303
Hersey Custom Shoe Company, 97, 303
HERSIZE, 248, 303
Hey, Dr. Dean (television program), 36
Hidalgo, 303
Higgs, Liz Curtis, 303
High Places, 86, 303
Hiking, 138
Hinsdale Furriers, 98, 303
Hitchcock Shoes, Inc., 97
Hodder and Stoughton, 303
Holliday, Jennifer, 178
Holy Cow, Inc., 77, 304
Homestead Furniture, 117, 304

Horseback riding, group, 21
The Horse's Mouth, 98, 304
Hot Off the Tour, 304
Hotels, 129
Household gadgets, 113–15
Hovis Jeans/Hoveland Manufacturing, 65, 304
How to Get Your Kid to Eat . . . But Not Too Much (Satter), 206, 260, 274
Howard, Dan, 304
Hue Q, 304
HUES (Hear Us Emerging Sisters), 194, 304
HUGS Affirmation Tapes, 217
HUGS Club News, 190
HUGS Fun Fitness Video-Gentle Physical Activity, 25
HUGS International, Inc., 21, 304
The Hungry Self: Women, Eating and Identity (Chernin), 206
Hunt Galleries, Inc., 117, 304
Hy Fishman Furs, 98, 304
Hysteria, 193, 304

I Like Me (Carlson), 273
I. Spiewak, 60–61, 304
IDEA Fitness Consultant, 24
Idrea Says "Yes You Can" (video), 25
If My Child Is Too Fat, What Should I Do About It? (booklet), 213, 275
Ikeda, Joanne, 265–68
Ilissa, 89, 304
Image consultants, 104
Imperial Wear, 59, 305
Impression Bridal, 89, 305
Improve Body Image-Develop Self Empowerment, 217
In Grand Form Enterprises, 305
In Grand Form with Jody Sandler (video), 26
In Search of Fullness: Women, Eating Disorders & Body Image, 217
Inclinator Co., 305
Independent Living Aids, Inc., 305

Innerworks/Food for Thought, 247, 305
Insurance, health and life, 45
International Fat Acceptance Network (IFAN), 245
International House of Pancakes, 132
International Male, 59, 305
International No Diet Coalition Directory of Resources, 213, 238
International No Diet Day, 237–38
Intestinal bypass, 344
Intimate Appeal, 77, 86, 305
Intimate Attitudes, 86, 305
Intimate Encounters, 86, 305
Invenco, 305
The Invisible Woman: Confronting Weight Prejudice (Goodman), 206
It's a Revolution, 72, 305
It's a Secret Plus, 86, 305
Ives, Burl, 178
I.Y.M. (video), 25, 304

The J, 89, 305
J. Jill, Ltd., 66, 306
J. Lumarel Corporation, 82, 306
J.C. Penney, 65, 306
J.C. Penney After Surgery Inner Fashions, 86
J.C. Penney Baby & You, 90
J.C. Penney Big Kids, 271
J.C. Penney Bridal Collection, 89
J.C. Penney Class Favorites, 271
J.C. Penney Fashion Influences, 72–73
J.C. Penney for Men/Big & Extra Tall/Workwear/Shirt and Tie Required, 59
J.C. Penney Scouts, 98, 271
J.C. Penney Simply for Sports, 20
J.C. Penney Uniforms and Scrubs, 50
J.C. Penney Workwear, 72
J.D. Products, 306
J W Ramàge, 66, 306
Jack Loews Theaters, 135

Size Wise Update!

Size Wise Update! will keep you ahead of the game when it comes to all of the issues covered in *Size Wise*—plus more! Published bimonthly, *Size Wise Update!* will provide you with:

- Closer, more detailed looks at products, services, organizations, and publications designed just for *Size Wise* readers. News on anything that can improve your life (and some of the scams that can't) will be found here.
- Celebrity interviews and personal glimpses into the lives of people who refuse to be defined by size alone.
- News from the front—activism, legislation, and lawsuits. Know who is standing up for your rights and who is learning not to tread on them.
- Medical updates—the latest on weight-loss drugs, doctor attitudes, and patient concerns. *Size Wise Update!* will help you to be a smart consumer when it comes to your health.
- Fashion news—including interviews with the designers who strive to provide us with smart, beautiful wardrobes. Keep up-to-date on all the new clothing resources for people over size 2X.
- Tips for stepping out into the world looking your absolute best. Hear from fashion and beauty consultants who specialize in enhancing the fuller face and figure.
- Media alerts—movies and television shows that include larger characters in a size-positive light . . . and some jabs at the ones who don't.

Size Wise is just the start. *Size Wise Update!* keeps you feeling great, looking spectacular, and in charge of your life.

- -

Don't miss a single issue. Subscribe now. Send a check or money order in the amount of $24 to Size Wise Update!, 1054 Los Osos Valley Road, Los Osos, CA 93402.

_____

Name

_____

Address

_____

City   State   Zip